TETSUYA TSUTSUI

PROPHECY

01

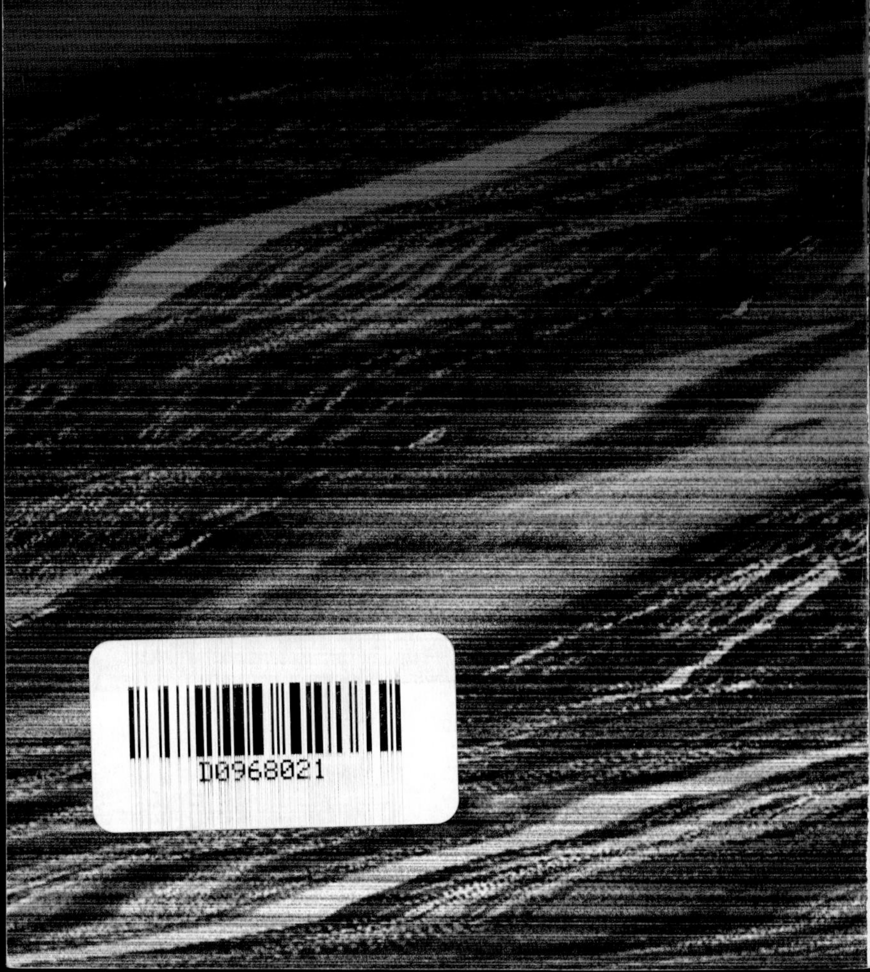

CONTENTS

File001 3

File002 37

File003 69

File004 97

File005 131

File006 163

File007 190

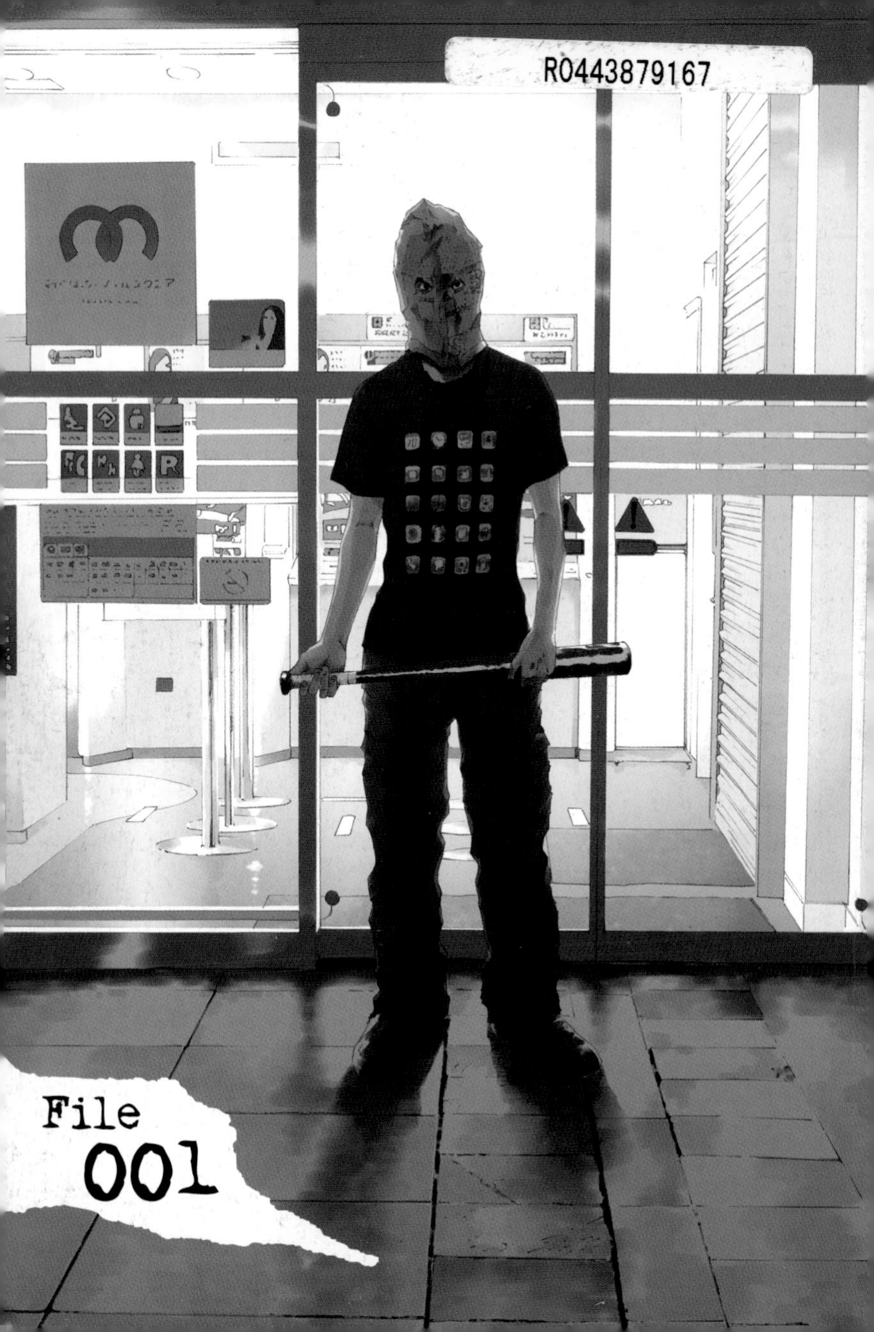
R0443879167
File
001

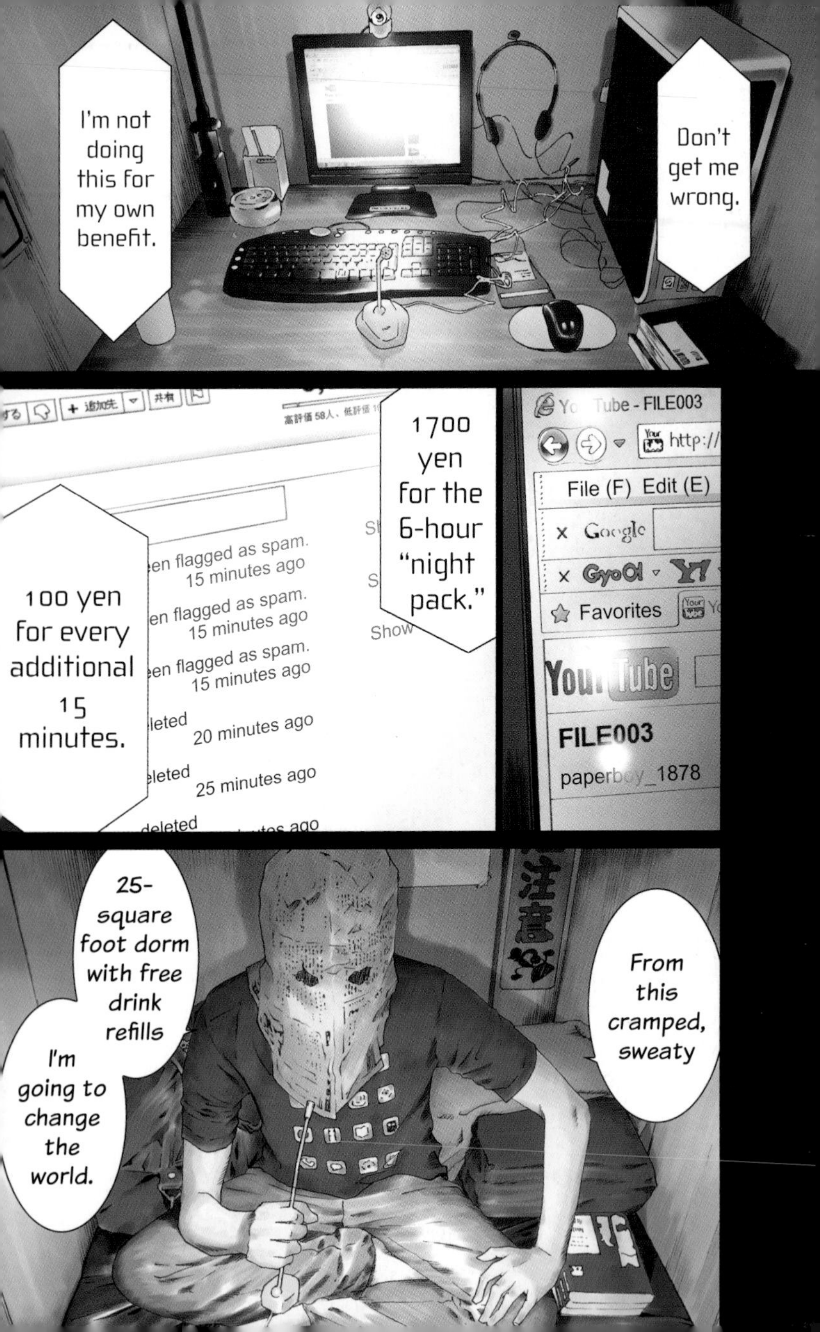
Don't get me wrong.
I'm not doing this for my own benefit.
File (F) Edit (E)
Google
Favorites
FILE003
1700 yen for the 6-hour "night pack."
100 yen for every additional 15 minutes.
From this cramped, sweaty
25-square foot dorm with free drink refills
I'm going to change the world.

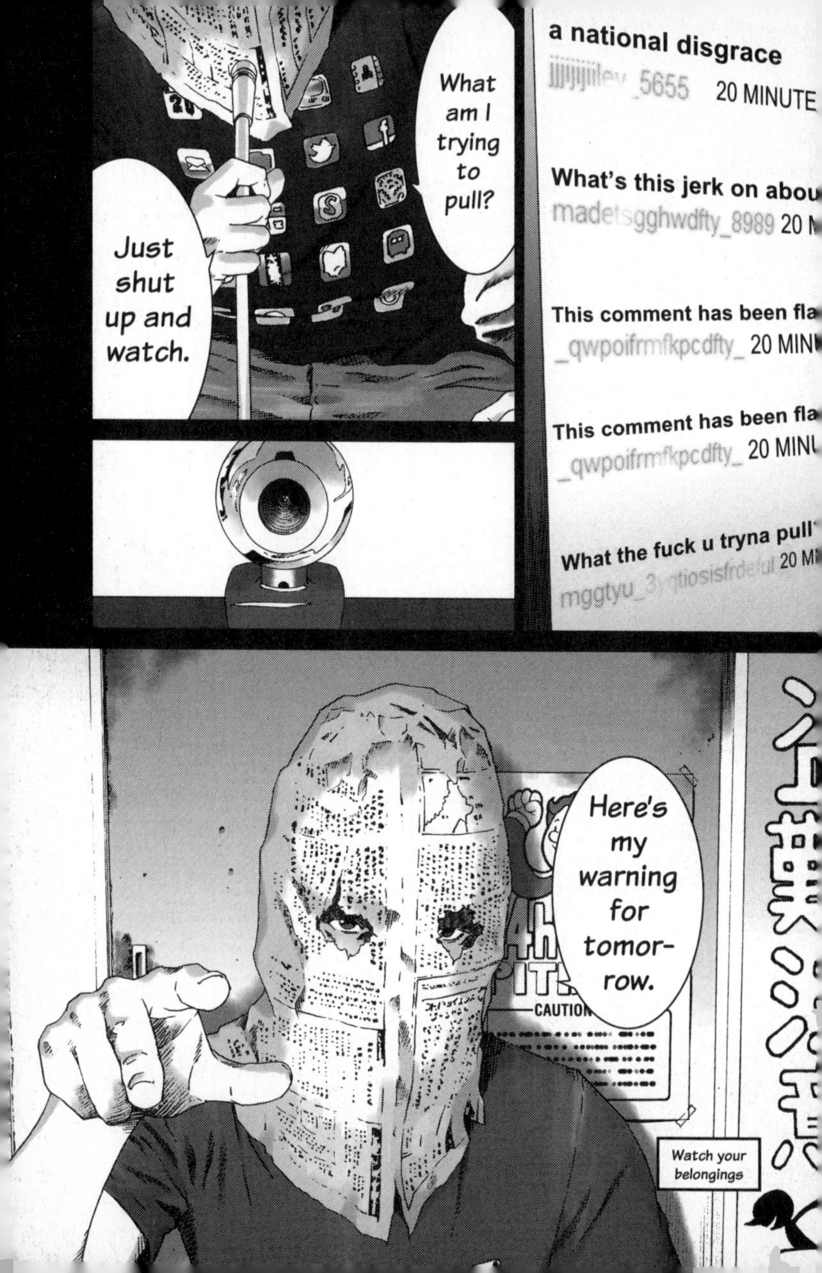
a national disgrace
20 MINUTE
What's this jerk on abou
madetsgghwdfty_8989 20 M
This comment has been fla
qwpoifrmfkpcdfty 20 MIN
This comment has been fla
qwpoifrmfkpcdfty 20 MINU
What the fuck u tryna pull
20 M
What am I trying to pull?
Just shut up and watch.
Here's my warning for tomorrow.
CAUTION
Watch your belongings

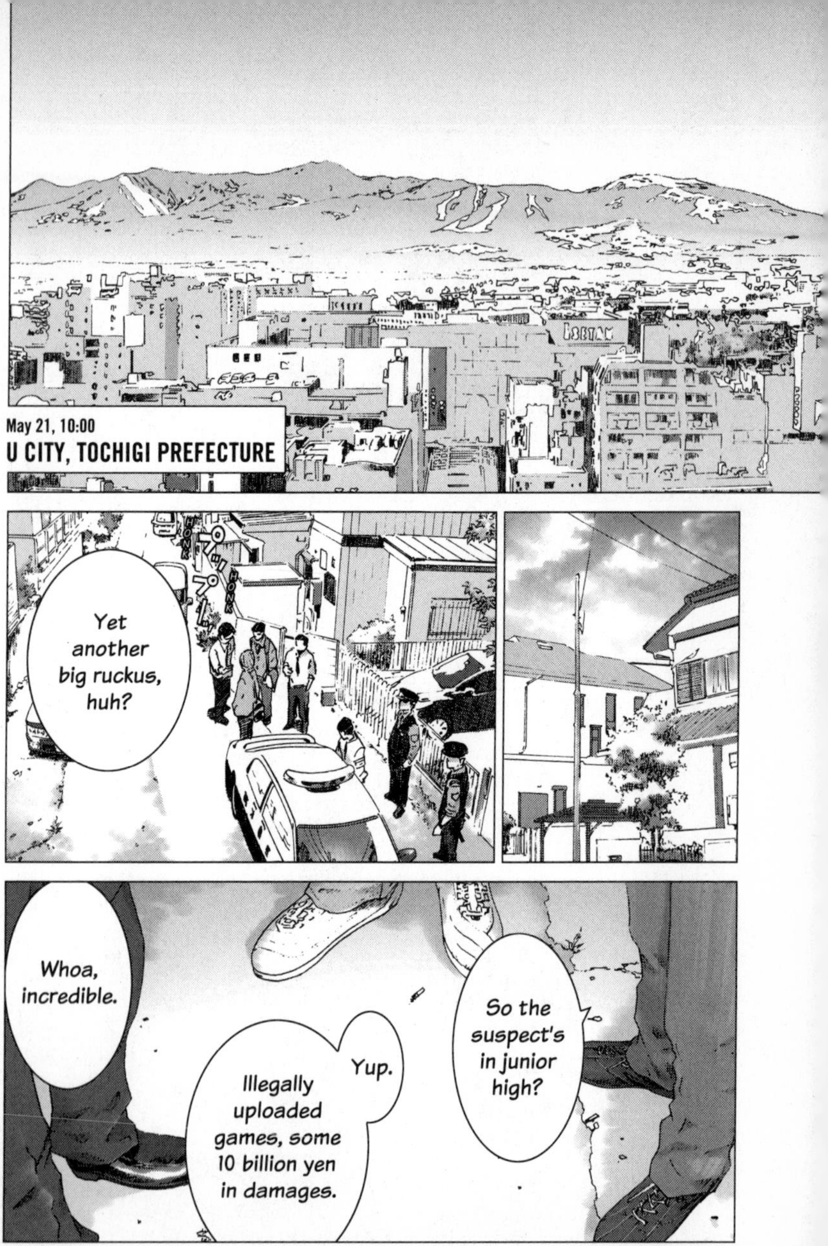
May 21, 10:00
U CITY, TOCHIGI PREFECTURE
HONK
HONK
Yet another big ruckus, huh?
So the suspect's in junior high?
Yup.
Illegally uploaded games, some 10 billion yen in damages.
Whoa, incredible.

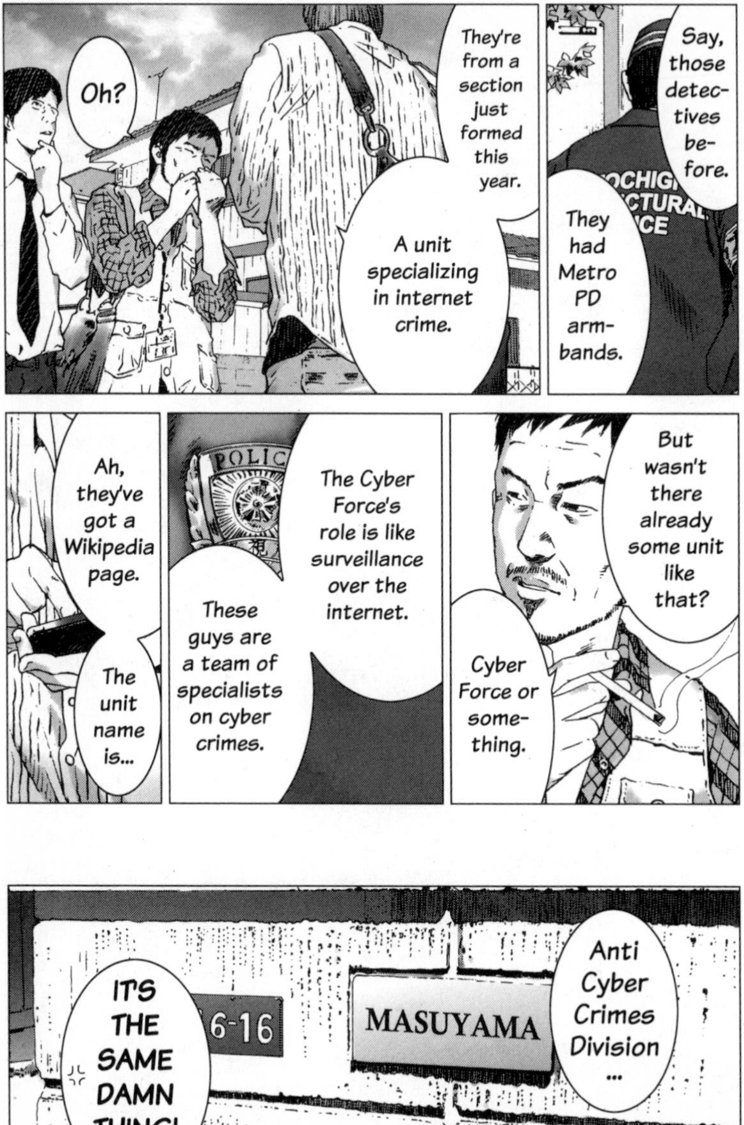
Say, those detectives before.
They had Metro PD armbands.
They're from a section just formed this year.
A unit specializing in internet crime.
Oh?
But wasn't there already some unit like that?
Cyber Force or something.
The Cyber Force's role is like surveillance over the internet.
These guys are a team of specialists on cyber crimes.
Ah, they've got a Wikipedia page.
The unit name is...
Anti Cyber Crimes Division...
MASUYAMA
6-16
IT'S THE SAME DAMN THING!

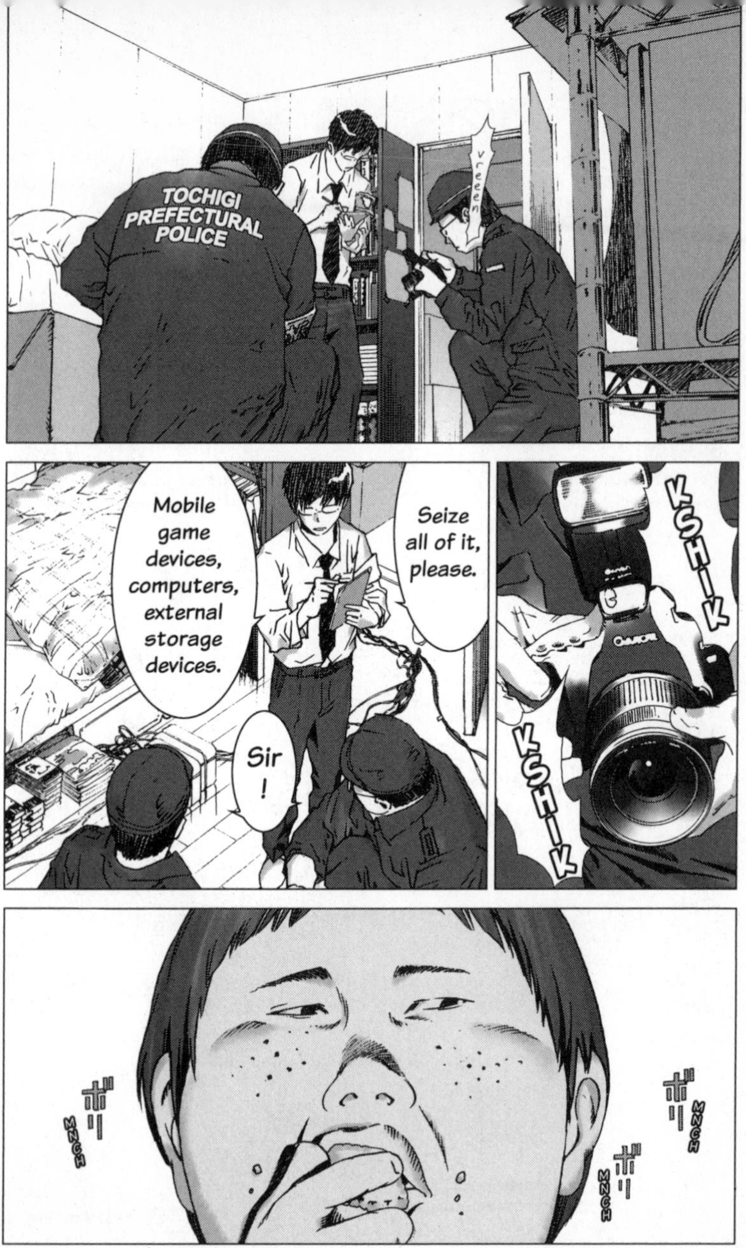
TOCHIGI PREFECTURAL POLICE
vreeen
KSHIK
KSHIK
Seize all of it, please.
Mobile game devices, computers, external storage devices.
Sir!
MNCH
MNCH
MNCH

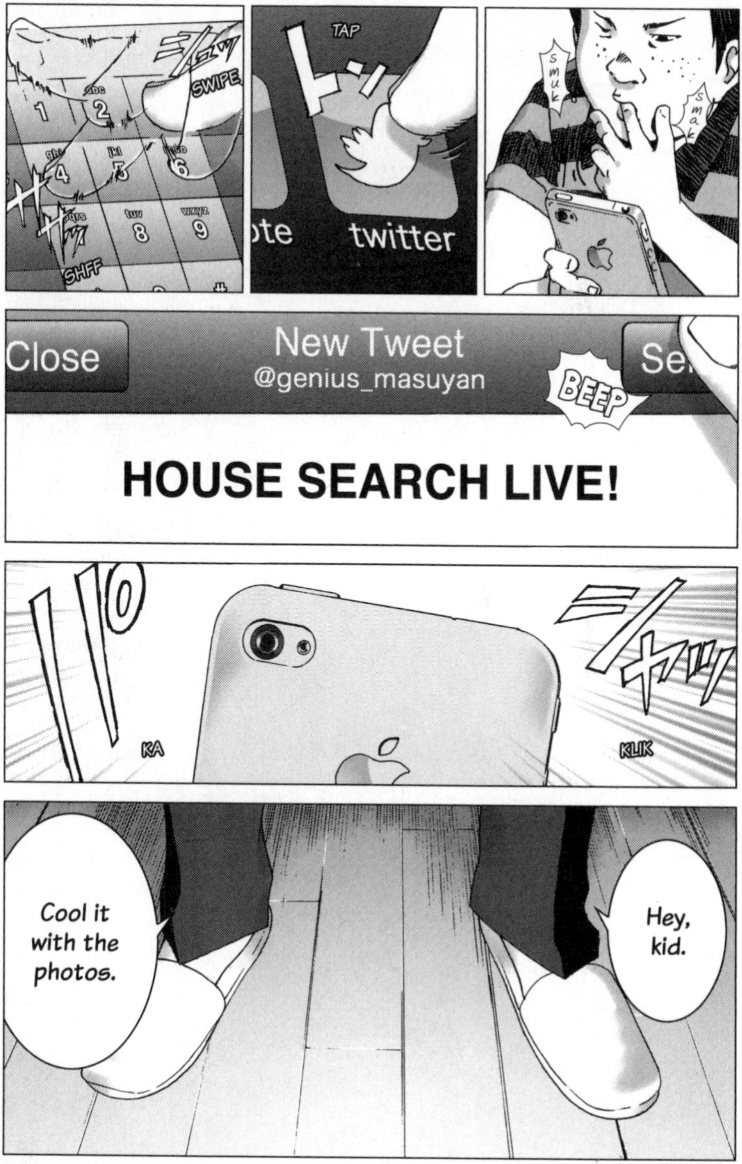
smuk
smak
TAP
twitter
SWIPE
SHFF
Close
New Tweet
@genius_masuyan
BEEP
HOUSE SEARCH LIVE!
KLIK
KA
Hey, kid.
Cool it with the photos.

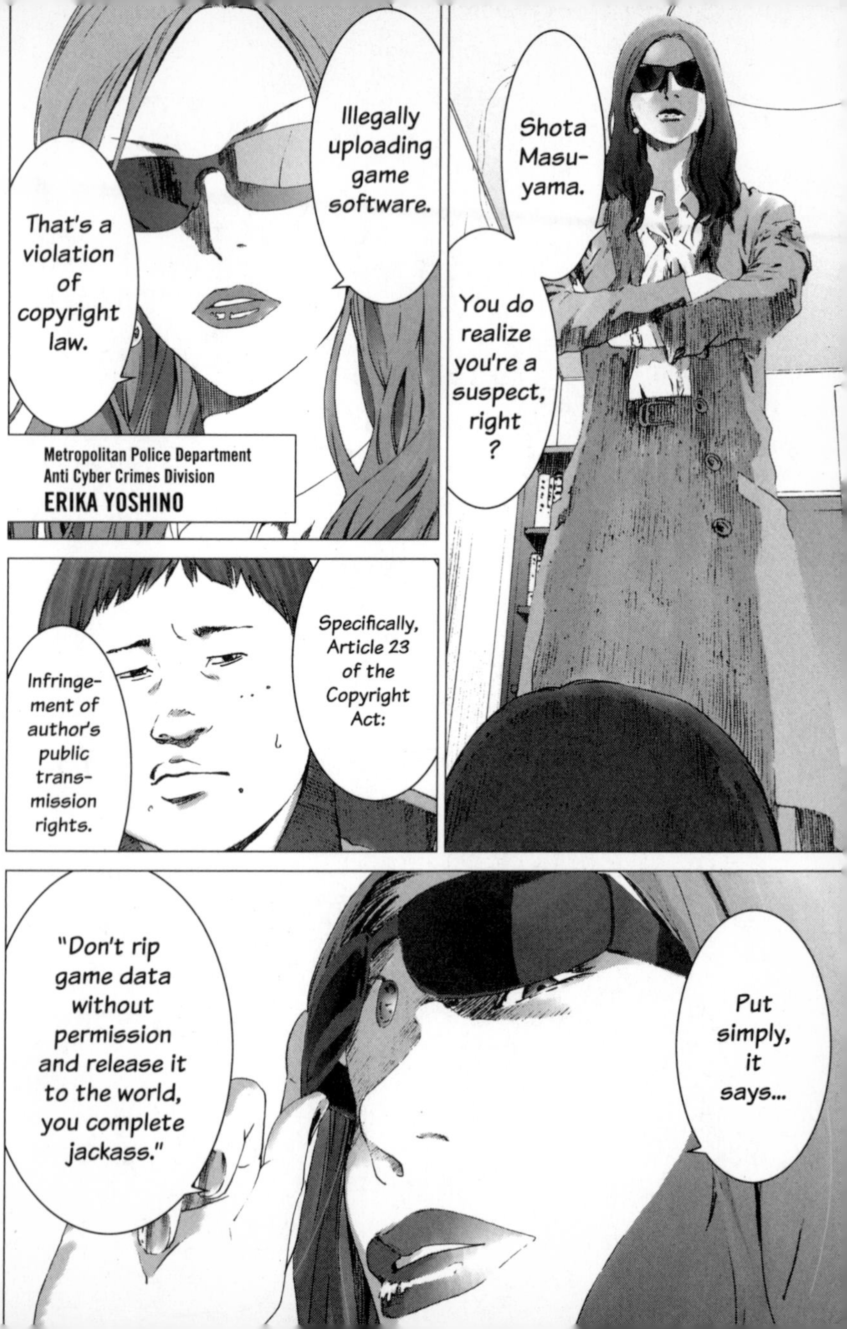
Shota Masu-yama.
You do realize you're a suspect, right?
Illegally uploading game software.
That's a violation of copyright law.
Metropolitan Police Department
Anti Cyber Crimes Division
ERIKA YOSHINO
Specifically, Article 23 of the Copyright Act:
Infringe-ment of author's public trans-mission rights.
Put simply, it says...
"Don't rip game data without permission and release it to the world, you complete jackass."

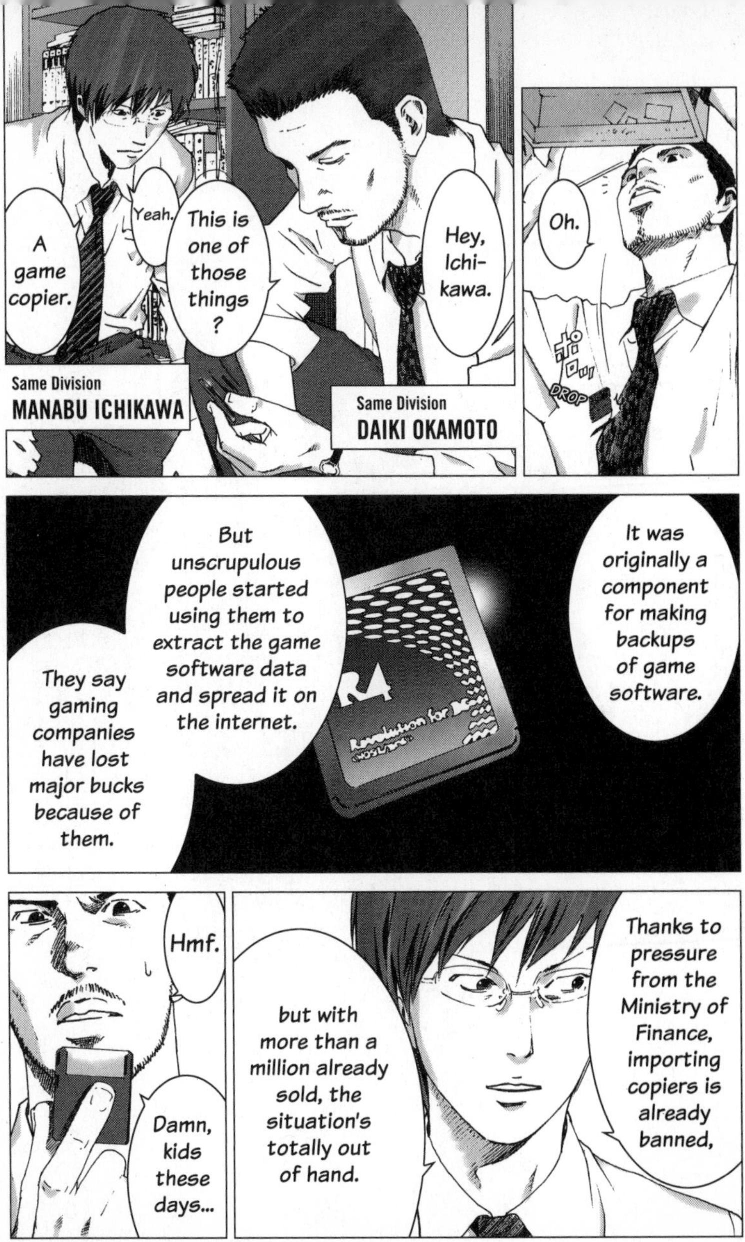
Oh.
DROP
Hey, Ichikawa.
This is one of those things?
Same Division
DAIKI OKAMOTO
Yeah.
A game copier.
Same Division
MANABU ICHIKAWA
It was originally a component for making backups of game software.
But unscrupulous people started using them to extract the game software data and spread it on the internet.
They say gaming companies have lost major bucks because of them.
Thanks to pressure from the Ministry of Finance, importing copiers is already banned,
but with more than a million already sold, the situation's totally out of hand.
Hmf.
Damn, kids these days...

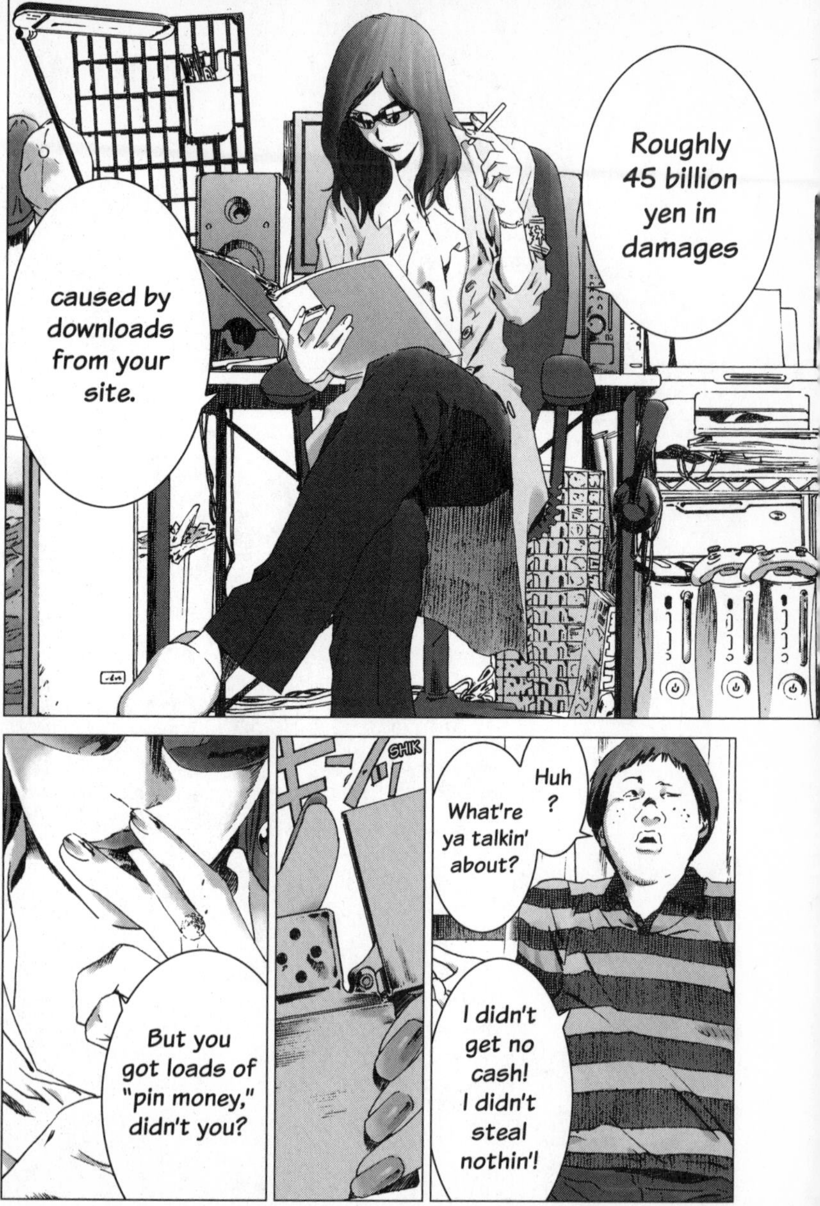
Roughly 45 billion yen in damages
caused by downloads from your site.
Huh?
What're ya talkin' about?
I didn't get no cash! I didn't steal nothin'!
SHIK
But you got loads of "pin money," didn't you?

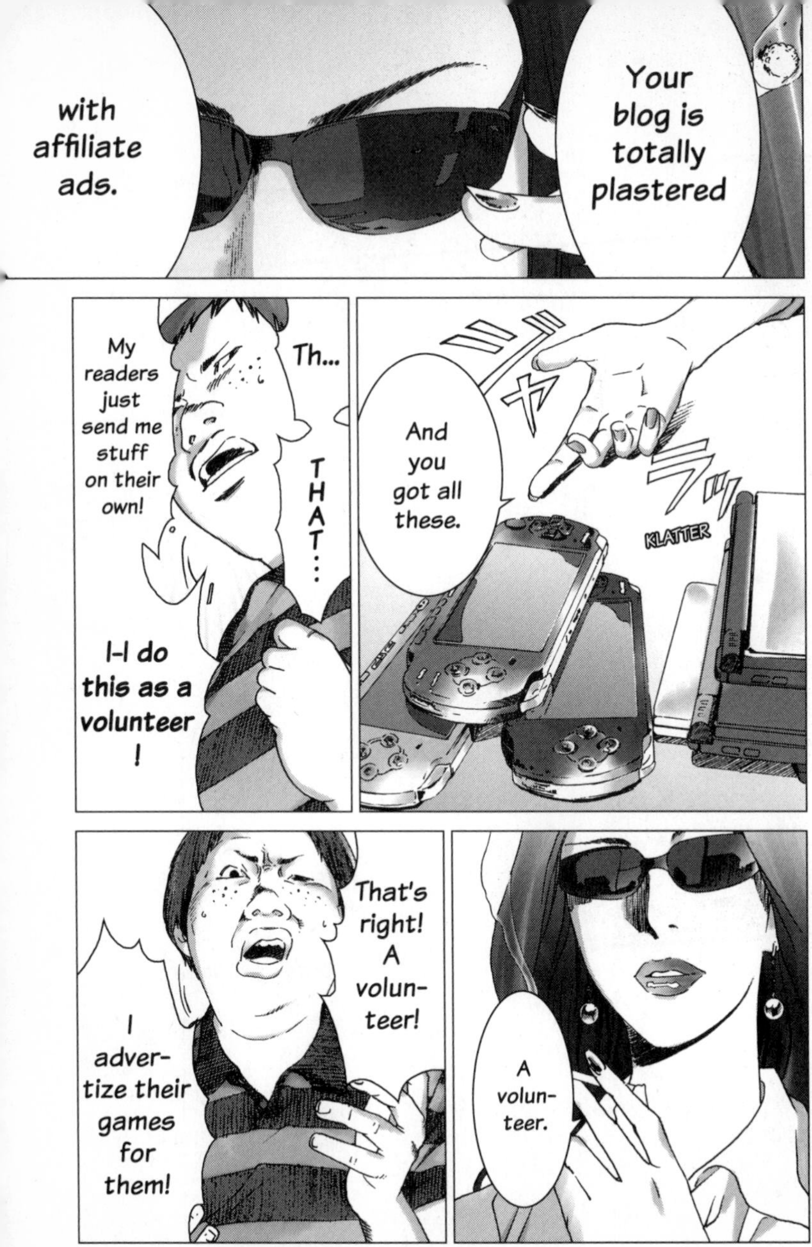
Your blog is totally plastered
with affiliate ads.
And you got all these.
KLATTER
Th...
THAT...
My readers just send me stuff on their own!
I-I do this as a volunteer!
A volunteer.
That's right! A volunteer!
I advertize their games for them!

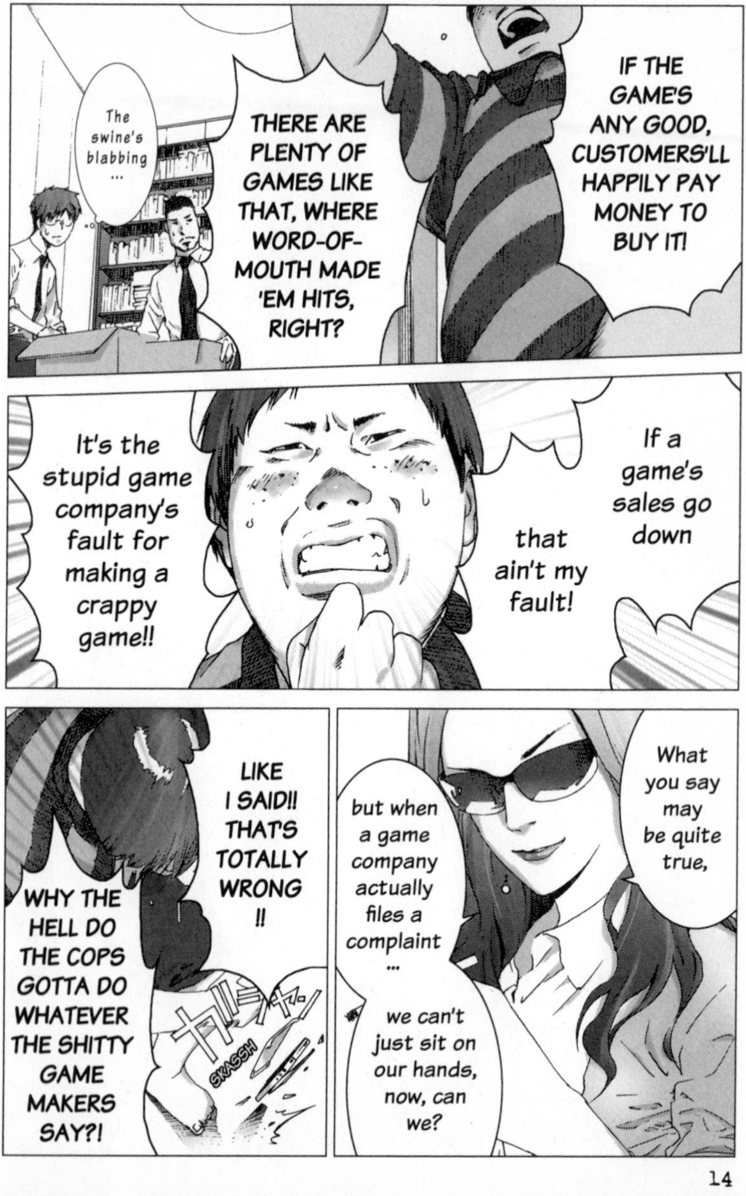
IF THE GAME'S ANY GOOD, CUSTOMERS'LL HAPPILY PAY MONEY TO BUY IT!
THERE ARE PLENTY OF GAMES LIKE THAT, WHERE WORD-OF-MOUTH MADE 'EM HITS, RIGHT?
The swine's blabbing ...
If a game's sales go down
that ain't my fault!
It's the stupid game company's fault for making a crappy game!!
What you say may be quite true,
but when a game company actually files a complaint ...
we can't just sit on our hands, now, can we?
LIKE I SAID!! THAT'S TOTALLY WRONG !!
WHY THE HELL DO THE COPS GOTTA DO WHATEVER THE SHITTY GAME MAKERS SAY?!
SKASSH

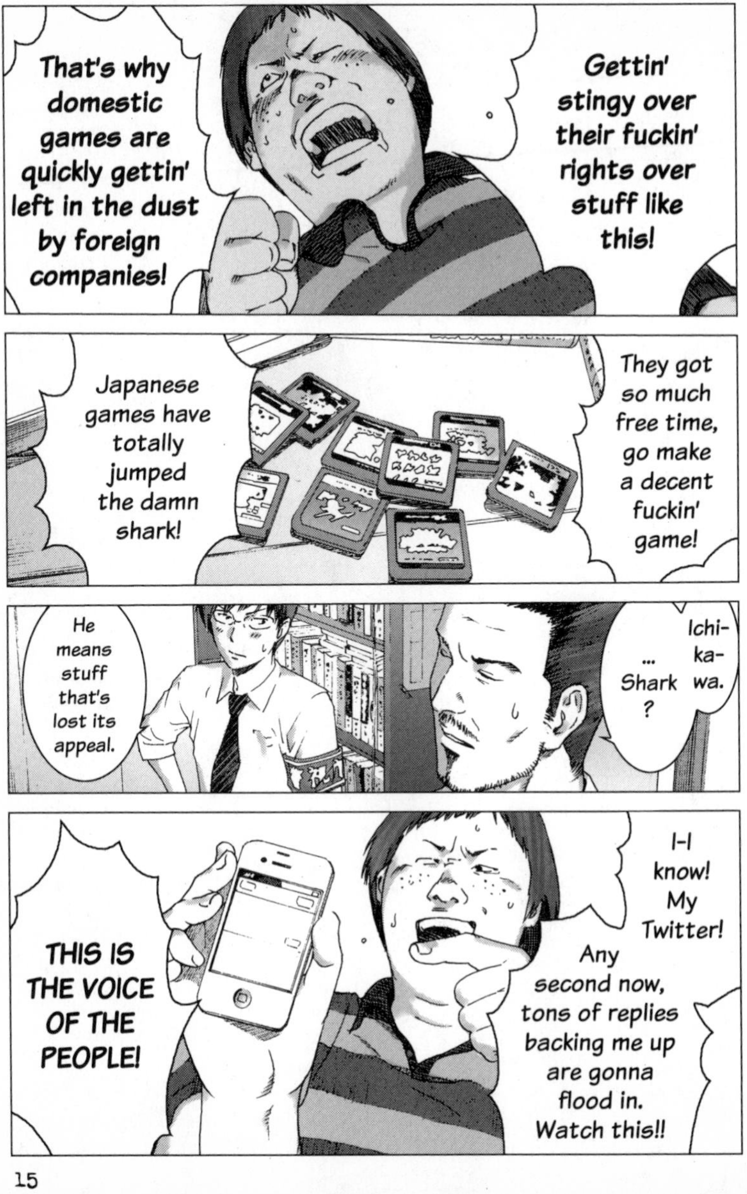
Gettin' stingy over their fuckin' rights over stuff like this!
That's why domestic games are quickly gettin' left in the dust by foreign companies!
They got so much free time, go make a decent fuckin' game!
Japanese games have totally jumped the damn shark!
Ichi-ka-wa.
... Shark ?
He means stuff that's lost its appeal.
I-I know! My Twitter!
Any second now, tons of replies backing me up are gonna flood in. Watch this!!
THIS IS THE VOICE OF THE PEOPLE!

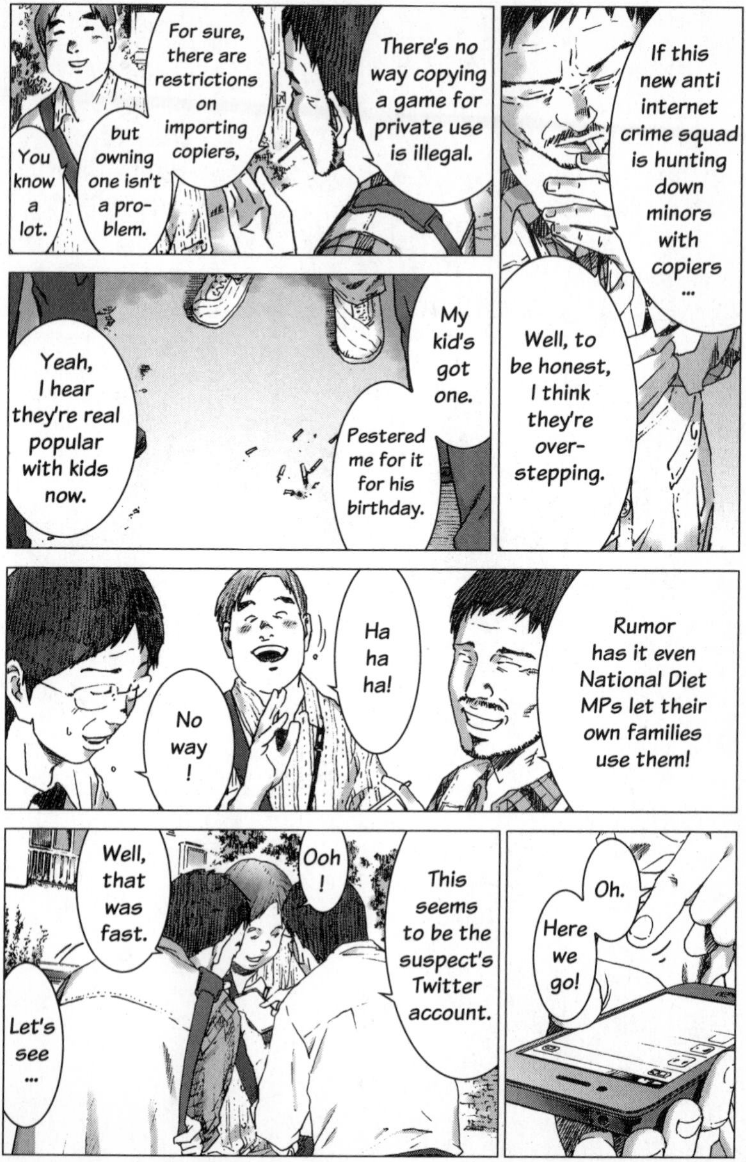
If this new anti internet crime squad is hunting down minors with copiers ...
Well, to be honest, I think they're over-stepping.
There's no way copying a game for private use is illegal.
For sure, there are restrictions on importing copiers,
but owning one isn't a pro-blem.
You know a lot.
My kid's got one.
Pestered me for it for his birthday.
Yeah, I hear they're real popular with kids now.
Rumor has it even National Diet MPs let their own families use them!
Ha ha ha!
No way!
Oh.
Here we go!
This seems to be the suspect's Twitter account.
Ooh!
Well, that was fast.
Let's see ...

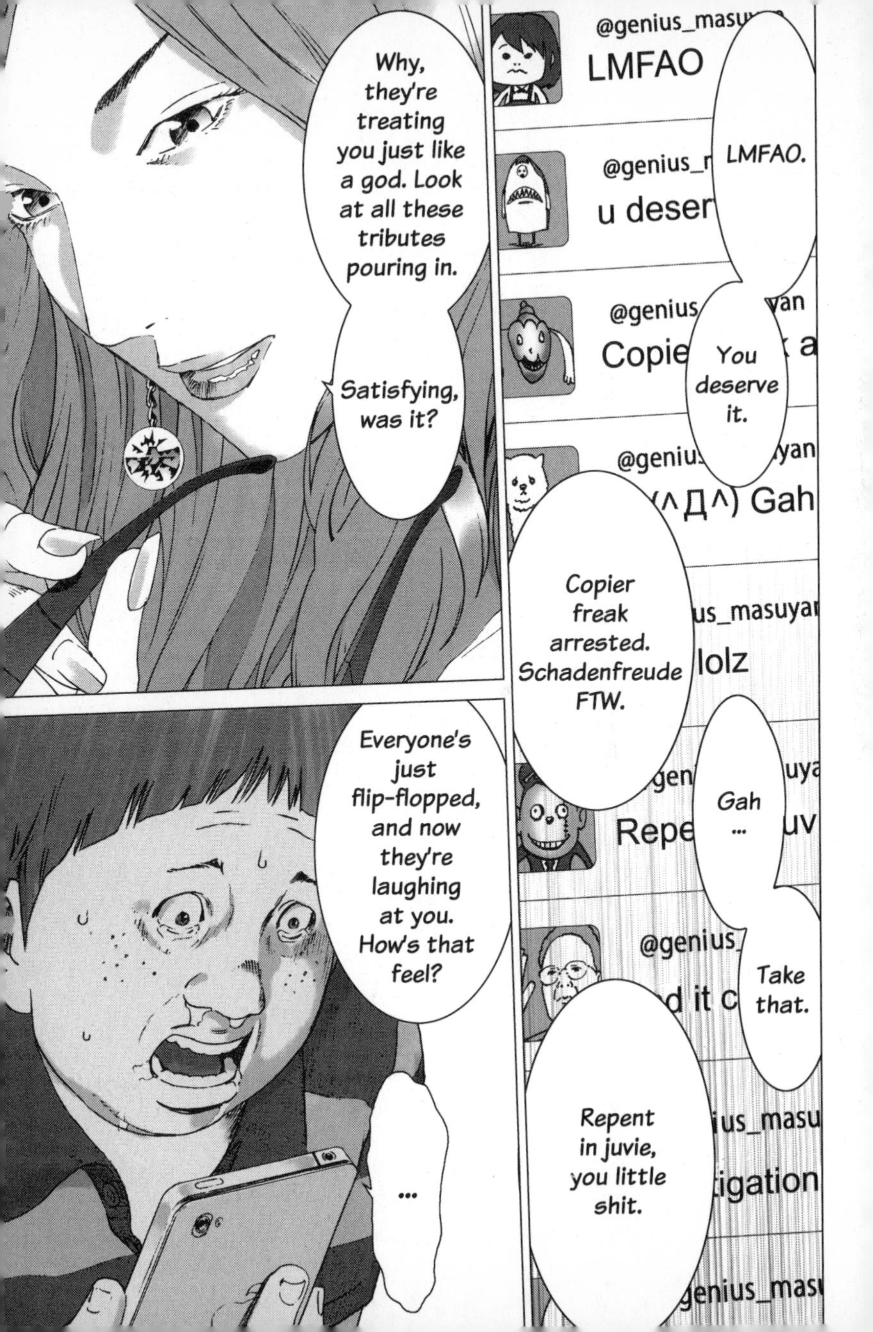
LMFAO.
You deserve it.
Copier freak arrested. Schadenfreude FTW.
Gah ...
Take that.
Repent in juvie, you little shit.
Why, they're treating you just like a god. Look at all these tributes pouring in.
Satisfying, was it?
Everyone's just flip-flopped, and now they're laughing at you. How's that feel?
...

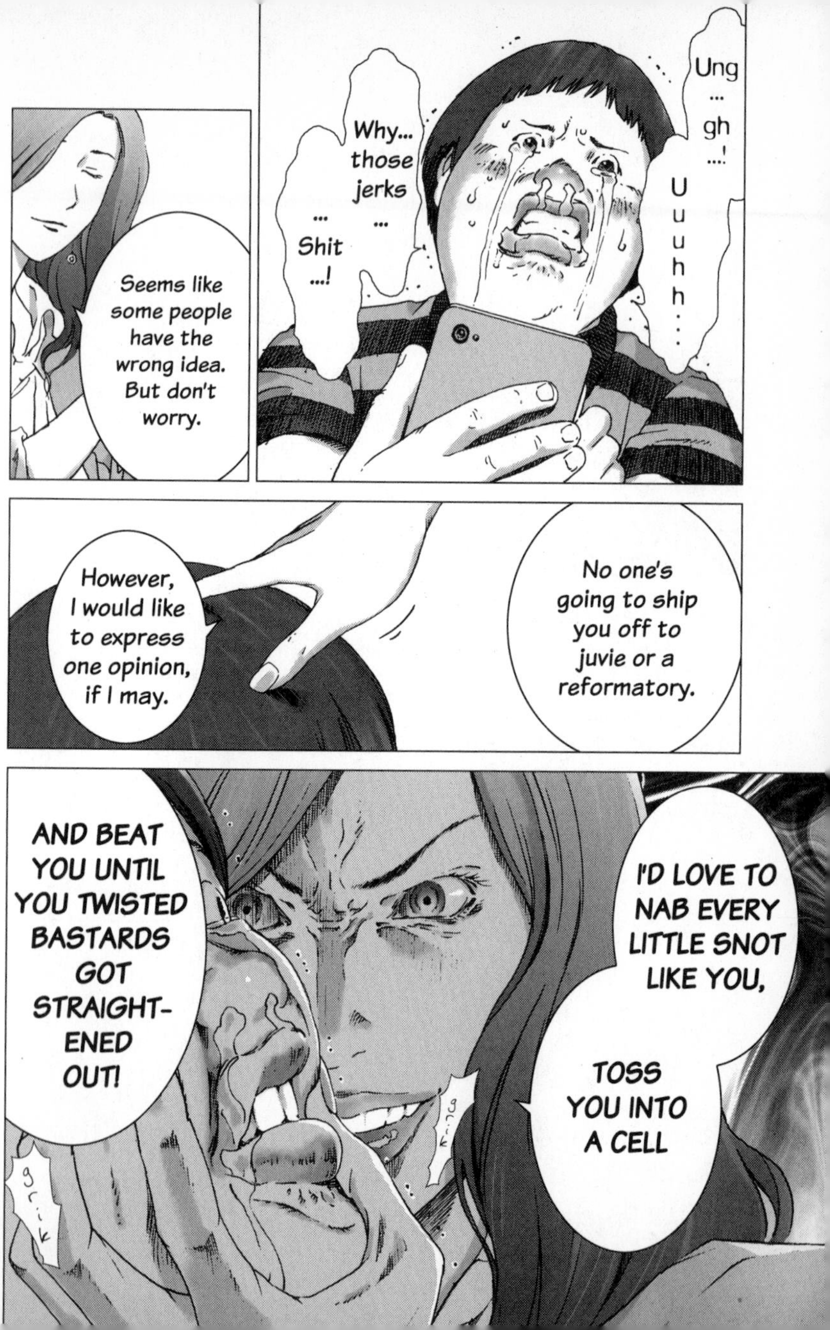
Ung ... gh ...!
Uuuhh...
Why... those jerks ... Shit ...!
Seems like some people have the wrong idea. But don't worry.
No one's going to ship you off to juvie or a reformatory.
However, I would like to express one opinion, if I may.
I'D LOVE TO NAB EVERY LITTLE SNOT LIKE YOU,
TOSS YOU INTO A CELL
AND BEAT YOU UNTIL YOU TWISTED BASTARDS GOT STRAIGHT-ENED OUT!
grik
grik

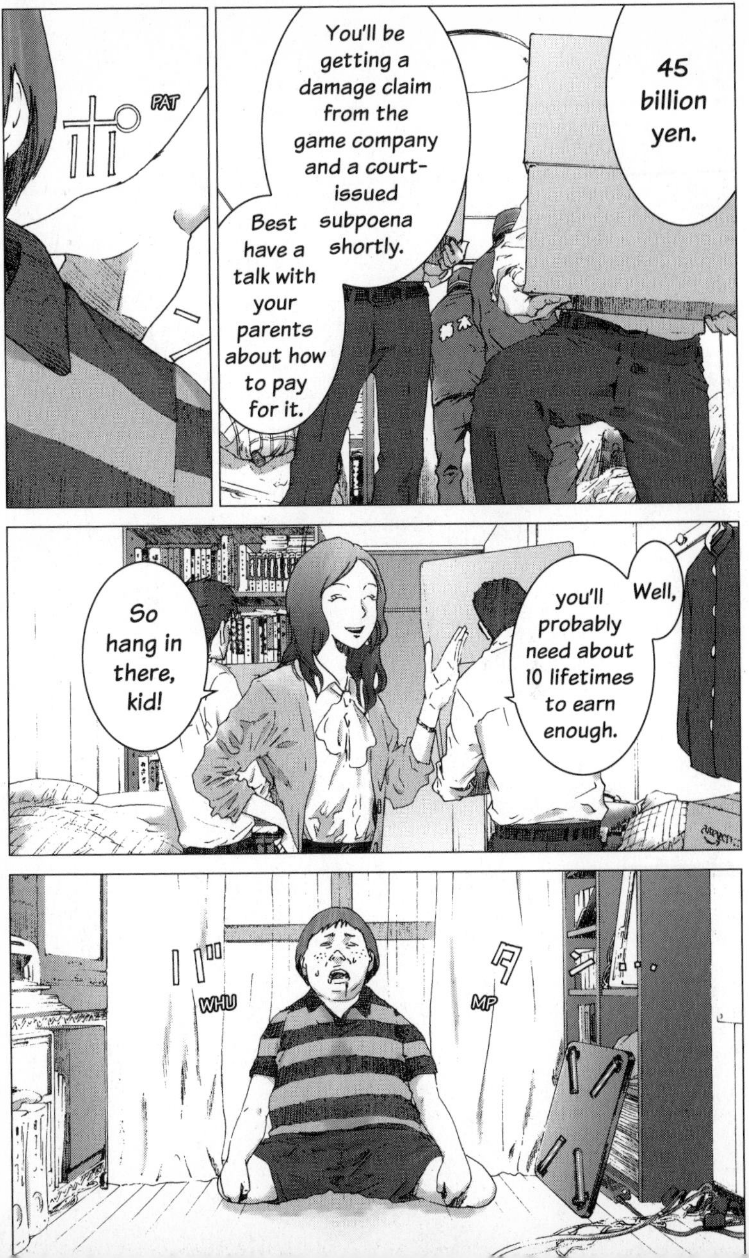
45 billion yen.
You'll be getting a damage claim from the game company and a court-issued subpoena shortly.
Best have a talk with your parents about how to pay for it.
PAT
Well, you'll probably need about 10 lifetimes to earn enough.
So hang in there, kid!
WHU
MP

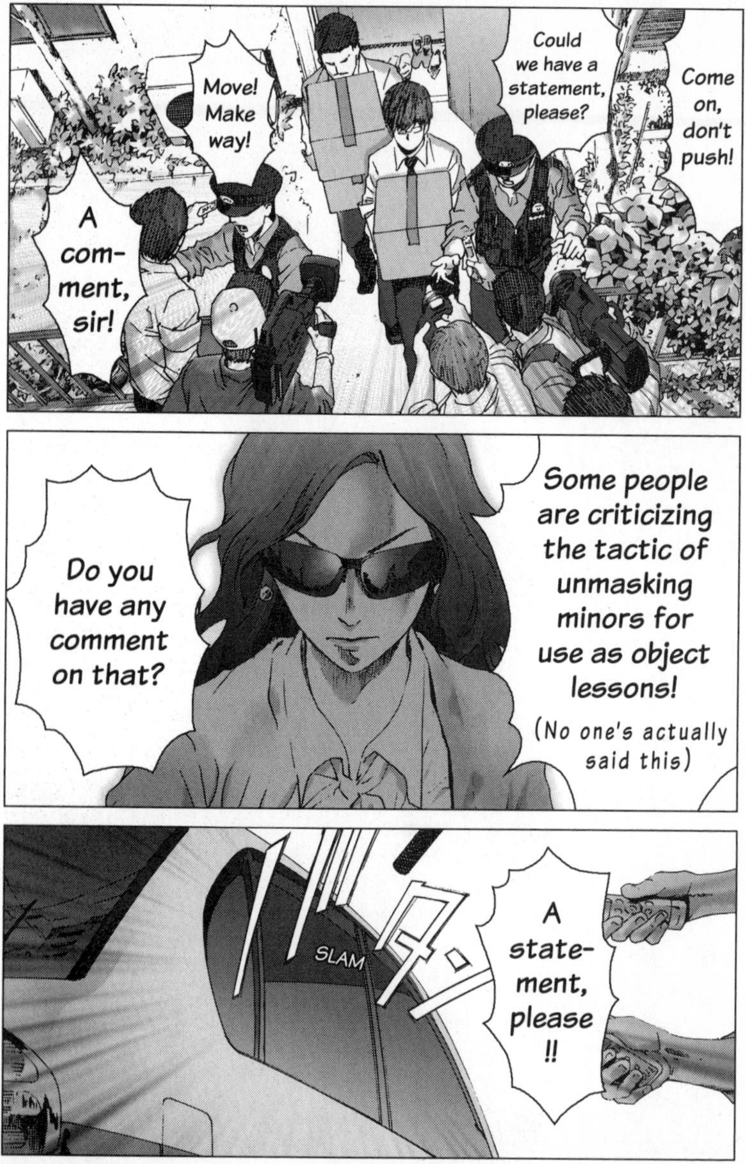
Come on, don't push!
Could we have a statement, please?
Move! Make way!
A com-ment, sir!
Some people are criticizing the tactic of unmasking minors for use as object lessons!
(No one's actually said this)
Do you have any comment on that?
A state-ment, please !!
SLAM

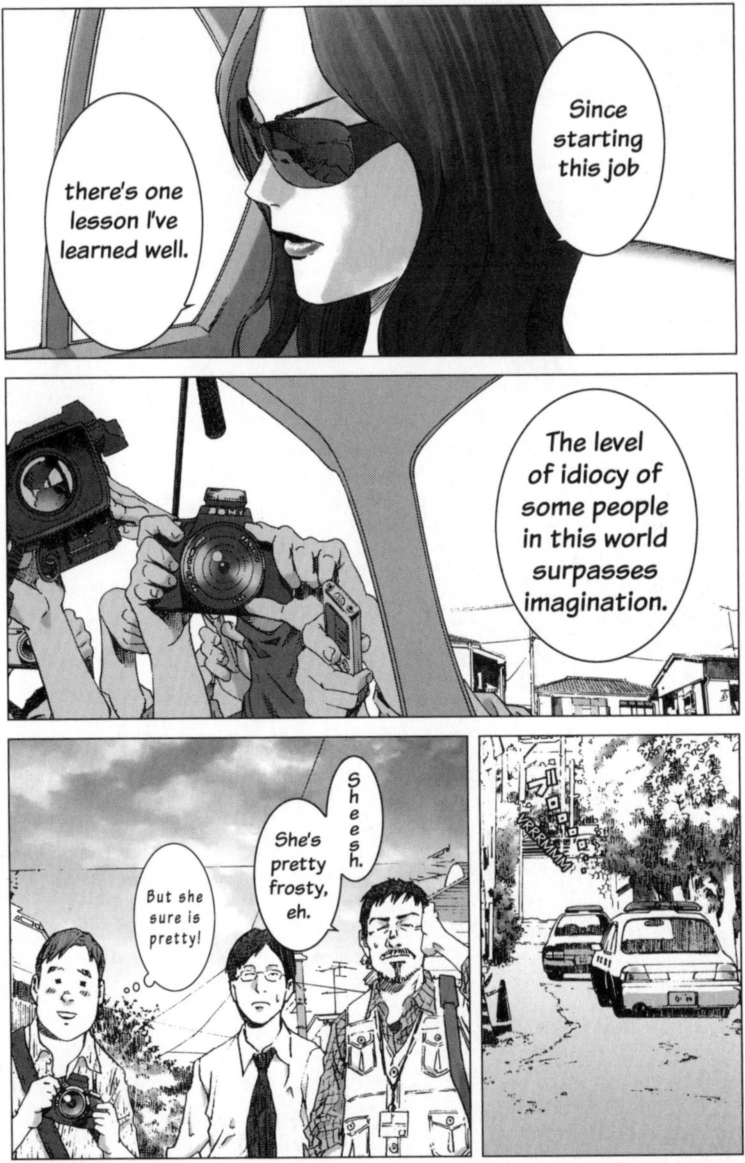

Since starting this job
there's one lesson I've learned well.
The level of idiocy of some people in this world surpasses imagination.
Sheesh.
She's pretty frosty, eh.
But she sure is pretty!

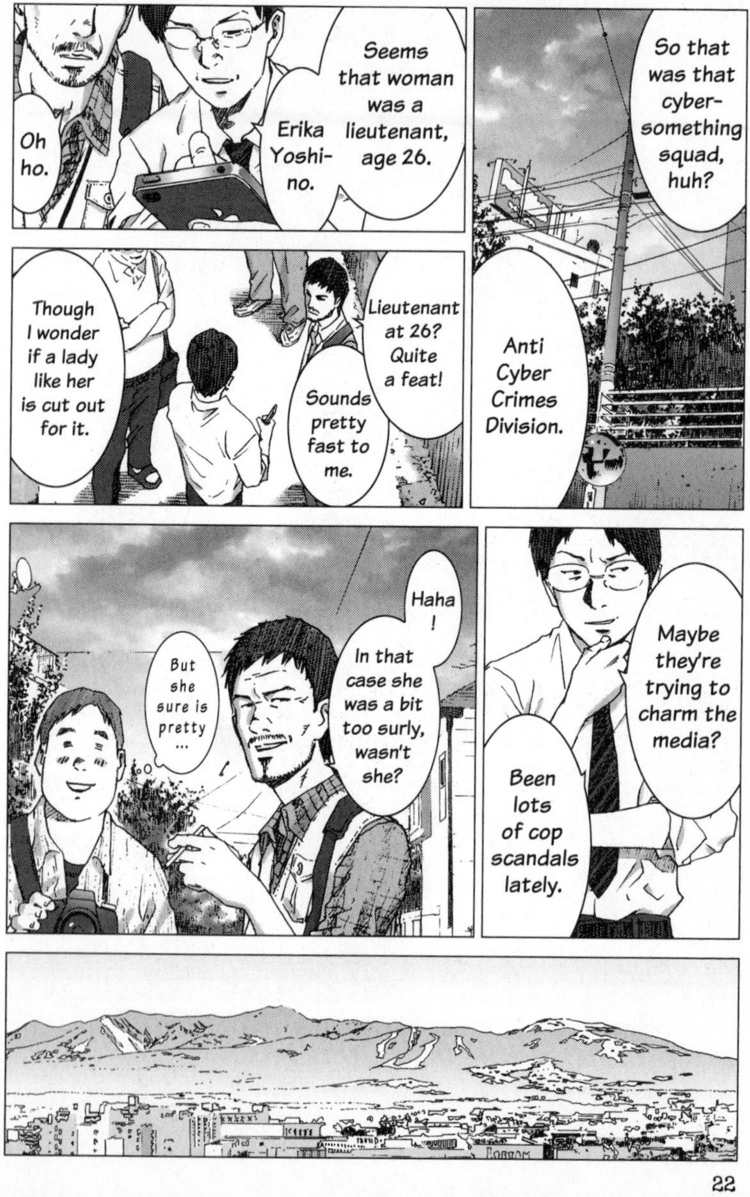
So that was that cyber-something squad, huh?
Anti Cyber Crimes Division.
Seems that woman was a lieutenant, age 26.
Erika Yoshi-no.
Oh ho.
Lieutenant at 26? Quite a feat!
Sounds pretty fast to me.
Though I wonder if a lady like her is cut out for it.
Maybe they're trying to charm the media?
Been lots of cop scandals lately.
Haha!
In that case she was a bit too surly, wasn't she?
But she sure is pretty...

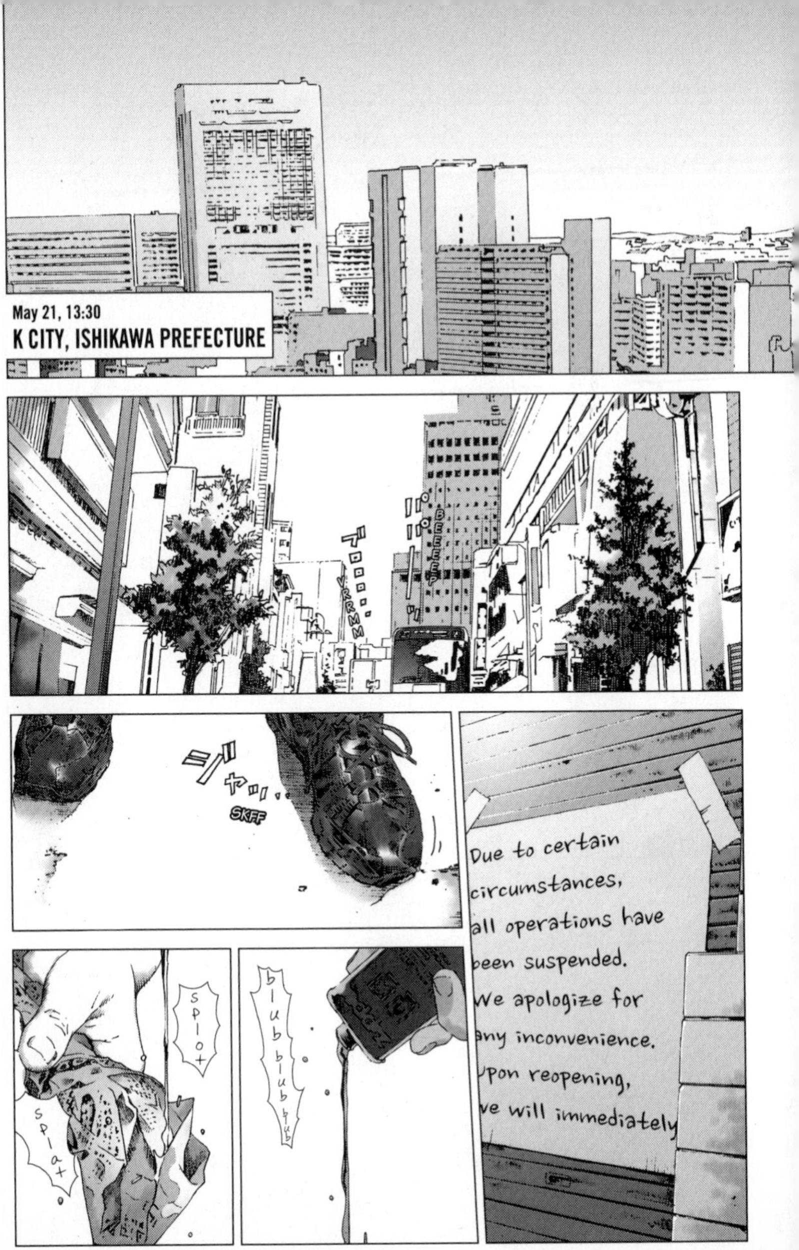
May 21, 13:30
K CITY, ISHIKAWA PREFECTURE
VRRMM
BEEEEP
Due to certain circumstances, all operations have been suspended. We apologize for any inconvenience. Upon reopening, we will immediately
SKFF
blub blub blub
splot
splat

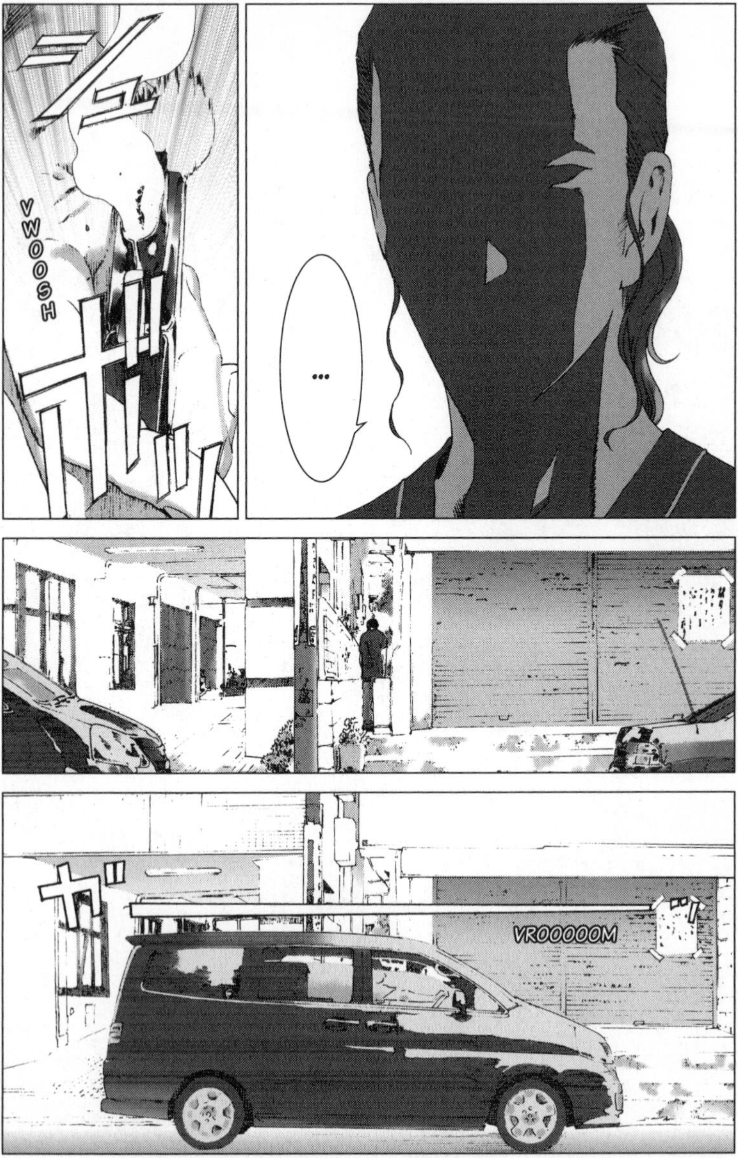
...
VWOOSH
VROOOOOM

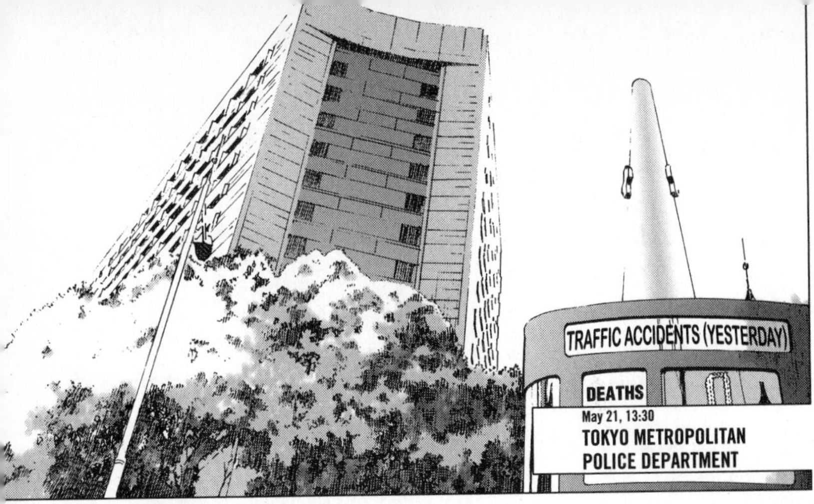
TRAFFIC ACCIDENTS (YESTERDAY)
DEATHS
May 21, 13:30
TOKYO METROPOLITAN POLICE DEPARTMENT

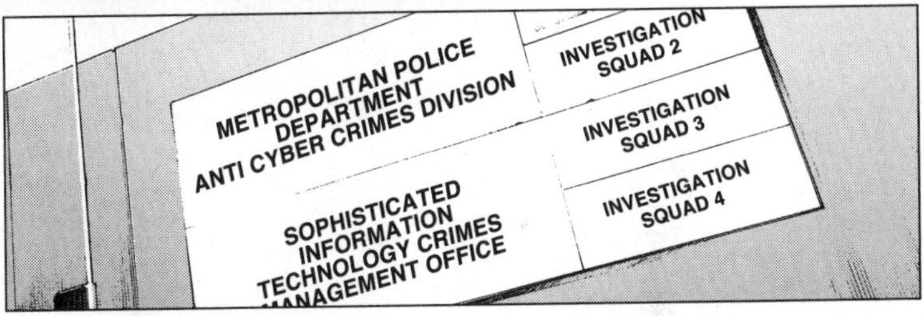
METROPOLITAN POLICE DEPARTMENT
ANTI CYBER CRIMES DIVISION
INVESTIGATION SQUAD 2
INVESTIGATION SQUAD 3
SOPHISTICATED INFORMATION TECHNOLOGY CRIMES MANAGEMENT OFFICE
INVESTIGATION SQUAD 4

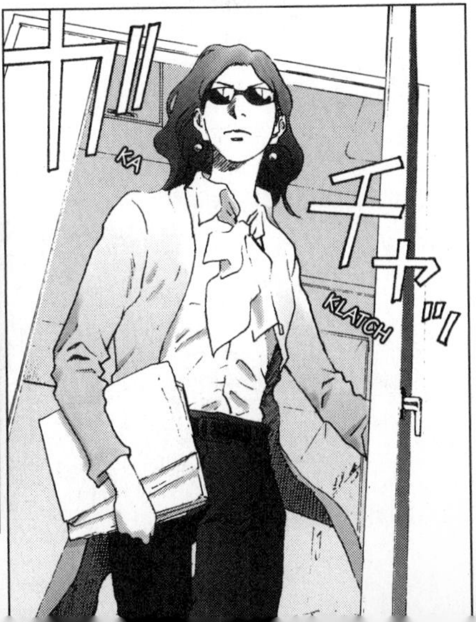
KA
KLATCH

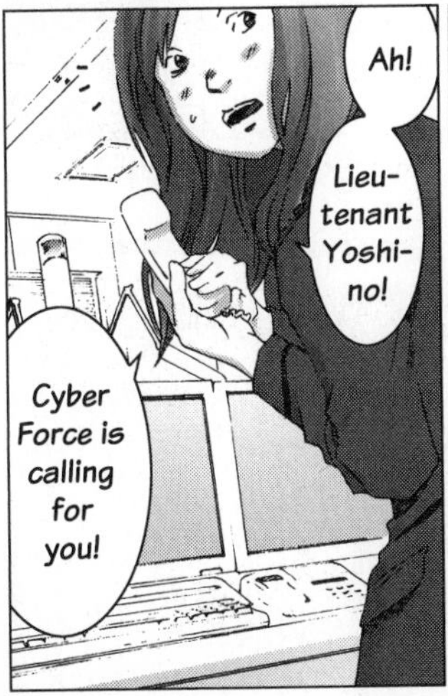
Ah!
Lieu-tenant Yoshi-no!
Cyber Force is calling for you!

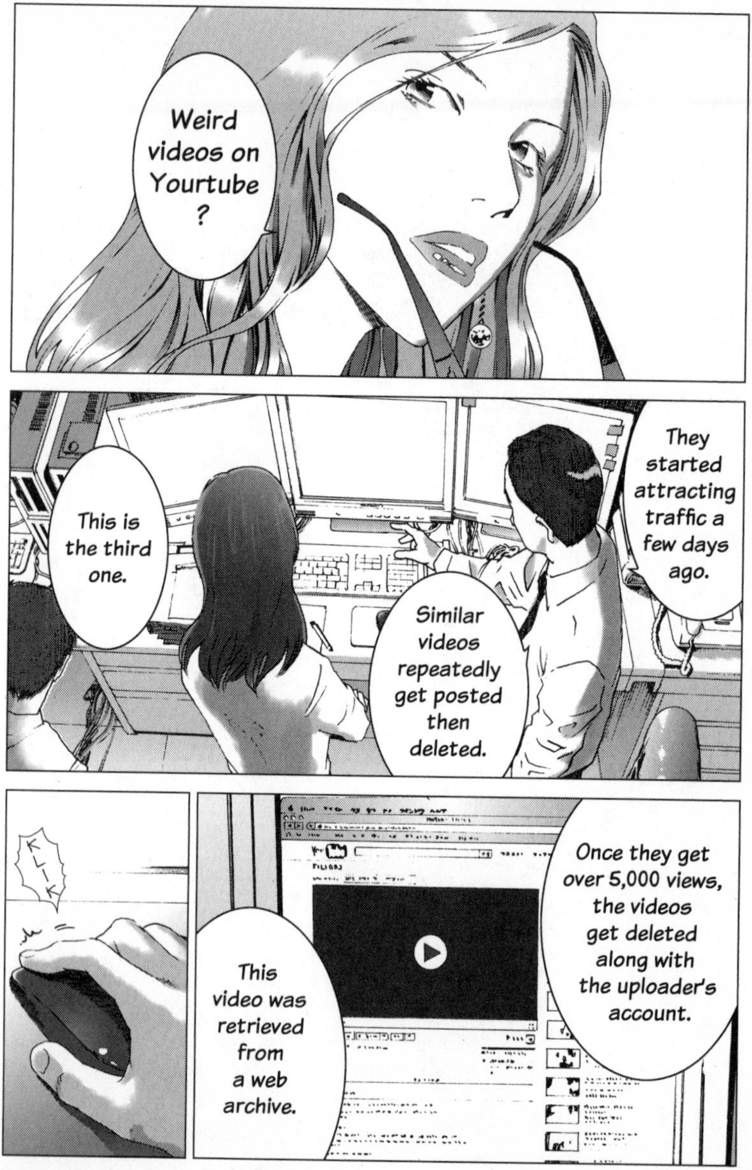
Weird videos on Yourtube ?
They started attracting traffic a few days ago.
Similar videos repeatedly get posted then deleted.
This is the third one.
Once they get over 5,000 views, the videos get deleted along with the uploader's account.
This video was retrieved from a web archive.
KLIK

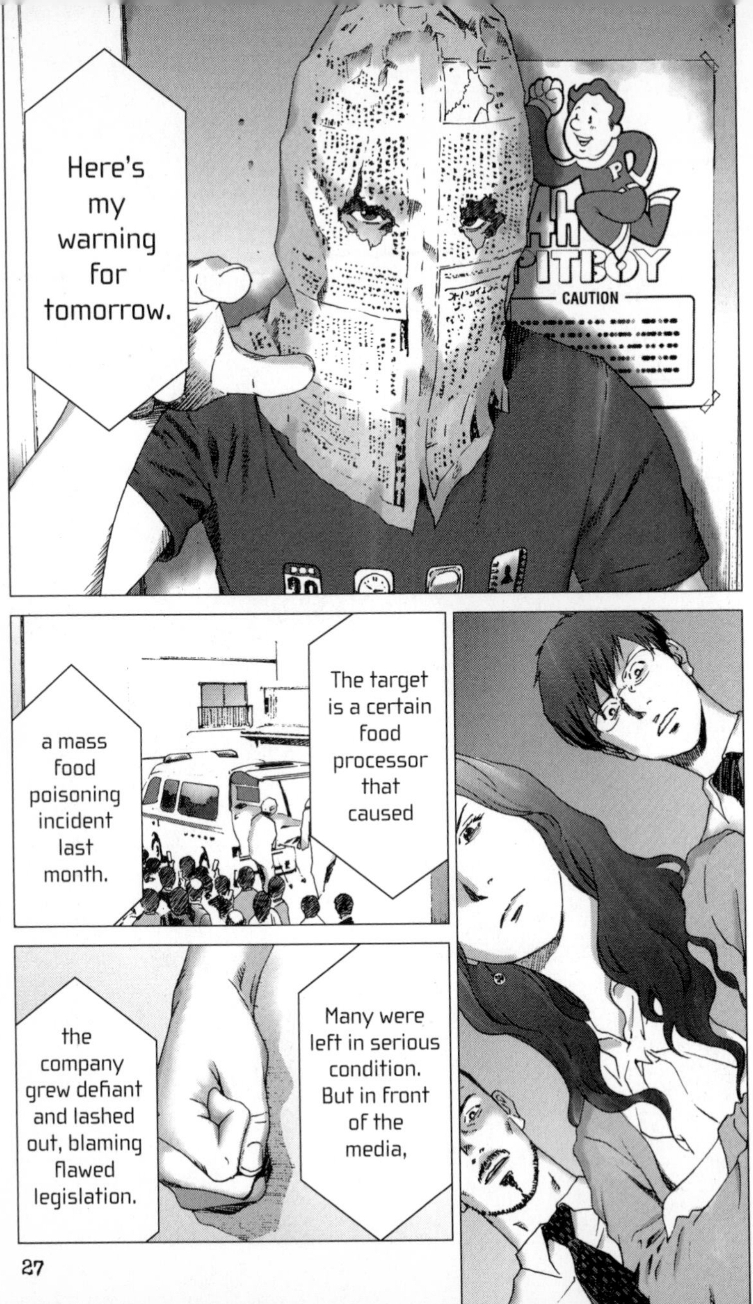
Here's my warning for tomorrow.
CAUTION
The target is a certain food processor that caused
a mass food poisoning incident last month.
Many were left in serious condition. But in front of the media,
the company grew defiant and lashed out, blaming flawed legislation.

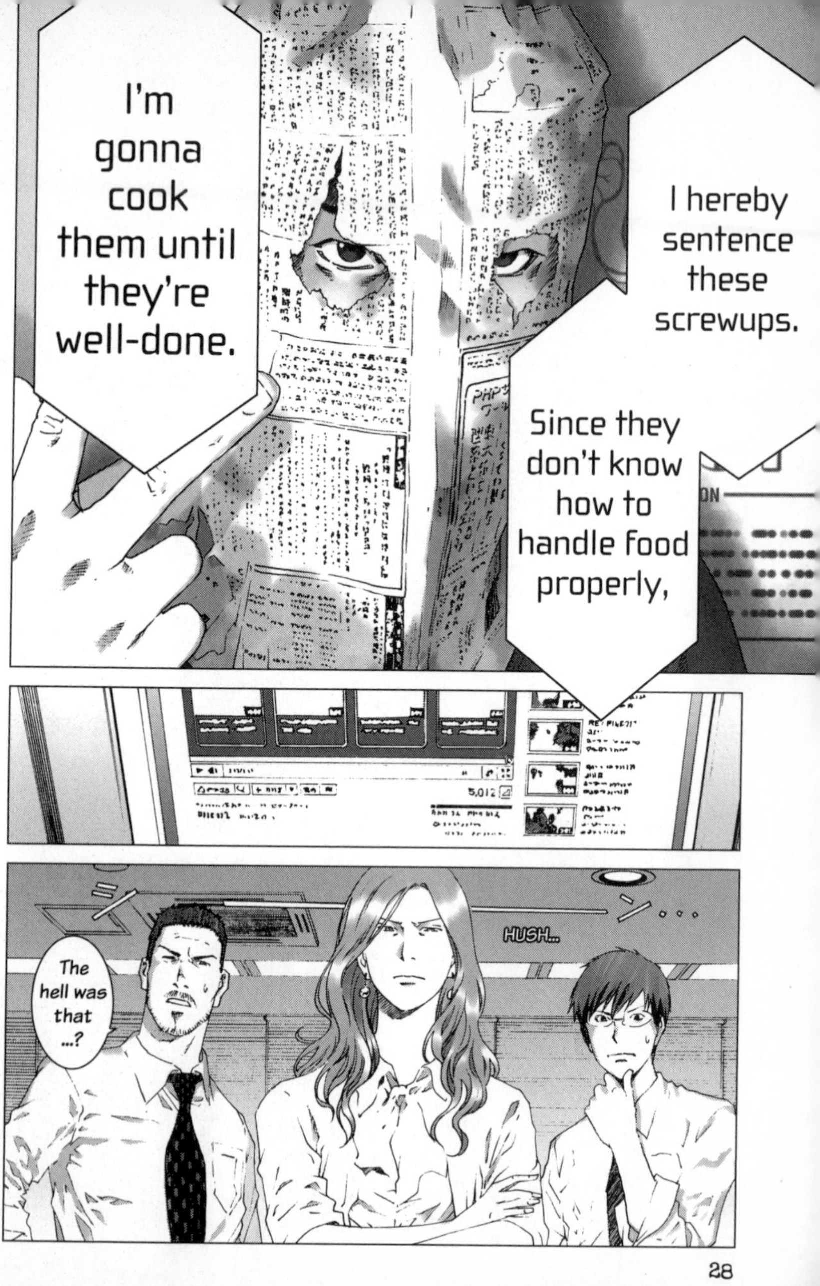
I hereby sentence these screwups.
Since they don't know how to handle food properly,
I'm gonna cook them until they're well-done.
HUSH...
The hell was that ...?

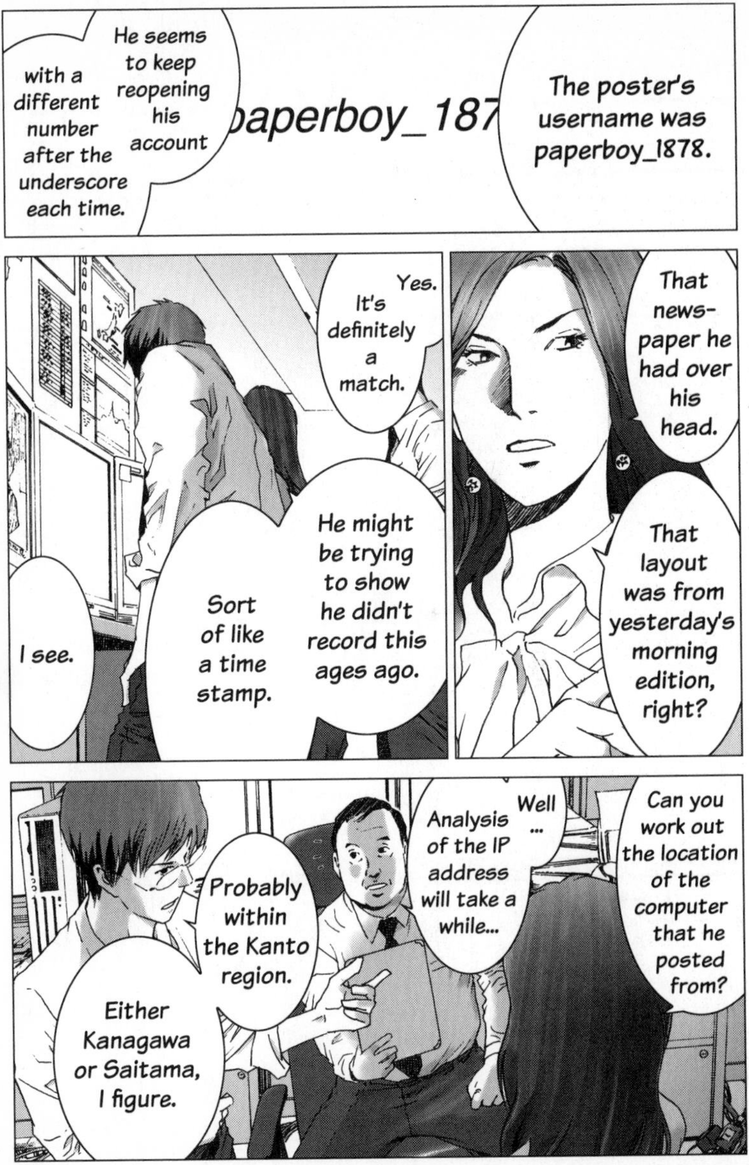
The poster's username was paperboy_1878.
He seems to keep reopening his account
with a different number after the underscore each time.
That news-paper he had over his head.
That layout was from yesterday's morning edition, right?
Yes. It's definitely a match.
He might be trying to show he didn't record this ages ago.
Sort of like a time stamp.
I see.
Can you work out the location of the computer that he posted from?
Well ...
Analysis of the IP address will take a while...
Probably within the Kanto region.
Either Kanagawa or Saitama, I figure.

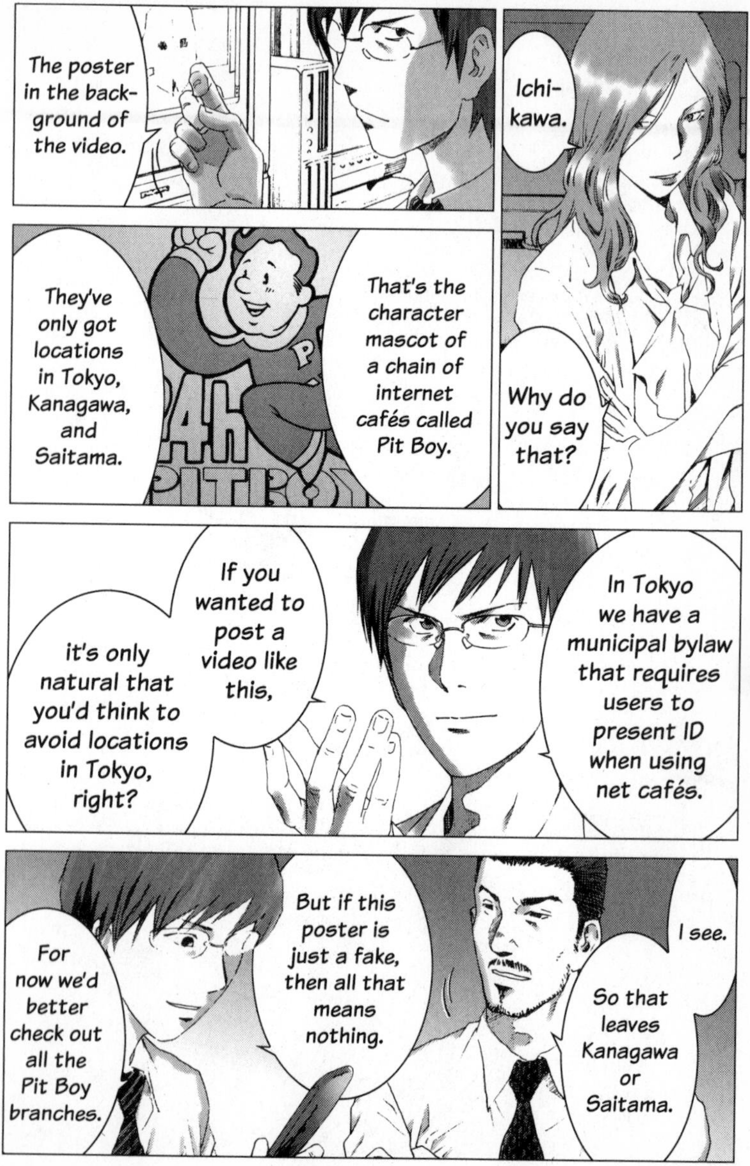
Ichi-kawa.
Why do you say that?
The poster in the back-ground of the video.
That's the character mascot of a chain of internet cafés called Pit Boy.
They've only got locations in Tokyo, Kanagawa, and Saitama.
In Tokyo we have a municipal bylaw that requires users to present ID when using net cafés.
If you wanted to post a video like this,
it's only natural that you'd think to avoid locations in Tokyo, right?
I see.
So that leaves Kanagawa or Saitama.
But if this poster is just a fake, then all that means nothing.
For now we'd better check out all the Pit Boy branches.

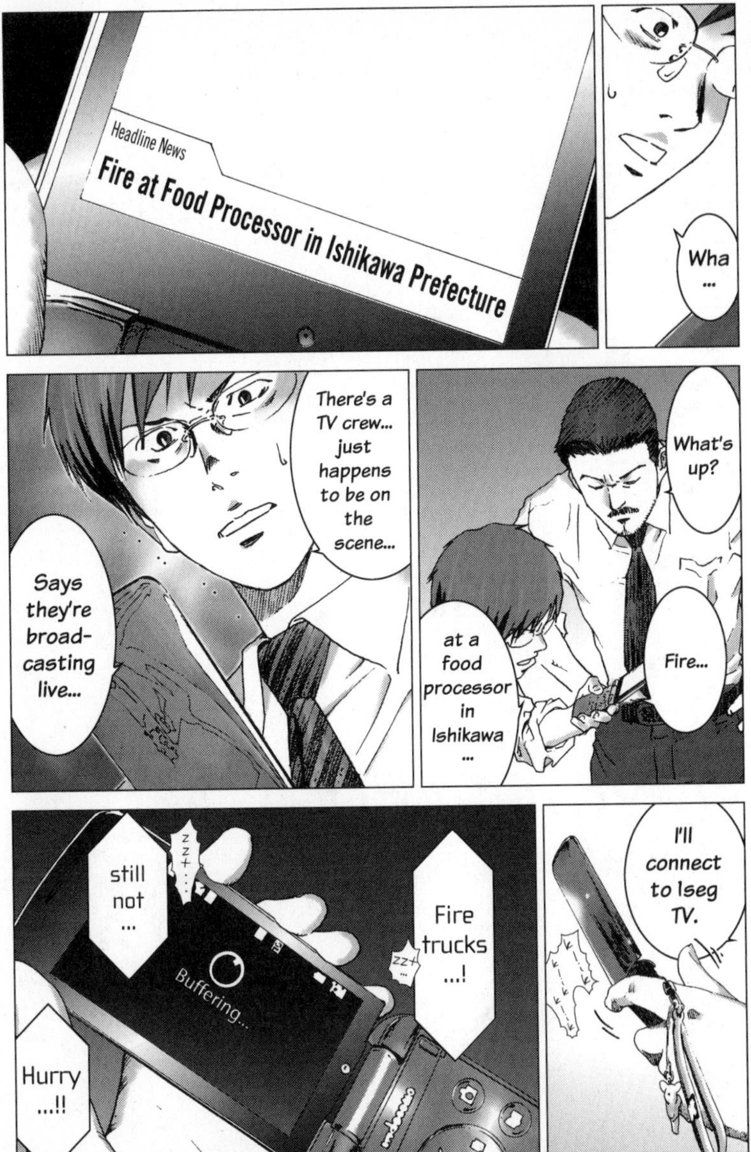

Wha ...
Headline News
Fire at Food Processor in Ishikawa Prefecture
What's up?
Fire...
at a food processor in Ishikawa ...
There's a TV crew... just happens to be on the scene...
Says they're broadcasting live...
I'll connect to Iseg TV.
Fire trucks ...!
still not ...
Buffering...
Hurry ...!!

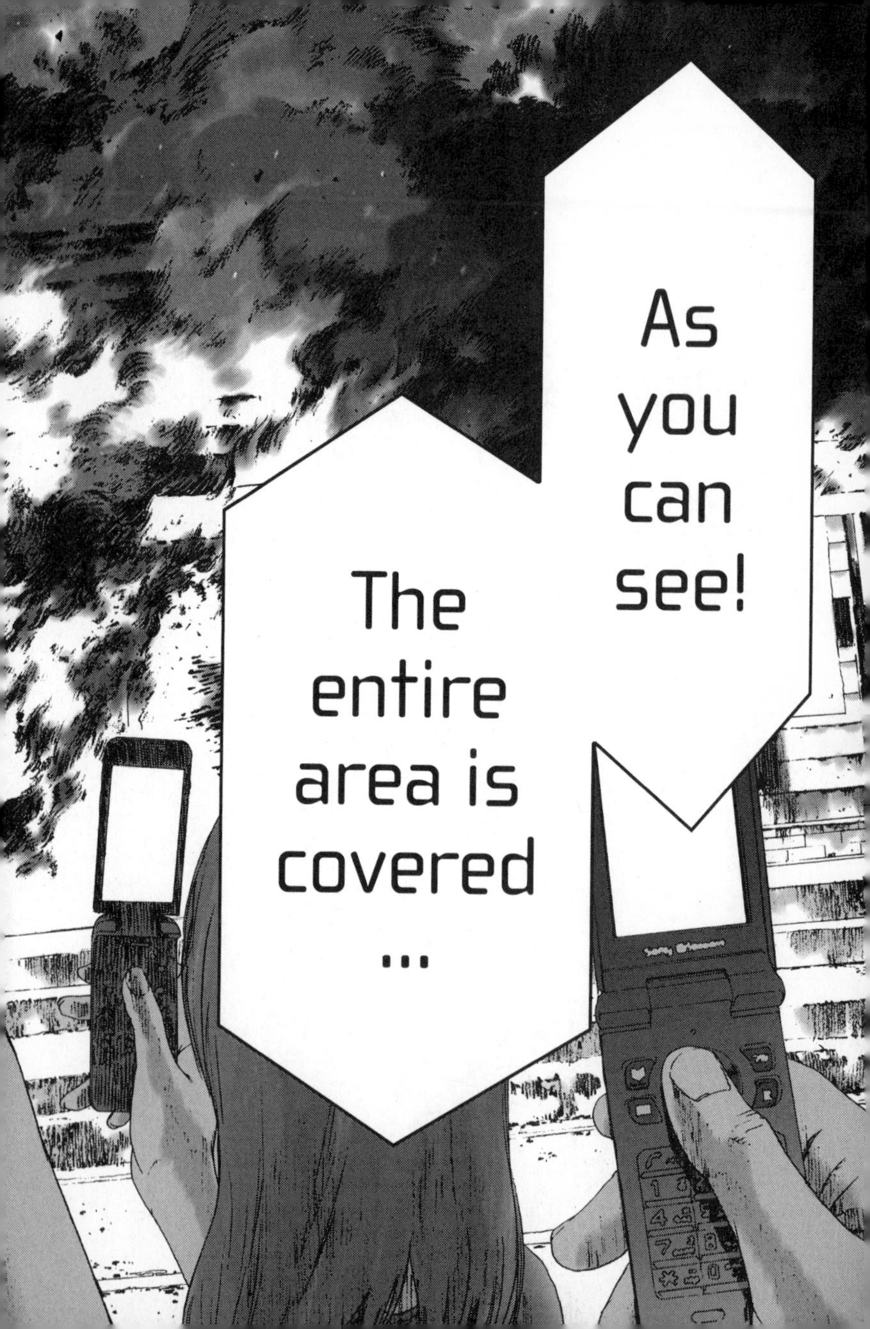
As you can see!
The entire area is covered ...

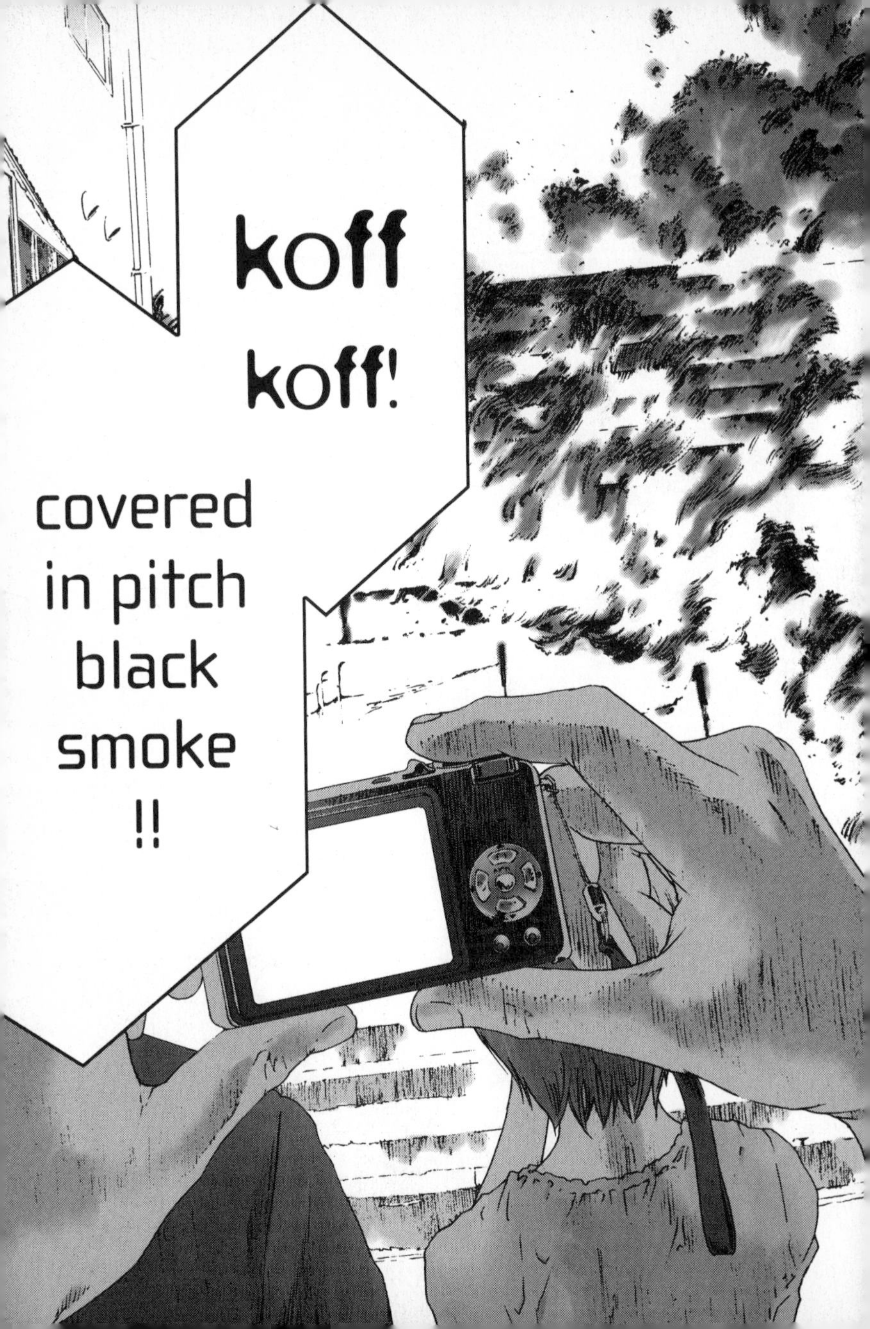
koff koff!
covered in pitch black smoke !!

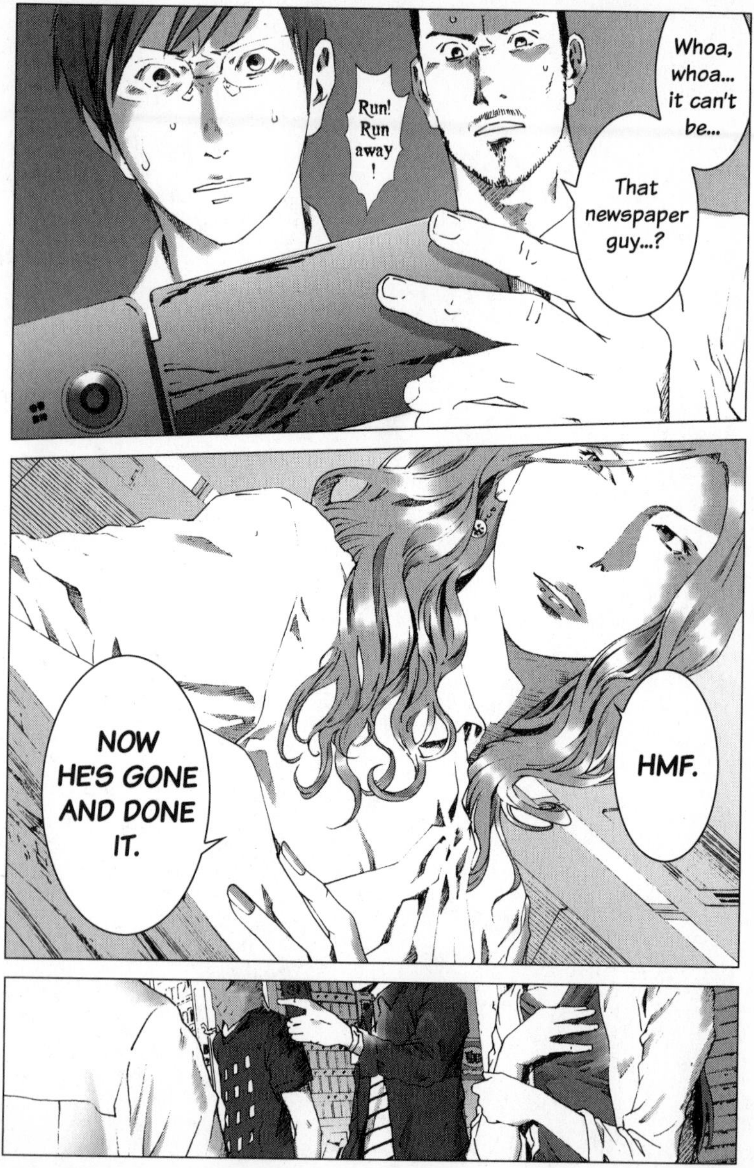
Whoa, whoa... it can't be...
That newspaper guy...?
Run! Run away!
HMF.
NOW HE'S GONE AND DONE IT.

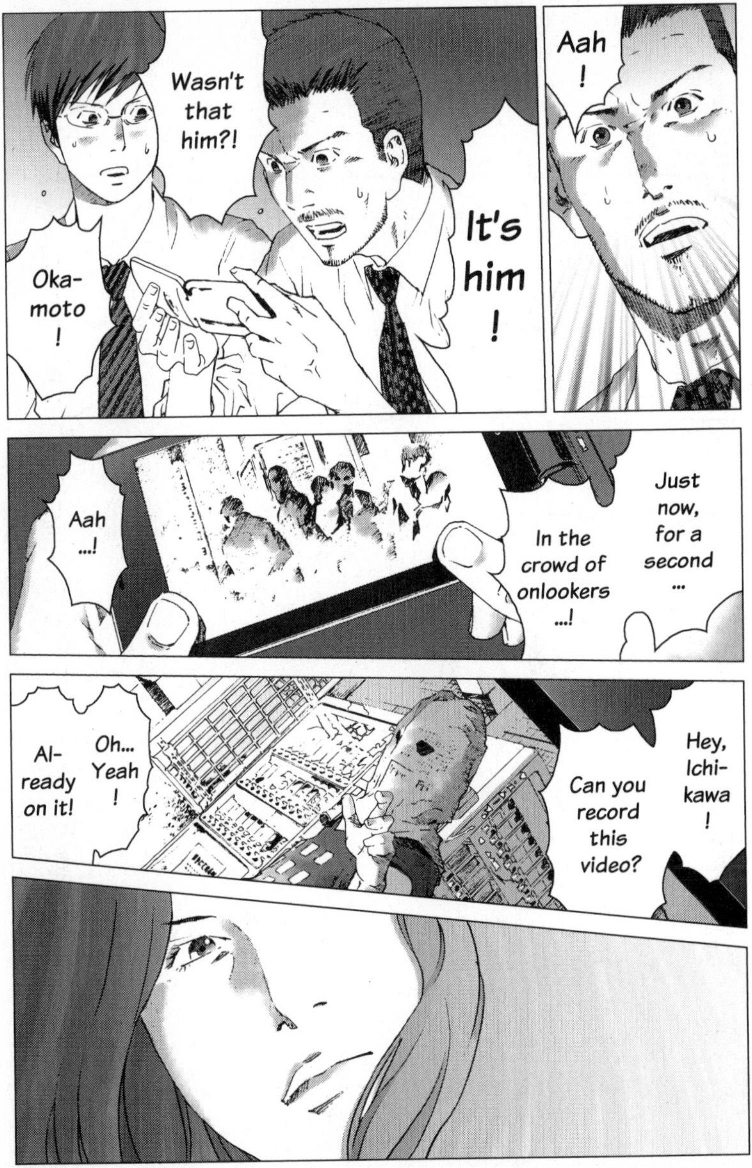
Aah!
Wasn't that him?!
It's him!
Okamoto!
Just now, for a second...
In the crowd of onlookers...!
Aah...!
Hey, Ichikawa!
Can you record this video?
Oh... Yeah!
Already on it!

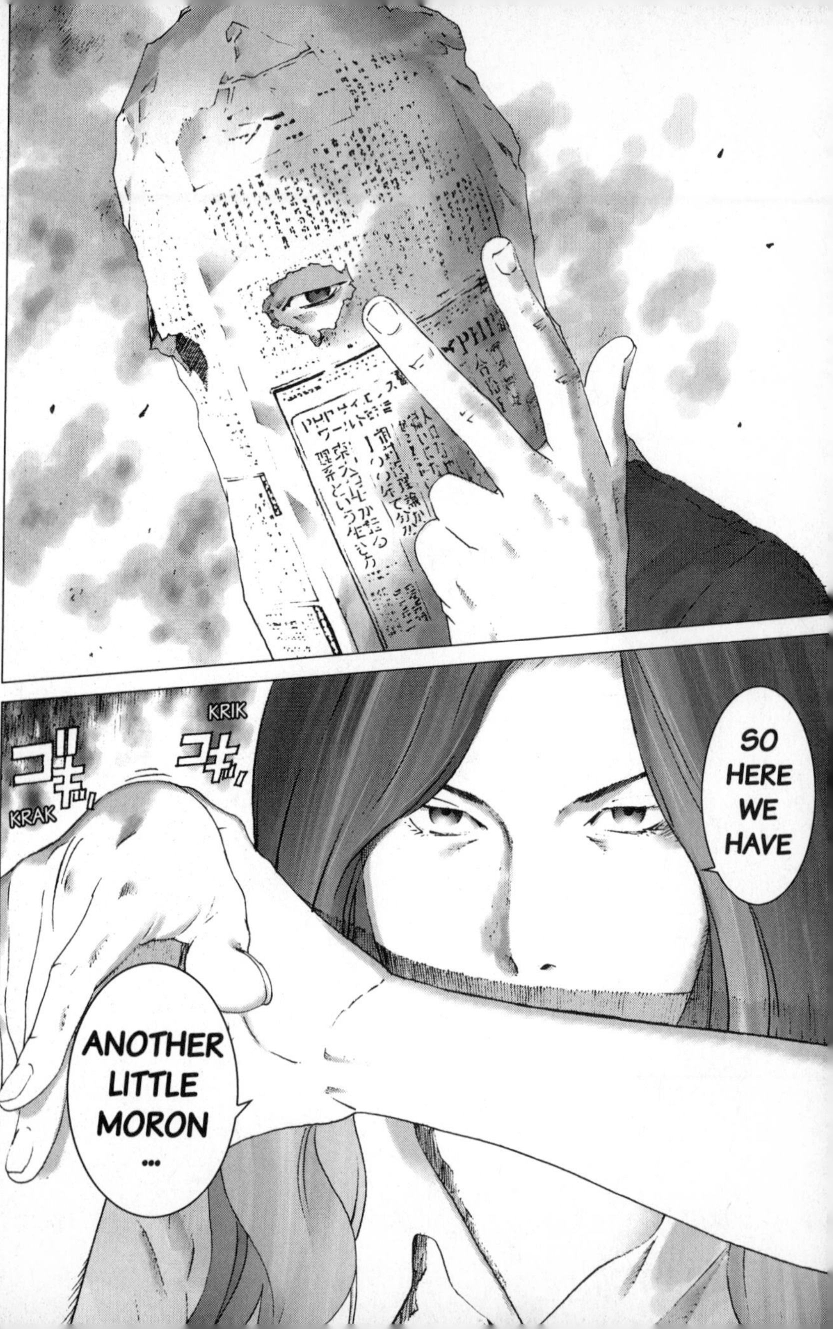
SO HERE WE HAVE
コキッ
KRIK
ゴキッ
KRAK
ANOTHER LITTLE MORON ...

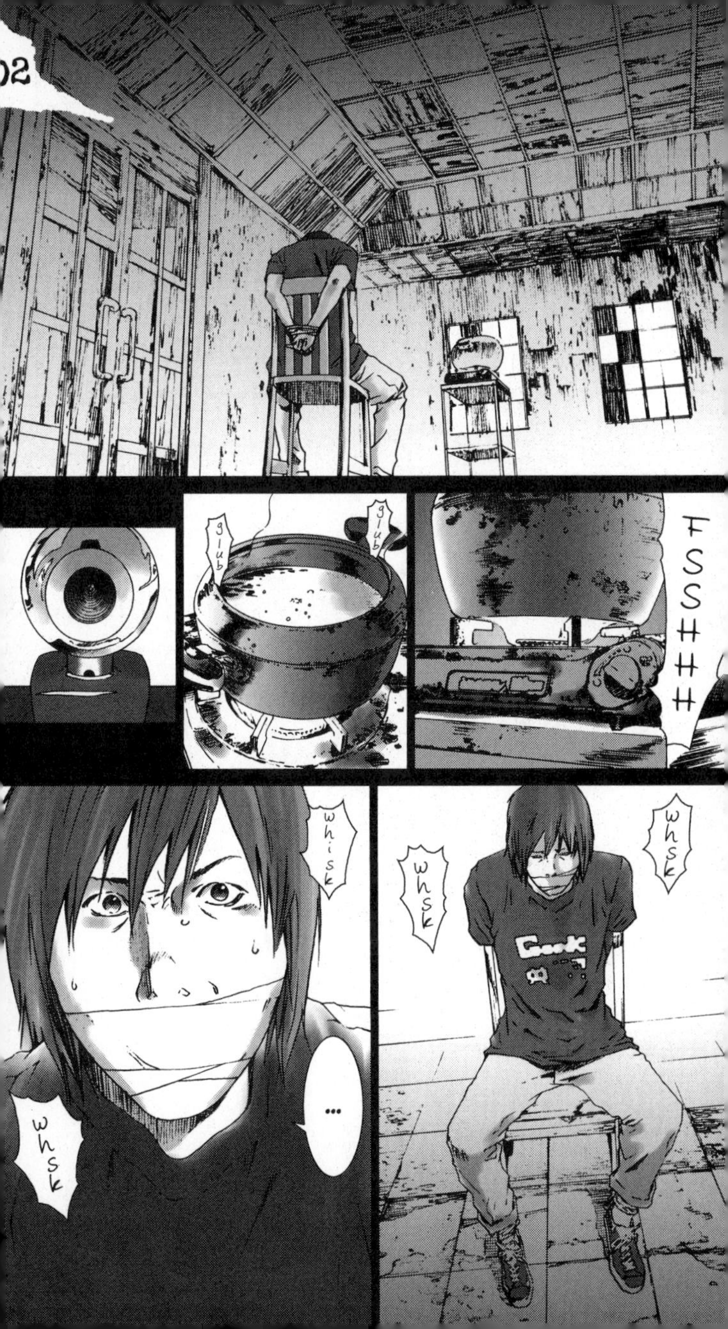
FSSHHH
glub
glub
whsk
whsk
whisk
...
whsk

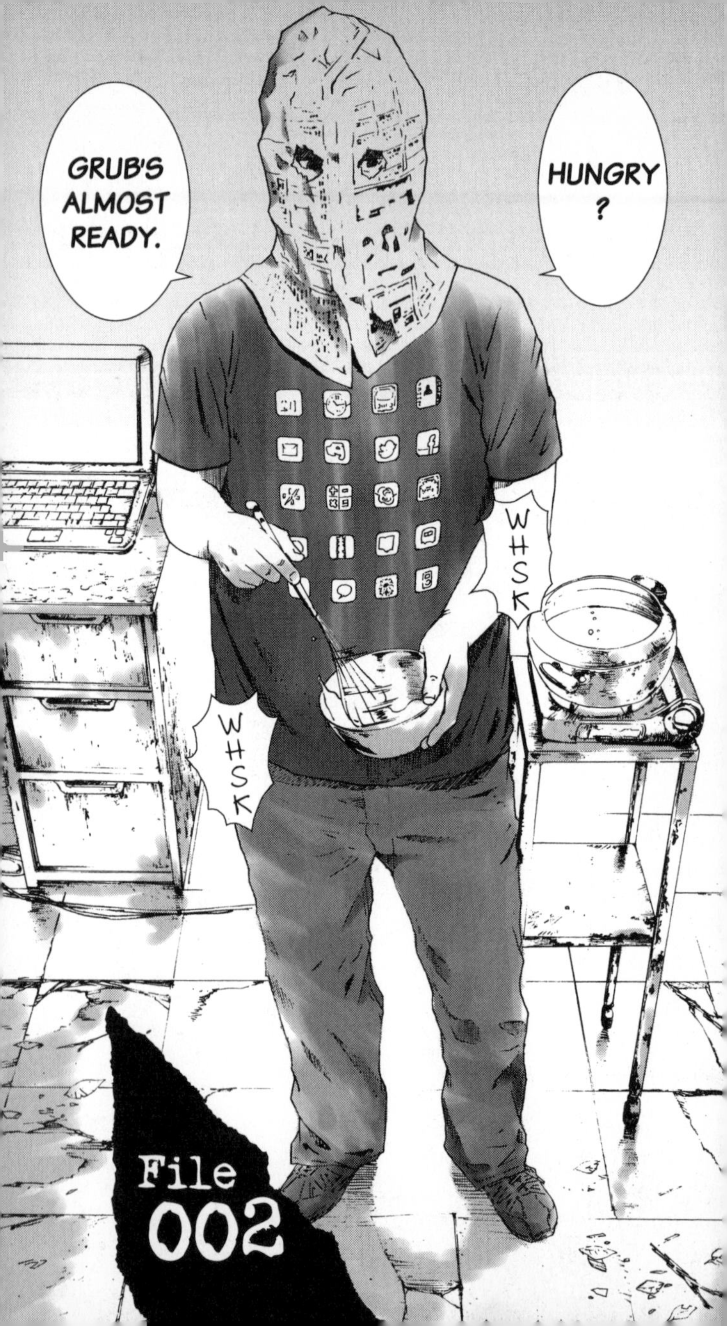
HUNGRY ?
GRUB'S ALMOST READY.
WHSK
WHSK
File 002

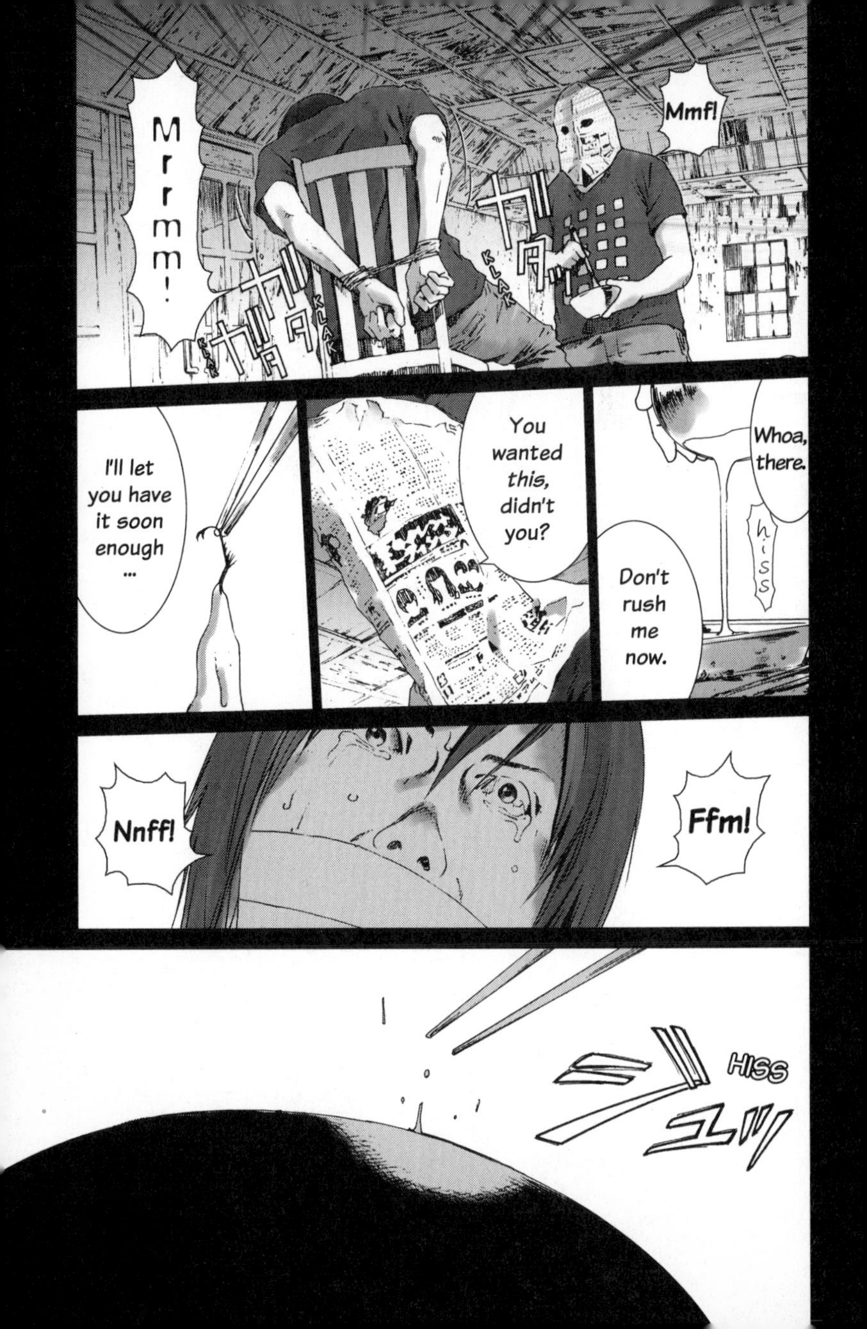
Mmf!
KLAK
KLAK
KLAK
Mrrmm!
Whoa, there.
hiss
Don't rush me now.
You wanted this, didn't you?
I'll let you have it soon enough ...
Ffm!
Nnff!
HISS

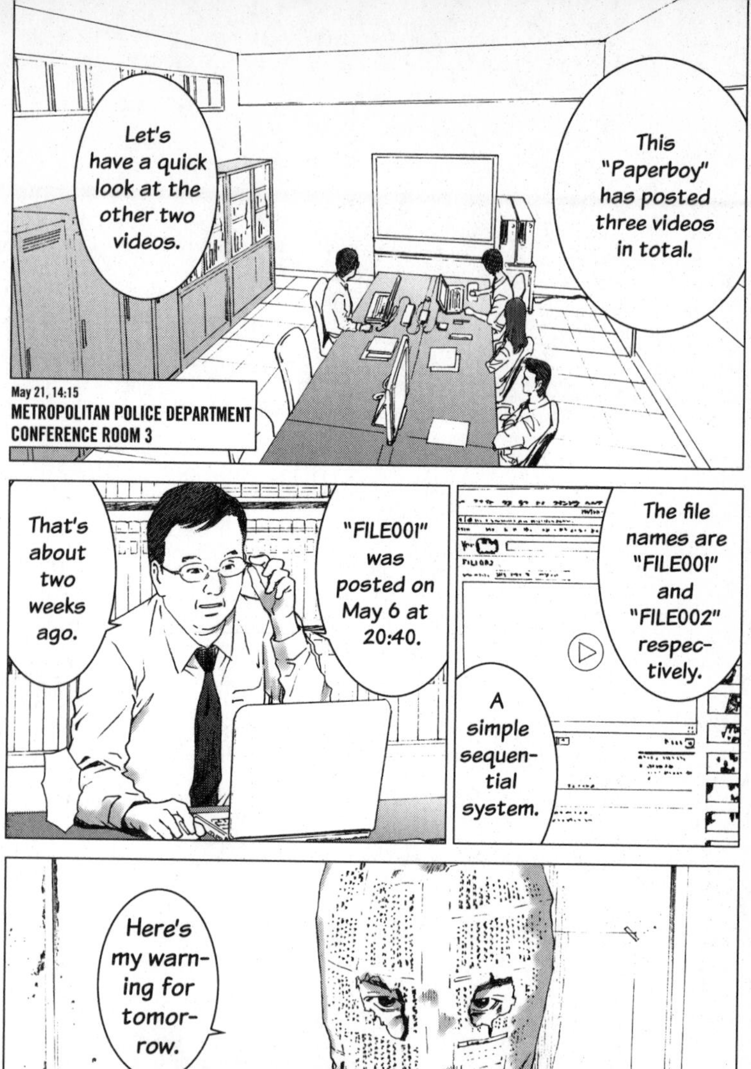
This "Paperboy" has posted three videos in total.
Let's have a quick look at the other two videos.
May 21, 14:15
METROPOLITAN POLICE DEPARTMENT CONFERENCE ROOM 3
The file names are "FILE001" and "FILE002" respectively.
A simple sequential system.
"FILE001" was posted on May 6 at 20:40.
That's about two weeks ago.
Here's my warning for tomorrow.

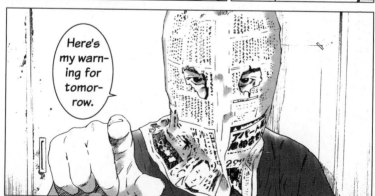

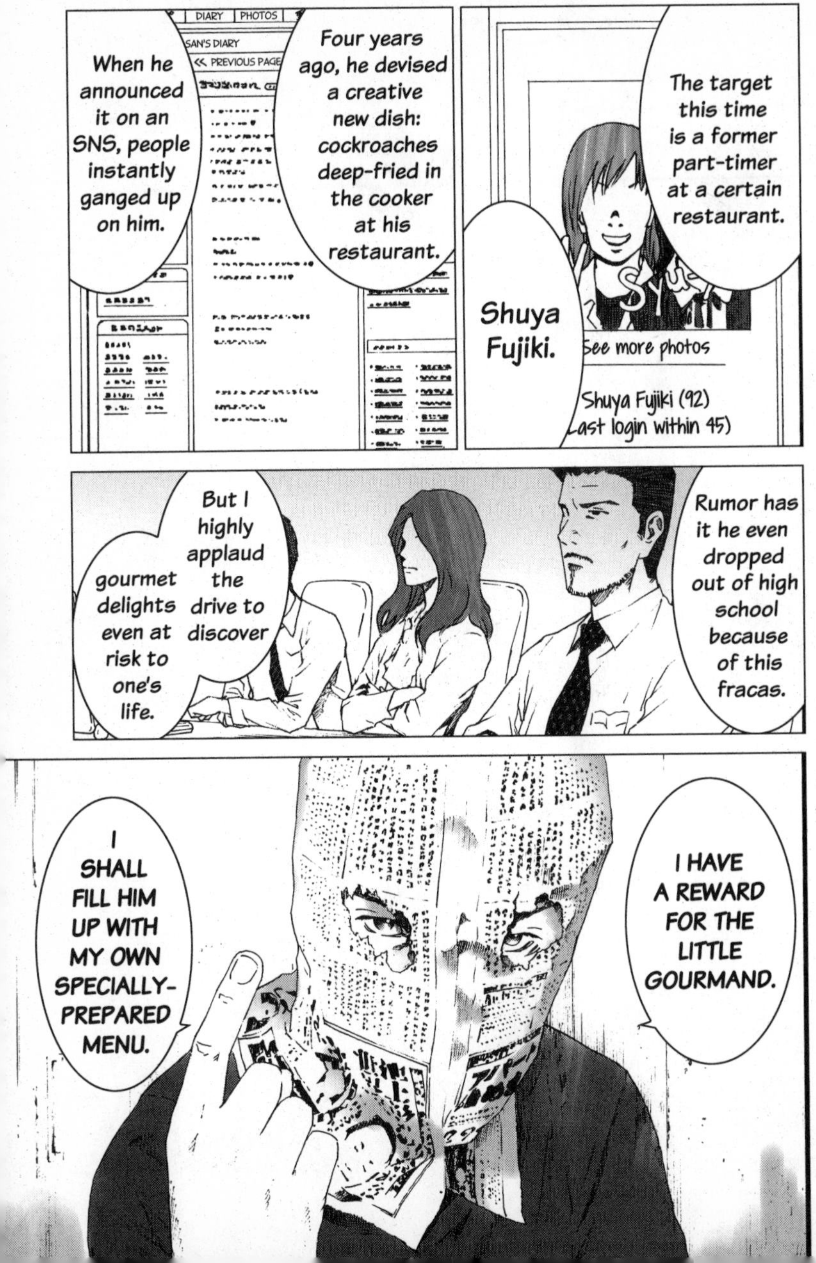

The target this time is a former part-timer at a certain restaurant.
Shuya Fujiki.
See more photos
Shuya Fujiki (92)
Last login within 45)
DIARY
PHOTOS
SAN'S DIARY
« PREVIOUS PAGE
Four years ago, he devised a creative new dish: cockroaches deep-fried in the cooker at his restaurant.
When he announced it on an SNS, people instantly ganged up on him.
Rumor has it he even dropped out of high school because of this fracas.
But I highly applaud the drive to discover gourmet delights even at risk to one's life.
I HAVE A REWARD FOR THE LITTLE GOURMAND.
I SHALL FILL HIM UP WITH MY OWN SPECIALLY-PREPARED MENU.

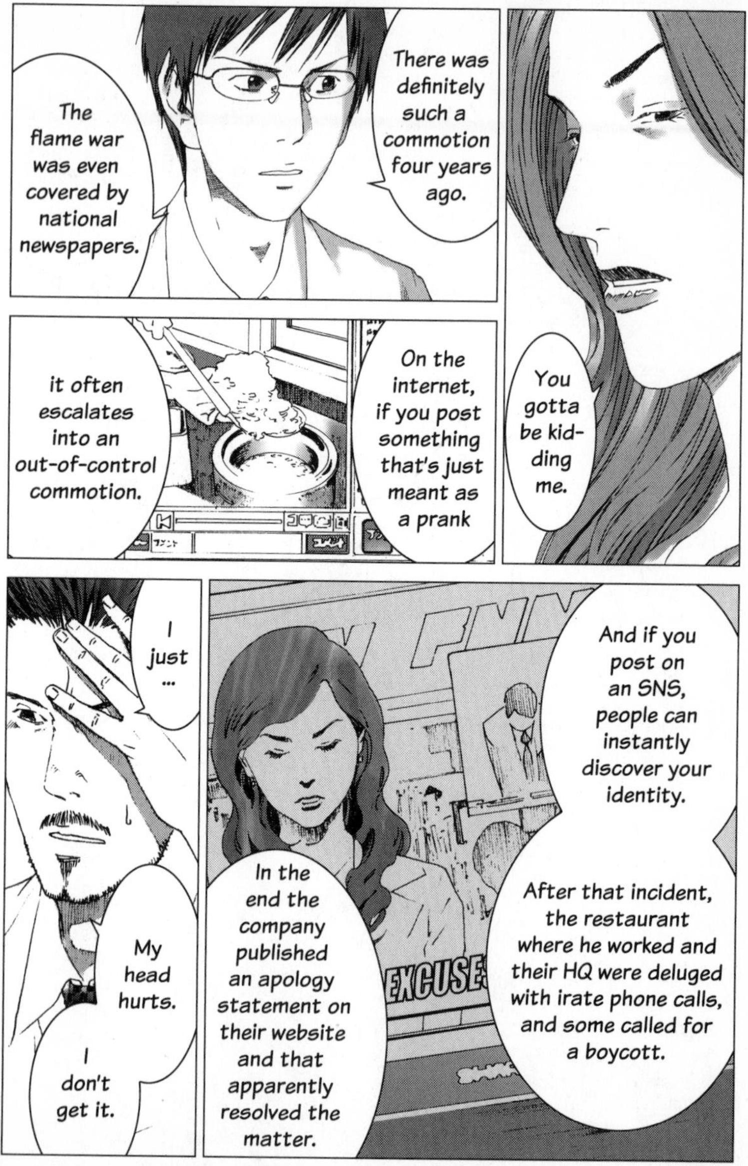
You gotta be kid-ding me.
There was definitely such a commotion four years ago.
The flame war was even covered by national newspapers.
On the internet, if you post something that's just meant as a prank
it often escalates into an out-of-control commotion.
And if you post on an SNS, people can instantly discover your identity.
EXCUSE
After that incident, the restaurant where he worked and their HQ were deluged with irate phone calls, and some called for a boycott.
In the end the company published an apology statement on their website and that apparently resolved the matter.
I just ...
My head hurts.
I don't get it.

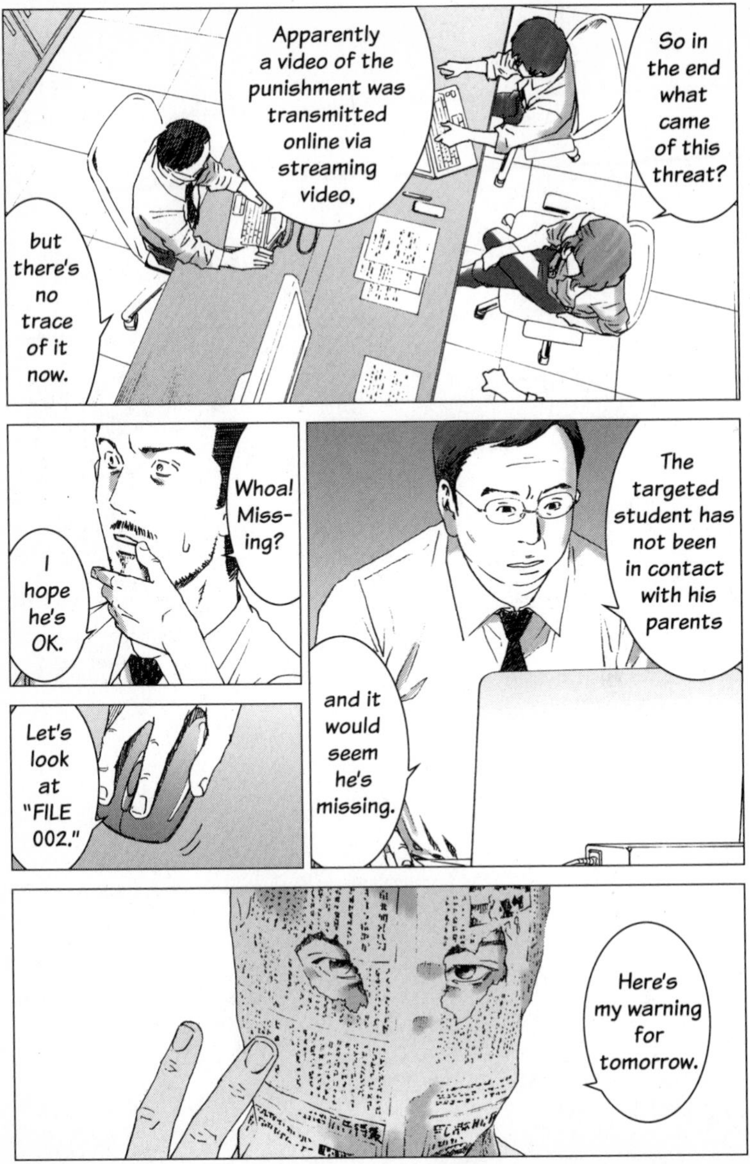
So in the end what came of this threat?
Apparently a video of the punishment was transmitted online via streaming video,
but there's no trace of it now.
The targeted student has not been in contact with his parents
and it would seem he's missing.
Whoa! Miss-ing?
I hope he's OK.
Let's look at "FILE 002."
Here's my warning for tomorrow.

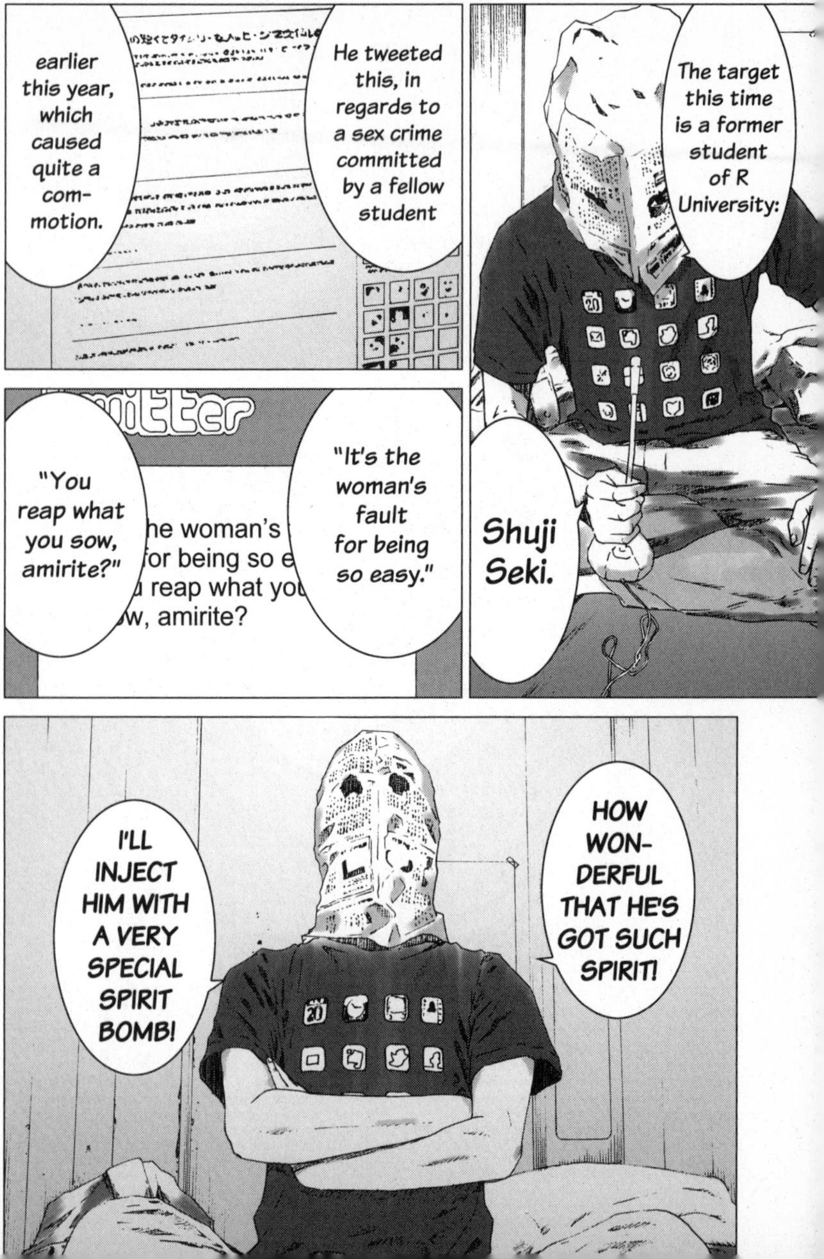
The target this time is a former student of R University:
Shuji Seki.
He tweeted this, in regards to a sex crime committed by a fellow student
earlier this year, which caused quite a com-motion.
"It's the woman's fault for being so easy."
"You reap what you sow, amirite?"
HOW WON-DERFUL THAT HE'S GOT SUCH SPIRIT!
I'LL INJECT HIM WITH A VERY SPECIAL SPIRIT BOMB!

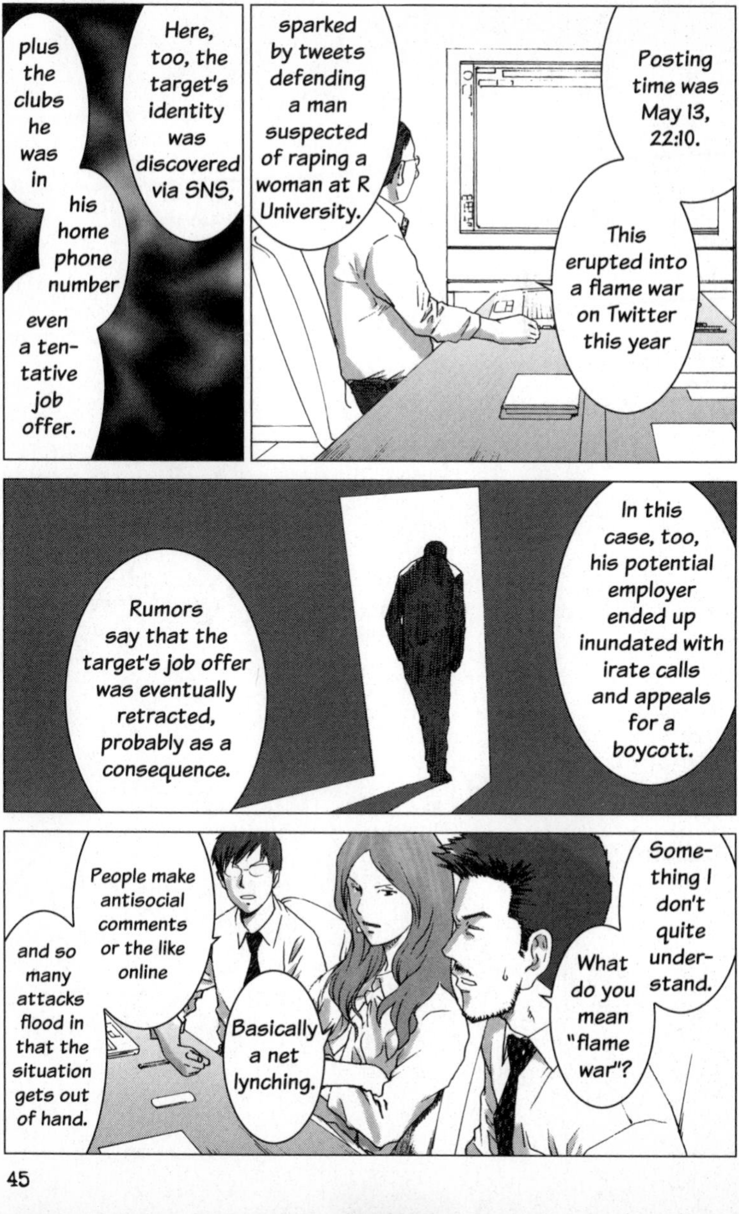
Posting time was May 13, 22:10.
This erupted into a flame war on Twitter this year
sparked by tweets defending a man suspected of raping a woman at R University.
Here, too, the target's identity was discovered via SNS,
plus the clubs he was in
his home phone number
even a ten-tative job offer.
In this case, too, his potential employer ended up inundated with irate calls and appeals for a boycott.
Rumors say that the target's job offer was eventually retracted, probably as a consequence.
Some-thing I don't quite under-stand.
What do you mean "flame war"?
Basically a net lynching.
People make antisocial comments or the like online
and so many attacks flood in that the situation gets out of hand.

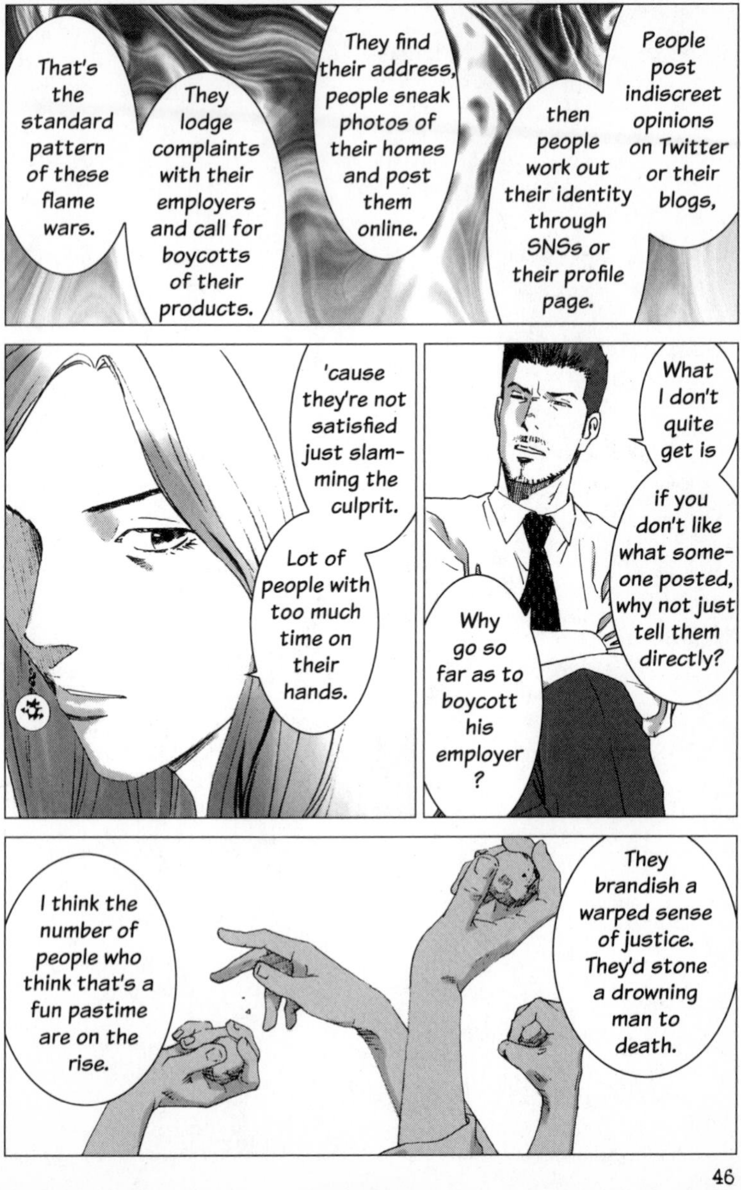
People post indiscreet opinions on Twitter or their blogs,
then people work out their identity through SNSs or their profile page.
They find their address, people sneak photos of their homes and post them online.
They lodge complaints with their employers and call for boycotts of their products.
That's the standard pattern of these flame wars.
What I don't quite get is
if you don't like what some-one posted, why not just tell them directly?
Why go so far as to boycott his employer?
'cause they're not satisfied just slam-ming the culprit.
Lot of people with too much time on their hands.
They brandish a warped sense of justice. They'd stone a drowning man to death.
I think the number of people who think that's a fun pastime are on the rise.

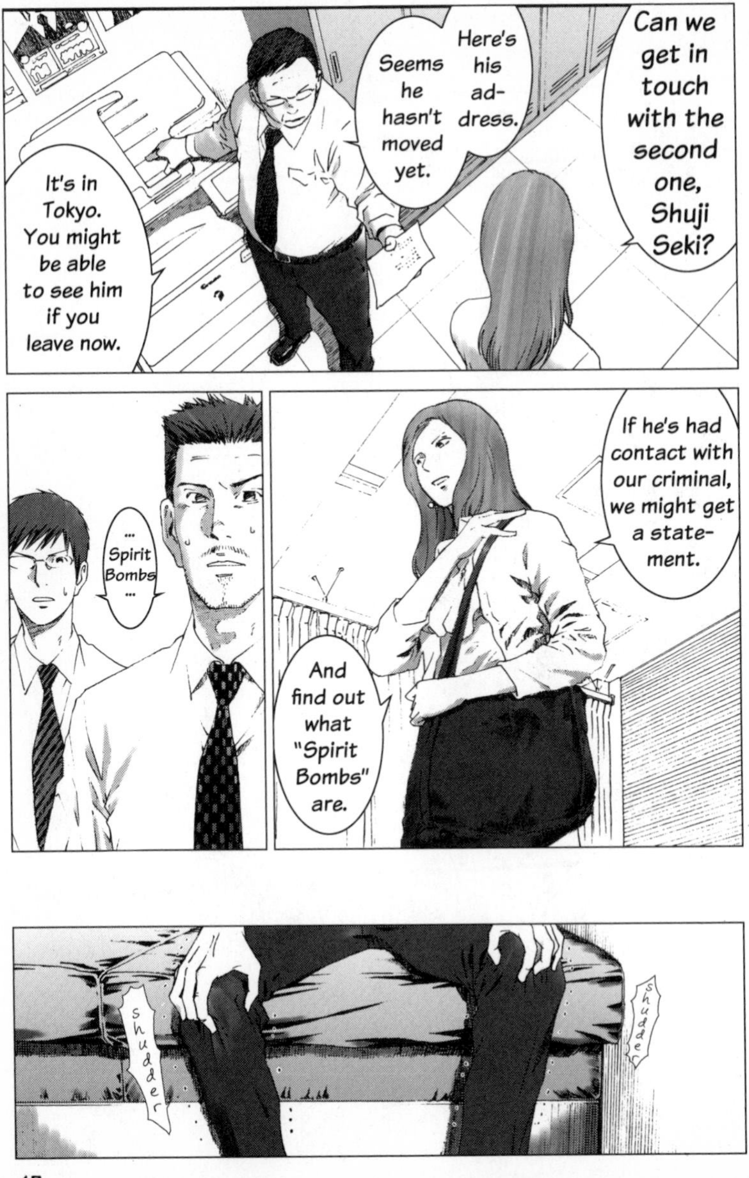
Can we get in touch with the second one, Shuji Seki?
Here's his ad-dress.
Seems he hasn't moved yet.
It's in Tokyo. You might be able to see him if you leave now.
If he's had contact with our criminal, we might get a state-ment.
And find out what "Spirit Bombs" are.
... Spirit Bombs ...
shudder
shudder

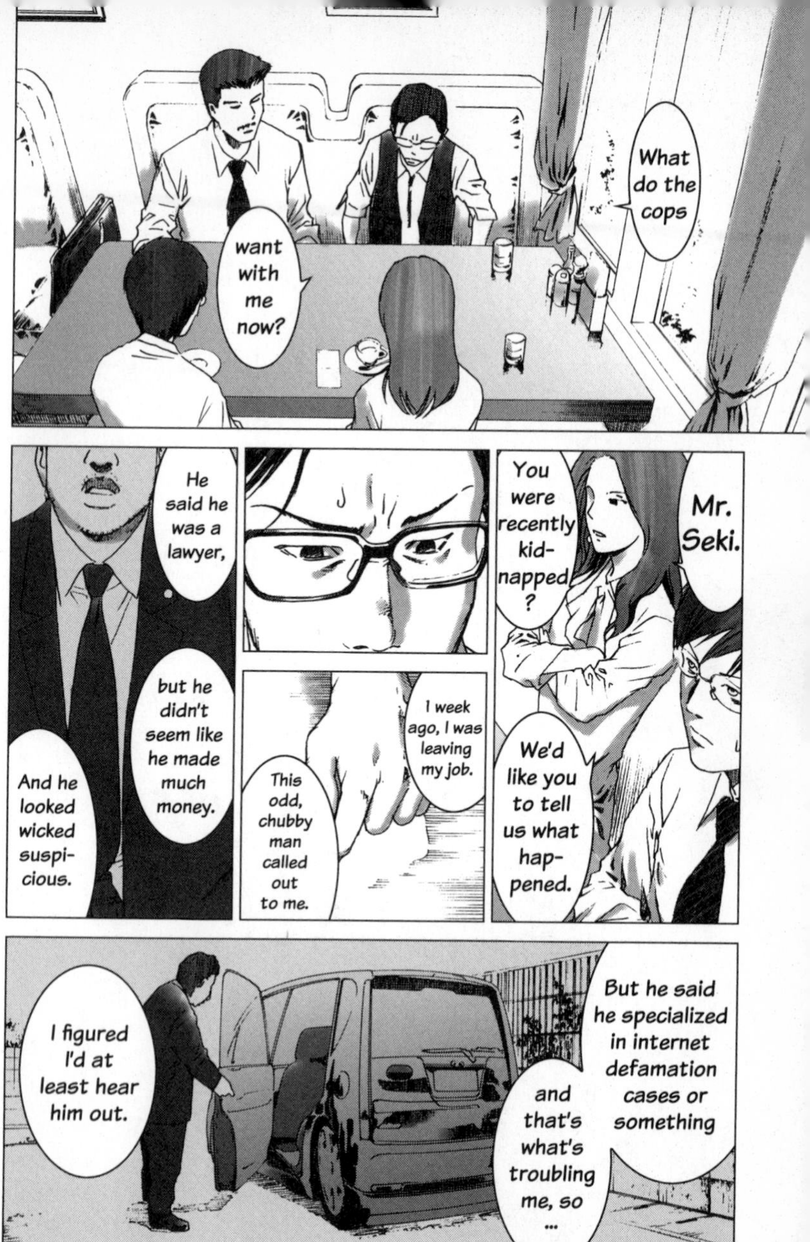
What do the cops
want with me now?
Mr. Seki.
You were recently kid-napped?
We'd like you to tell us what hap-pened.
1 week ago, I was leaving my job.
This odd, chubby man called out to me.
He said he was a lawyer,
but he didn't seem like he made much money.
And he looked wicked suspi-cious.
But he said he specialized in internet defamation cases or something
and that's what's troubling me, so ...
I figured I'd at least hear him out.

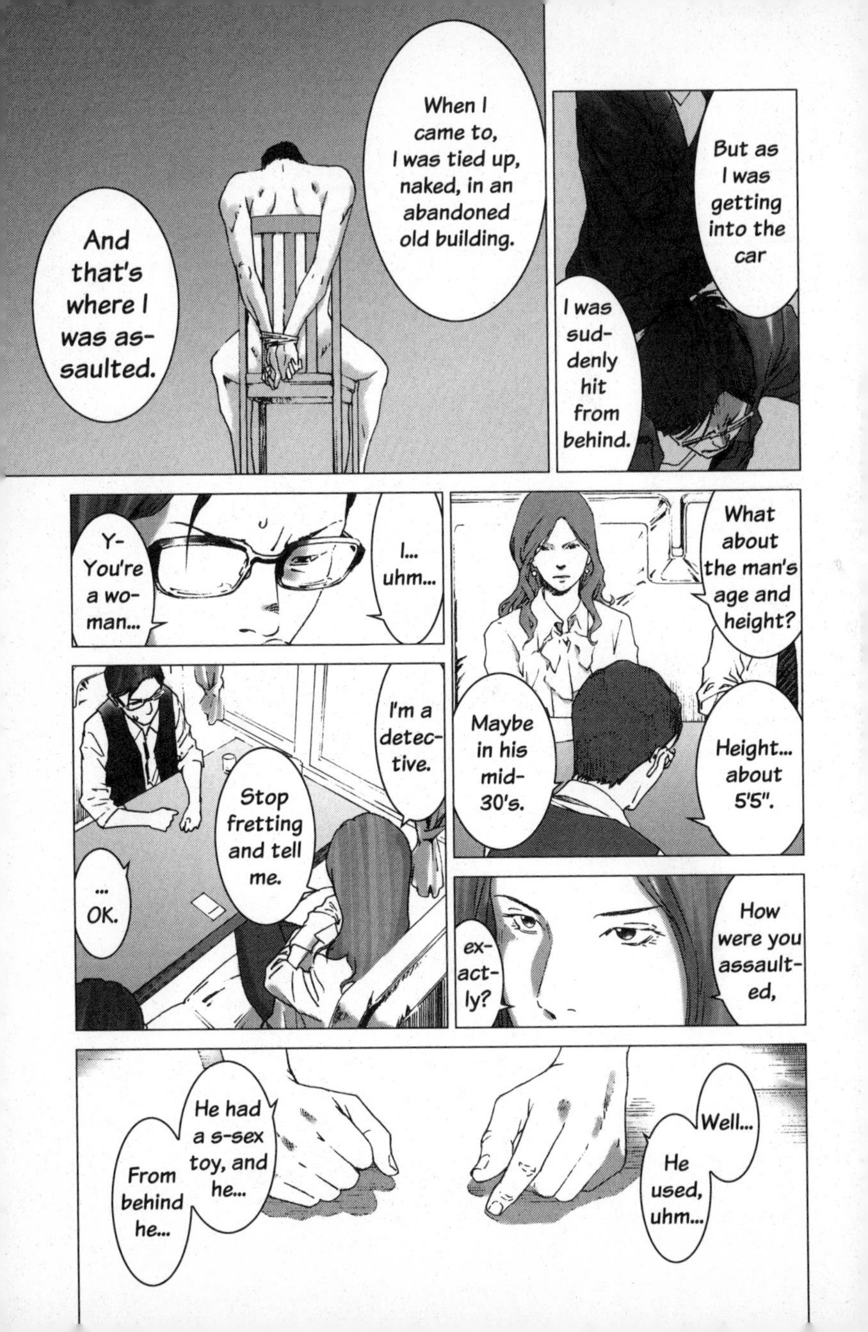

But as I was getting into the car
I was suddenly hit from behind.
When I came to, I was tied up, naked, in an abandoned old building.
And that's where I was assaulted.
What about the man's age and height?
Height... about 5'5".
Maybe in his mid-30's.
How were you assault-ed,
ex-act-ly?
I... uhm...
Y-You're a wo-man...
I'm a detec-tive.
Stop fretting and tell me.
... OK.
Well...
He used, uhm...
He had a s-sex toy, and he...
From behind he...

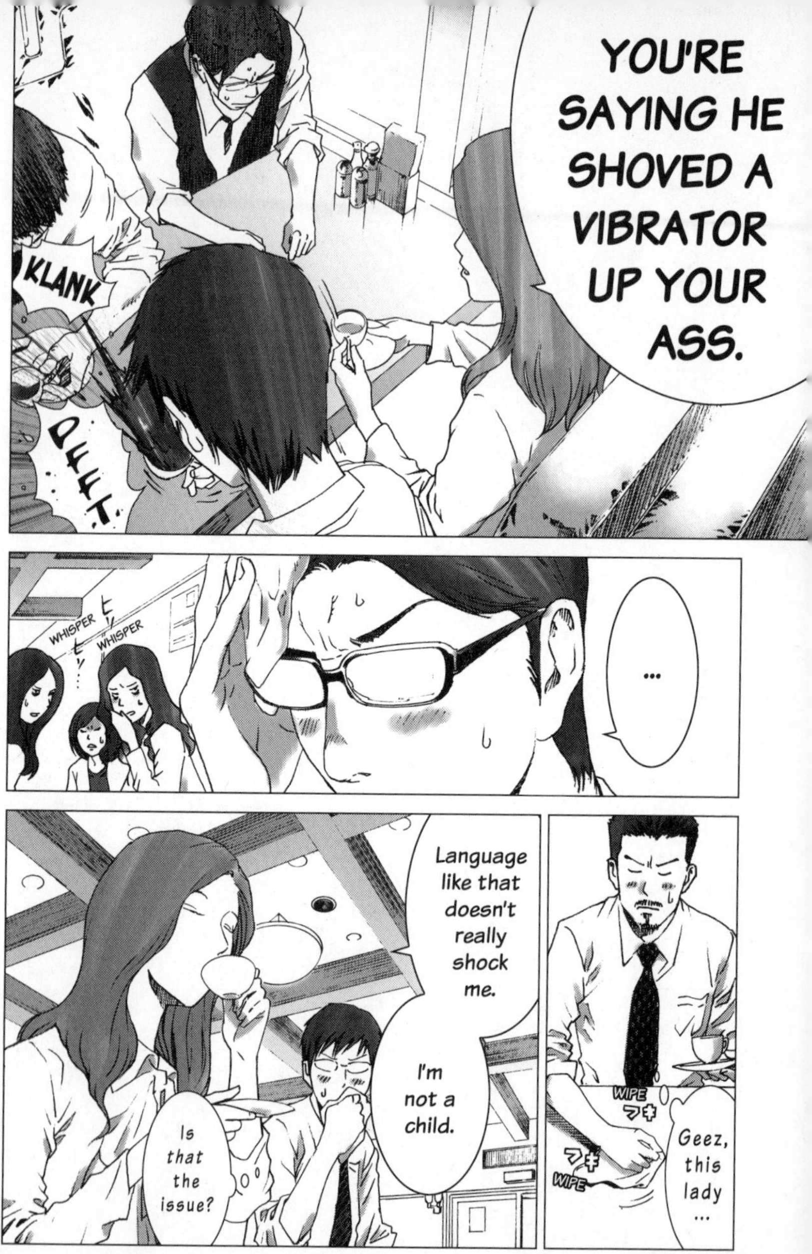
YOU'RE SAYING HE SHOVED A VIBRATOR UP YOUR ASS.
KLANK
DFFFT
...
WHISPER
WHISPER
WIPE
フキ
フキ
WIPE
Geez, this lady ...
Language like that doesn't really shock me.
I'm not a child.
Is that the issue?

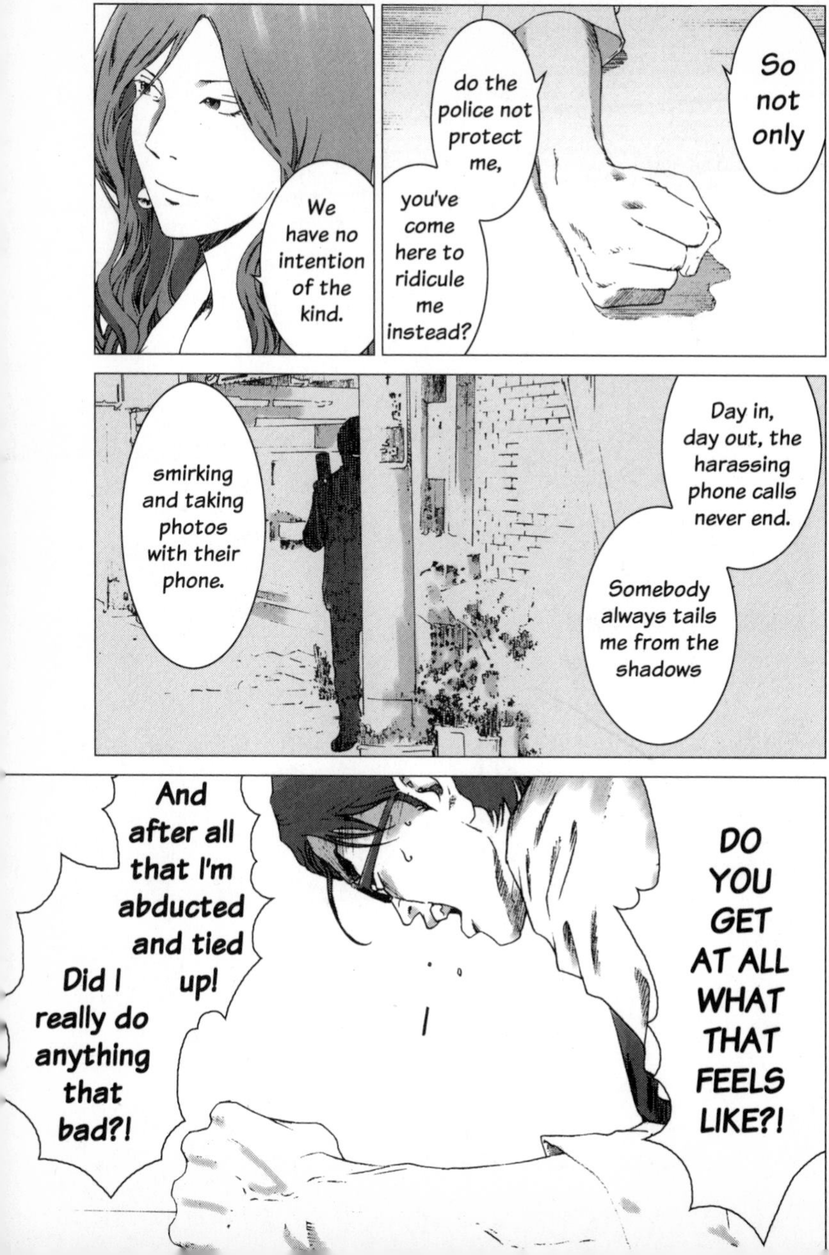
So not only
do the police not protect me,
you've come here to ridicule me instead?
We have no intention of the kind.
Day in, day out, the harassing phone calls never end.
Somebody always tails me from the shadows
smirking and taking photos with their phone.
DO YOU GET AT ALL WHAT THAT FEELS LIKE?!
And after all that I'm abducted and tied up!
Did I really do anything that bad?!

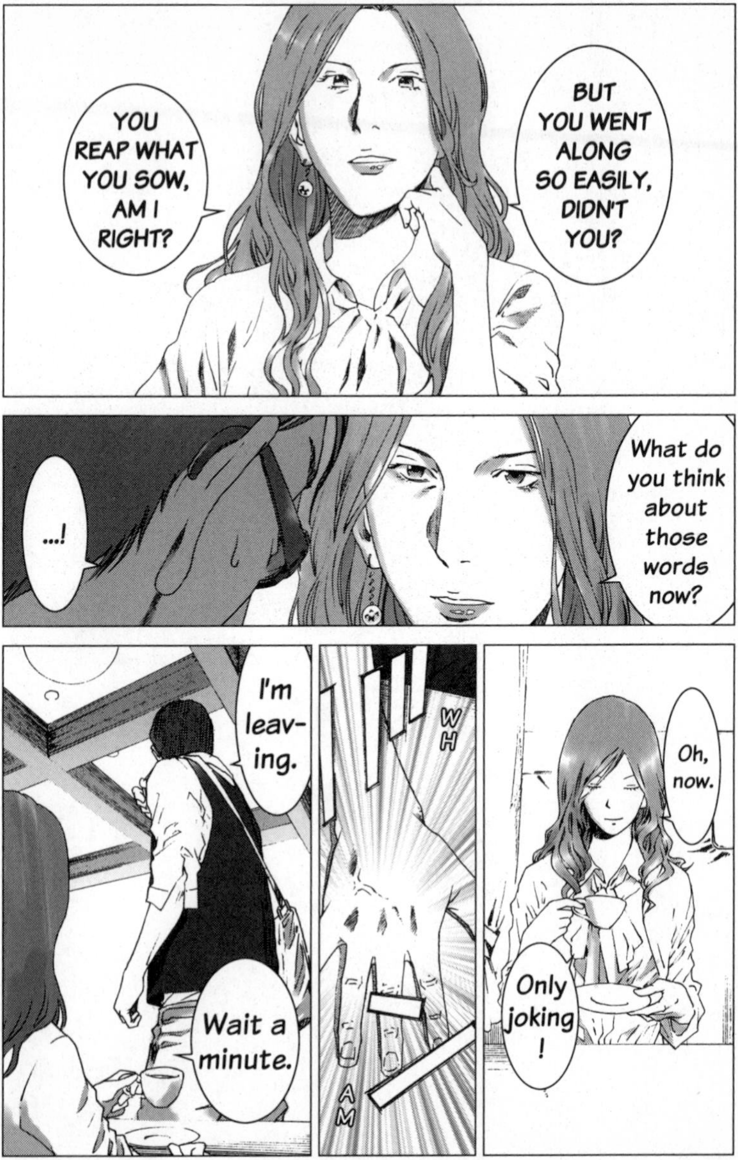
BUT YOU WENT ALONG SO EASILY, DIDN'T YOU?
YOU REAP WHAT YOU SOW, AM I RIGHT?
What do you think about those words now?
...!
Oh, now.
Only joking!
WHAM
I'm leav-ing.
Wait a minute.

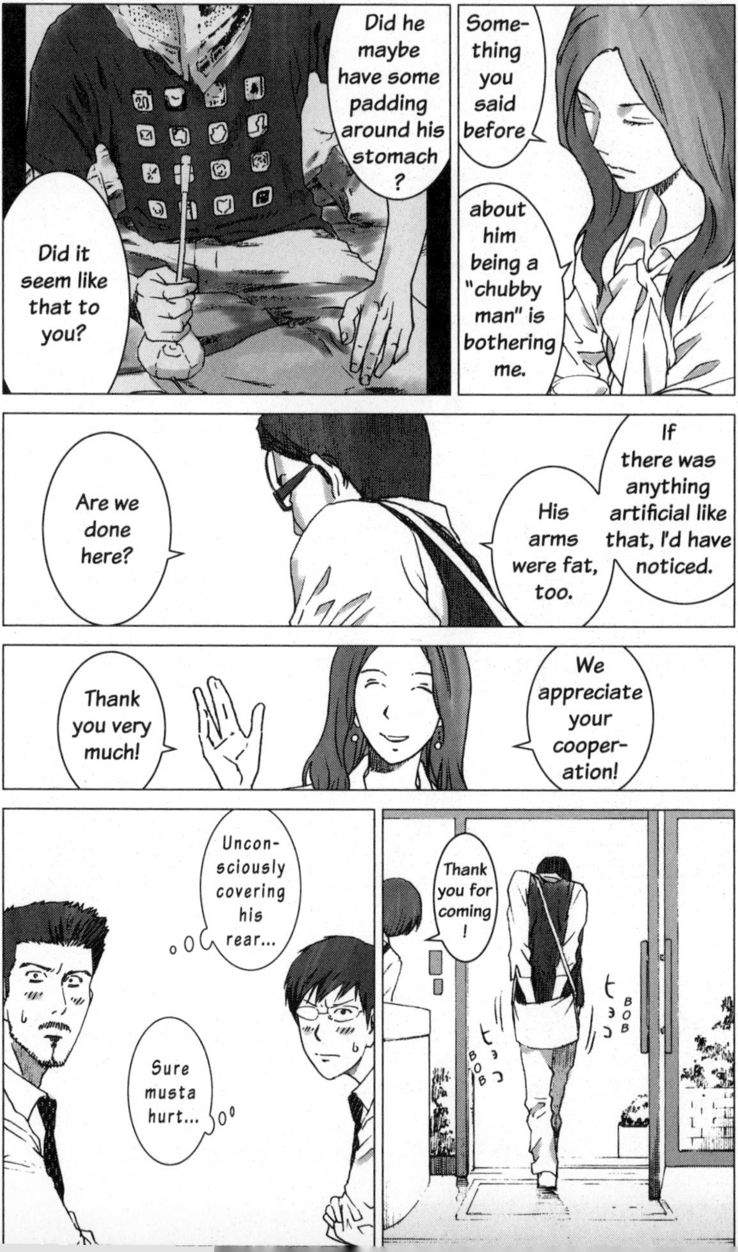

Something you said before
about him being a "chubby man" is bothering me.
Did he maybe have some padding around his stomach?
Did it seem like that to you?
If there was anything artificial like that, I'd have noticed.
His arms were fat, too.
Are we done here?
We appreciate your cooperation!
Thank you very much!
Thank you for coming!
BOB
BOB
Unconsciously covering his rear...
Sure musta hurt...

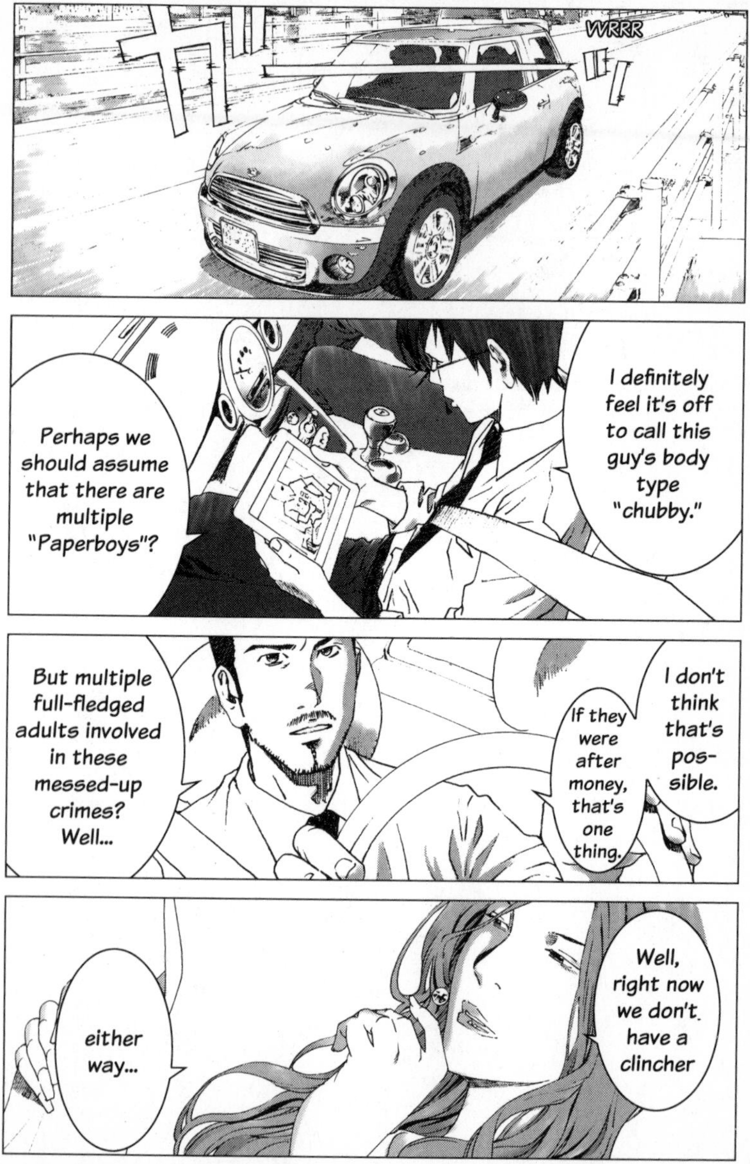
WRRR
I definitely feel it's off to call this guy's body type "chubby."
Perhaps we should assume that there are multiple "Paperboys"?
I don't think that's pos-sible.
If they were after money, that's one thing.
But multiple full-fledged adults involved in these messed-up crimes? Well...
Well, right now we don't have a clincher
either way...

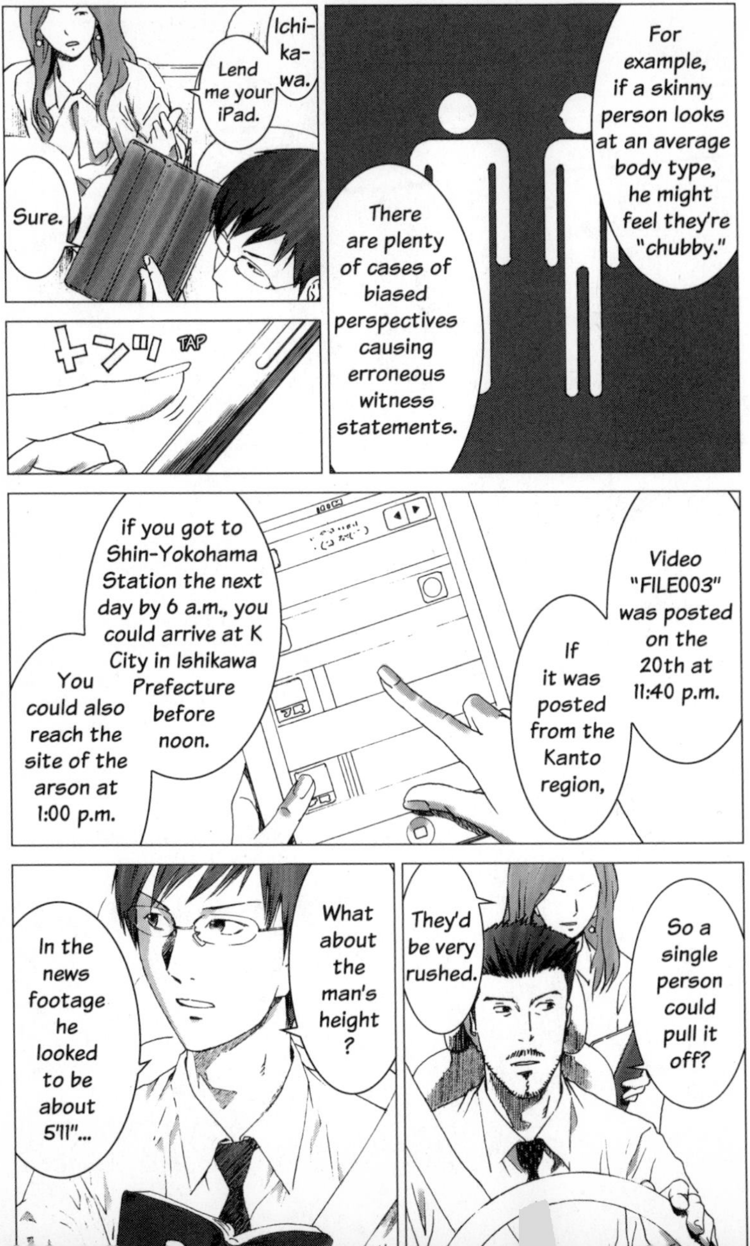
For example, if a skinny person looks at an average body type, he might feel they're "chubby."
There are plenty of cases of biased perspectives causing erroneous witness statements.
Ichi-ka-wa.
Lend me your iPad.
Sure.
TAP
Video "FILE003" was posted on the 20th at 11:40 p.m.
If it was posted from the Kanto region,
if you got to Shin-Yokohama Station the next day by 6 a.m., you could arrive at K City in Ishikawa Prefecture before noon.
You could also reach the site of the arson at 1:00 p.m.
So a single person could pull it off?
They'd be very rushed.
What about the man's height?
In the news footage he looked to be about 5'11"...

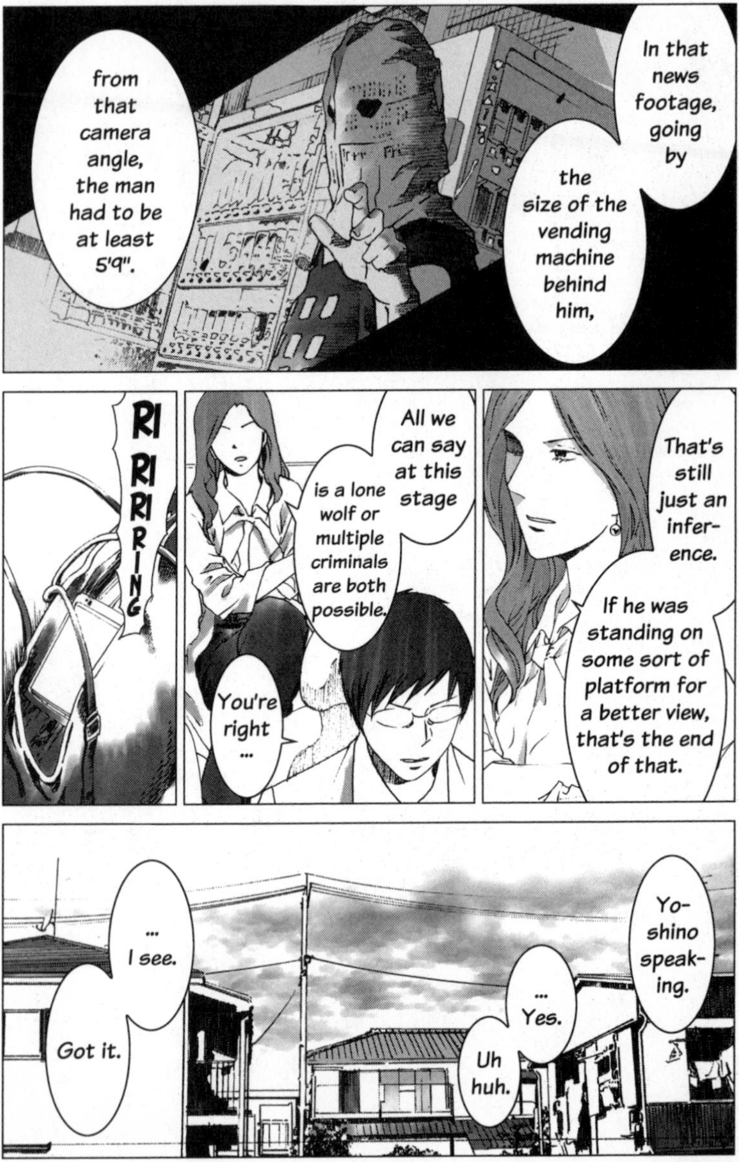
In that news footage, going by
the size of the vending machine behind him,
from that camera angle, the man had to be at least 5'9".
That's still just an inference.
If he was standing on some sort of platform for a better view, that's the end of that.
All we can say at this stage
is a lone wolf or multiple criminals are both possible.
You're right ...
RI RI RI RIRING
Yo-shino speak-ing.
... Yes.
Uh huh.
... I see.
Got it.

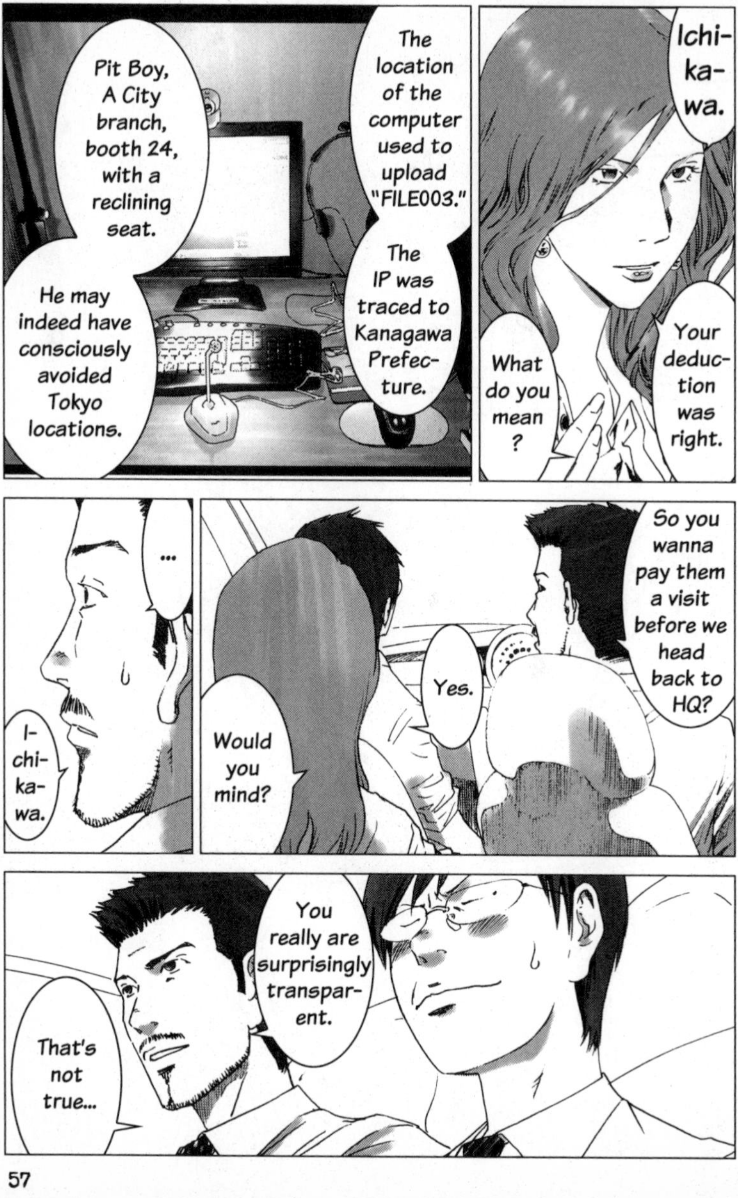
Ichikawa.
Your deduction was right.
What do you mean?
The location of the computer used to upload "FILE003."
The IP was traced to Kanagawa Prefecture.
Pit Boy, A City branch, booth 24, with a reclining seat.
He may indeed have consciously avoided Tokyo locations.
So you wanna pay them a visit before we head back to HQ?
Yes.
Would you mind?
...
I-chi-ka-wa.
You really are surprisingly transparent.
That's not true...

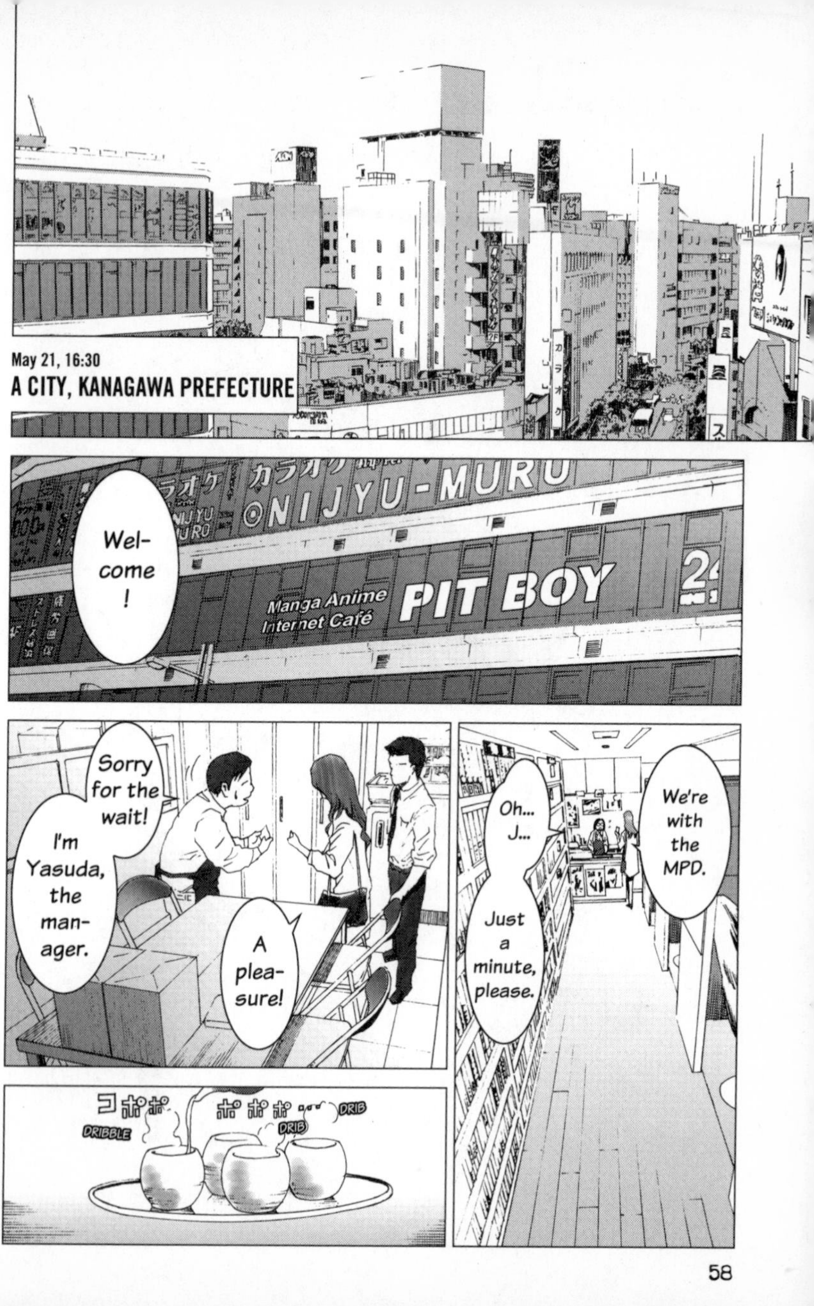
May 21, 16:30
A CITY, KANAGAWA PREFECTURE
ONIJYU-MURO
PIT BOY
Manga Anime Internet Café
Welcome!
We're with the MPD.
Oh... J...
Just a minute, please.
Sorry for the wait!
I'm Yasuda, the manager.
A pleasure!
DRIB
DRIB
DRIBBLE

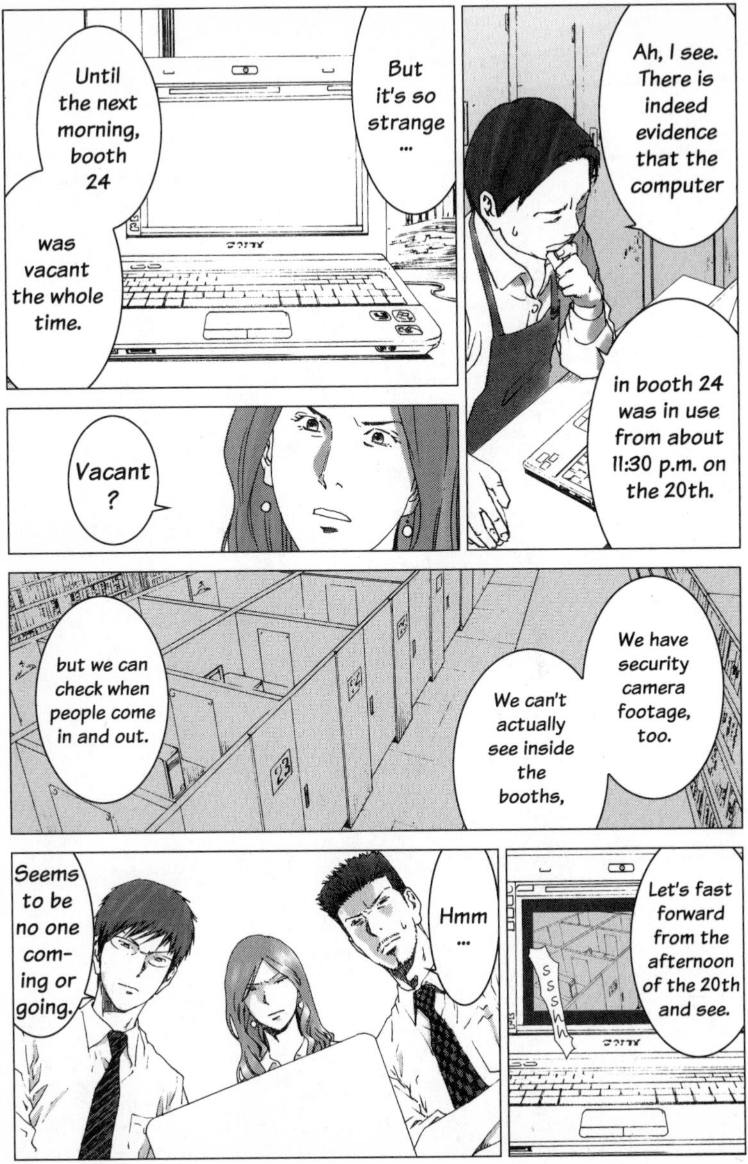
Ah, I see. There is indeed evidence that the computer
in booth 24 was in use from about 11:30 p.m. on the 20th.
But it's so strange ...
Until the next morning, booth 24
was vacant the whole time.
Vacant?
We have security camera footage, too.
We can't actually see inside the booths,
but we can check when people come in and out.
Let's fast forward from the afternoon of the 20th and see.
SSSWH
Hmm ...
Seems to be no one com-ing or going.

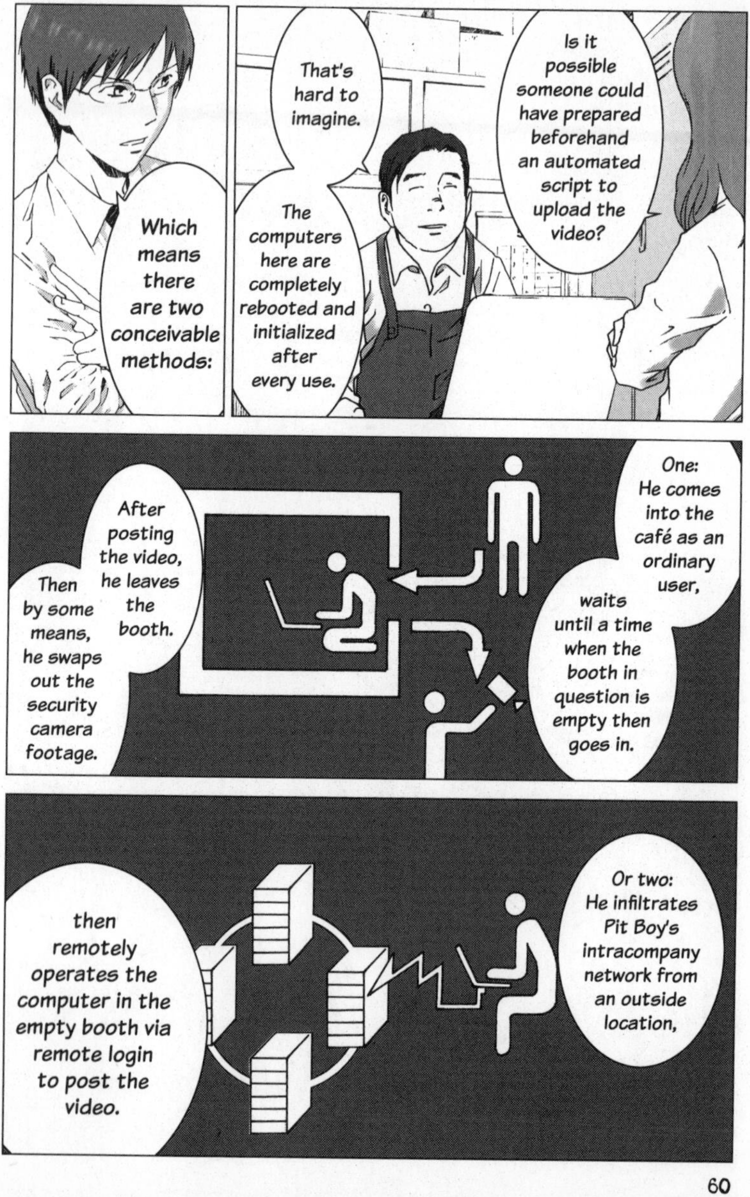

Is it possible someone could have prepared beforehand an automated script to upload the video?
That's hard to imagine.
The computers here are completely rebooted and initialized after every use.
Which means there are two conceivable methods:
One: He comes into the café as an ordinary user,
waits until a time when the booth in question is empty then goes in.
After posting the video, he leaves the booth.
Then by some means, he swaps out the security camera footage.
Or two: He infiltrates Pit Boy's intracompany network from an outside location,
then remotely operates the computer in the empty booth via remote login to post the video.

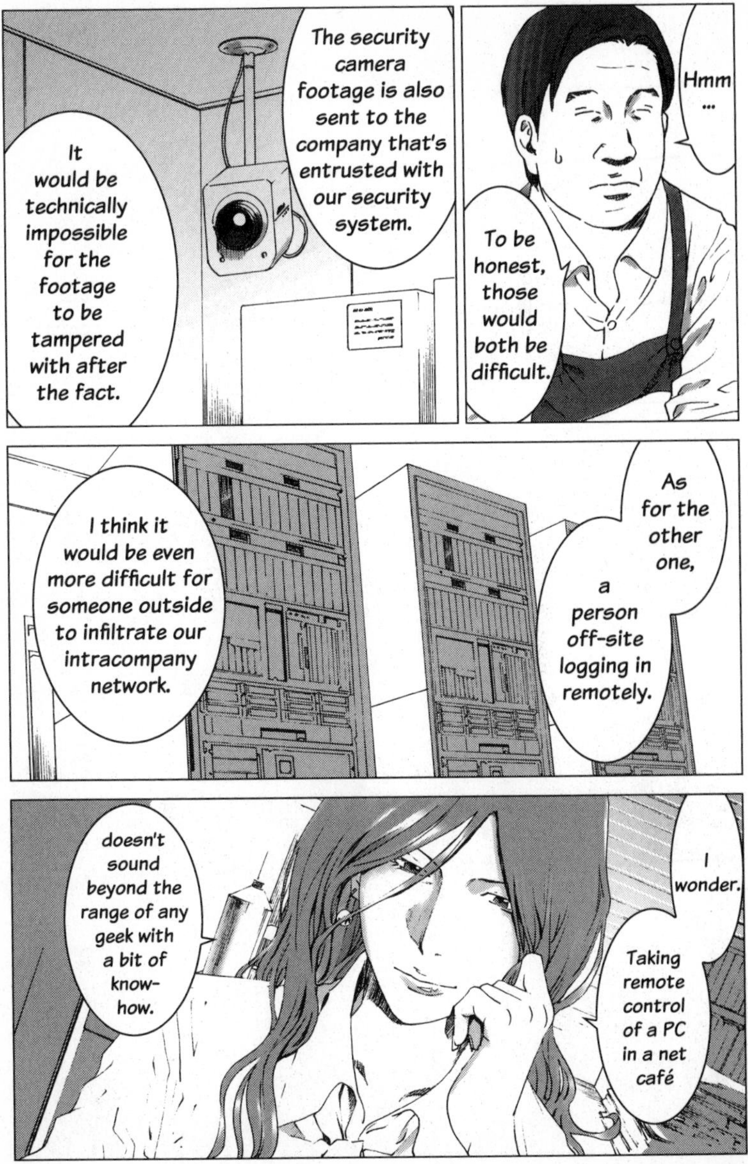
Hmm...
To be honest, those would both be difficult.
The security camera footage is also sent to the company that's entrusted with our security system.
It would be technically impossible for the footage to be tampered with after the fact.
As for the other one, a person off-site logging in remotely.
I think it would be even more difficult for someone outside to infiltrate our intracompany network.
I wonder.
Taking remote control of a PC in a net café
doesn't sound beyond the range of any geek with a bit of know-how.

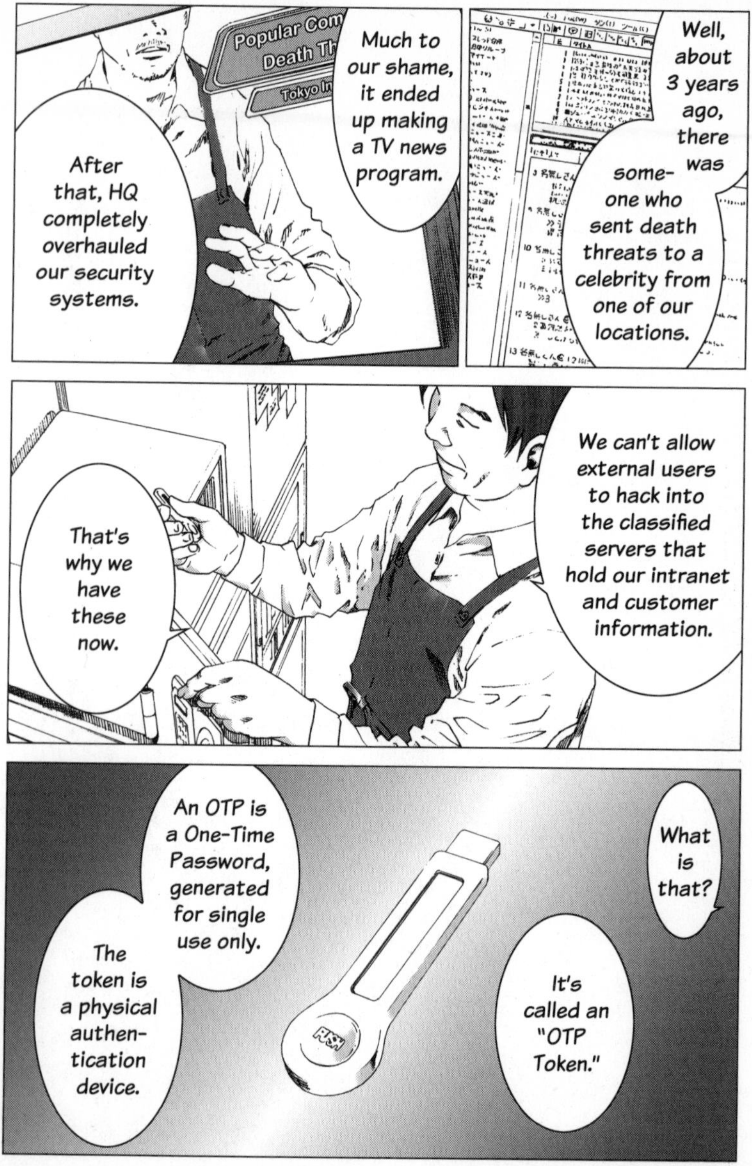
Well, about 3 years ago, there was some-one who sent death threats to a celebrity from one of our locations.
Much to our shame, it ended up making a TV news program.
After that, HQ completely overhauled our security systems.
We can't allow external users to hack into the classified servers that hold our intranet and customer information.
That's why we have these now.
What is that?
It's called an "OTP Token."
An OTP is a One-Time Password, generated for single use only.
The token is a physical authen-tication device.

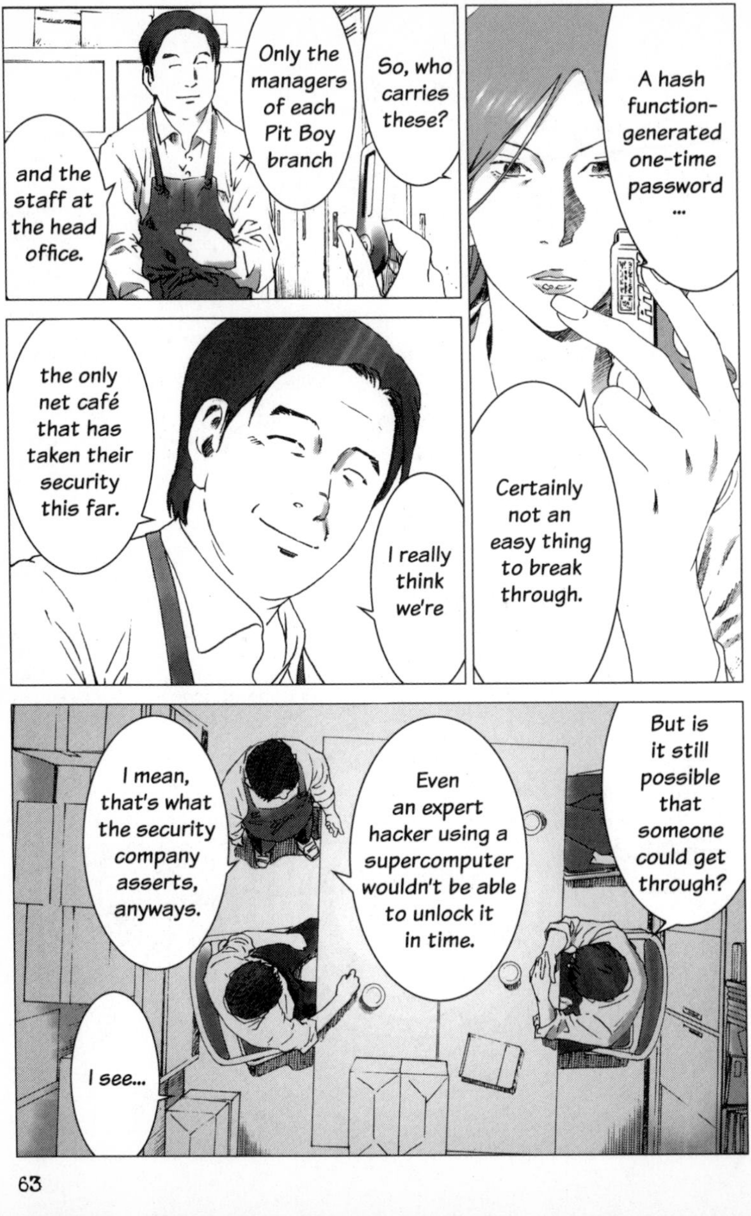
A hash function-generated one-time password...
Certainly not an easy thing to break through.
So, who carries these?
Only the managers of each Pit Boy branch
and the staff at the head office.
I really think we're
the only net café that has taken their security this far.
But is it still possible that someone could get through?
Even an expert hacker using a supercomputer wouldn't be able to unlock it in time.
I mean, that's what the security company asserts, anyways.
I see...

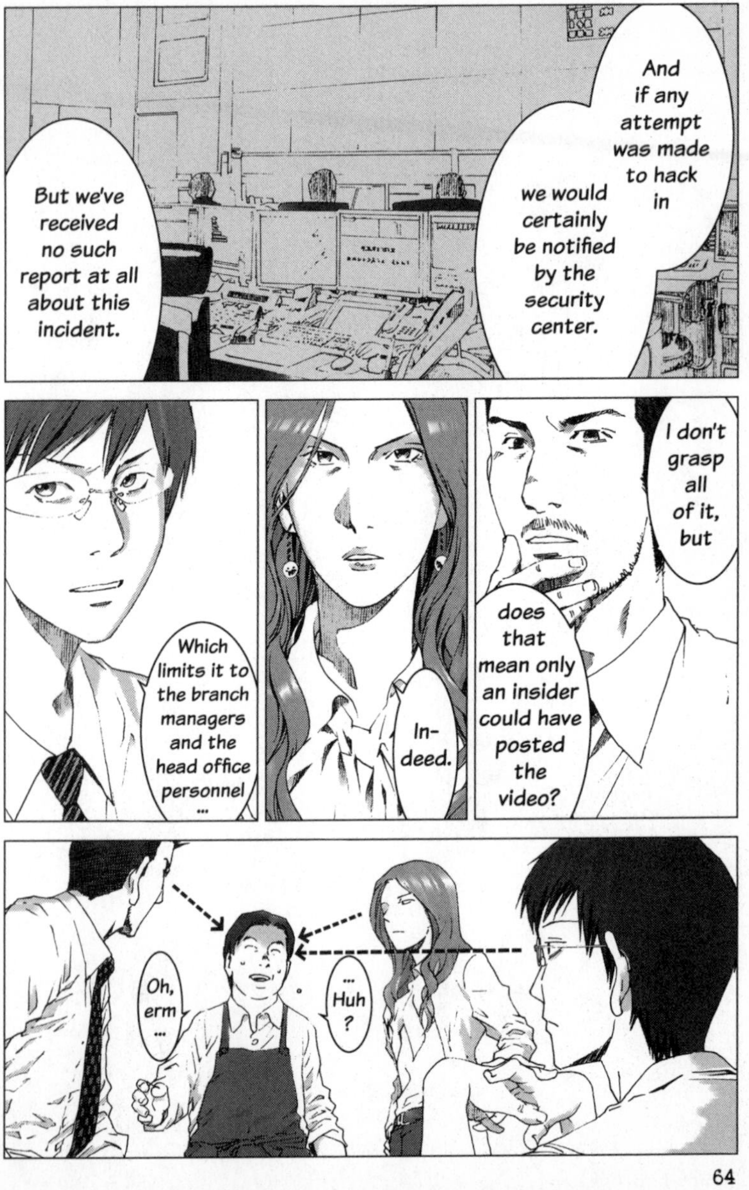
And if any attempt was made to hack in
we would certainly be notified by the security center.
But we've received no such report at all about this incident.
I don't grasp all of it, but
does that mean only an insider could have posted the video?
In- deed.
Which limits it to the branch managers and the head office personnel ...
... Huh ?
Oh, erm ...

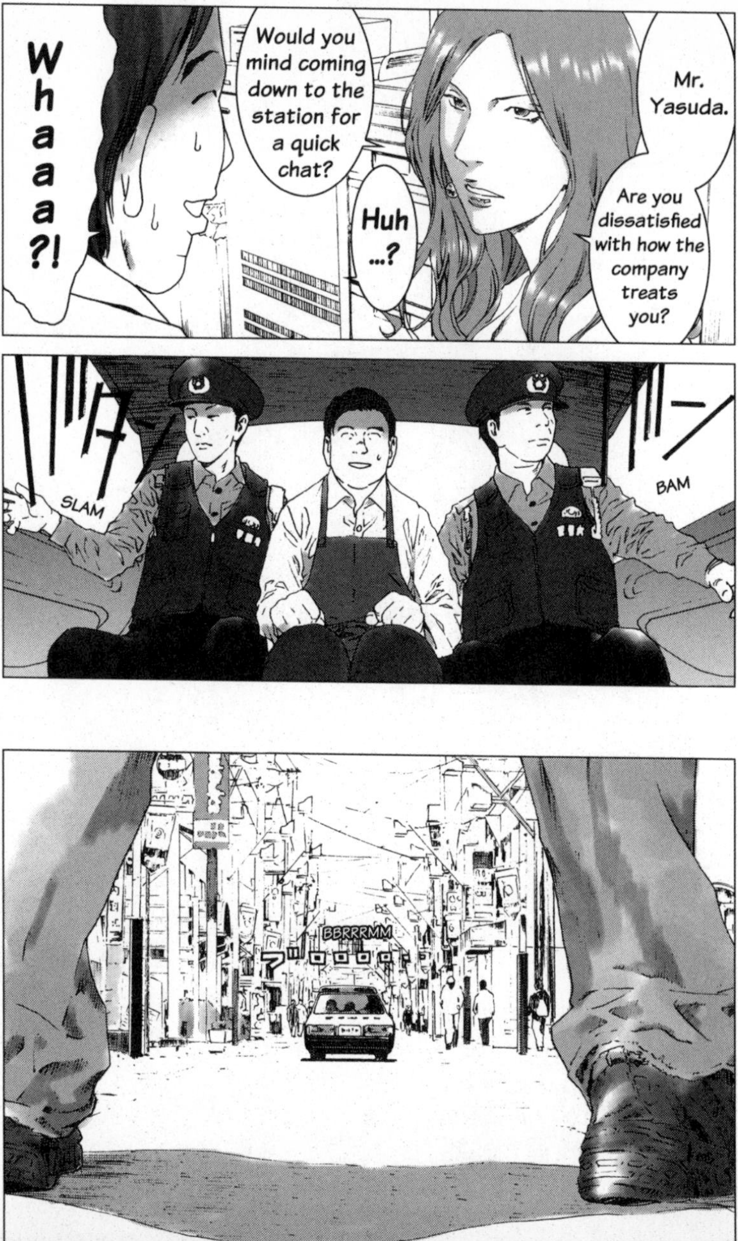
Mr. Yasuda.
Are you dissatisfied with how the company treats you?
Huh ...?
Would you mind coming down to the station for a quick chat?
Whaaaa?!
BAM
SLAM
BBRRRMM

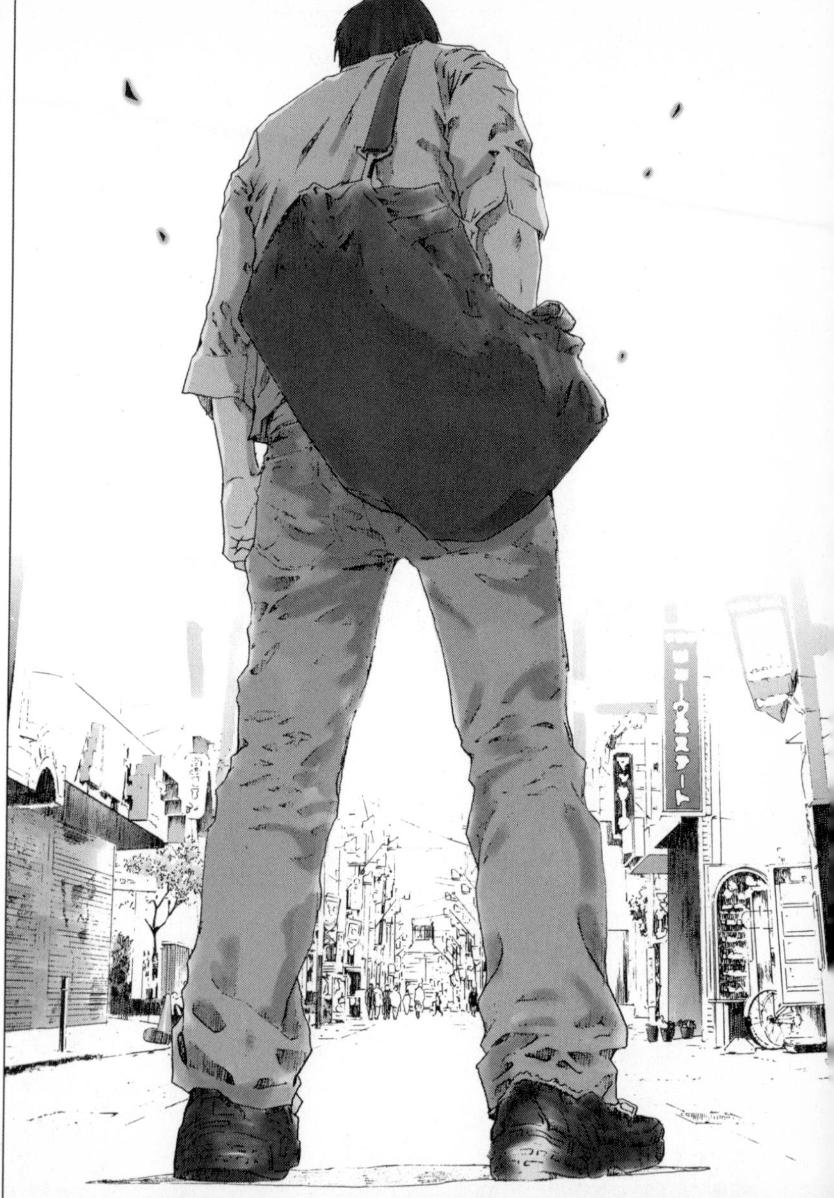

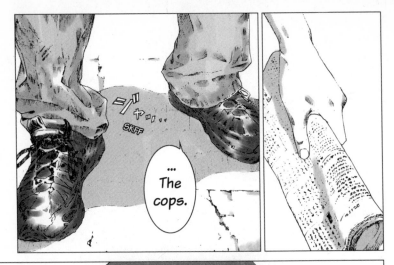

...
The cops.

Faster than I'd expected.

PROPHECY

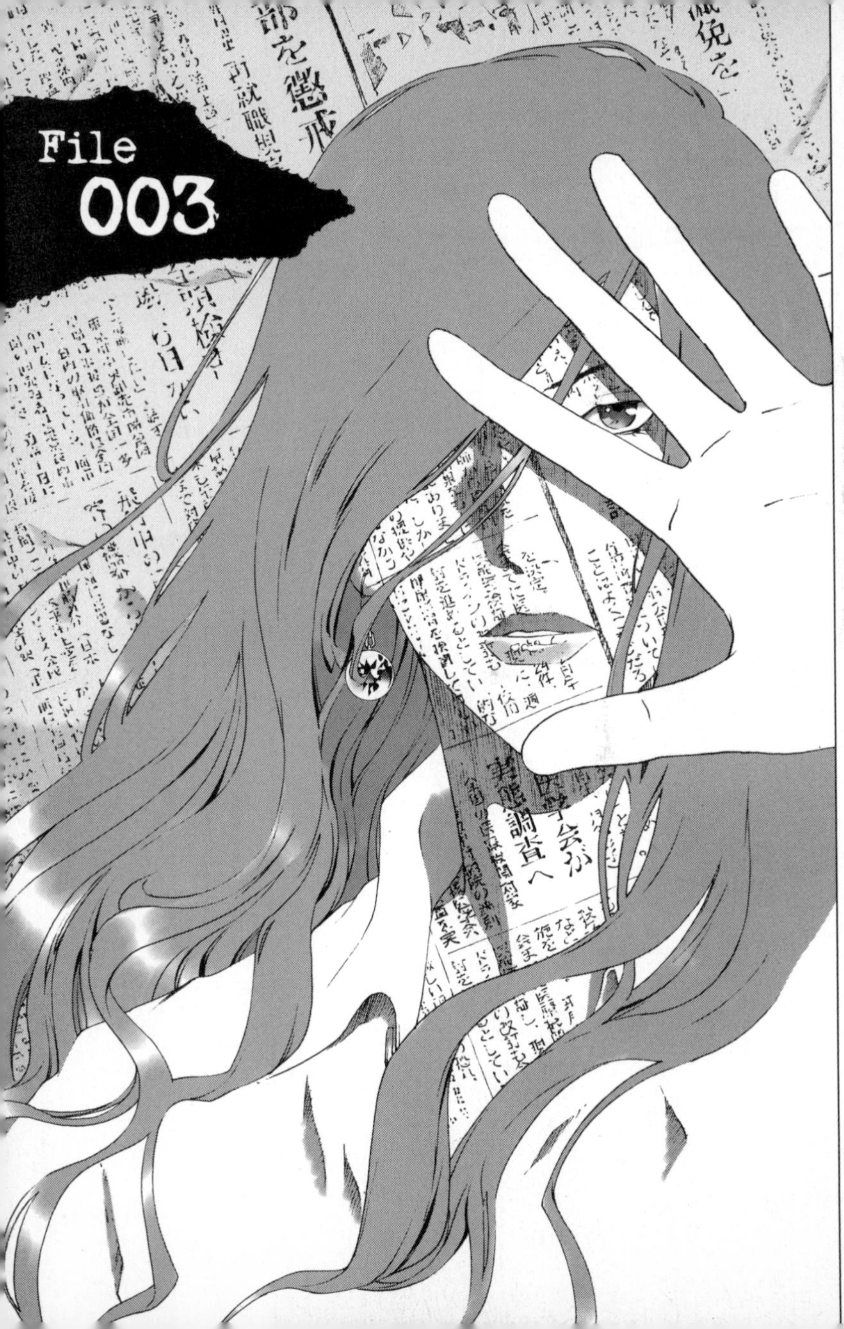
File
003

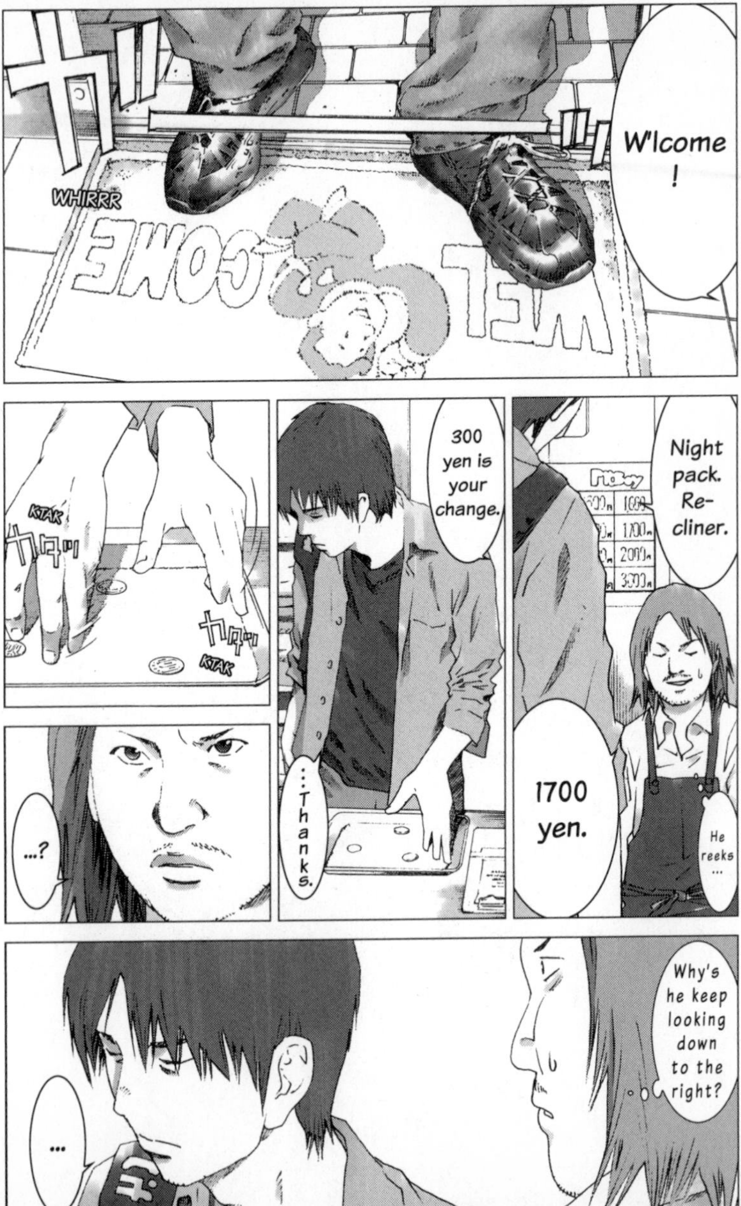
W'lcome !
WHIRRR
Night pack. Re-cliner.
1700 yen.
He reeks ...
300 yen is your change.
...Thanks.
KTAK
KTAK
...?
Why's he keep looking down to the right?
...

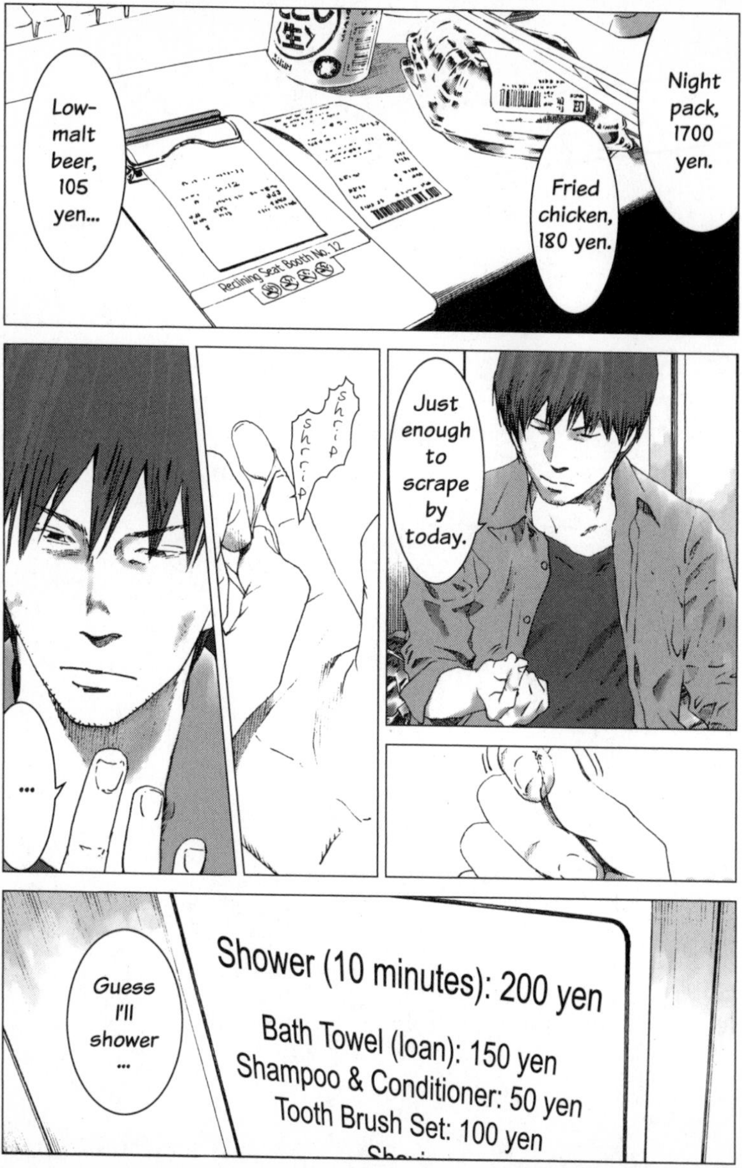
Night pack, 1700 yen.
Fried chicken, 180 yen.
Low-malt beer, 105 yen...
Reclining Seat Booth No. 12
Just enough to scrape by today.
shrrip shrrip
...
Shower (10 minutes): 200 yen
Bath Towel (loan): 150 yen
Shampoo & Conditioner: 50 yen
Tooth Brush Set: 100 yen
Guess I'll shower...

GLUE
SNFFF...
SNFFF...

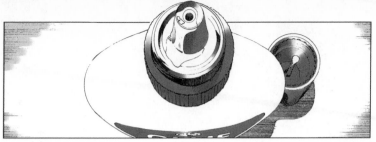

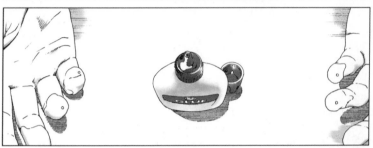

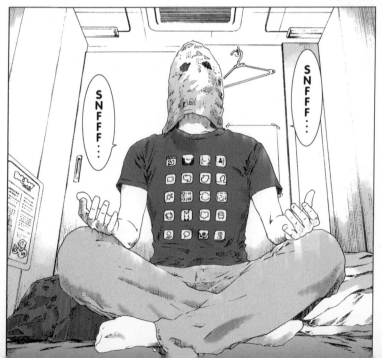

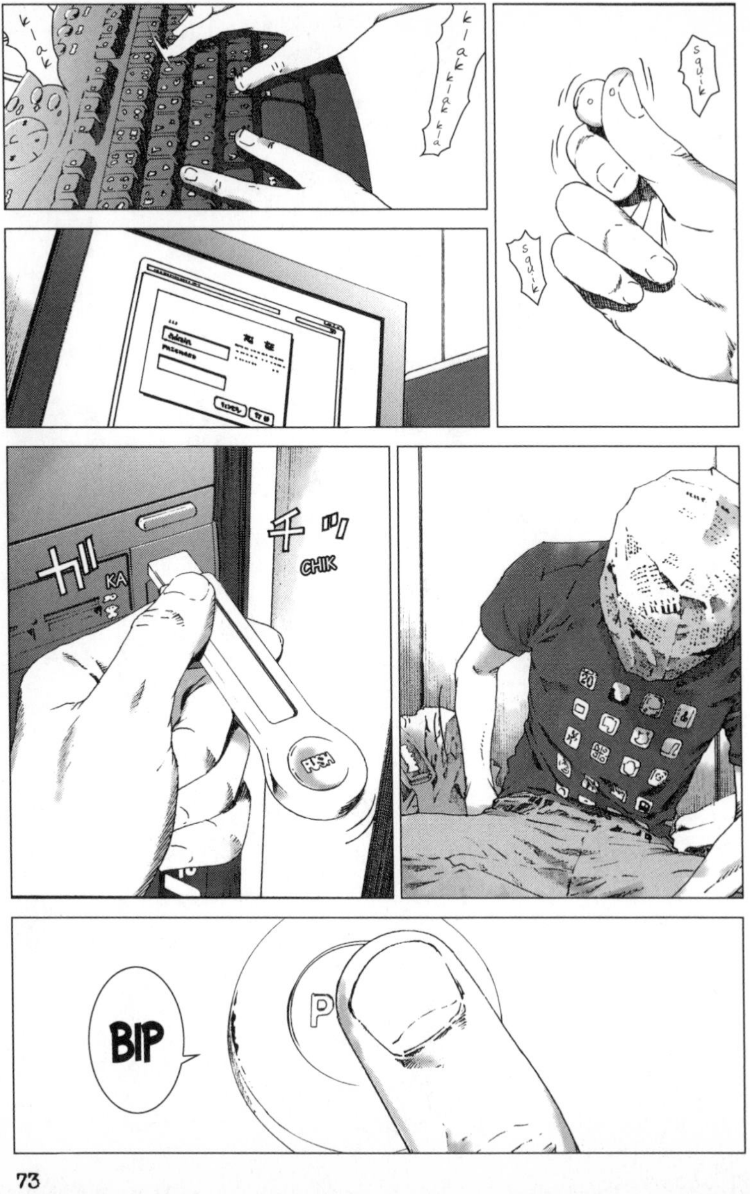
squik
squik
klakklakkla
klak
チリ
CHIK
カリ
KA
PUSH
BIP
P

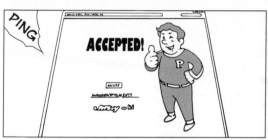

BLINK
PING
ACCEPTED!
Now to search for an empty booth
in one of the 12 branches in Kanagawa and Saitama.
KRAK
#8 recliner booth, W City branch, Saitama.
How about this one today?
KLIK

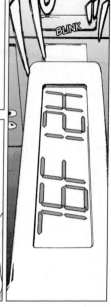

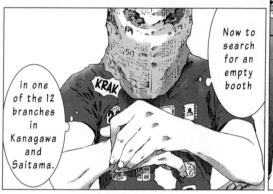

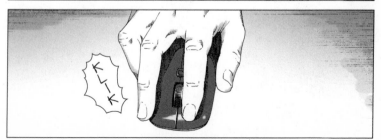

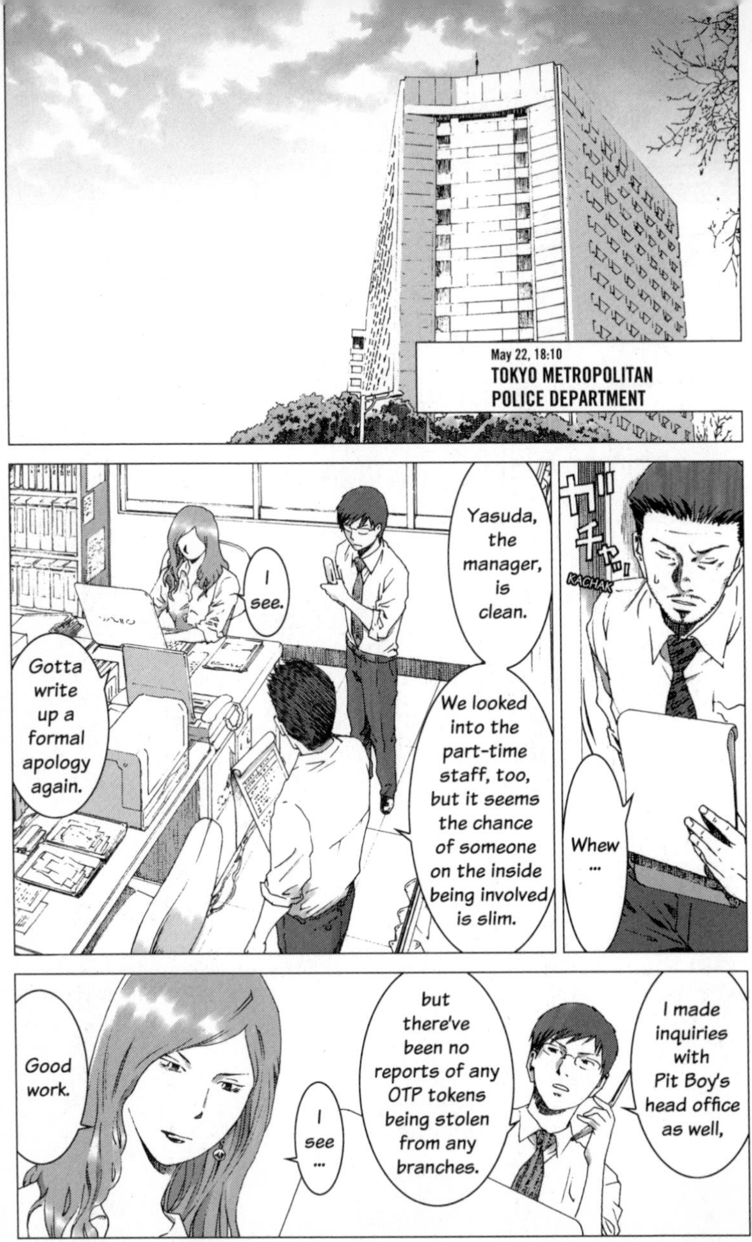
May 22, 18:10
TOKYO METROPOLITAN POLICE DEPARTMENT
KACHAK
Whew ...
Yasuda, the manager, is clean.
We looked into the part-time staff, too, but it seems the chance of someone on the inside being involved is slim.
I see.
Gotta write up a formal apology again.
I made inquiries with Pit Boy's head office as well,
but there've been no reports of any OTP tokens being stolen from any branches.
I see ...
Good work.

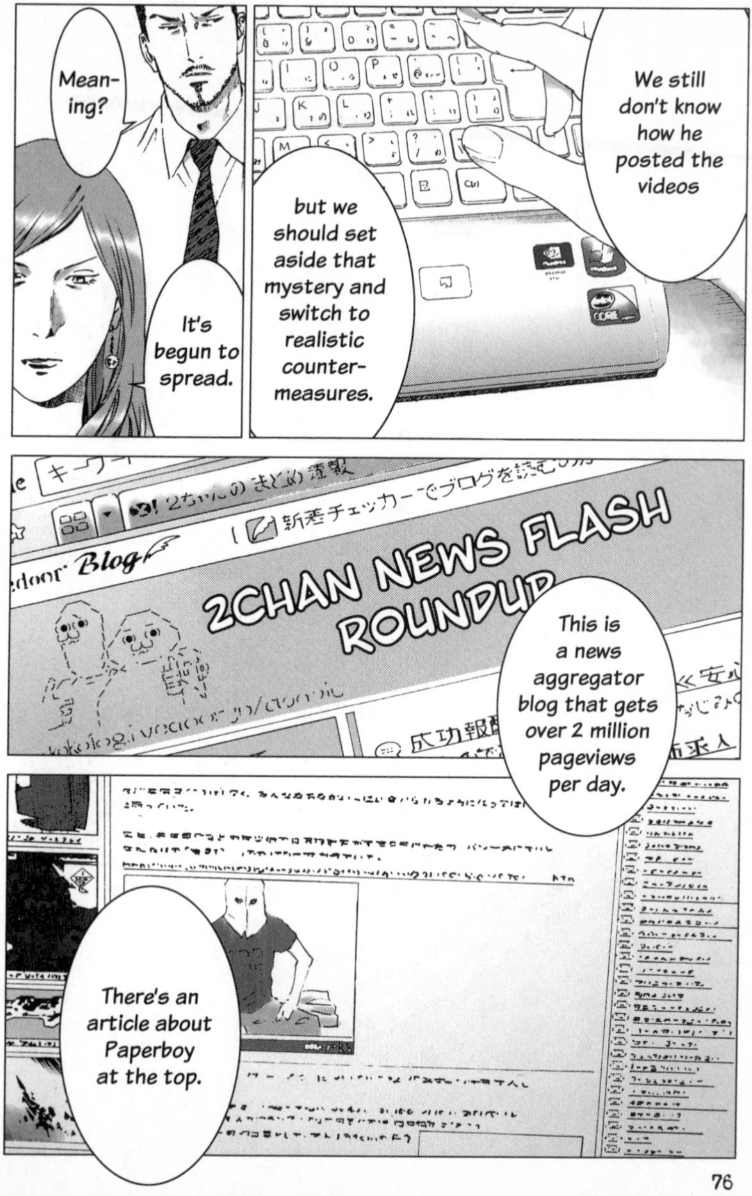
We still don't know how he posted the videos
but we should set aside that mystery and switch to realistic counter-measures.
Meaning?
It's begun to spread.
2CHAN NEWS FLASH ROUNDUP
This is a news aggregator blog that gets over 2 million pageviews per day.
There's an article about Paperboy at the top.

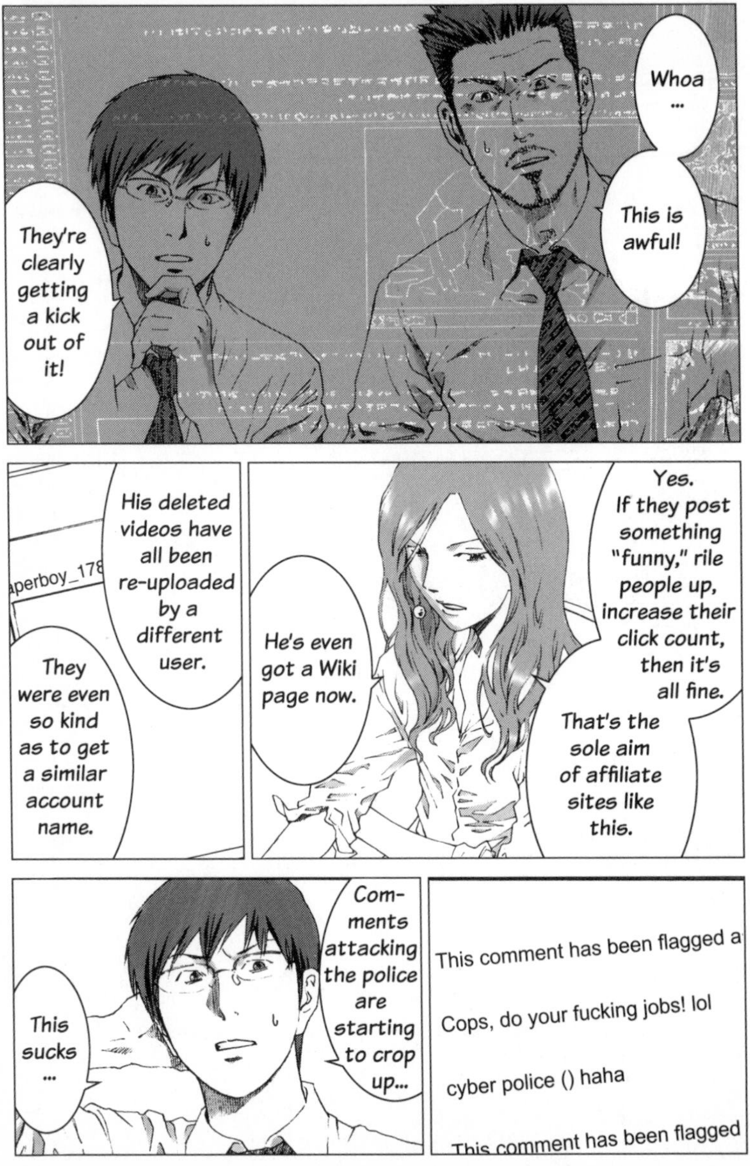
Whoa ...
This is awful!
They're clearly getting a kick out of it!
Yes. If they post something "funny," rile people up, increase their click count, then it's all fine.
That's the sole aim of affiliate sites like this.
He's even got a Wiki page now.
His deleted videos have all been re-uploaded by a different user.
They were even so kind as to get a similar account name.
This comment has been flagged a
Cops, do your fucking jobs! lol
cyber police () haha
This comment has been flagged
Com-ments attacking the police are starting to crop up...
This sucks ...

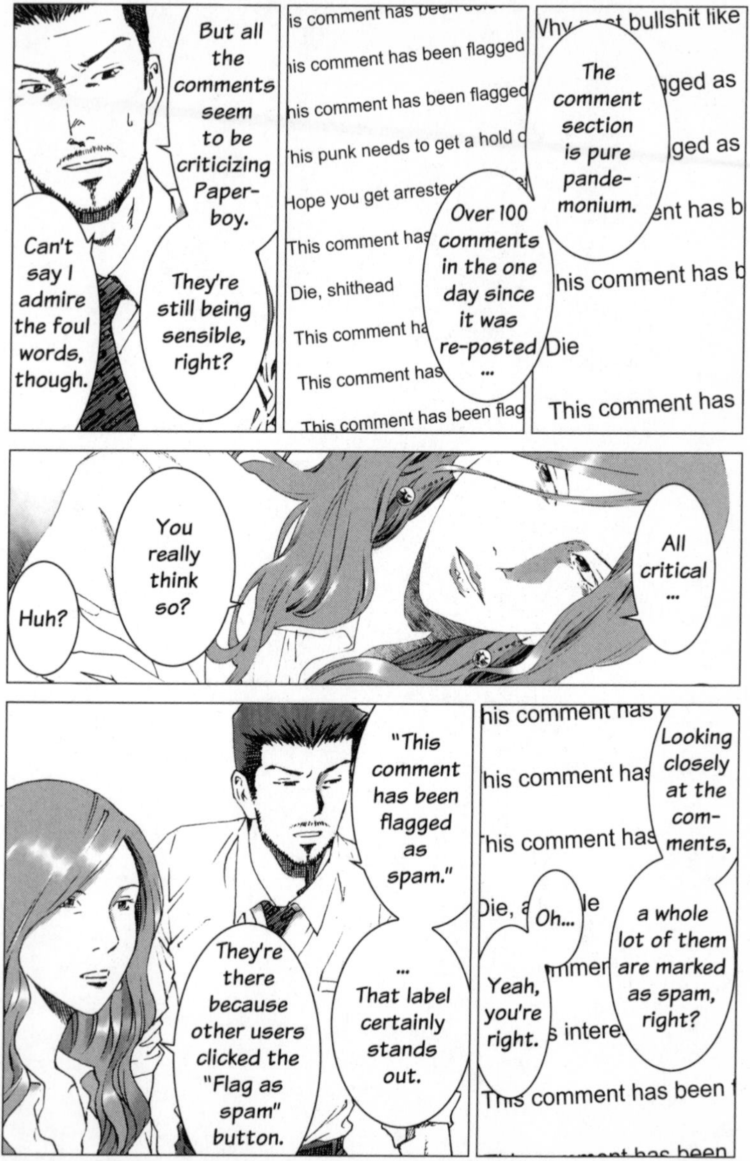
The comment section is pure pandemonium.
Over 100 comments in the one day since it was re-posted ...
But all the comments seem to be criticizing Paperboy.
They're still being sensible, right?
Can't say I admire the foul words, though.
All critical ...
You really think so?
Huh?
Looking closely at the comments,
a whole lot of them are marked as spam, right?
Oh...
Yeah, you're right.
"This comment has been flagged as spam."
... That label certainly stands out.
They're there because other users clicked the "Flag as spam" button.

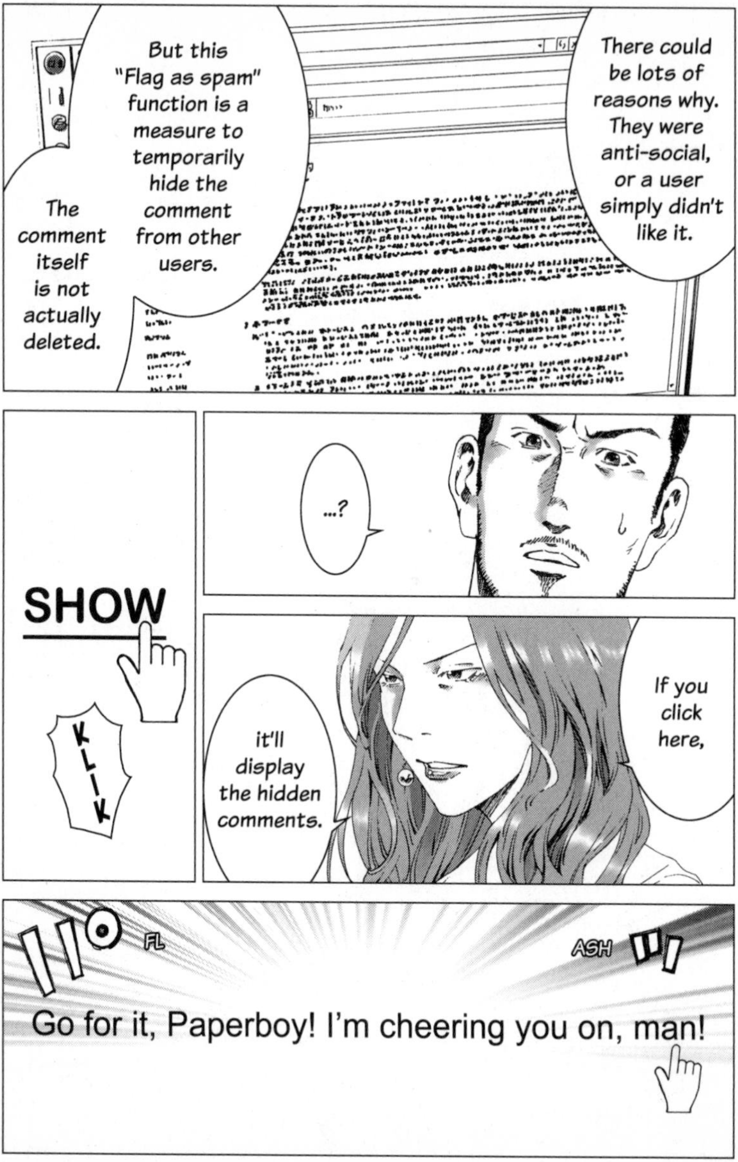
There could be lots of reasons why. They were anti-social, or a user simply didn't like it.
But this "Flag as spam" function is a measure to temporarily hide the comment from other users.
The comment itself is not actually deleted.
...?
If you click here,
it'll display the hidden comments.
SHOW
KLIK
FLASH
Go for it, Paperboy! I'm cheering you on, man!

I wish you'd come punish some people at my school, dude. Some of the teachers are pieces of shit.

Hide

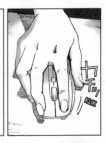

This newspaper guy is awesome! lol

watching ur video makes me feel brand new

That cockroach thing cracked me up! rofl

This comment has been flagged as spam.   Show

...!

got your back

Do it!

You're a her

Paperboy

I got you

Off the chain but it's hilarious!

This comment has been flagged

This comment has been flagged

This comment has been fl

THESE PEOPLE ...

This comment has been flagg

mment has been flagged as sp

ment has b   d as sp

ment has   d as s

ent has b   ged as s

mment has been flagged as s

ment has been flagged as

nt has been flagged as

d as

WHAT THE...

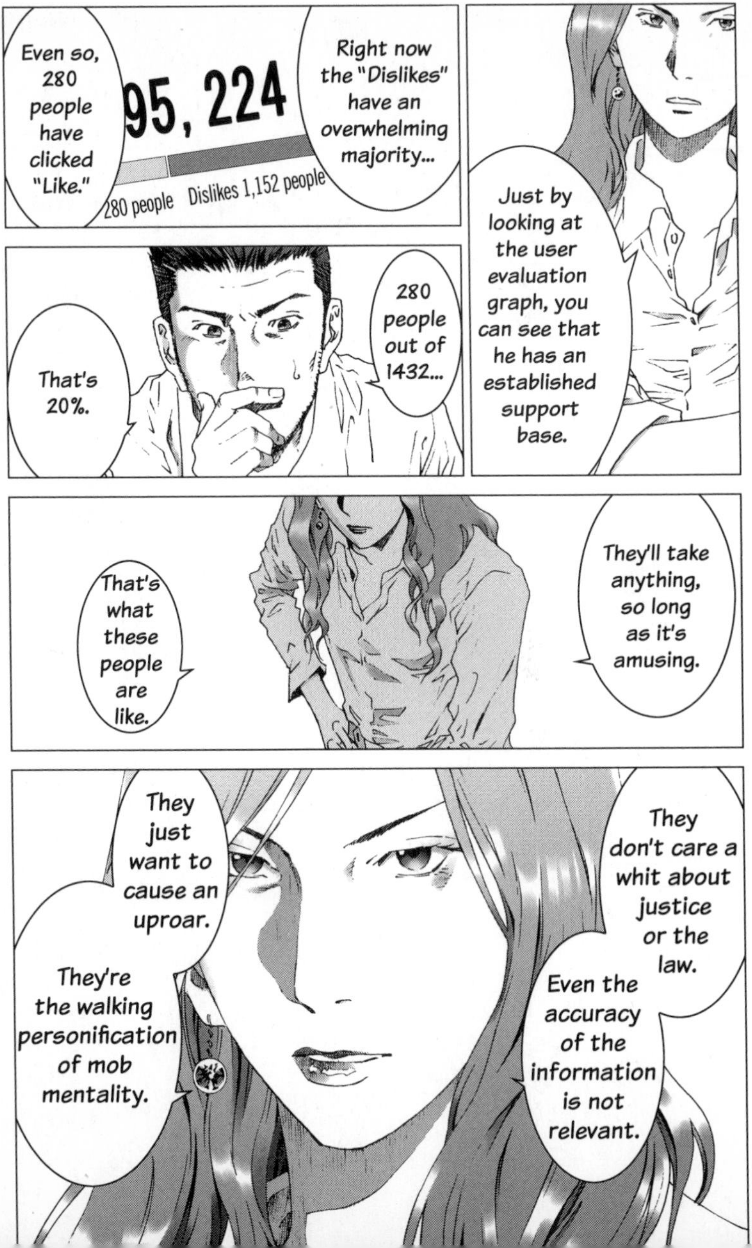
Just by looking at the user evaluation graph, you can see that he has an established support base.
Right now the "Dislikes" have an overwhelming majority...
95, 224
280 people Dislikes 1,152 people
Even so, 280 people have clicked "Like."
280 people out of 1432...
That's 20%.
They'll take anything, so long as it's amusing.
That's what these people are like.
They don't care a whit about justice or the law.
They just want to cause an uproar.
Even the accuracy of the information is not relevant.
They're the walking personification of mob mentality.

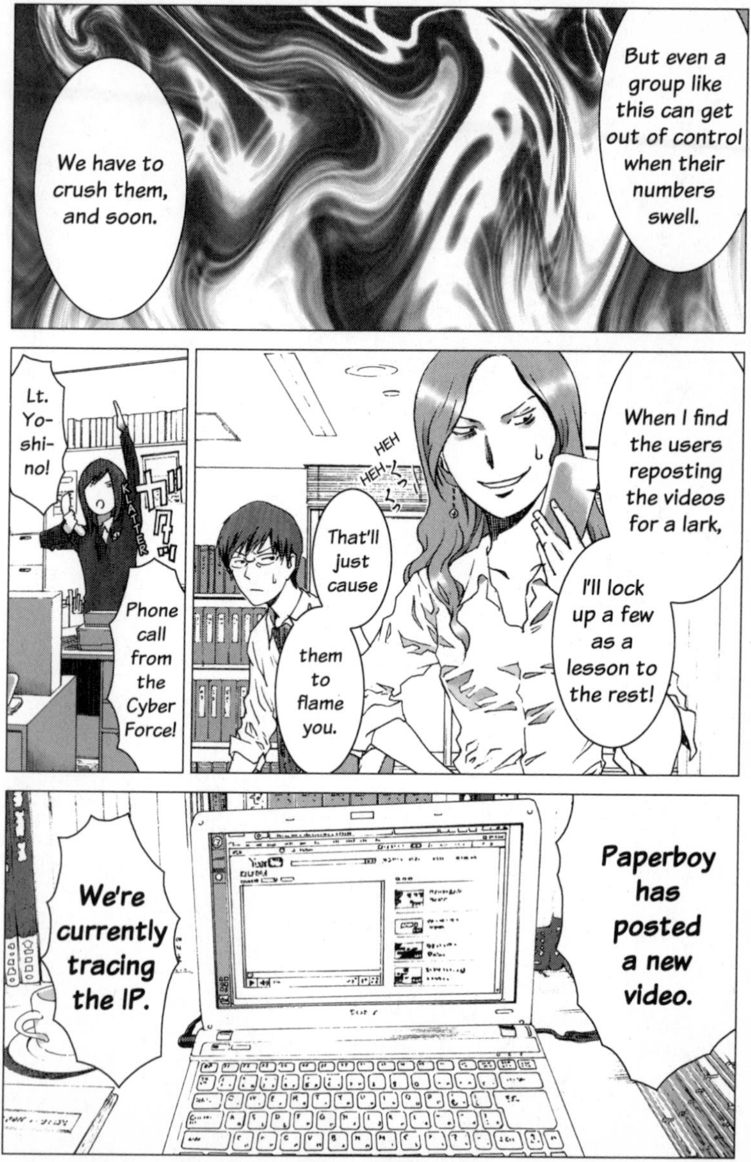
But even a group like this can get out of control when their numbers swell.
We have to crush them, and soon.
When I find the users reposting the videos for a lark,
I'll lock up a few as a lesson to the rest!
HEH HEH
That'll just cause them to flame you.
Lt. Yo-shi-no!
KLATTER
Phone call from the Cyber Force!
Paperboy has posted a new video.
We're currently tracing the IP.

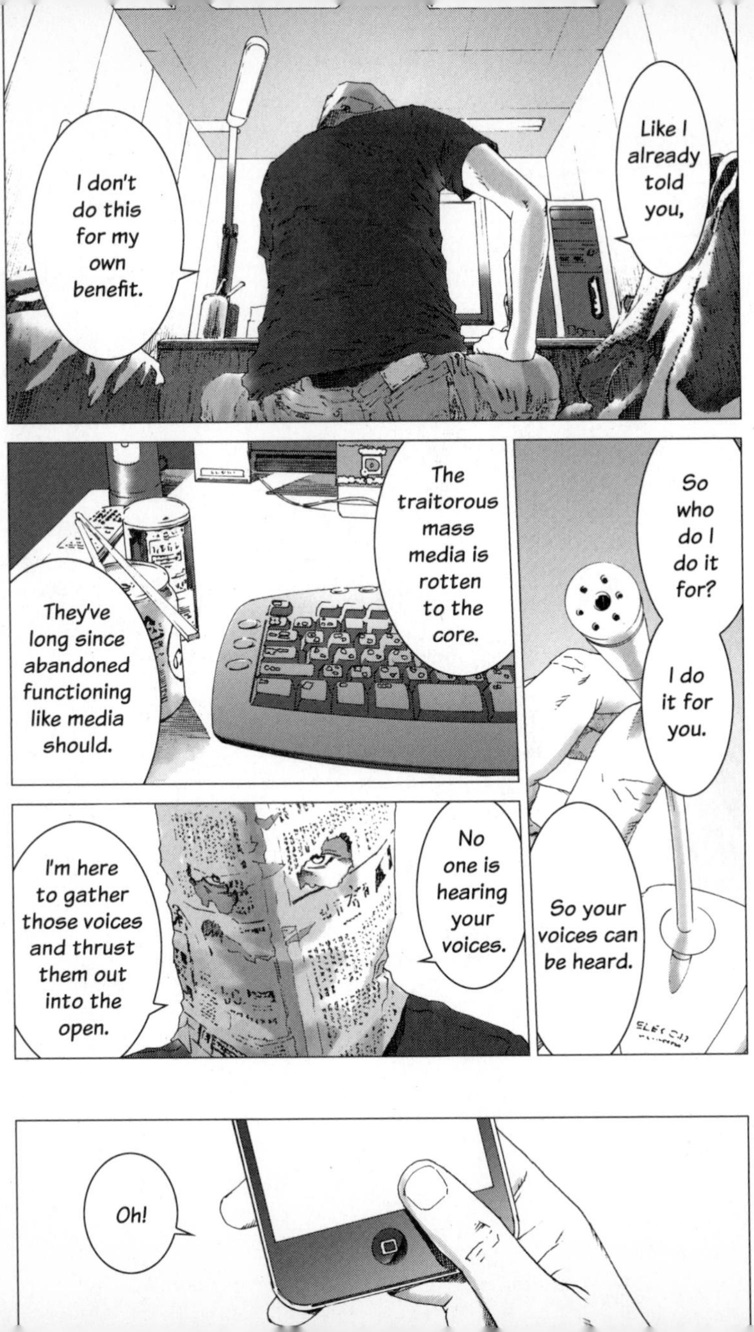
Like I already told you,
I don't do this for my own benefit.
So who do I do it for?
I do it for you.
So your voices can be heard.
The traitorous mass media is rotten to the core.
They've long since abandoned functioning like media should.
No one is hearing your voices.
I'm here to gather those voices and thrust them out into the open.
Oh!

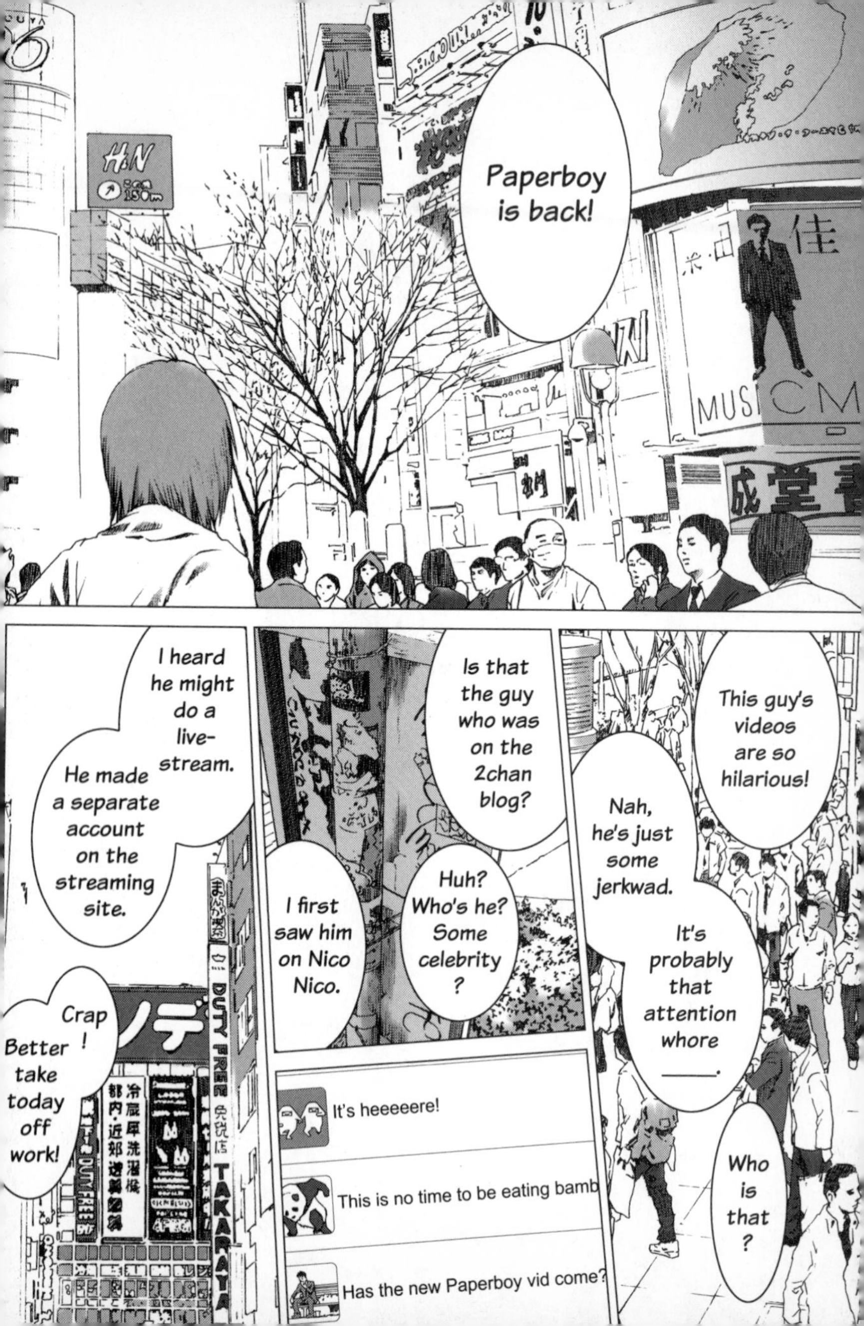
Paperboy is back!
This guy's videos are so hilarious!
Nah, he's just some jerkwad.
It's probably that attention whore ____.
Who is that?
Is that the guy who was on the 2chan blog?
Huh? Who's he? Some celebrity?
I first saw him on Nico Nico.
It's heeeeere!
This is no time to be eating bamb
Has the new Paperboy vid come?
I heard he might do a live-stream.
He made a separate account on the streaming site.
Crap! Better take today off work!

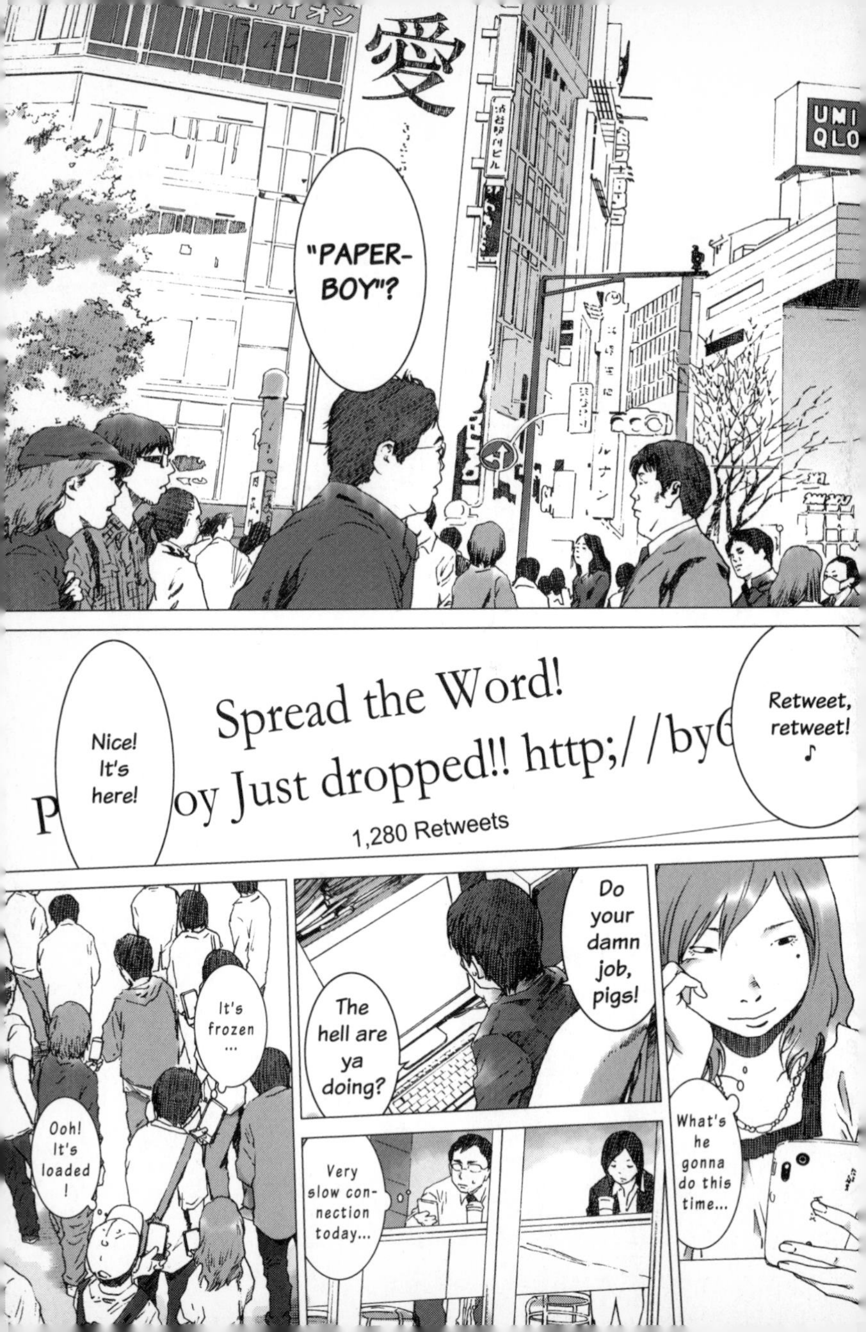
愛
UNI QLO
"PAPER-BOY"?
Retweet, retweet! ♪
Spread the Word!
P oy Just dropped!! http;/ /by6
1,280 Retweets
Nice! It's here!
What's he gonna do this time...
Do your damn job, pigs!
The hell are ya doing?
Very slow con-nection today...
It's frozen ...
Ooh! It's loaded !

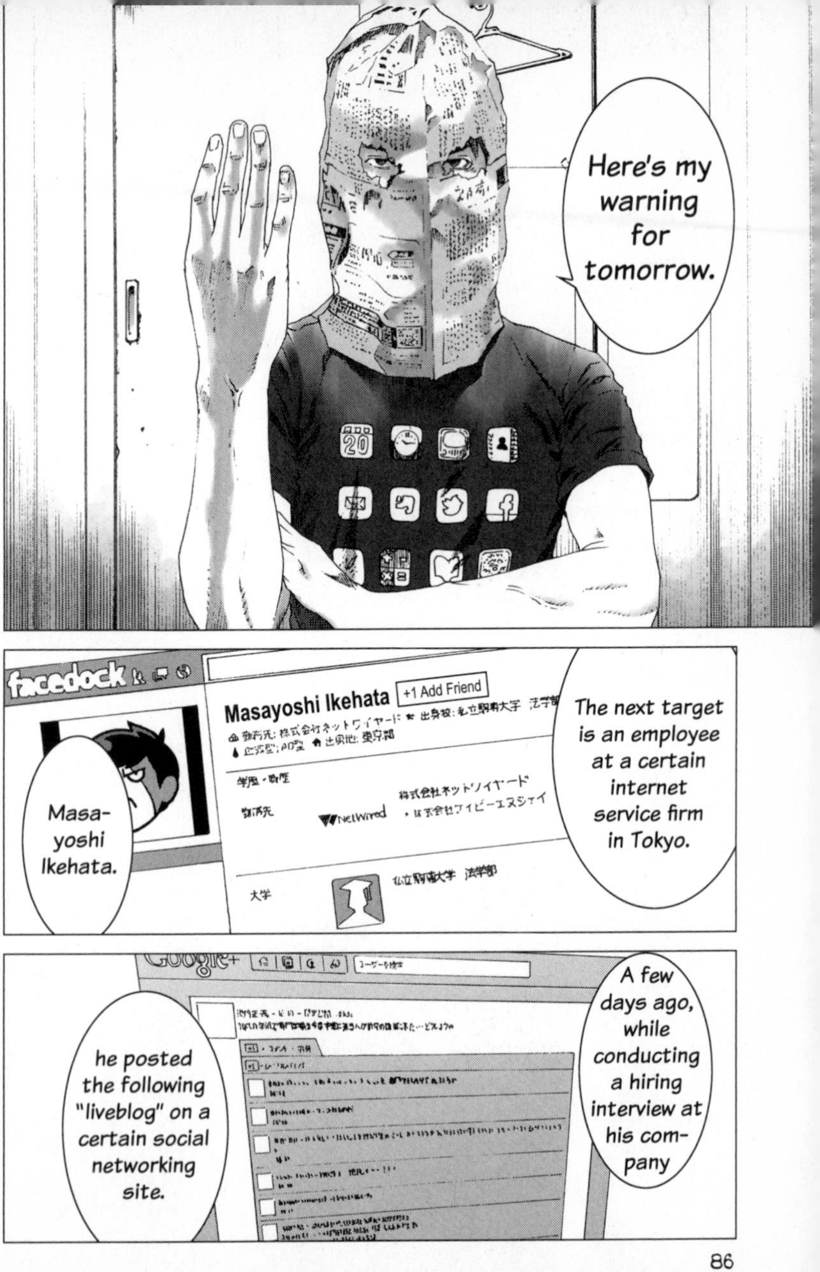
Here's my warning for tomorrow.
facedock
Masayoshi Ikehata
+1 Add Friend
NetWired
The next target is an employee at a certain internet service firm in Tokyo.
Masa-yoshi Ikehata.
A few days ago, while conducting a hiring interview at his com-pany
he posted the following "liveblog" on a certain social networking site.

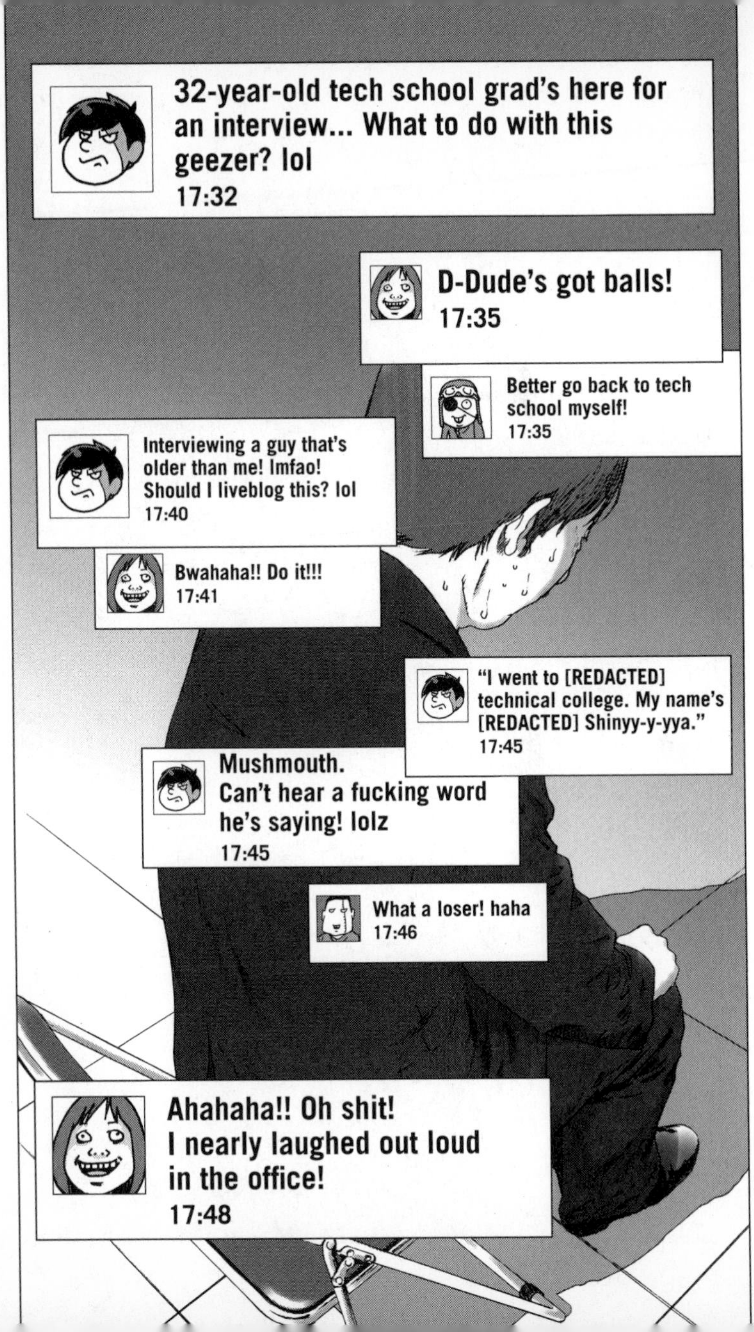
32-year-old tech school grad's here for an interview... What to do with this geezer? lol
17:32
D-Dude's got balls!
17:35
Better go back to tech school myself!
17:35
Interviewing a guy that's older than me! lmfao! Should I liveblog this? lol
17:40
Bwahaha!! Do it!!!
17:41
"I went to [REDACTED] technical college. My name's [REDACTED] Shinyy-y-yya."
17:45
Mushmouth.
Can't hear a fucking word he's saying! lolz
17:45
What a loser! haha
17:46
Ahahaha!! Oh shit!
I nearly laughed out loud in the office!
17:48

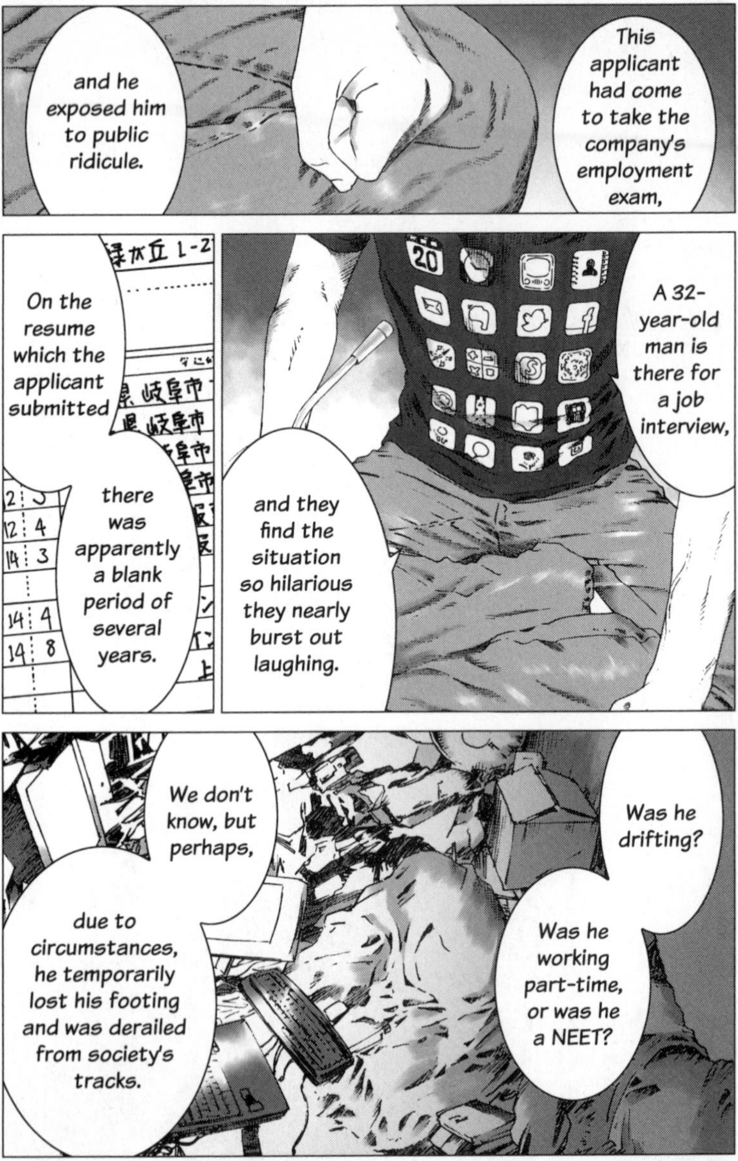
This applicant had come to take the company's employment exam,
and he exposed him to public ridicule.
A 32-year-old man is there for a job interview,
and they find the situation so hilarious they nearly burst out laughing.
On the resume which the applicant submitted
there was apparently a blank period of several years.
Was he drifting?
Was he working part-time, or was he a NEET?
We don't know, but perhaps,
due to circumstances, he temporarily lost his footing and was derailed from society's tracks.

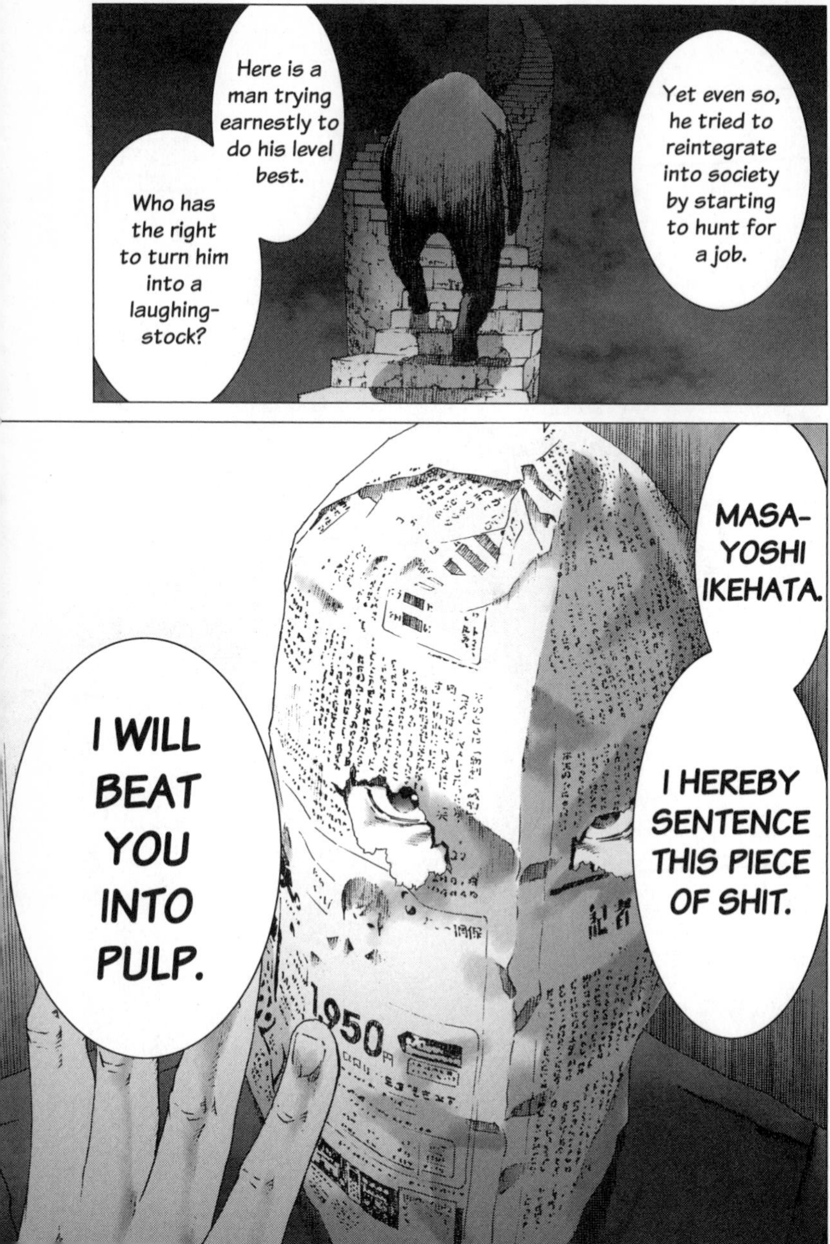
Yet even so, he tried to reintegrate into society by starting to hunt for a job.
Here is a man trying earnestly to do his level best.
Who has the right to turn him into a laughing-stock?
MASA-YOSHI IKEHATA.
I HEREBY SENTENCE THIS PIECE OF SHIT.
I WILL BEAT YOU INTO PULP.

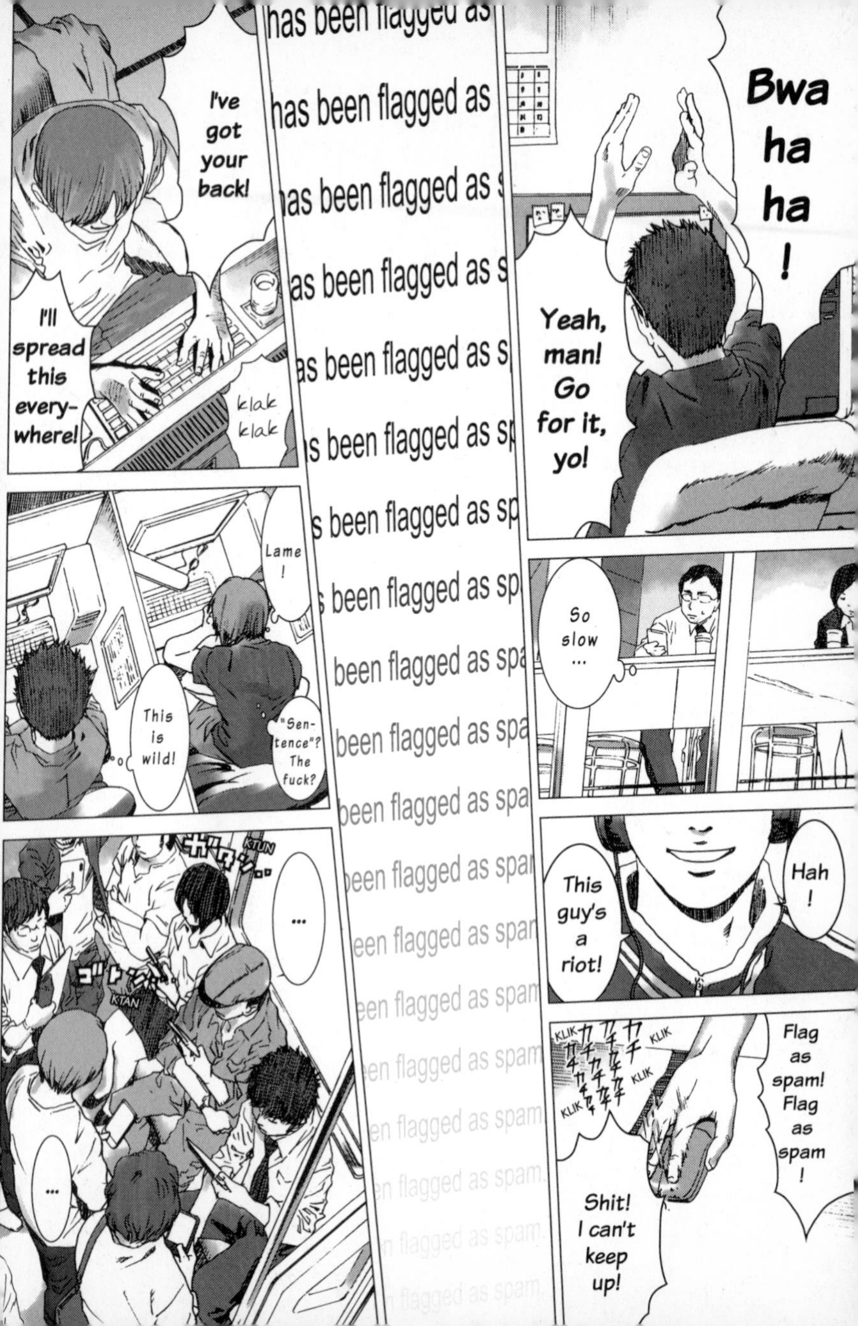
Bwa ha ha!
Yeah, man! Go for it, yo!
So slow...
Hah!
This guy's a riot!
KLIK KLIK KLIK KLIK
Flag as spam! Flag as spam!
Shit! I can't keep up!
has been flagged as
has been flagged as
has been flagged as s
as been flagged as s
as been flagged as sp
as been flagged as sp
s been flagged as sp
s been flagged as sp
been flagged as spa
been flagged as spa
been flagged as spa
been flagged as spam
een flagged as spam
een flagged as spam
een flagged as spam
en flagged as spam
en flagged as spam.
n flagged as spam.
n flagged as spam.
flagged as spam.
I've got your back!
I'll spread this everywhere!
klak klak
Lame!
"Sentence"? The fuck?
This is wild!
KTUN
...
KTAN
...

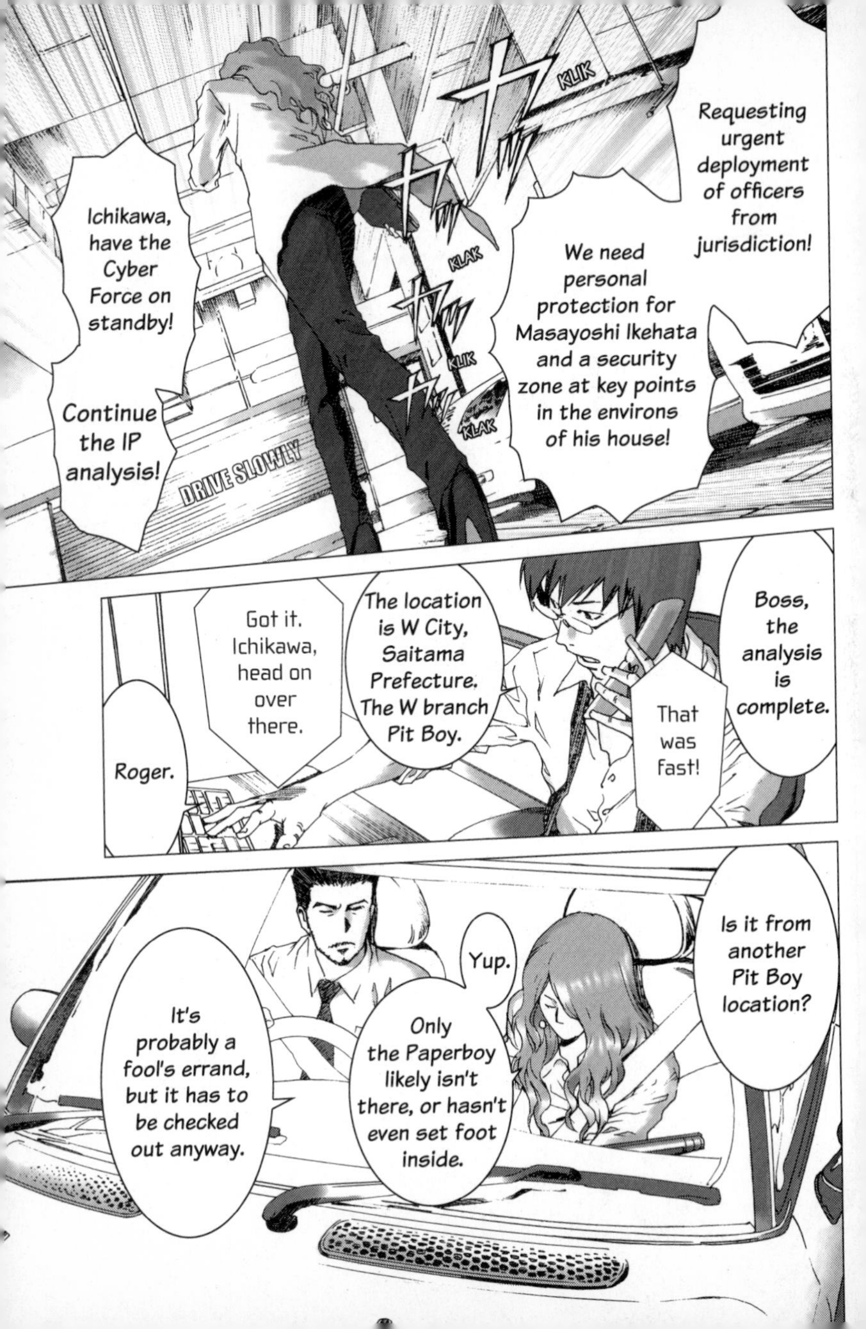

KLIK
Requesting urgent deployment of officers from jurisdiction!
We need personal protection for Masayoshi Ikehata and a security zone at key points in the environs of his house!
KLAK
KLIK
KLAK
Ichikawa, have the Cyber Force on standby!
Continue the IP analysis!
DRIVE SLOWLY
Boss, the analysis is complete.
That was fast!
The location is W City, Saitama Prefecture. The W branch Pit Boy.
Got it. Ichikawa, head on over there.
Roger.
Is it from another Pit Boy location?
Yup.
Only the Paperboy likely isn't there, or hasn't even set foot inside.
It's probably a fool's errand, but it has to be checked out anyway.

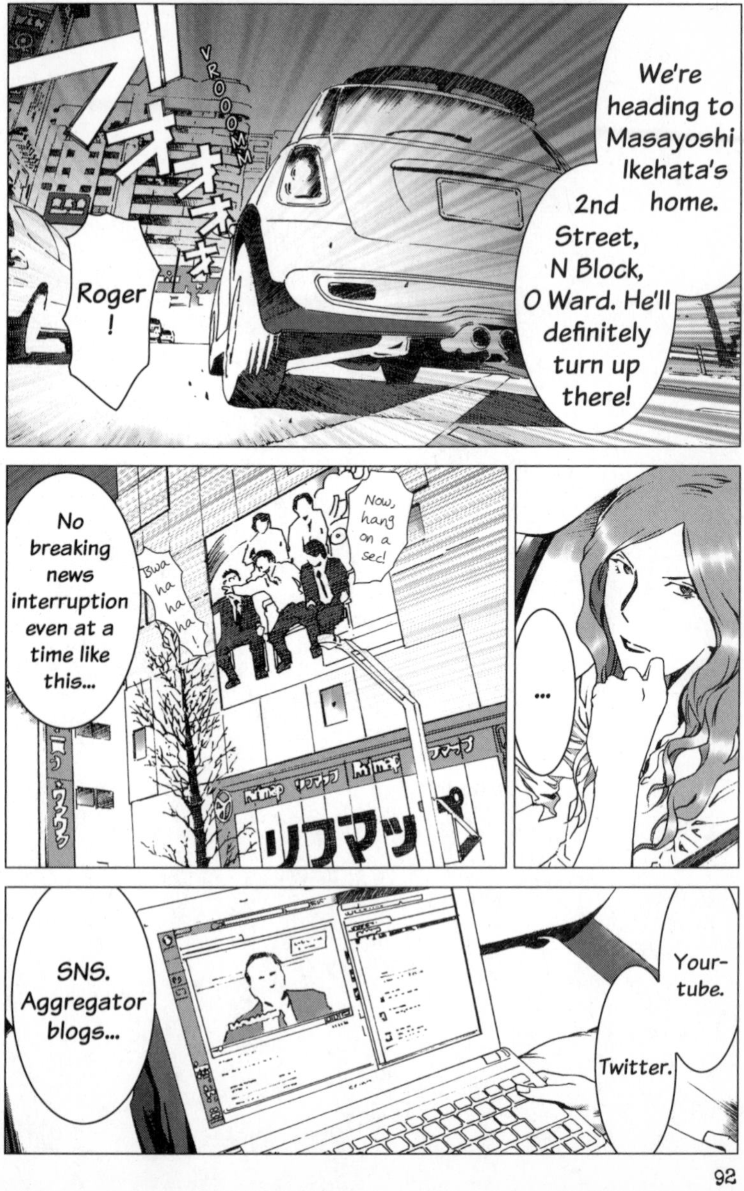
VROOOMM
We're heading to Masayoshi Ikehata's home. 2nd Street, N Block, O Ward. He'll definitely turn up there!
Roger!
...
Now, hang on a sec!
Bwa ha ha ha!
No breaking news interruption even at a time like this...
Your-tube.
Twitter.
SNS. Aggregator blogs...

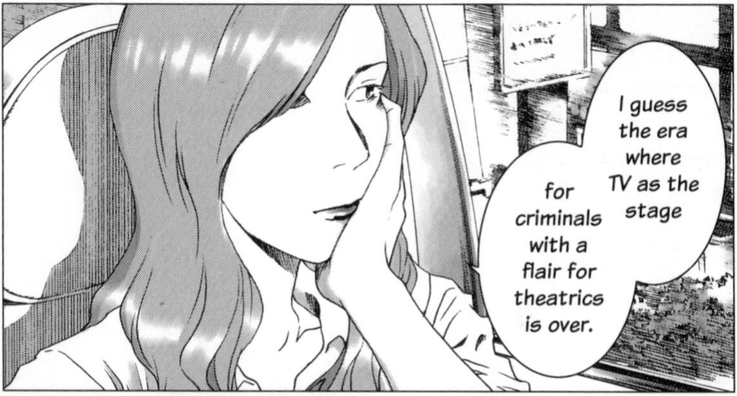
I guess the era where TV as the stage
for criminals with a flair for theatrics is over.

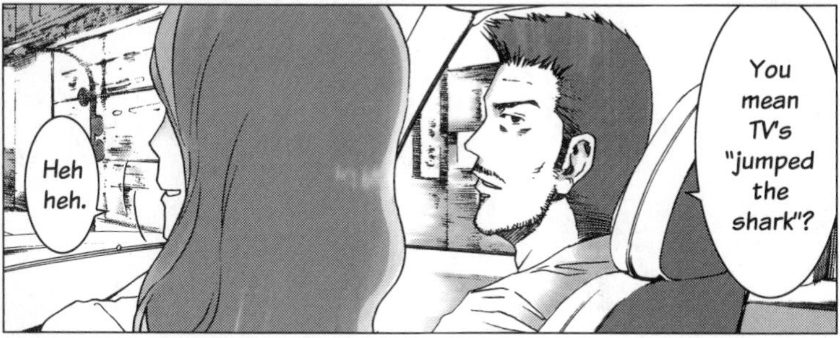
You mean TV's "jumped the shark"?
Heh heh.

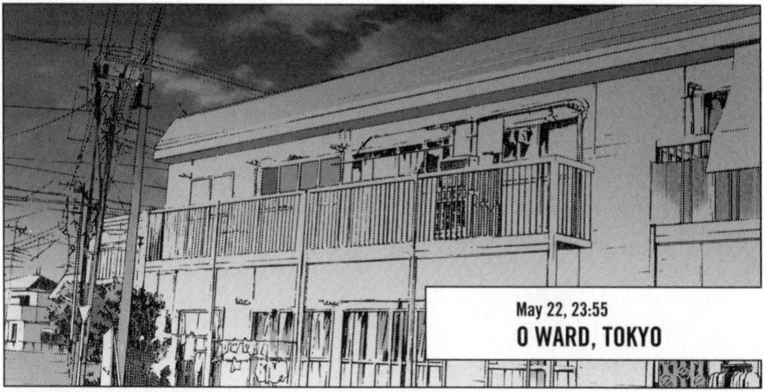
May 22, 23:55
O WARD, TOKYO

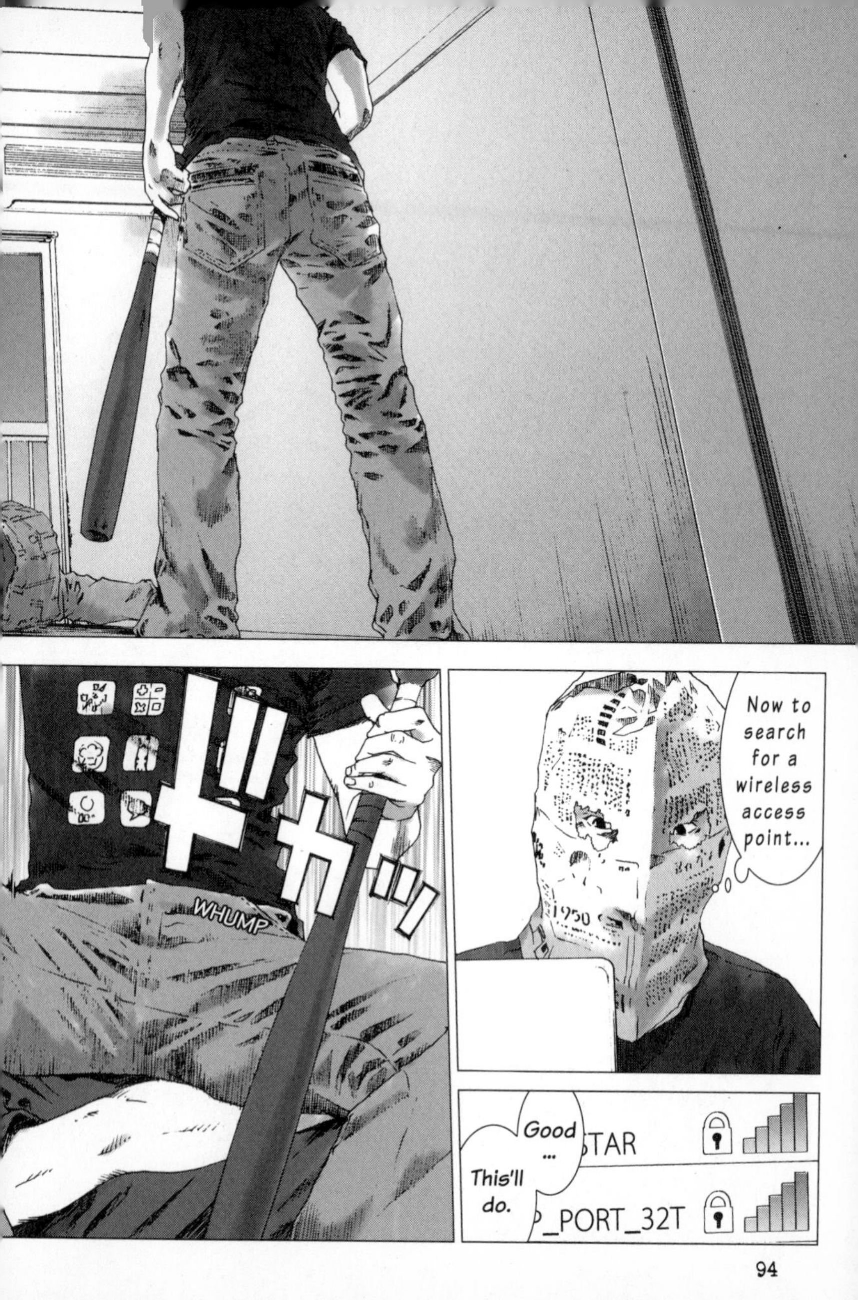
Now to search for a wireless access point...
Good ...
This'll do.
STAR
_PORT_32T
WHUMP

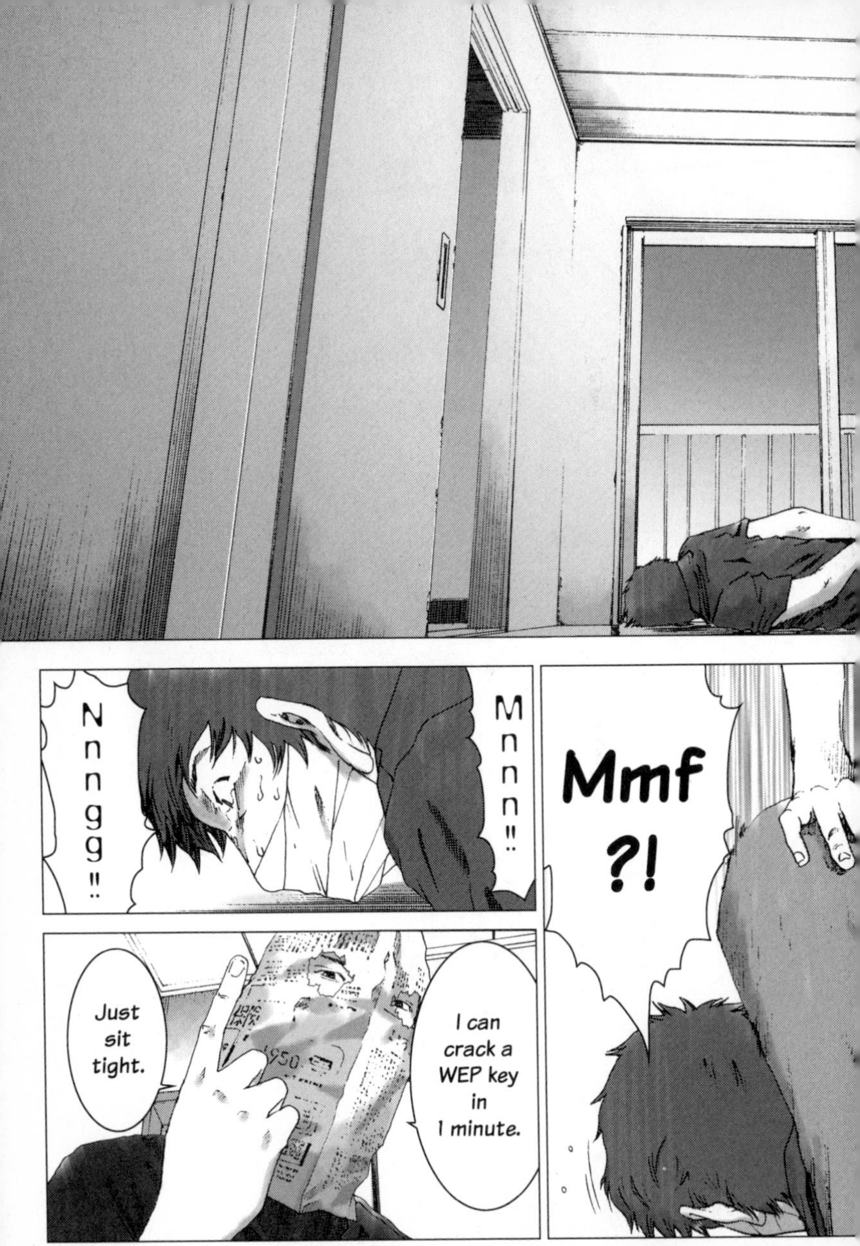
Mmf ?!
Mnnn!!
Nnngg!!
I can crack a WEP key in 1 minute.
Just sit tight.

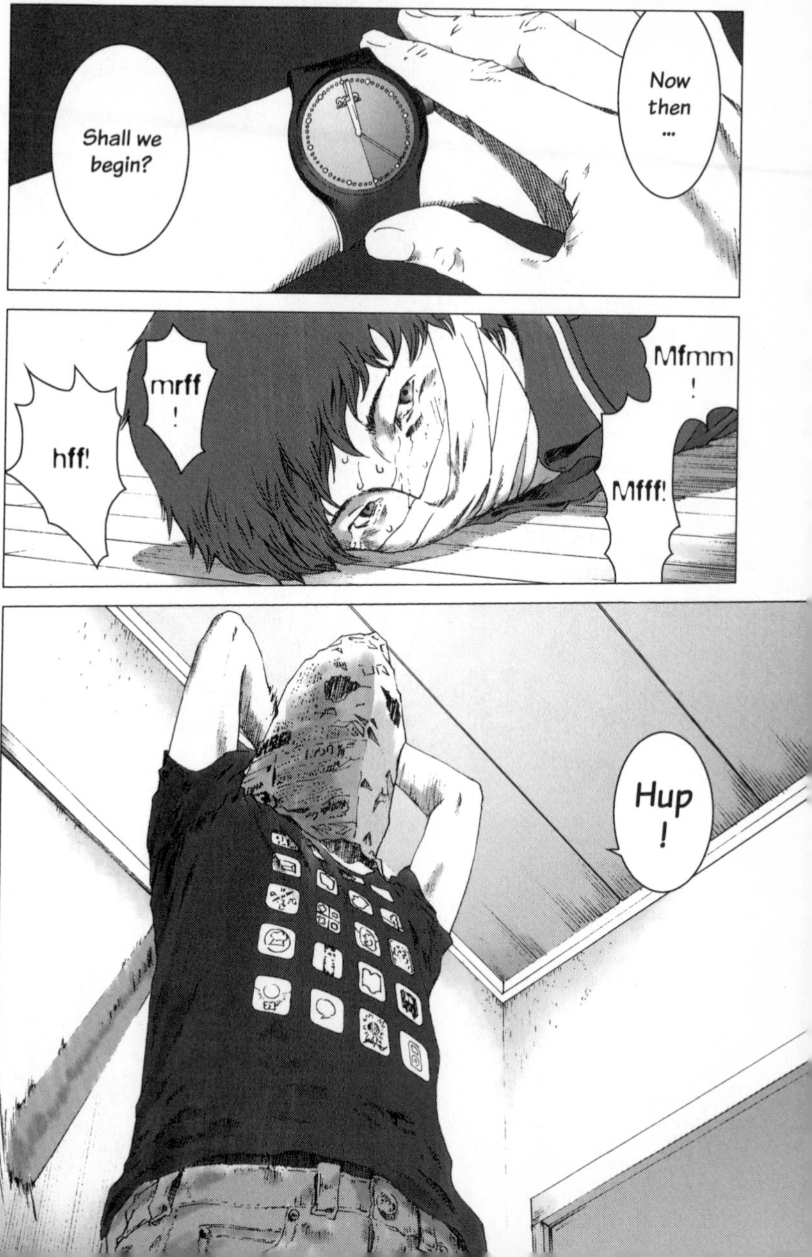
Now then ...
Shall we begin?
Mfmm!
Mfff!
mrff!
hff!
Hup!

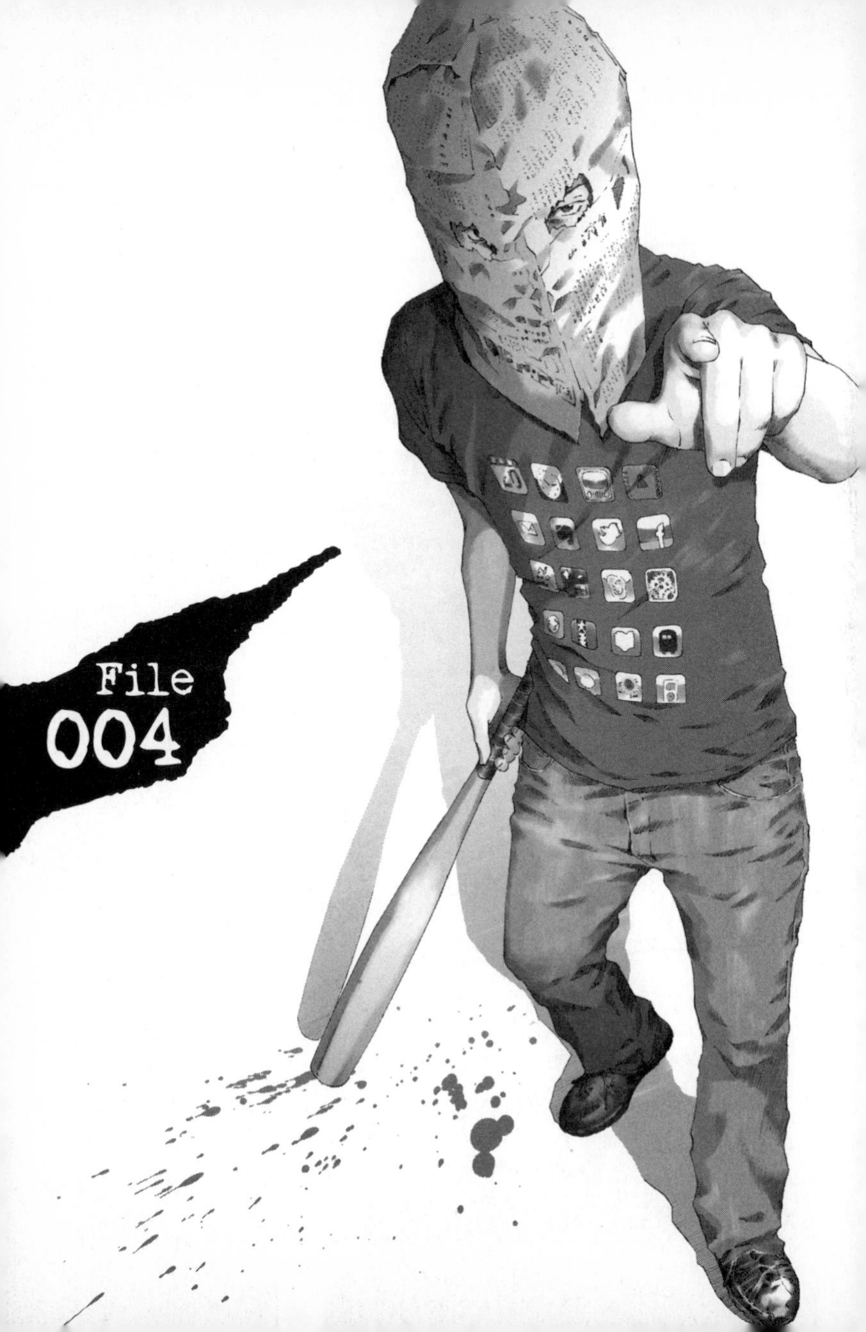
File
004

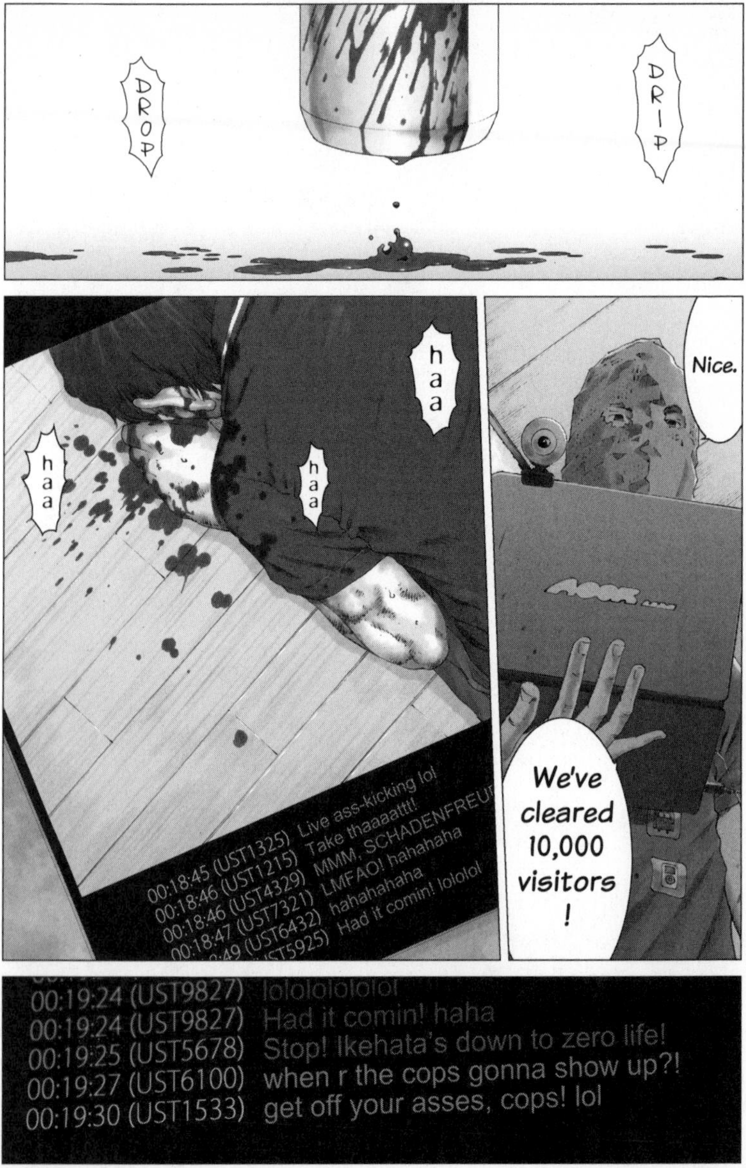
DRIP
DROP
Nice.
We've cleared 10,000 visitors!
haa
haa
haa
00:18:45 (UST1325) Live ass-kicking lol
00:18:46 (UST1215) Take thaaaattt!
00:18:46 (UST4329) MMM, SCHADENFREU
00:18:47 (UST7321) LMFAO! hahahaha
(UST6432) hahahahaha
(UST5925) Had it comin! lololol
00:19:24 (UST9827) lolololololol
00:19:24 (UST9827) Had it comin! haha
00:19:25 (UST5678) Stop! Ikehata's down to zero life!
00:19:27 (UST6100) when r the cops gonna show up?!
00:19:30 (UST1533) get off your asses, cops! lol

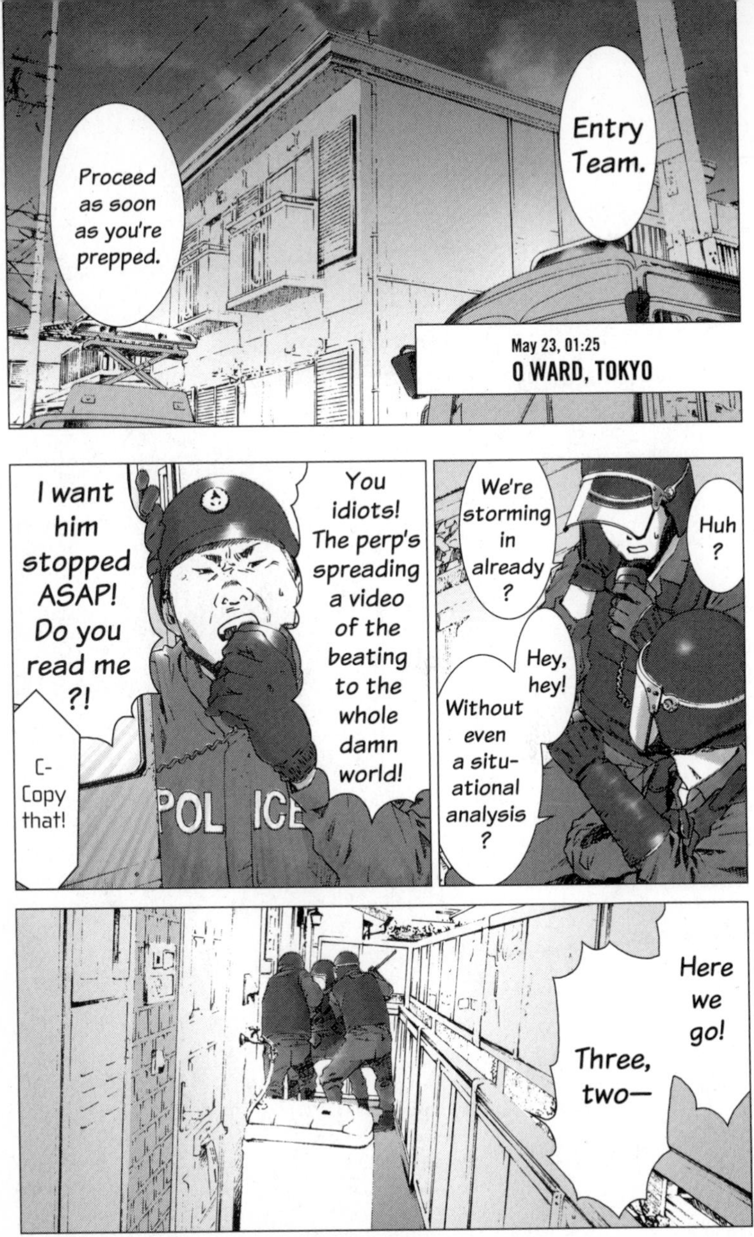

Entry Team.
Proceed as soon as you're prepped.
May 23, 01:25
O WARD, TOKYO
Huh?
We're storming in already?
Hey, hey!
Without even a situ-ational analysis?
You idiots! The perp's spreading a video of the beating to the whole damn world!
I want him stopped ASAP! Do you read me?!
C- Copy that!
POLICE
Here we go!
Three, two—

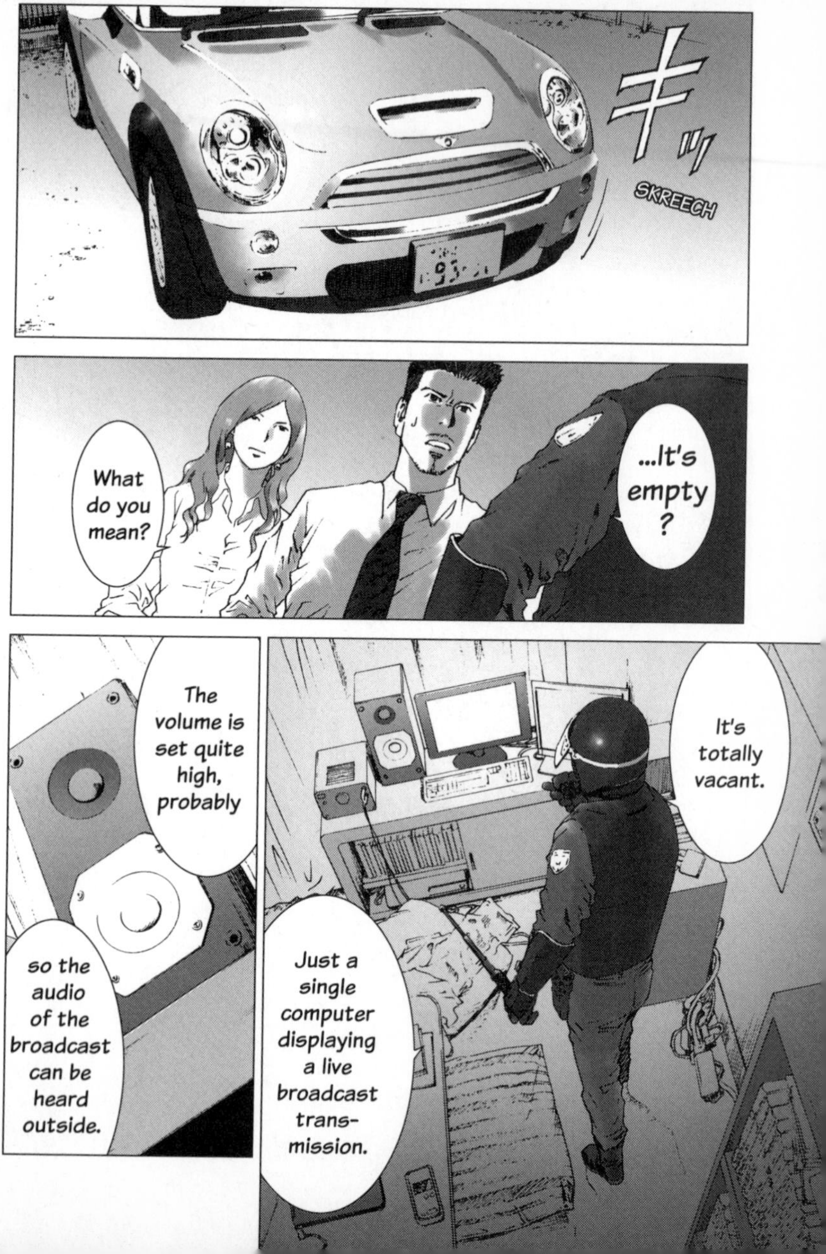
キッ
SKREECH
...It's empty?
What do you mean?
It's totally vacant.
Just a single computer displaying a live broadcast trans-mission.
The volume is set quite high, probably
so the audio of the broadcast can be heard outside.

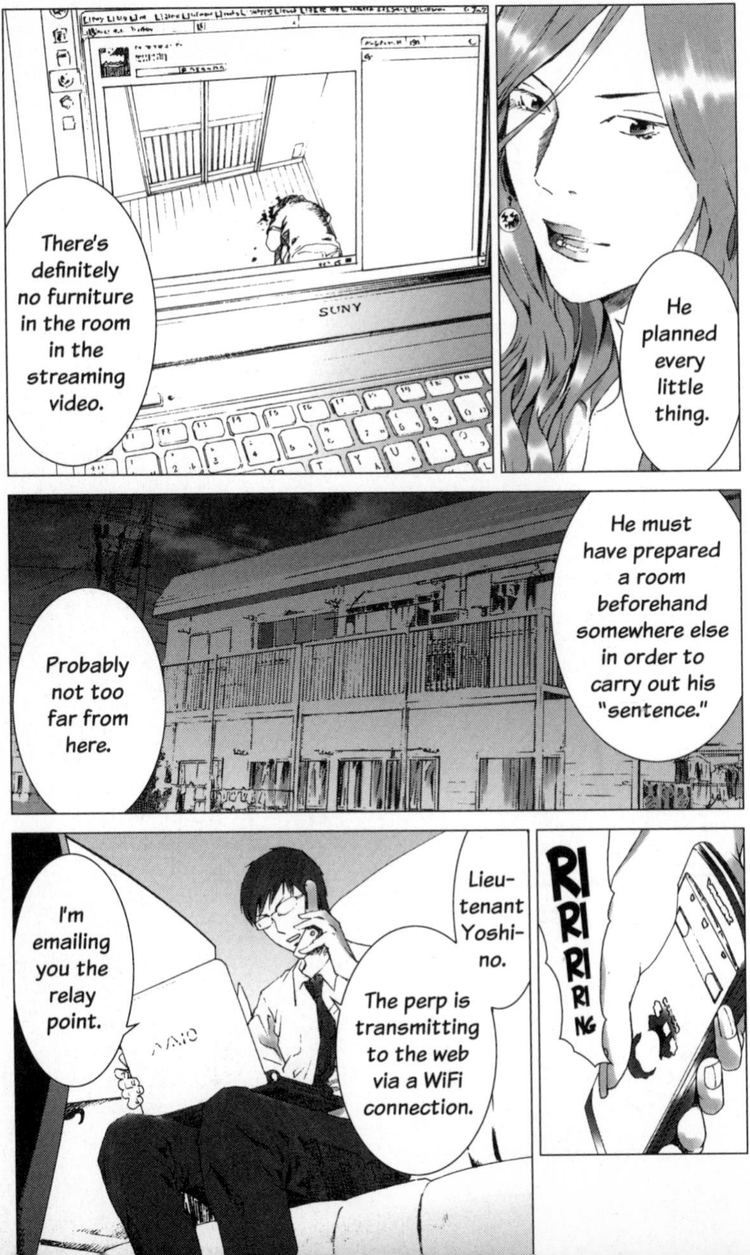
He planned every little thing.
There's definitely no furniture in the room in the streaming video.
SUNY
He must have prepared a room beforehand somewhere else in order to carry out his "sentence."
Probably not too far from here.
RIRIRIRING
Lieu-tenant Yoshi-no.
The perp is transmitting to the web via a WiFi connection.
I'm emailing you the relay point.

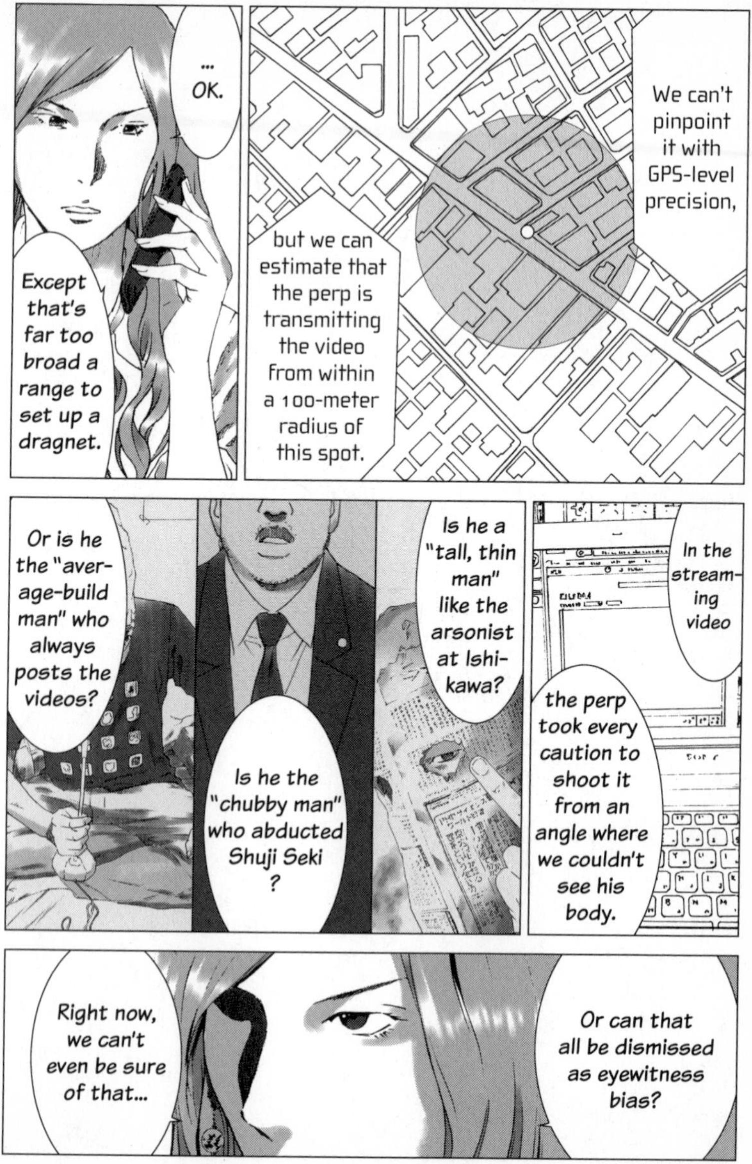
We can't pinpoint it with GPS-level precision,
but we can estimate that the perp is transmitting the video from within a 100-meter radius of this spot.
... OK.
Except that's far too broad a range to set up a dragnet.
In the streaming video
the perp took every caution to shoot it from an angle where we couldn't see his body.
Is he a "tall, thin man" like the arsonist at Ishikawa?
Is he the "chubby man" who abducted Shuji Seki ?
Or is he the "average-build man" who always posts the videos?
Or can that all be dismissed as eyewitness bias?
Right now, we can't even be sure of that...

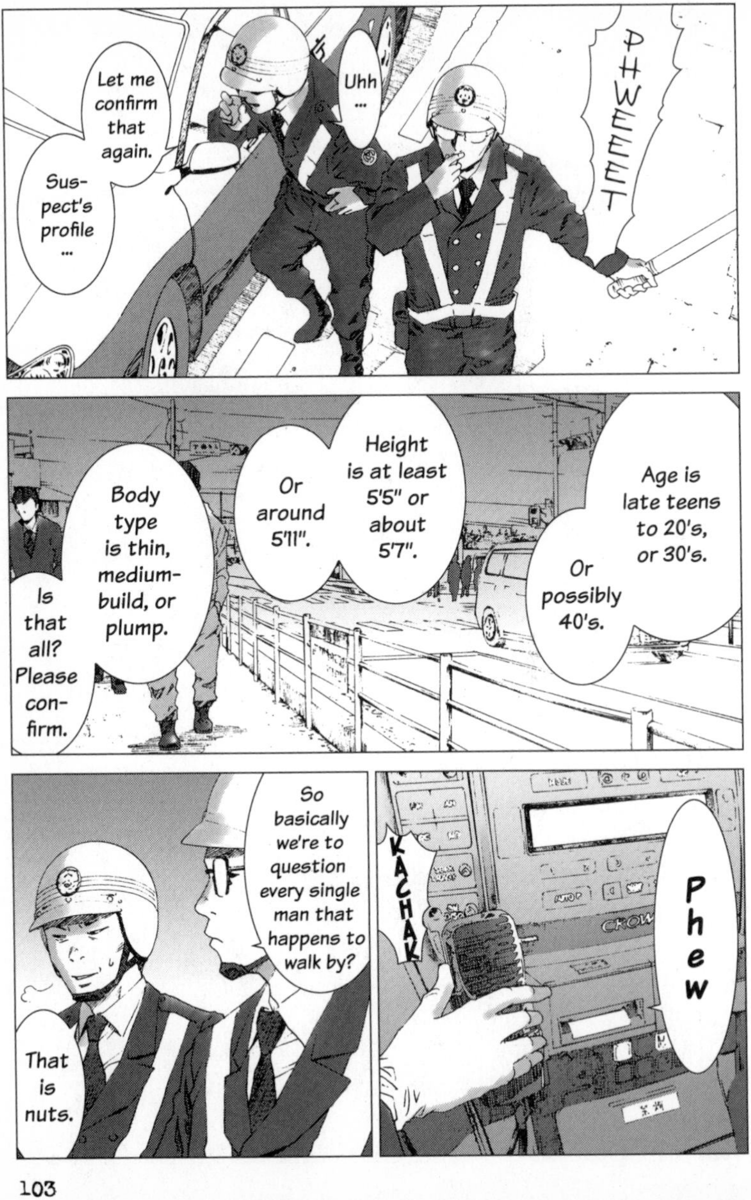
PHWEEEET
Uhh ...
Let me confirm that again.
Sus-pect's profile ...
Age is late teens to 20's, or 30's.
Or possibly 40's.
Height is at least 5'5" or about 5'7".
Or around 5'11".
Body type is thin, medium-build, or plump.
Is that all? Please con-firm.
Phew
KACHAK
So basically we're to question every single man that happens to walk by?
That is nuts.

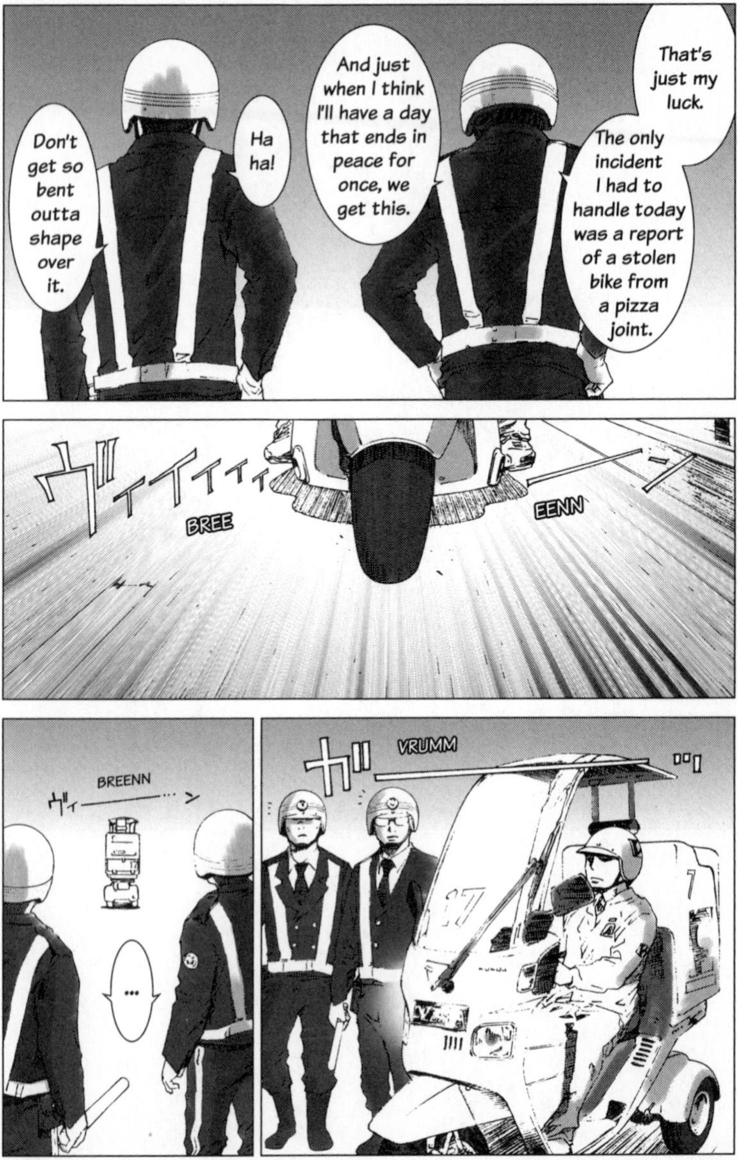
That's just my luck.
The only incident I had to handle today was a report of a stolen bike from a pizza joint.
And just when I think I'll have a day that ends in peace for once, we get this.
Ha ha!
Don't get so bent outta shape over it.
BREE
EENN
VRUMM
ヴィ
BREENN
...

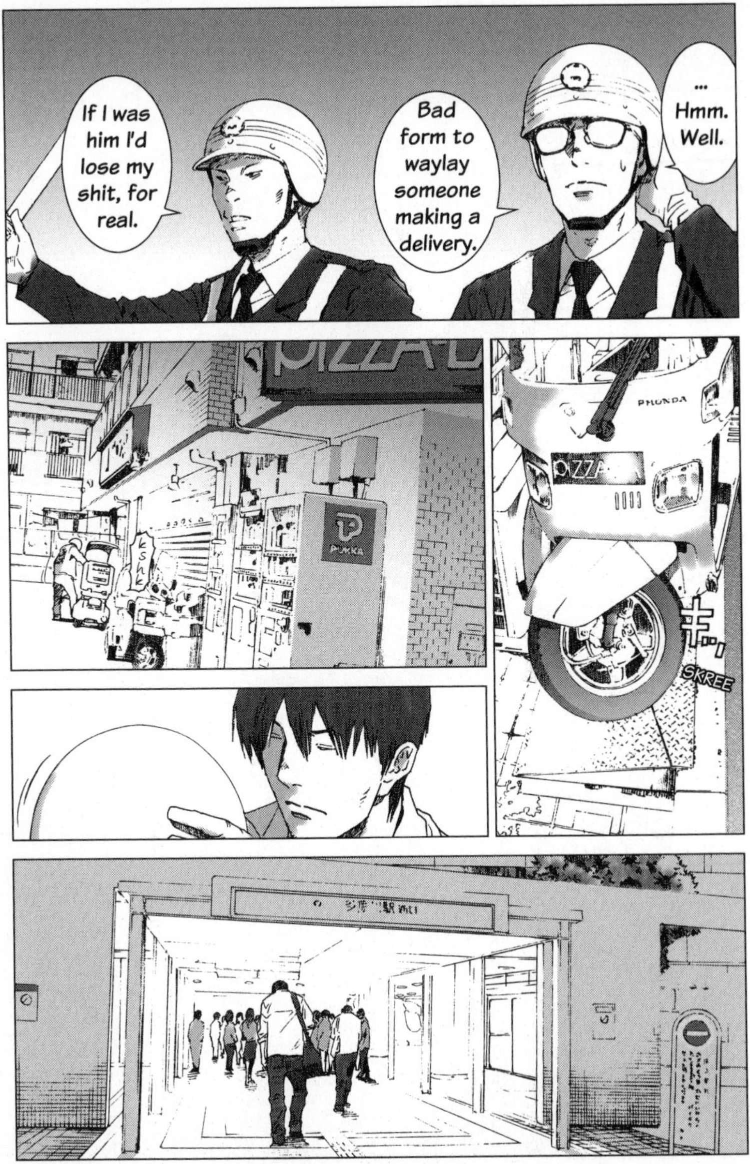
... Hmm. Well.
Bad form to waylay someone making a delivery.
If I was him I'd lose my shit, for real.
PHONDA
SKREE
PUKKA
kshk

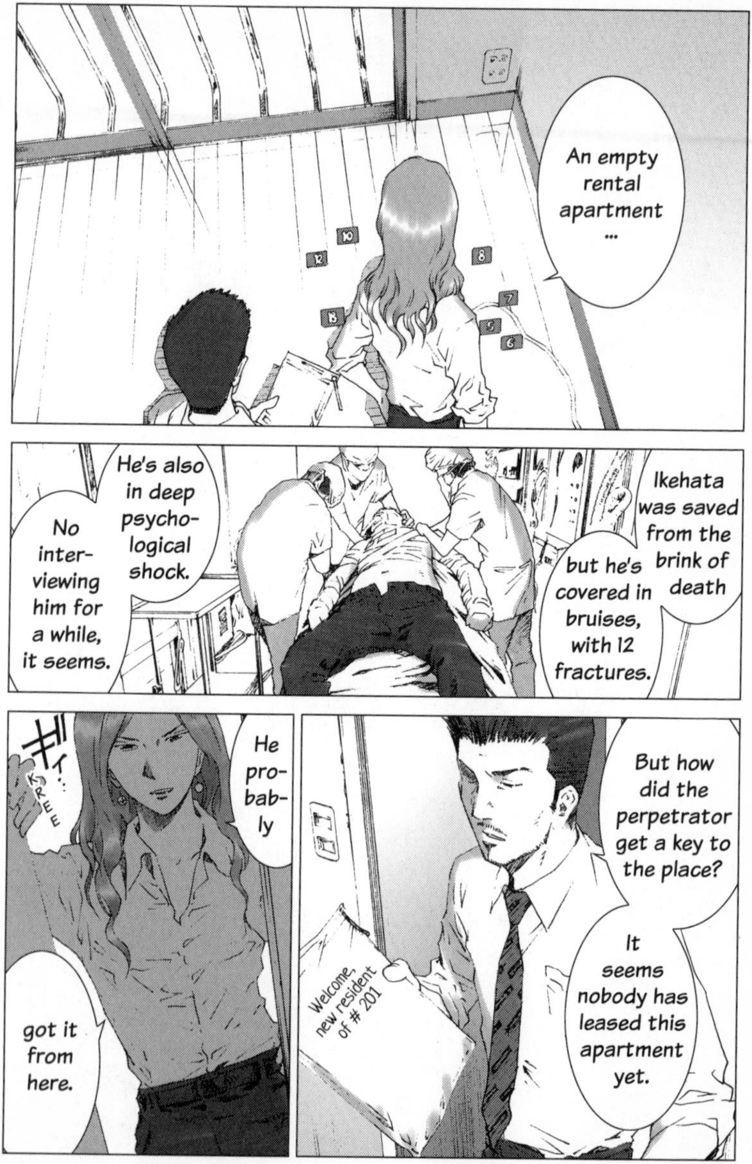
An empty rental apartment ...
Ikehata was saved from the brink of death
but he's covered in bruises, with 12 fractures.
He's also in deep psycho-logical shock.
No inter-viewing him for a while, it seems.
But how did the perpetrator get a key to the place?
It seems nobody has leased this apartment yet.
Welcome, new resident of # 201
KREE
He pro-bab-ly
got it from here.

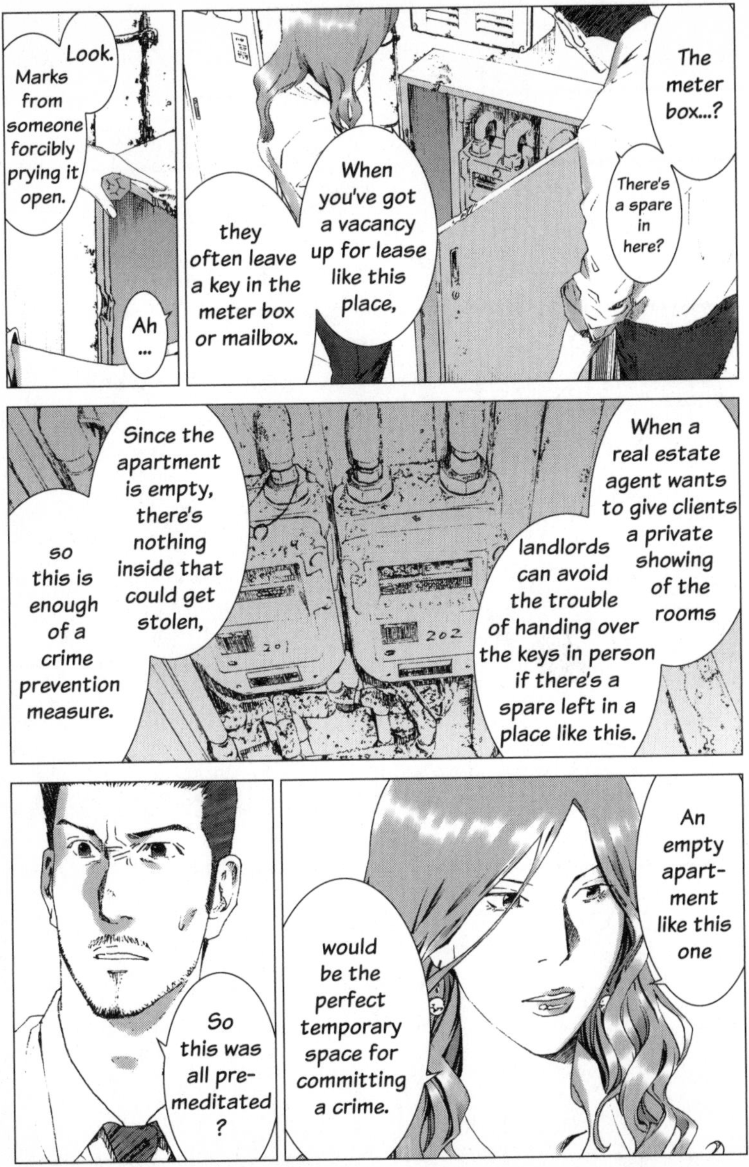

The meter box...?
There's a spare in here?
When you've got a vacancy up for lease like this place,
they often leave a key in the meter box or mailbox.
Look. Marks from someone forcibly prying it open.
Ah ...
When a real estate agent wants to give clients a private showing of the rooms
landlords can avoid the trouble of handing over the keys in person if there's a spare left in a place like this.
Since the apartment is empty, there's nothing inside that could get stolen,
so this is enough of a crime prevention measure.
An empty apartment like this one
would be the perfect temporary space for committing a crime.
So this was all premeditated?

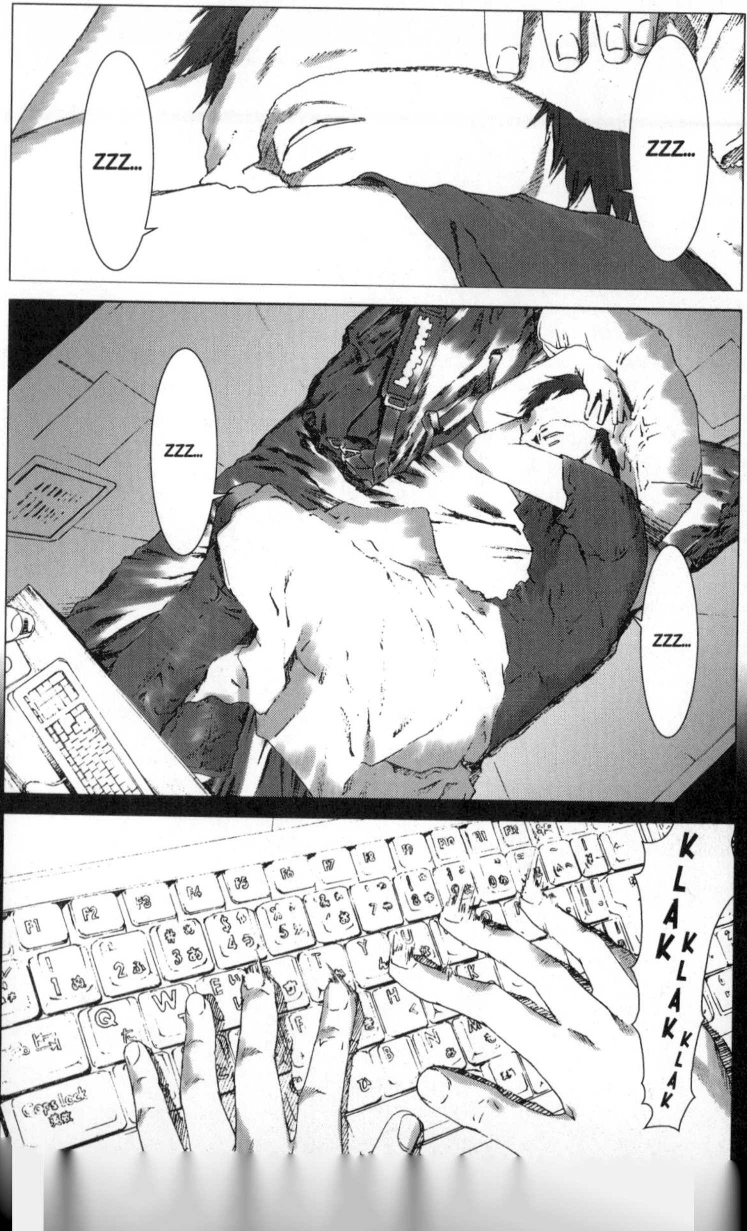
ZZZ...
ZZZ...
ZZZ...
ZZZ...
KLAK
KLAK
KLAK

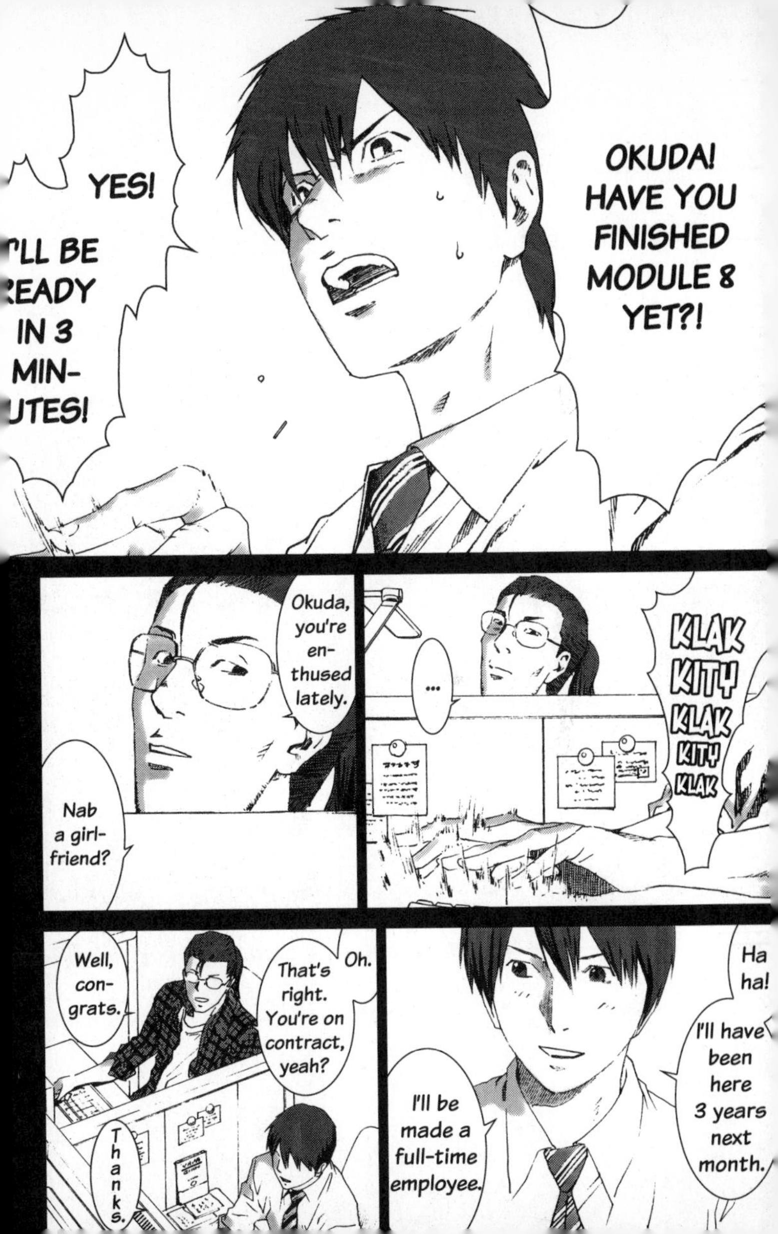
OKUDA! HAVE YOU FINISHED MODULE 8 YET?!
YES!
I'LL BE READY IN 3 MIN-UTES!
KLAK KITY KLAK KITY KLAK
...
Okuda, you're en-thused lately.
Nab a girl-friend?
Ha ha!
I'll have been here 3 years next month.
I'll be made a full-time employee.
Oh.
That's right. You're on contract, yeah?
Well, con-grats.
Thanks.

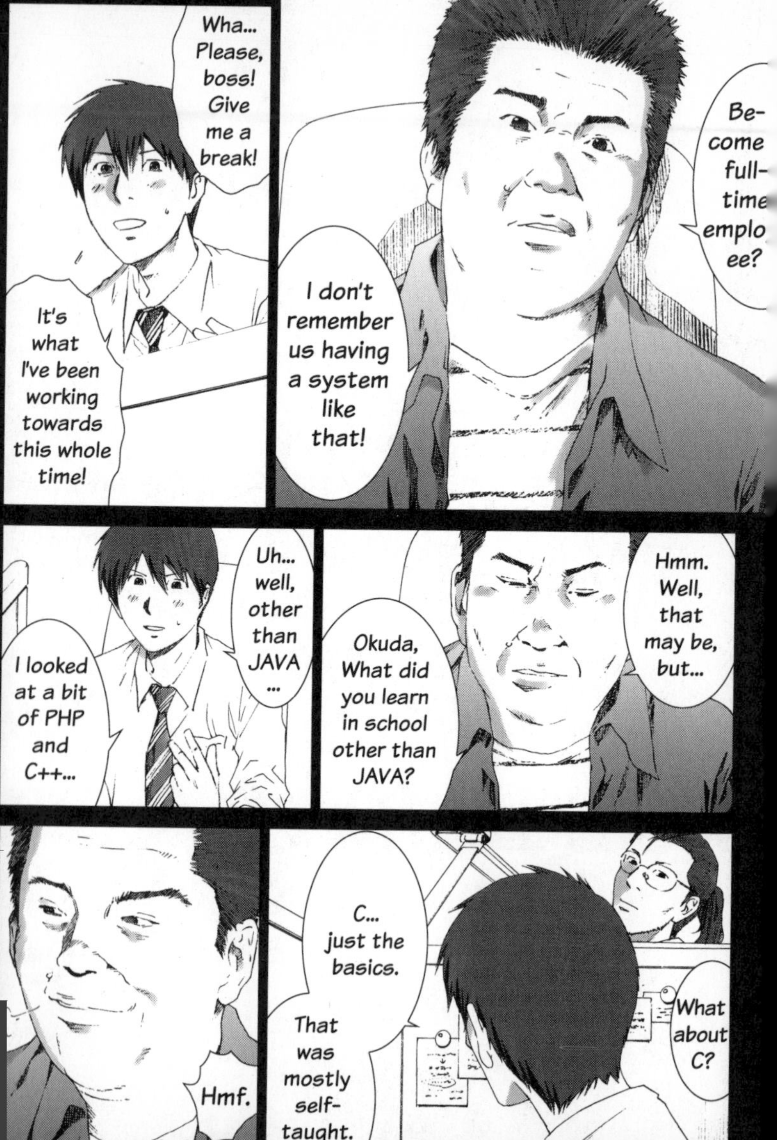
Be-come full-time employee?
I don't remember us having a system like that!
Wha... Please, boss! Give me a break!
It's what I've been working towards this whole time!
Hmm. Well, that may be, but...
Okuda, What did you learn in school other than JAVA?
Uh... well, other than JAVA ...
I looked at a bit of PHP and C++...
What about C?
C... just the basics.
That was mostly self-taught.
Hmf.

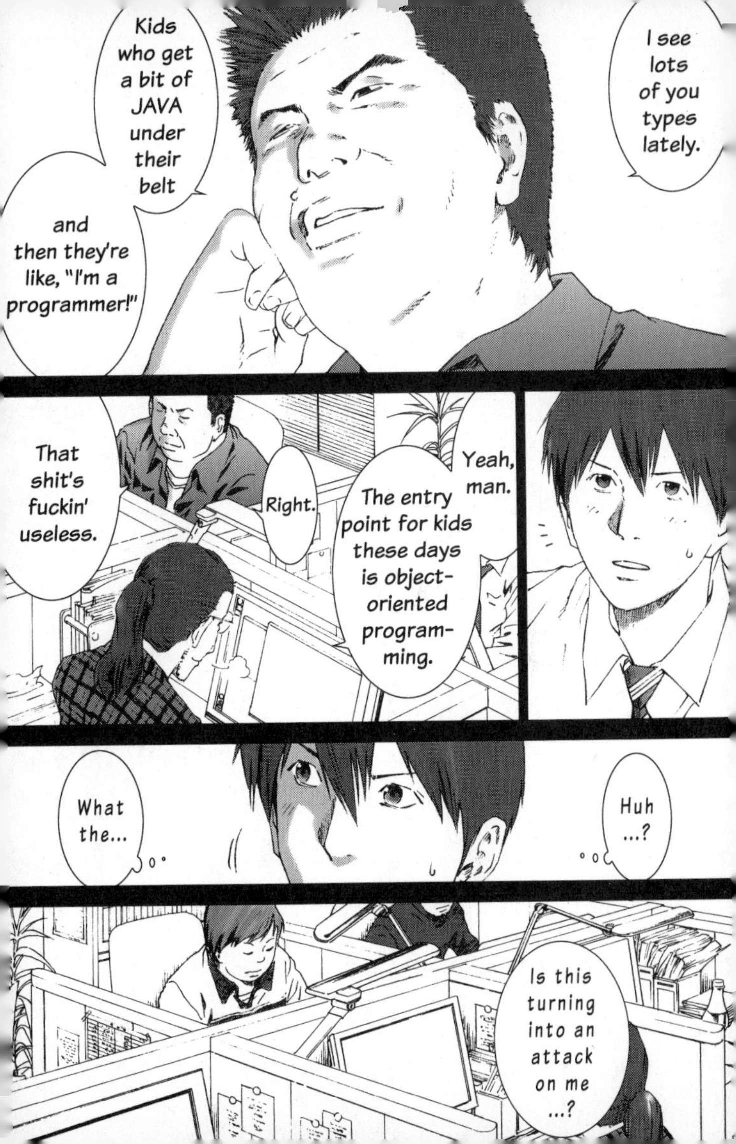
I see lots of you types lately.
Kids who get a bit of JAVA under their belt
and then they're like, "I'm a programmer!"
Yeah, man.
The entry point for kids these days is object-oriented program-ming.
Right.
That shit's fuckin' useless.
Huh ...?
What the...
Is this turning into an attack on me ...?

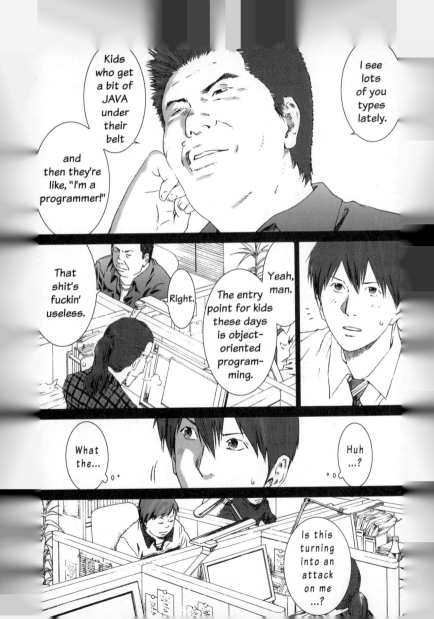

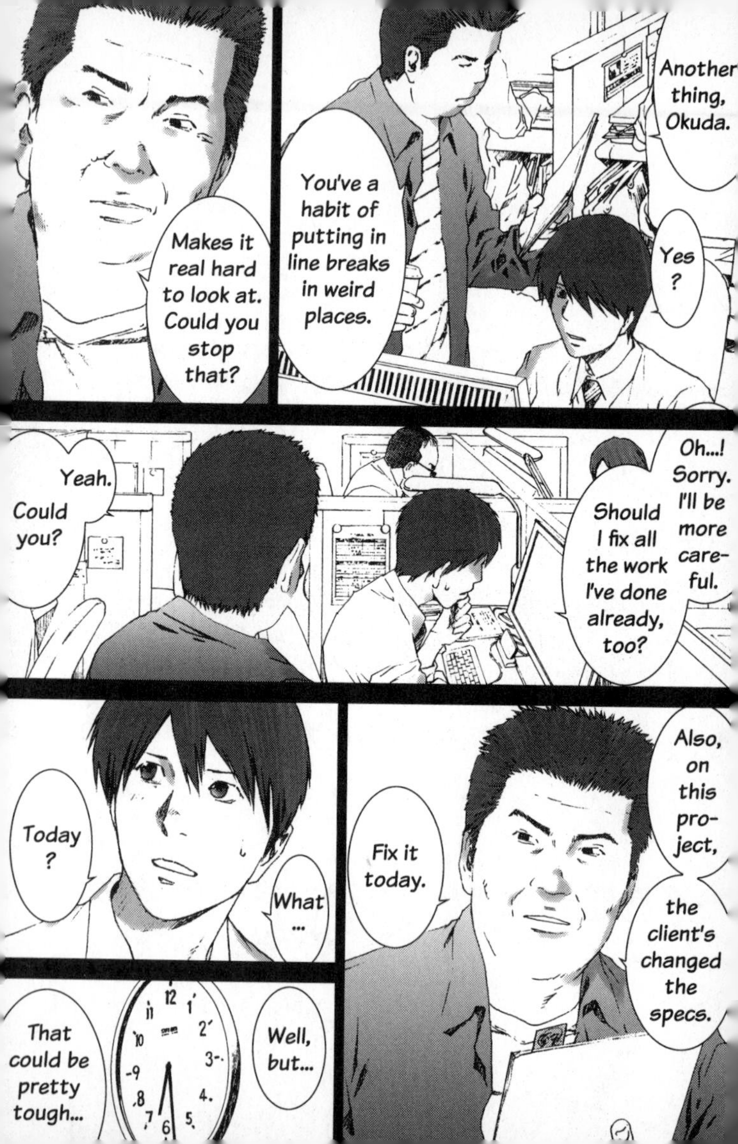

Another thing, Okuda.
Yes?
You've a habit of putting in line breaks in weird places.
Makes it real hard to look at. Could you stop that?
Oh...! Sorry. I'll be more care-ful.
Should I fix all the work I've done already, too?
Yeah. Could you?
Also, on this pro-ject,
the client's changed the specs.
Fix it today.
What...
Today?
Well, but...
That could be pretty tough...

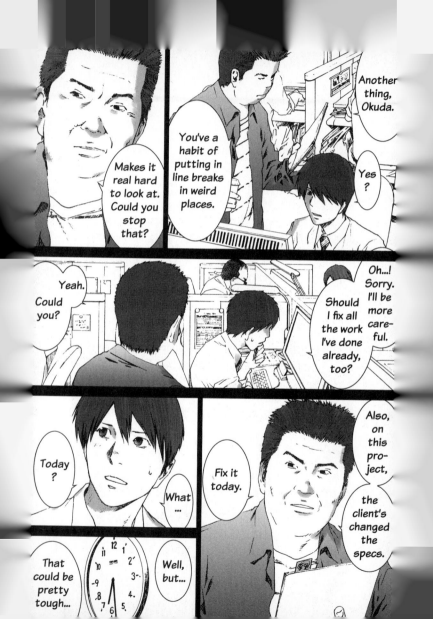

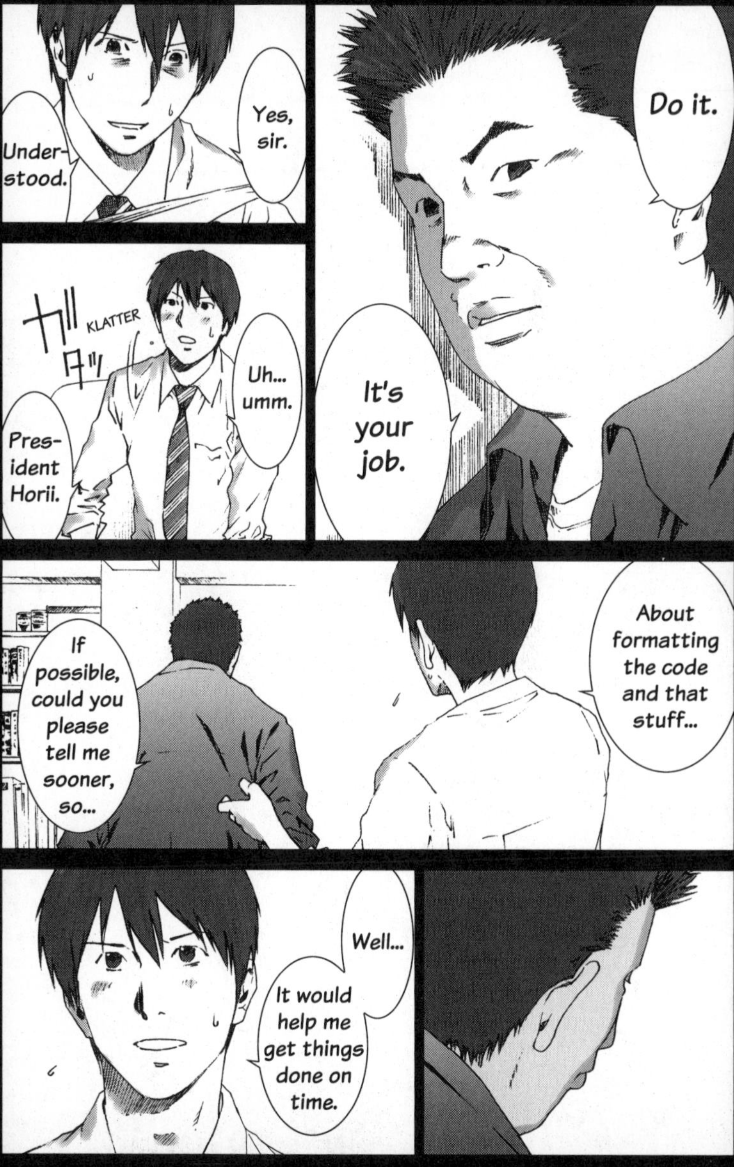
Do it.
It's your job.
Yes, sir.
Understood.
ガタッ KLATTER
Uh... umm.
President Horii.
About formatting the code and that stuff...
If possible, could you please tell me sooner, so...
Well...
It would help me get things done on time.

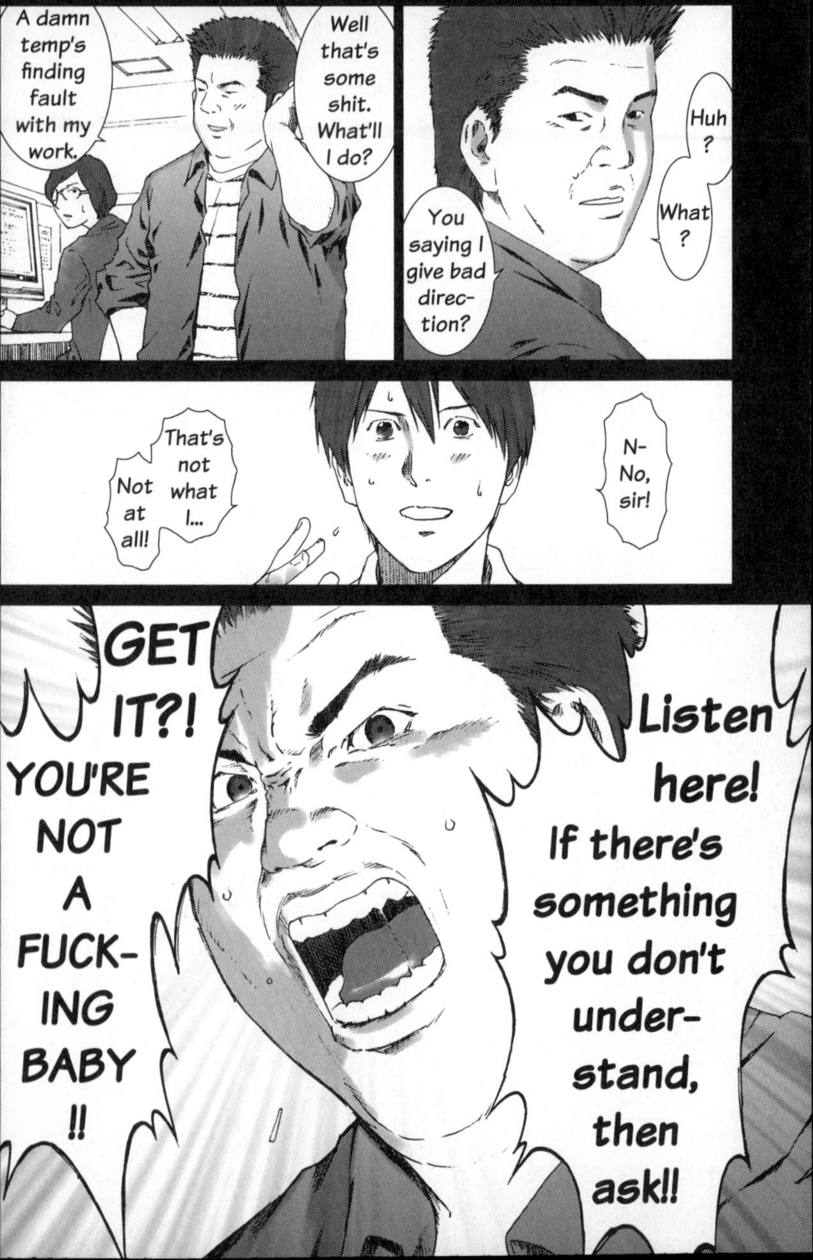
Huh?
What?
You saying I give bad direction?
Well that's some shit. What'll I do?
A damn temp's finding fault with my work.
N- No, sir!
That's not what I...
Not at all!
Listen here!
If there's something you don't under-stand, then ask!!
YOU'RE NOT A FUCK-ING BABY!!
GET IT?!

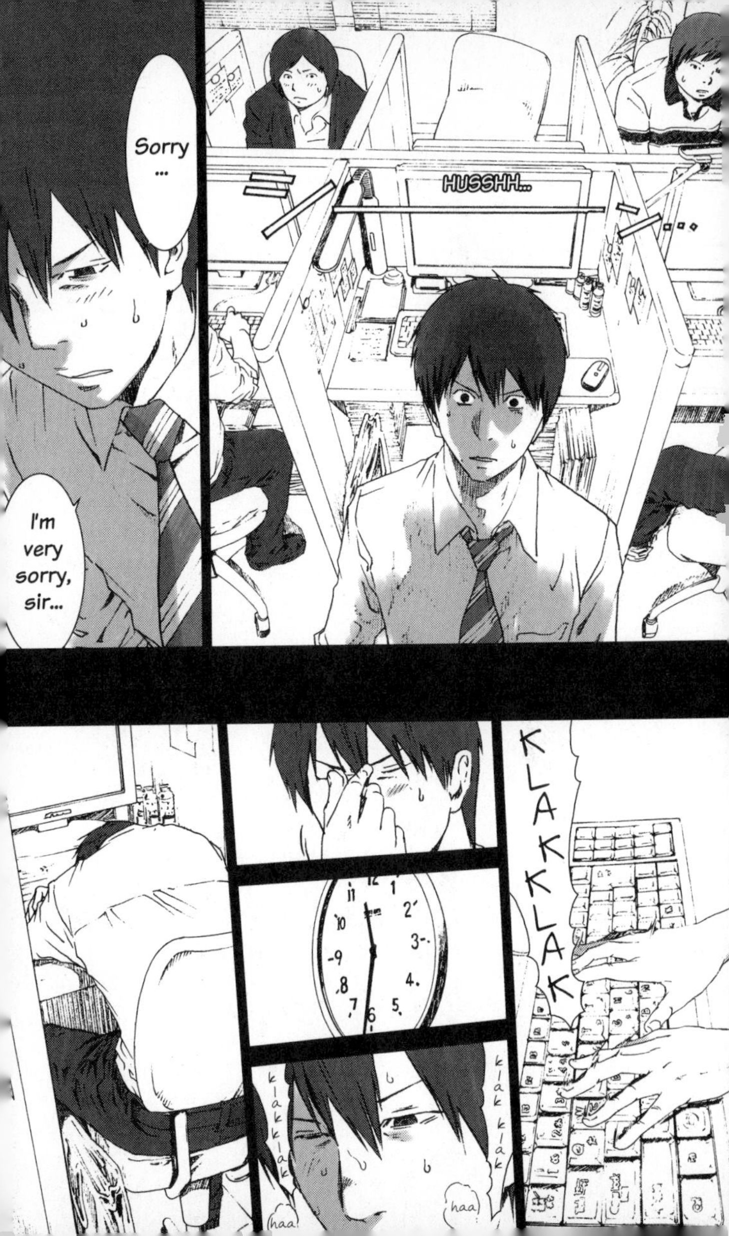
HUSSHH...
Sorry ...
I'm very sorry, sir...
KLAKKLAK
klak klak
klakklak
haa
haa

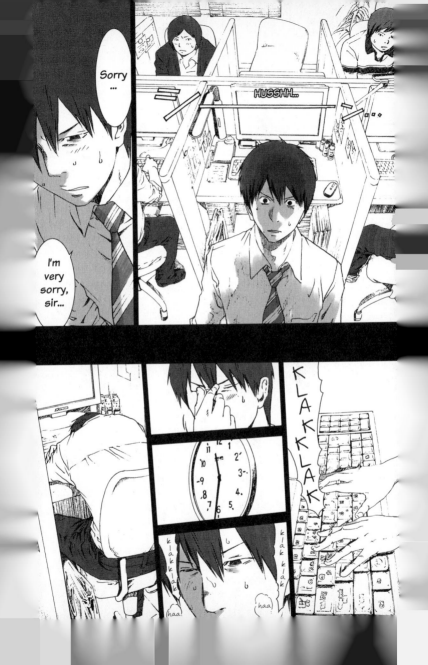

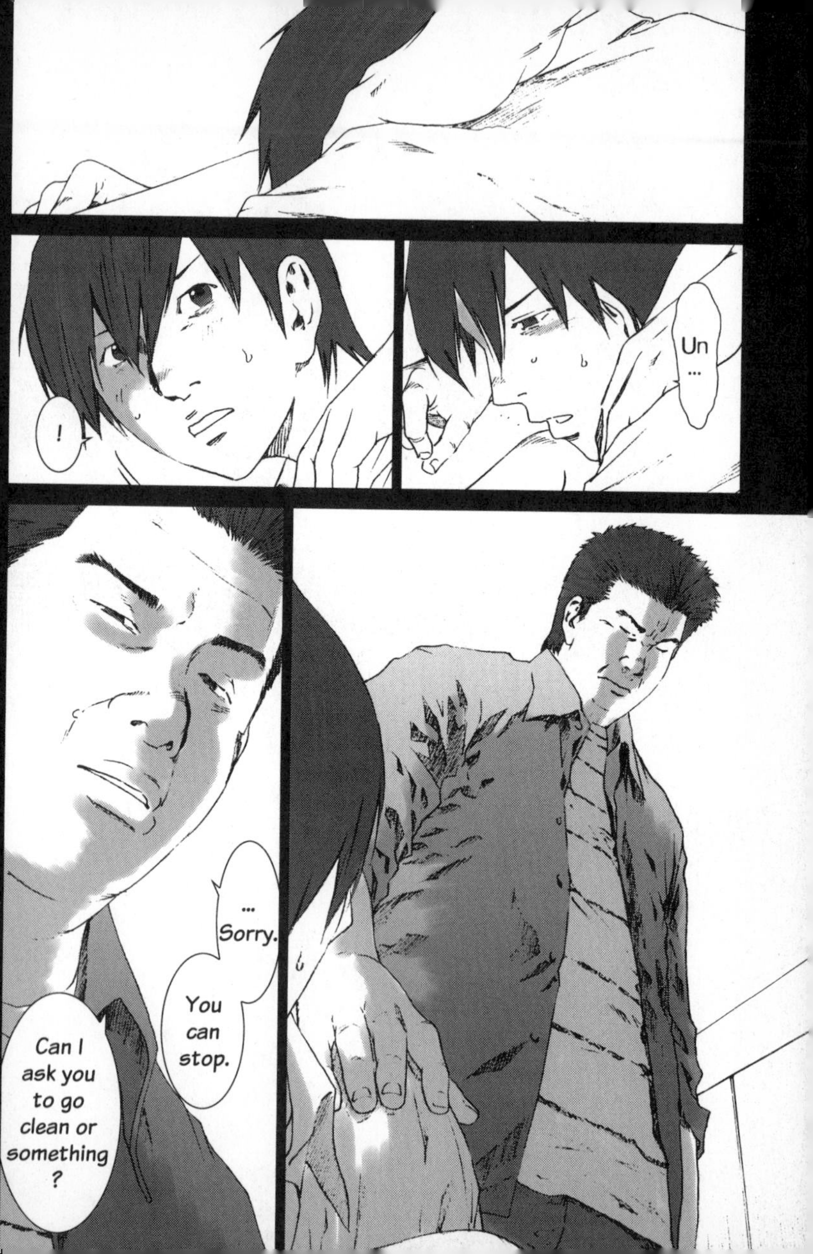
Un ...
!
... Sorry.
You can stop.
Can I ask you to go clean or something?

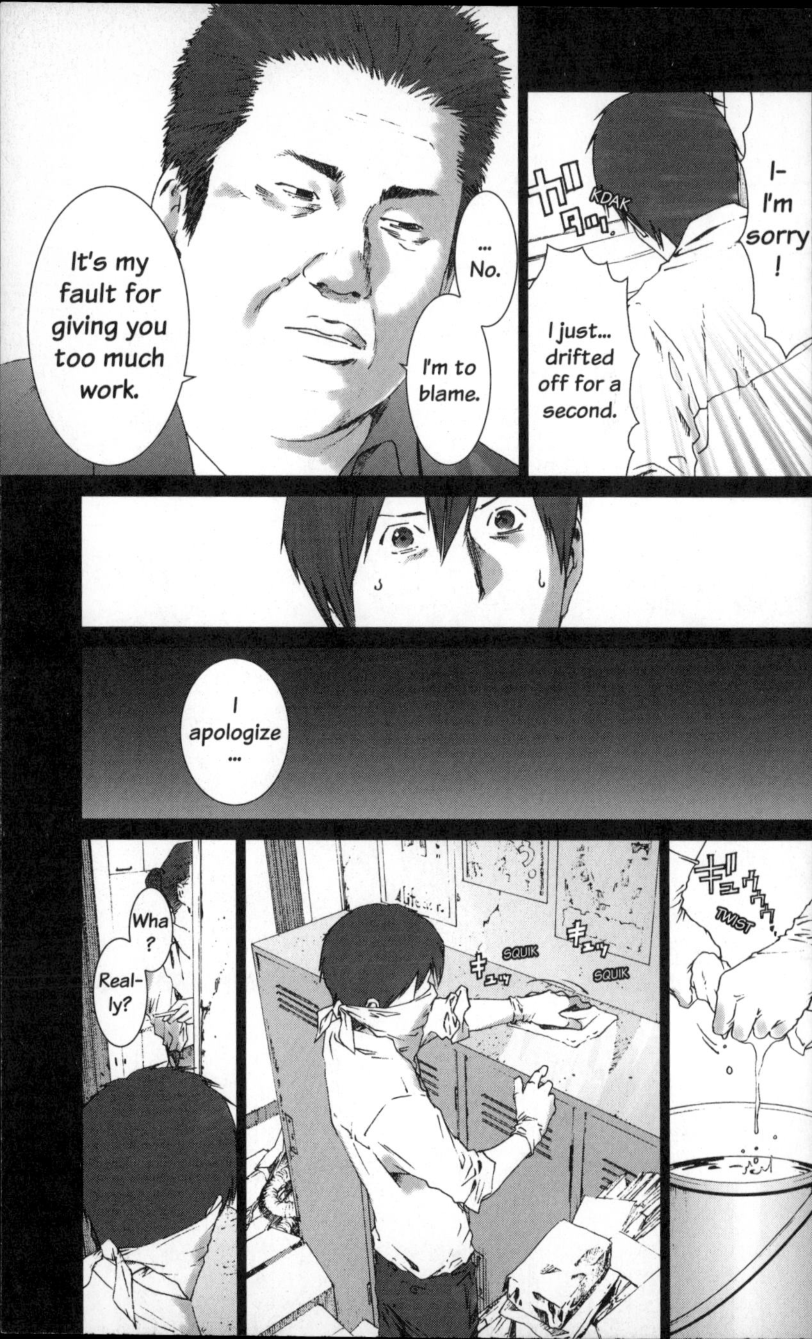
I- I'm sorry!
KDAK
I just... drifted off for a second.
... No.
I'm to blame.
It's my fault for giving you too much work.
I apologize ...
TWIST
SQUIK
SQUIK
Wha?
Real-ly?

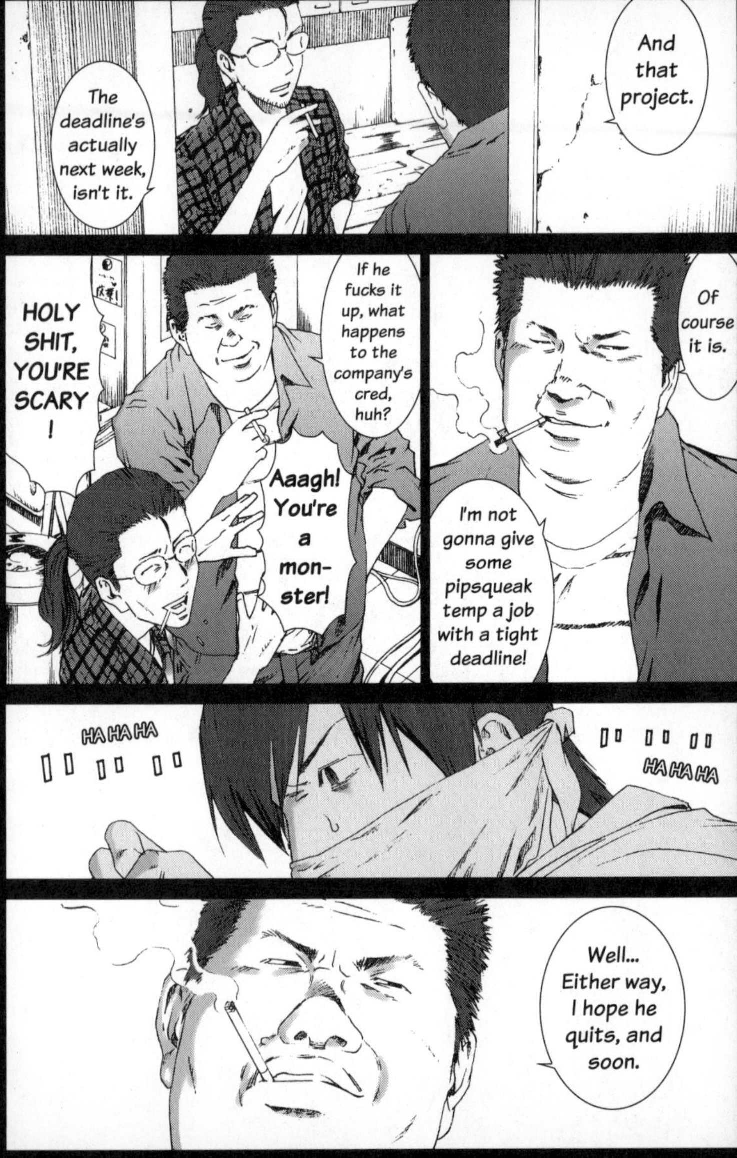
And that project.
The deadline's actually next week, isn't it.
Of course it is.
I'm not gonna give some pipsqueak temp a job with a tight deadline!
If he fucks it up, what happens to the company's cred, huh?
Aaagh! You're a mon-ster!
HOLY SHIT, YOU'RE SCARY!
HA HA HA
HA HA HA
Well... Either way, I hope he quits, and soon.

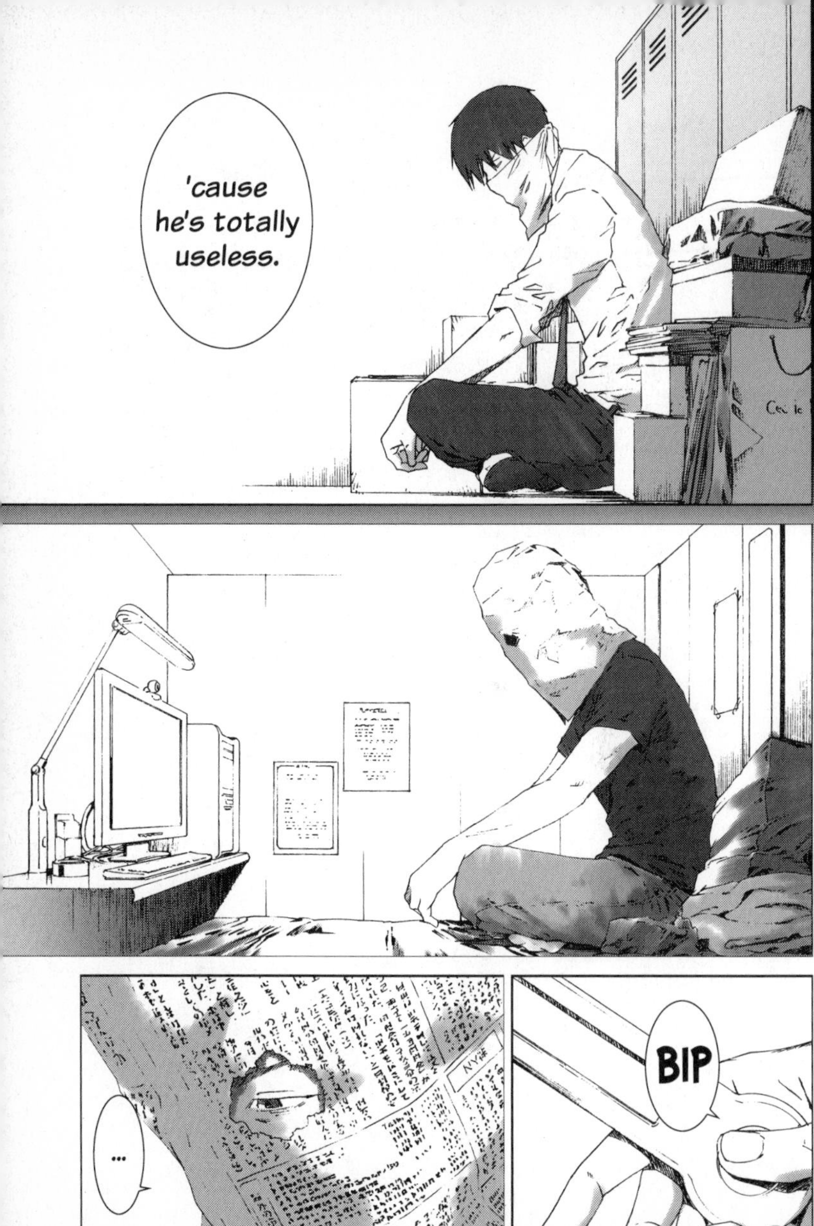
'cause he's totally useless.
BIP
...

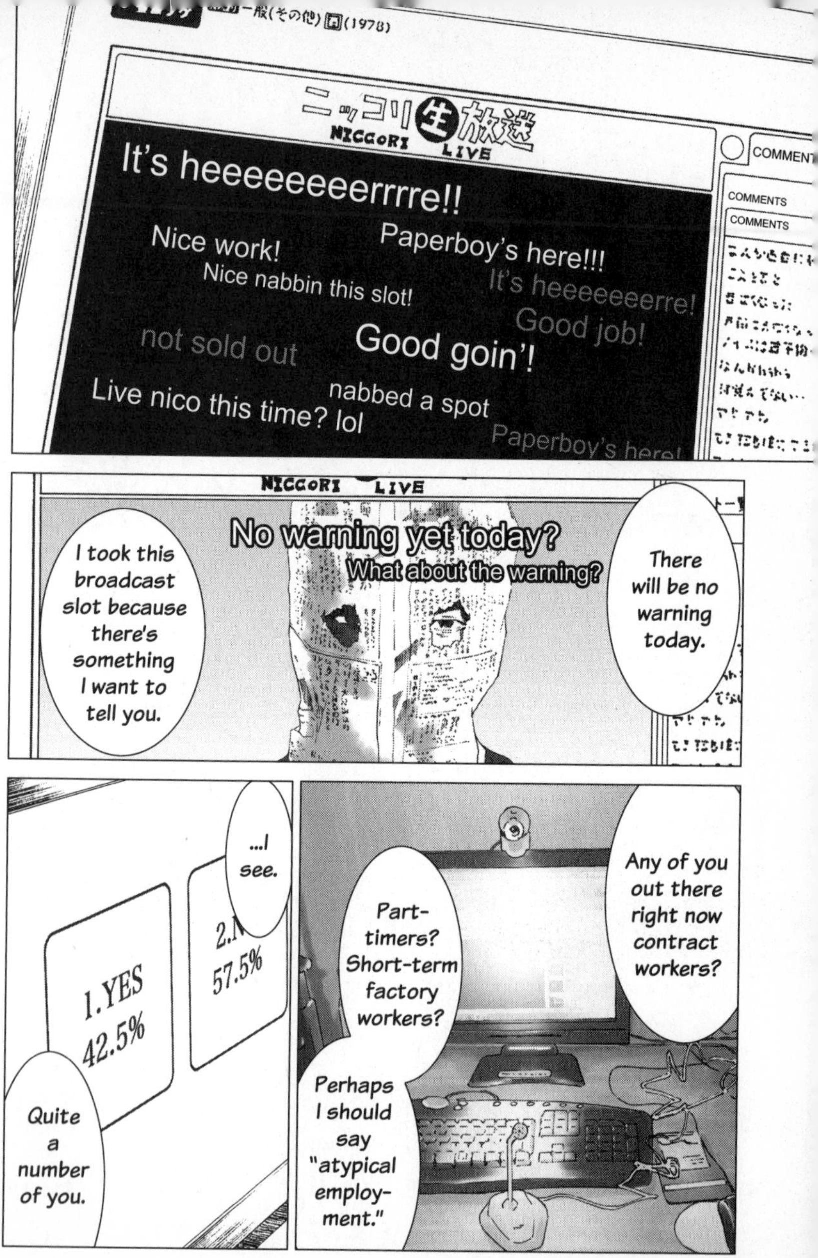
一般(その他) (1978)
ニッコリ生放送
NICCORI LIVE
COMMENT
COMMENTS
COMMENTS
It's heeeeeeeerrrre!!
Paperboy's here!!!
Nice work!
Nice nabbin this slot!
It's heeeeeeerre!
Good job!
Good goin'!
not sold out
nabbed a spot
Live nico this time? lol
Paperboy's here!
NICCORI LIVE
There will be no warning today.
No warning yet today?
What about the warning?
I took this broadcast slot because there's something I want to tell you.
Any of you out there right now contract workers?
Part-timers? Short-term factory workers?
Perhaps I should say "atypical employment."
...I see.
1. YES 42.5%
57.5%
Quite a number of you.

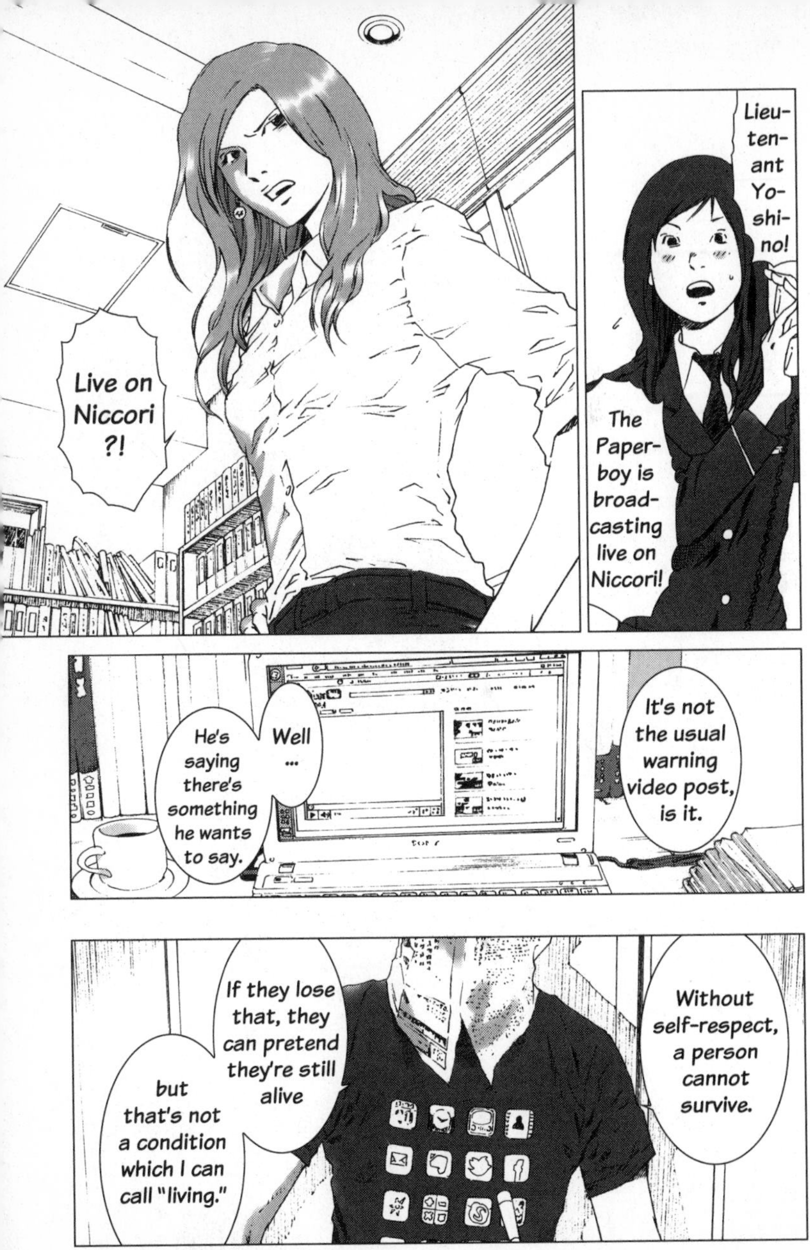
Lieutenant Yoshino!
The Paperboy is broadcasting live on Niccori!
Live on Niccori ?!
It's not the usual warning video post, is it.
Well ...
He's saying there's something he wants to say.
Without self-respect, a person cannot survive.
If they lose that, they can pretend they're still alive
but that's not a condition which I can call "living."

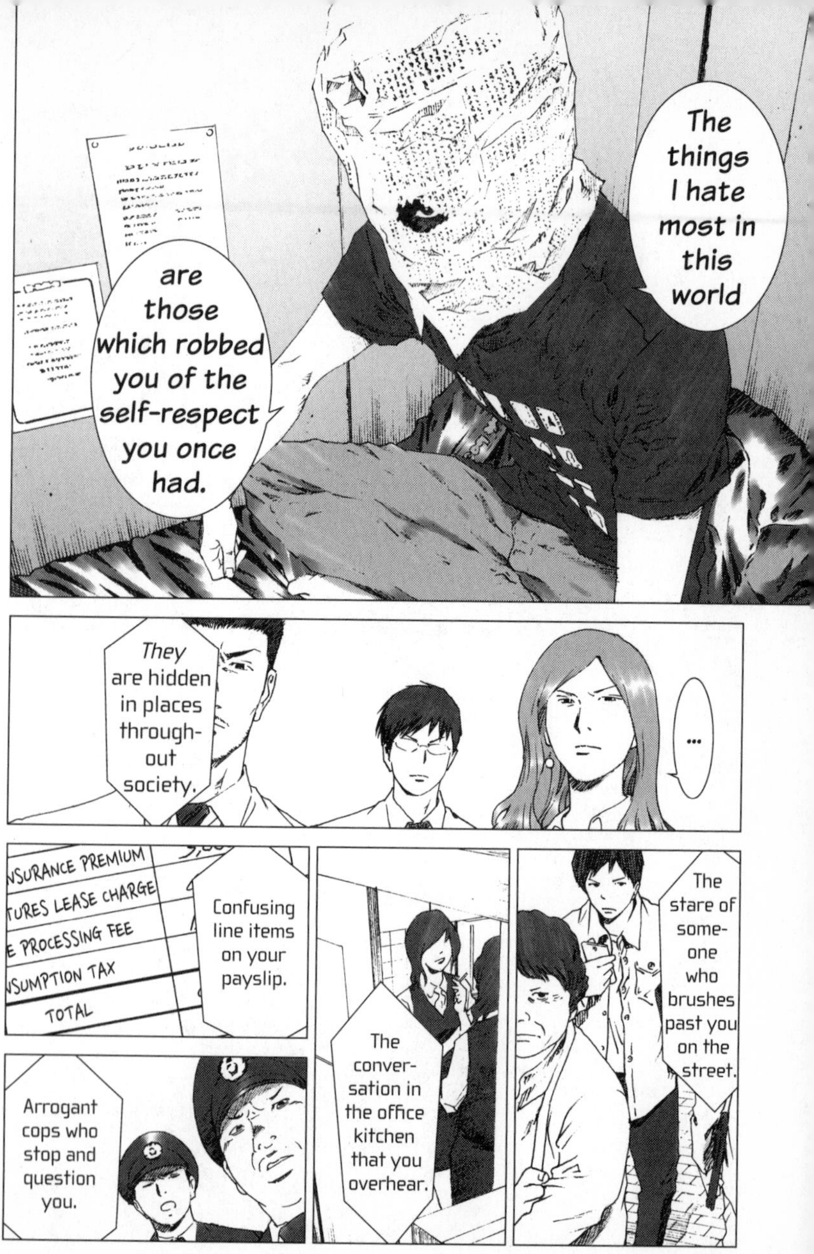
The things I hate most in this world
are those which robbed you of the self-respect you once had.
...
They are hidden in places through-out society.
The stare of some-one who brushes past you on the street.
The conver-sation in the office kitchen that you overhear.
NSURANCE PREMIUM
TURES LEASE CHARGE
E PROCESSING FEE
NSUMPTION TAX
TOTAL
Confusing line items on your payslip.
Arrogant cops who stop and question you.

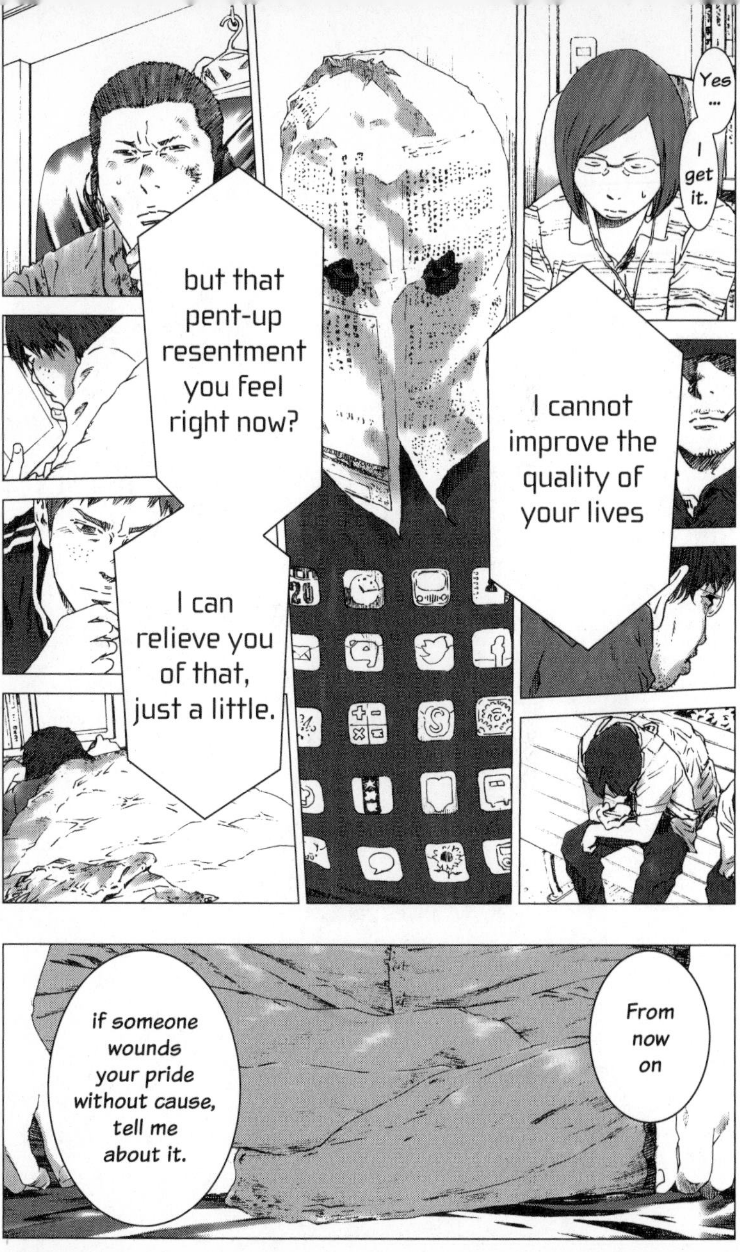
Yes... I get it.
I cannot improve the quality of your lives
but that pent-up resentment you feel right now?
I can relieve you of that, just a little.
From now on
if someone wounds your pride without cause, tell me about it.

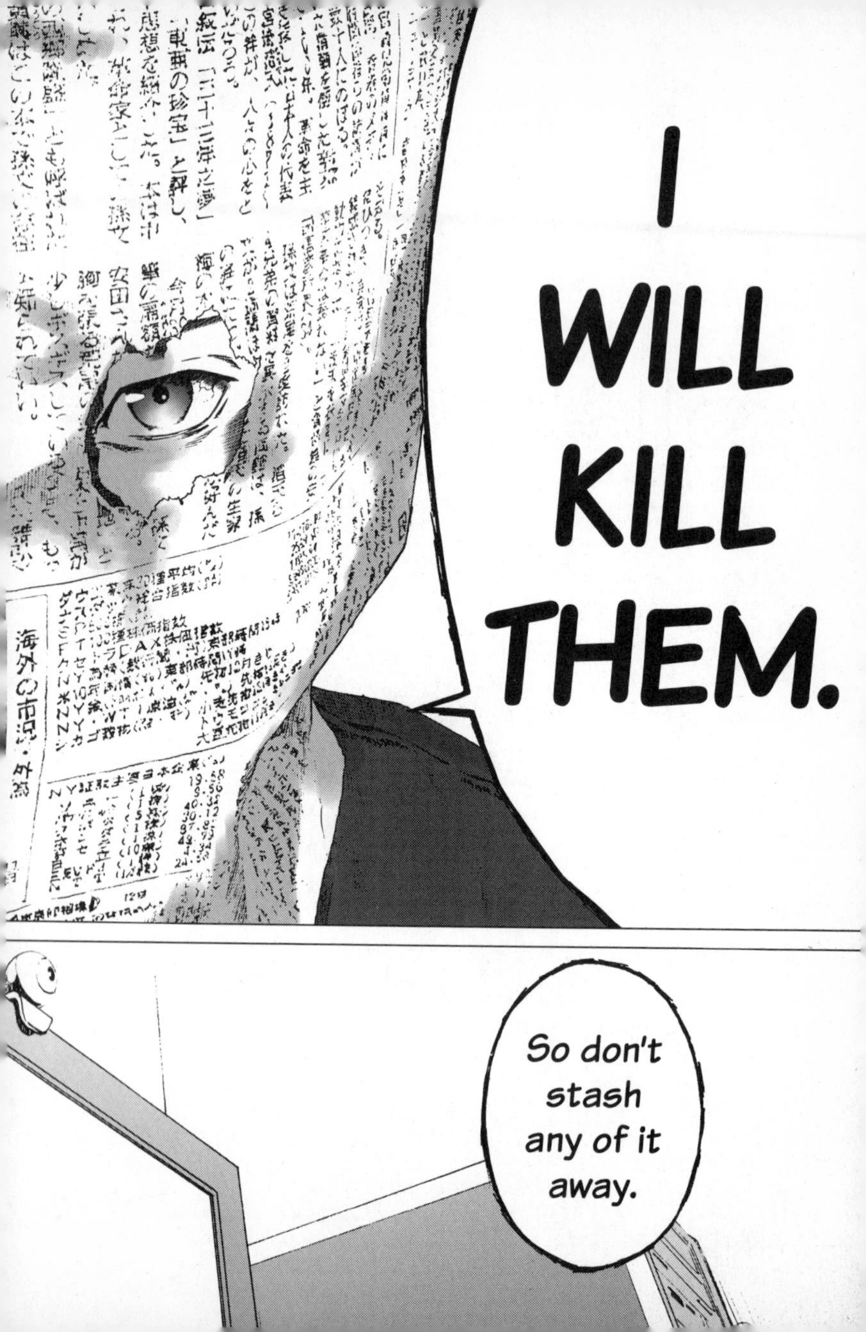
I WILL KILL THEM.
So don't stash any of it away.

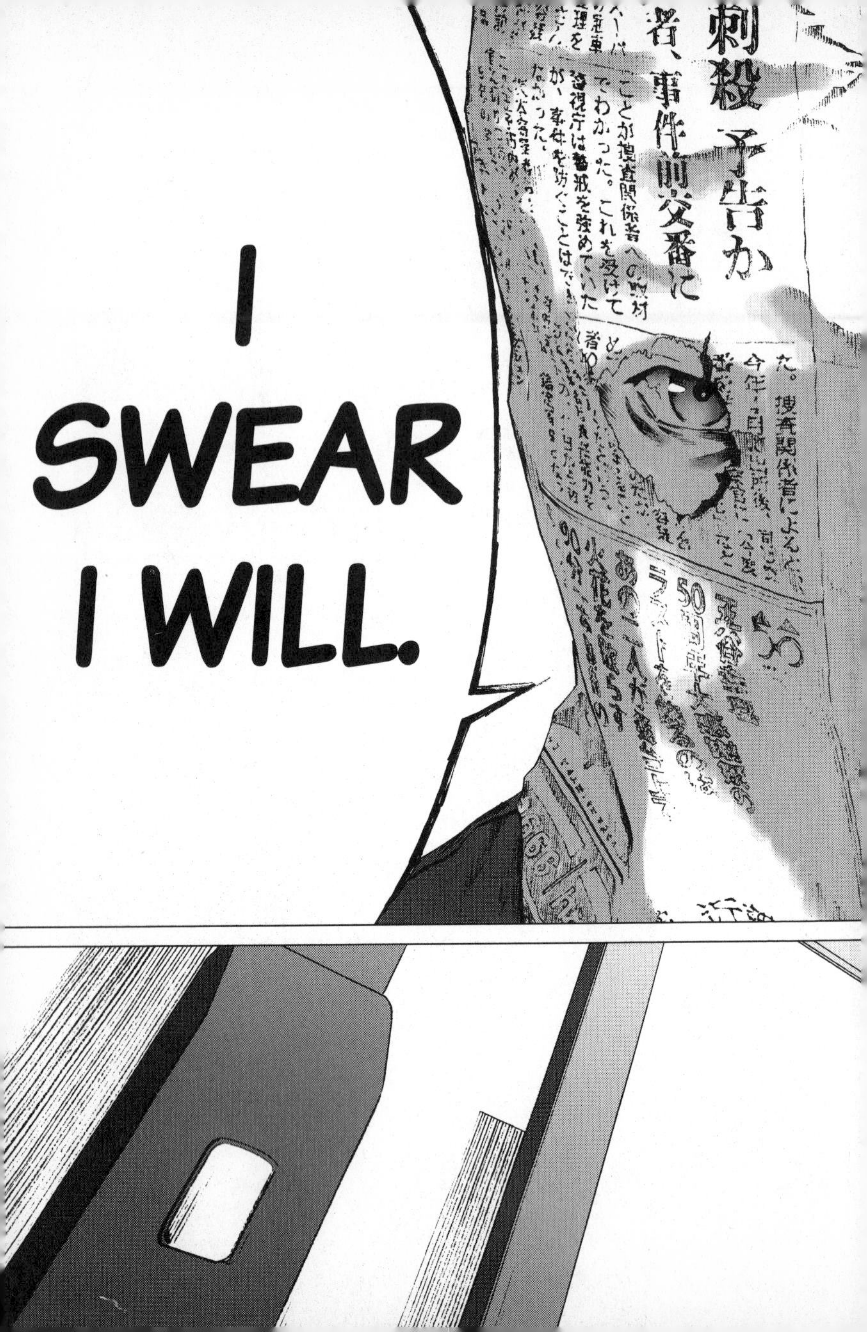
刺殺予告か
者、事件前交番に
I SWEAR I WILL.

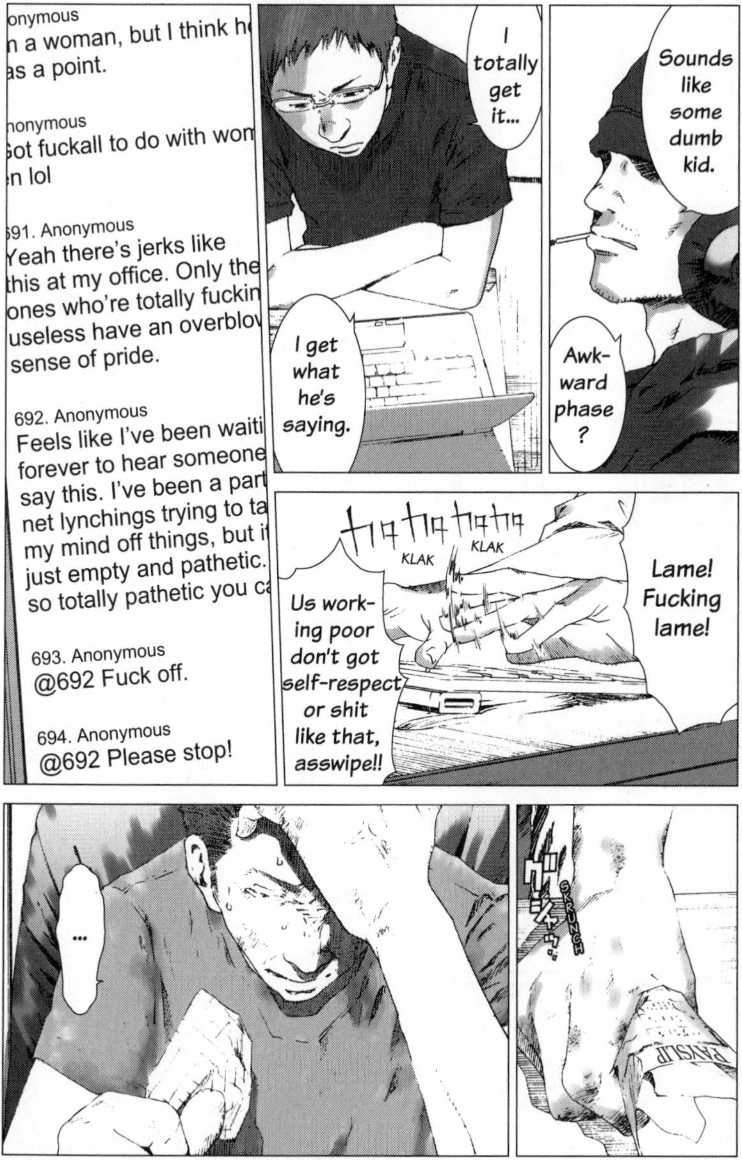
Sounds like some dumb kid.
Awk-ward phase?
I totally get it...
I get what he's saying.
KLAK
KLAK
Lame! Fucking lame!
Us work-ing poor don't got self-respect or shit like that, asswipe!!
onymous
n a woman, but I think h
as a point.
nonymous
Got fuckall to do with wom
n lol
691. Anonymous
Yeah there's jerks like
this at my office. Only the
ones who're totally fuckin
useless have an overblov
sense of pride.
692. Anonymous
Feels like I've been waiti
forever to hear someone
say this. I've been a part
net lynchings trying to ta
my mind off things, but it
just empty and pathetic.
so totally pathetic you c
693. Anonymous
@692 Fuck off.
694. Anonymous
@692 Please stop!
SKRUNCH
PAYSLIP
...

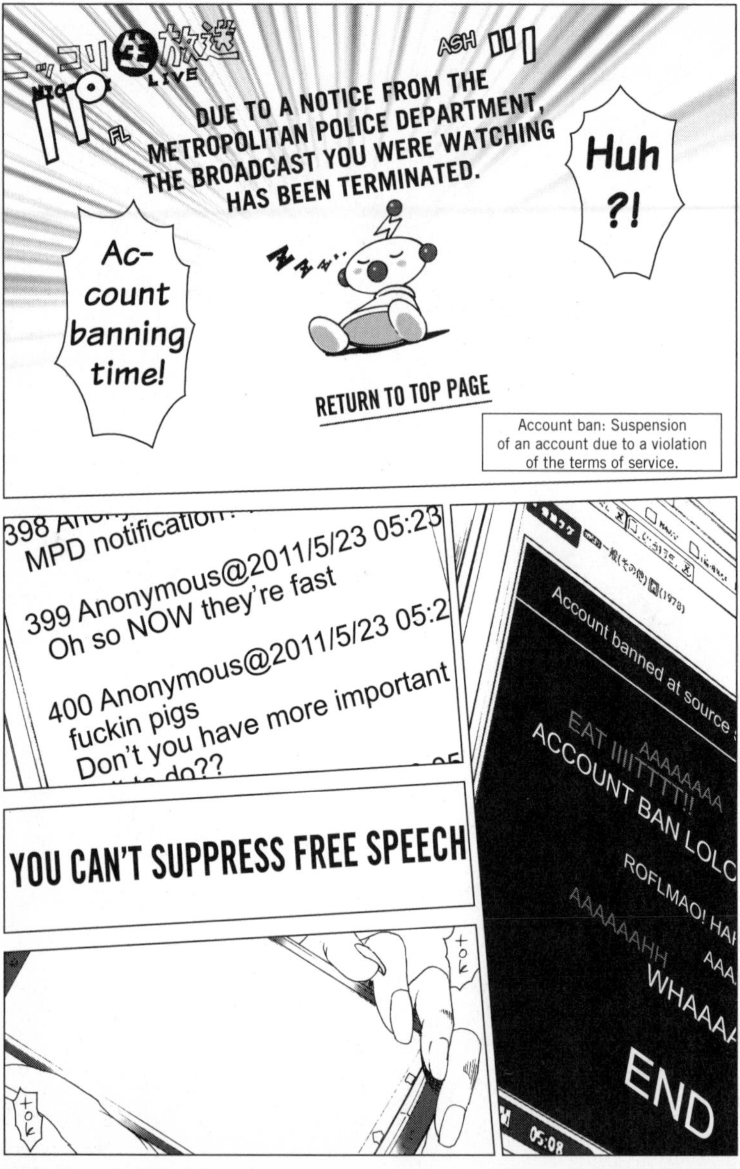
ASH
LIVE
DUE TO A NOTICE FROM THE METROPOLITAN POLICE DEPARTMENT, THE BROADCAST YOU WERE WATCHING HAS BEEN TERMINATED.
Huh ?!
Ac- count banning time!
RETURN TO TOP PAGE
Account ban: Suspension of an account due to a violation of the terms of service.
Account banned at source
AAAAAAAA
EAT IIIIITTTT!!
ACCOUNT BAN LOLC
ROFLMAO! HAH
AAAAAAAHH
AAA
WHAAAA
END
05:08
MPD notification
399 Anonymous@2011/5/23 05:23
Oh so NOW they're fast
400 Anonymous@2011/5/23 05:2
fuckin pigs
Don't you have more important
YOU CAN'T SUPPRESS FREE SPEECH
tok
tok

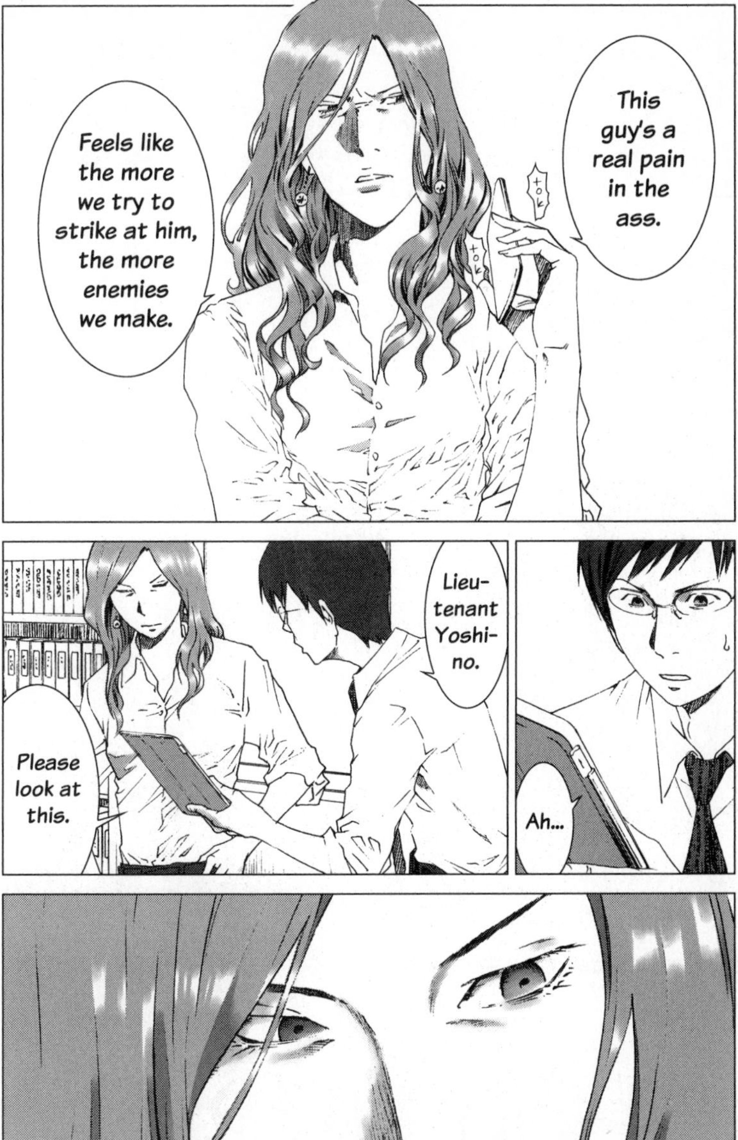
This guy's a real pain in the ass.
tok
tok
Feels like the more we try to strike at him, the more enemies we make.
Ah...
Lieu-tenant Yoshi-no.
Please look at this.

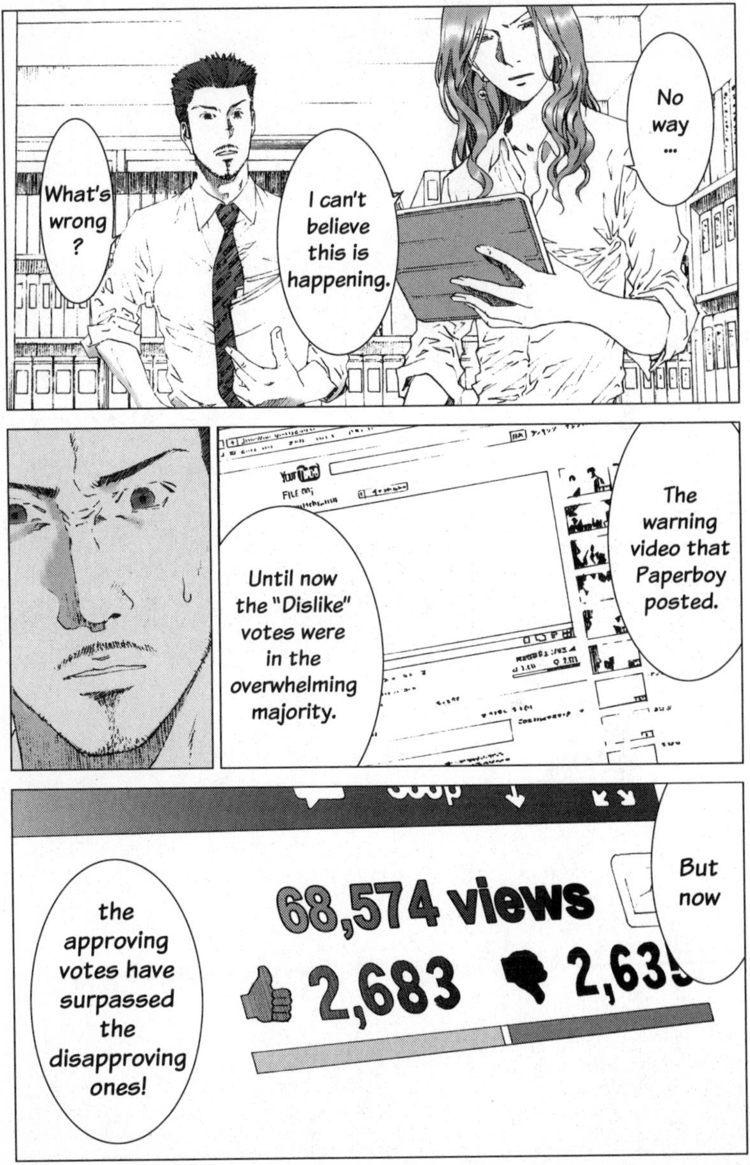
No way …
I can't believe this is happening.
What's wrong?
The warning video that Paperboy posted.
Until now the "Dislike" votes were in the overwhelming majority.
But now
68,574 views
2,683
the approving votes have surpassed the disapproving ones!

PROPHECY

File 005

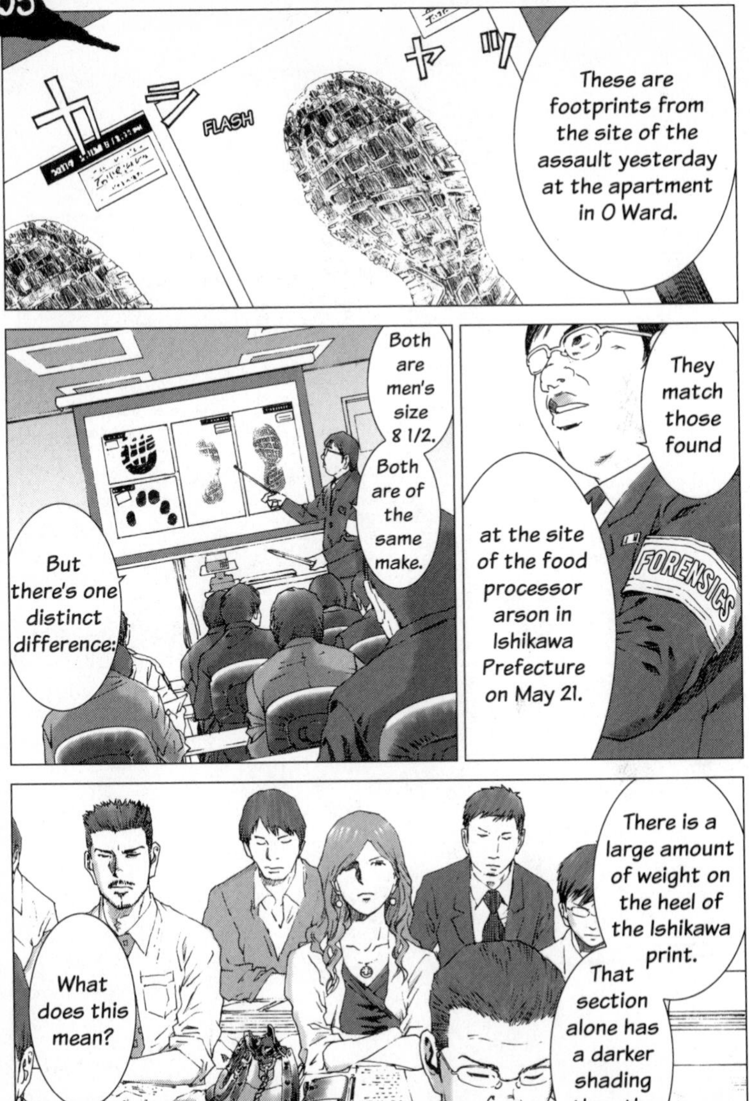
FLASH
These are footprints from the site of the assault yesterday at the apartment in O Ward.
They match those found
at the site of the food processor arson in Ishikawa Prefecture on May 21.
FORENSICS
Both are men's size 8 1/2.
Both are of the same make.
But there's one distinct difference:
There is a large amount of weight on the heel of the Ishikawa print.
That section alone has a darker shading than the rest.
What does this mean?

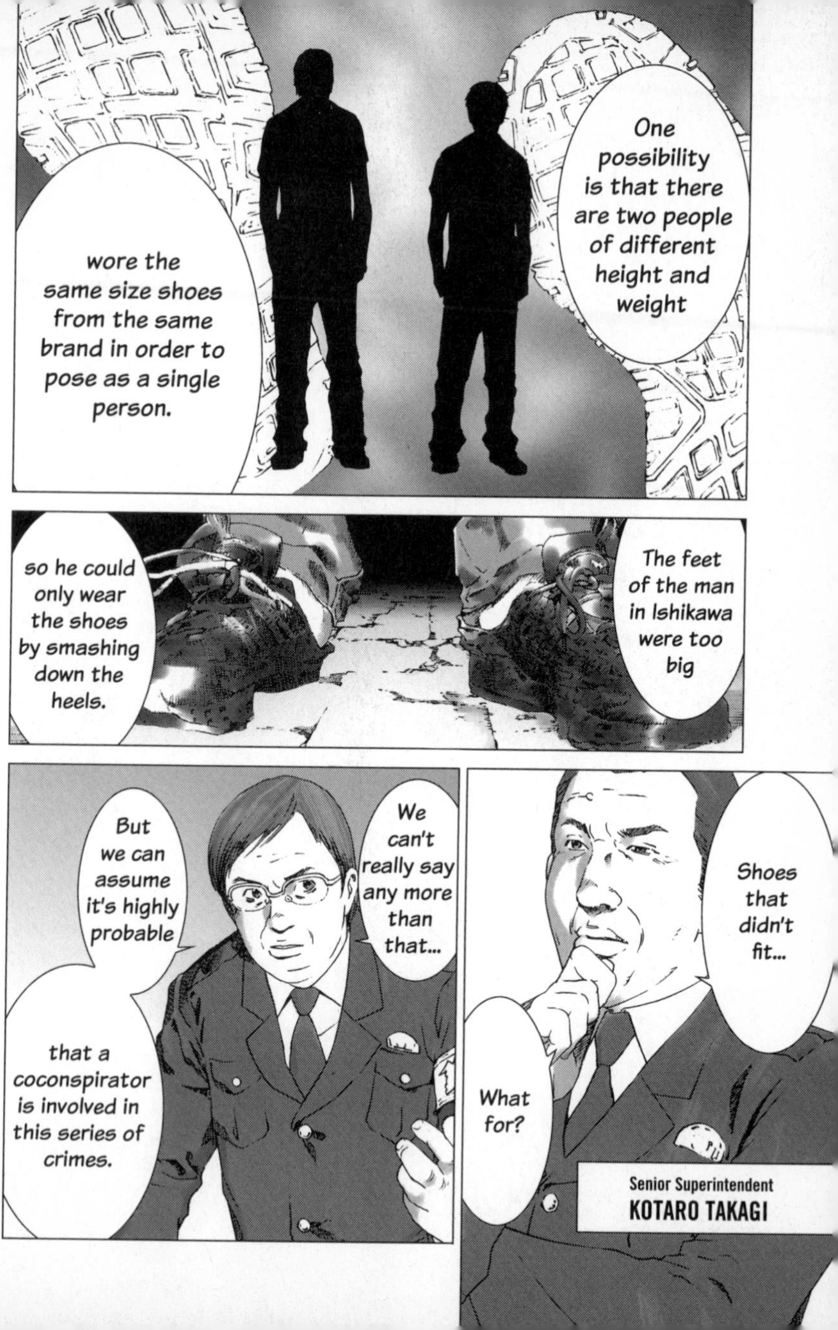
One possibility is that there are two people of different height and weight
wore the same size shoes from the same brand in order to pose as a single person.
The feet of the man in Ishikawa were too big
so he could only wear the shoes by smashing down the heels.
Shoes that didn't fit...
What for?
Senior Superintendent
KOTARO TAKAGI
We can't really say any more than that...
But we can assume it's highly probable
that a coconspirator is involved in this series of crimes.

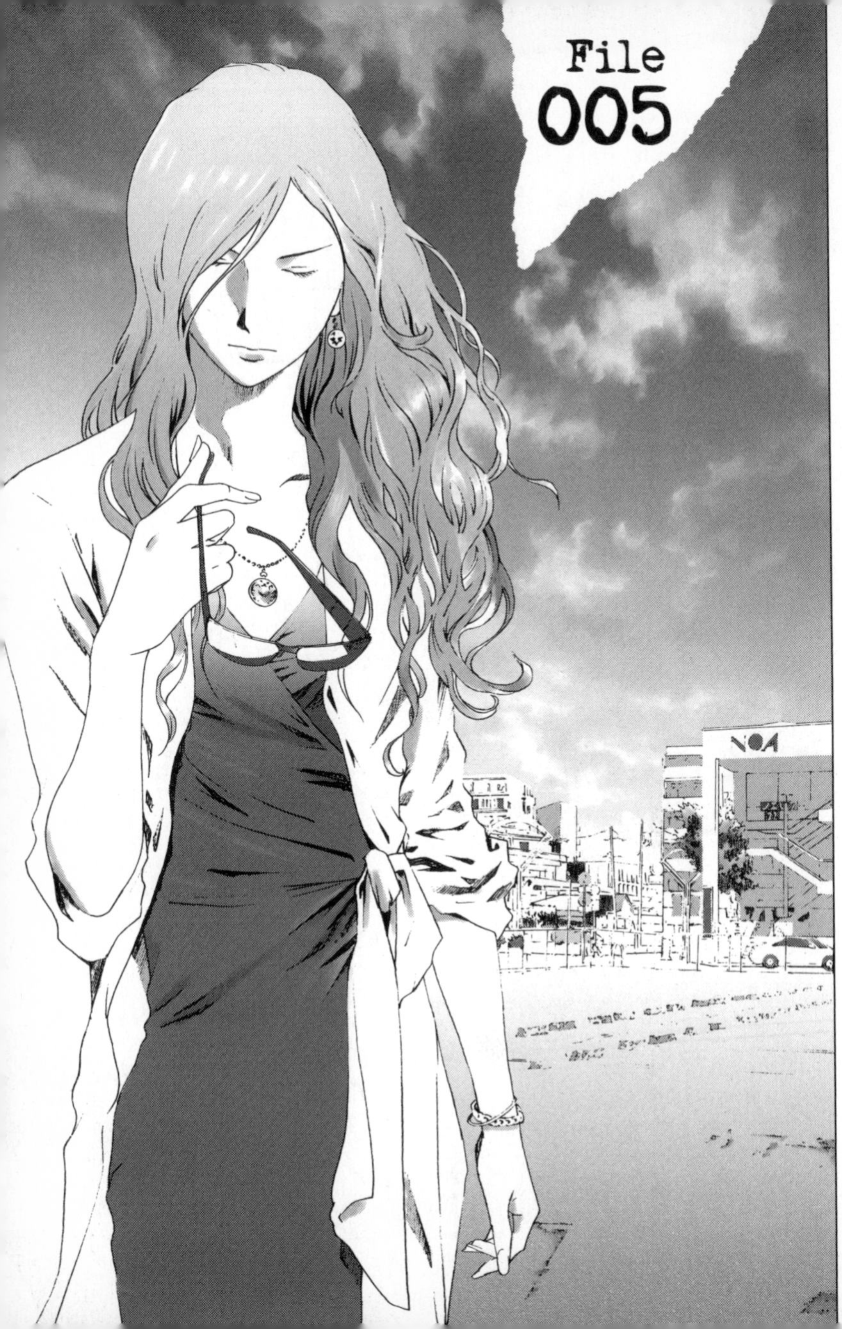
File
005
NOA

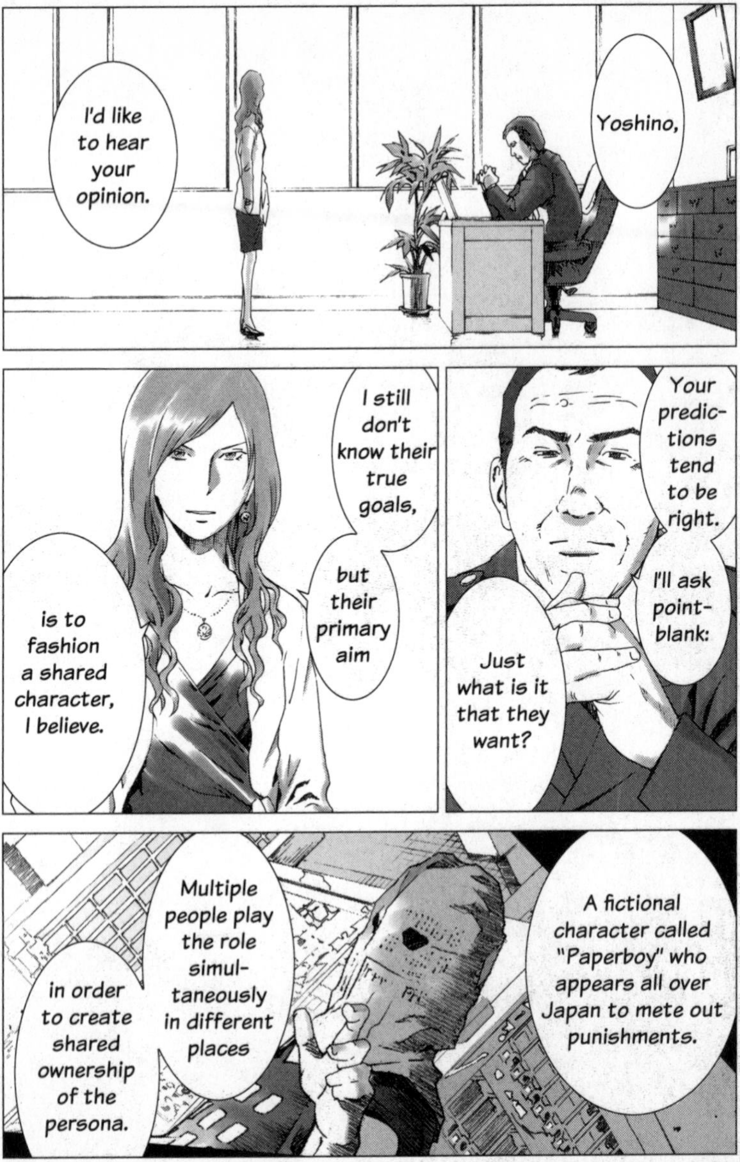
Yoshino,
I'd like to hear your opinion.
Your predic-tions tend to be right.
I'll ask point-blank:
Just what is it that they want?
I still don't know their true goals,
but their primary aim
is to fashion a shared character, I believe.
A fictional character called "Paperboy" who appears all over Japan to mete out punishments.
Multiple people play the role simul-taneously in different places
in order to create shared ownership of the persona.

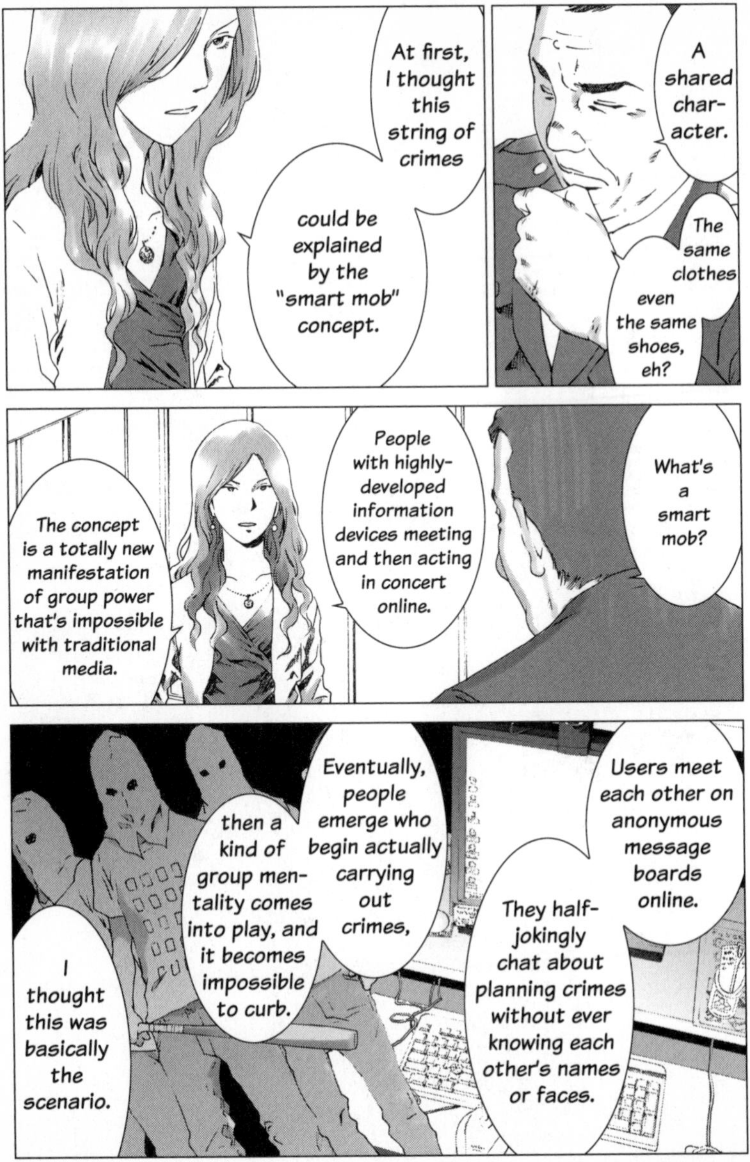
A shared character.
The same clothes
even the same shoes, eh?
At first, I thought this string of crimes
could be explained by the "smart mob" concept.
What's a smart mob?
People with highly-developed information devices meeting and then acting in concert online.
The concept is a totally new manifestation of group power that's impossible with traditional media.
Users meet each other on anonymous message boards online.
They half-jokingly chat about planning crimes without ever knowing each other's names or faces.
Eventually, people emerge who begin actually carrying out crimes,
then a kind of group mentality comes into play, and it becomes impossible to curb.
I thought this was basically the scenario.

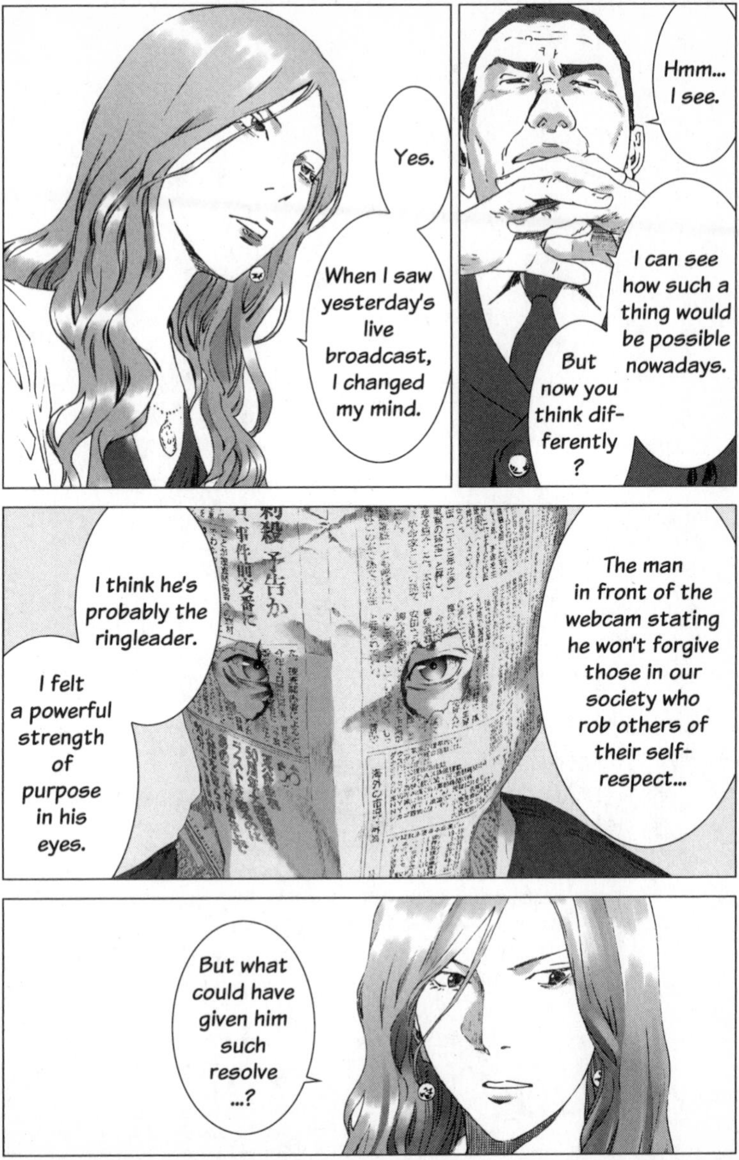
Hmm... I see.
I can see how such a thing would be possible nowadays.
But now you think differently?
Yes.
When I saw yesterday's live broadcast, I changed my mind.
The man in front of the webcam stating he won't forgive those in our society who rob others of their self-respect...
I think he's probably the ringleader.
I felt a powerful strength of purpose in his eyes.
But what could have given him such resolve ...?

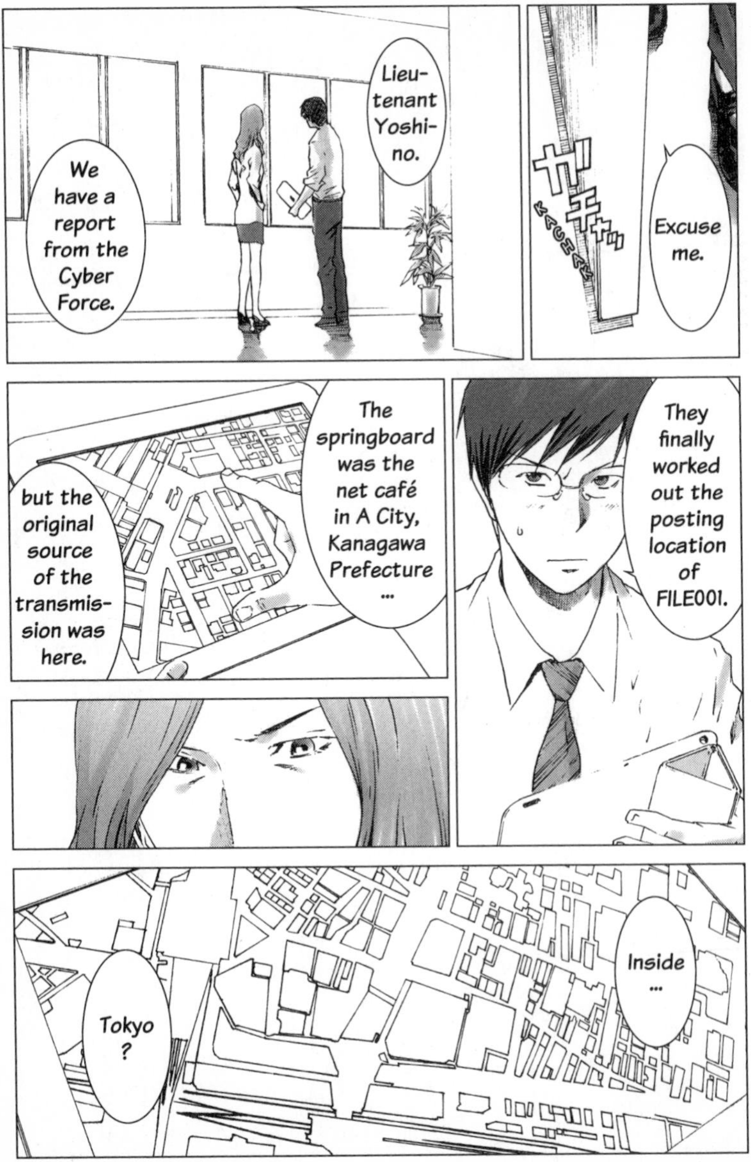
KACHAK
Excuse me.
Lieutenant Yoshino.
We have a report from the Cyber Force.
They finally worked out the posting location of FILE001.
The springboard was the net café in A City, Kanagawa Prefecture ...
but the original source of the transmission was here.
Inside ...
Tokyo ?

May 23, 14:00
M TOWN, TOKYO

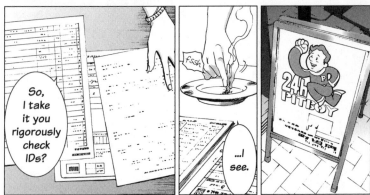

So, I take it you rigorously check IDs?

...I see.

I applied by the law!

Yes, of course!

"Abide," you mean.

KAPOP

138

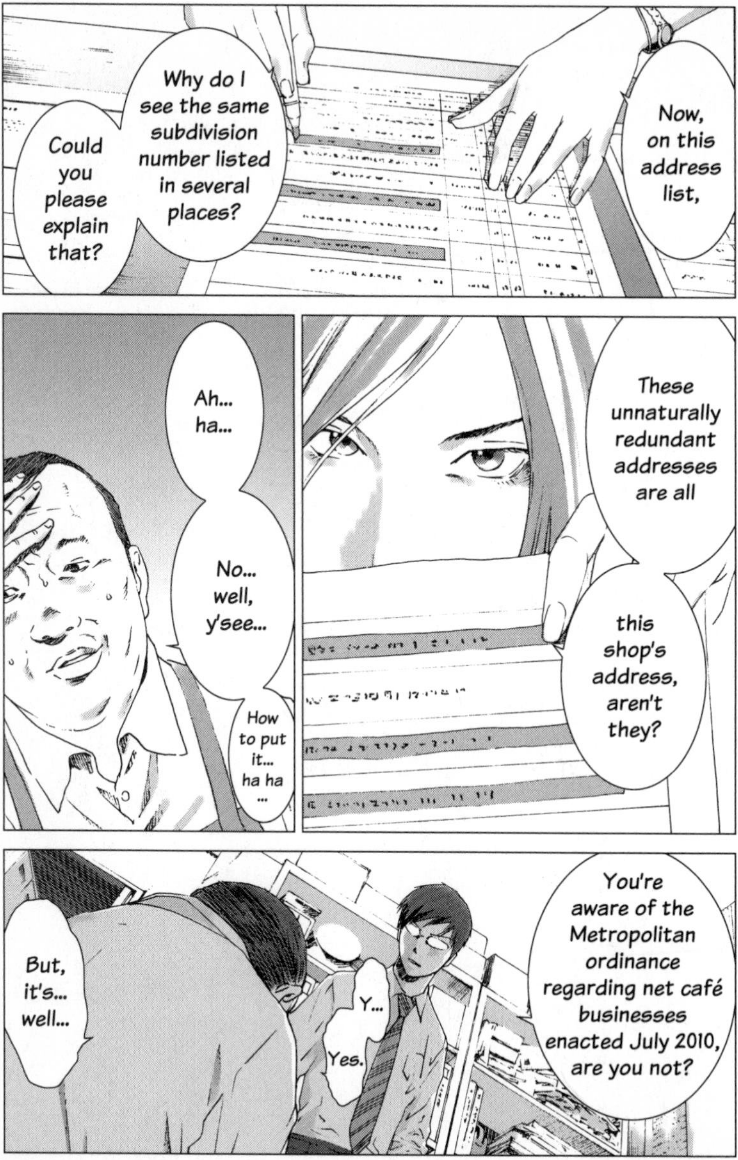
Now, on this address list,
Why do I see the same subdivision number listed in several places?
Could you please explain that?
These unnaturally redundant addresses are all
this shop's address, aren't they?
Ah... ha...
No... well, y'see...
How to put it... ha ha ...
You're aware of the Metropolitan ordinance regarding net café businesses enacted July 2010, are you not?
Y...
Yes.
But, it's... well...

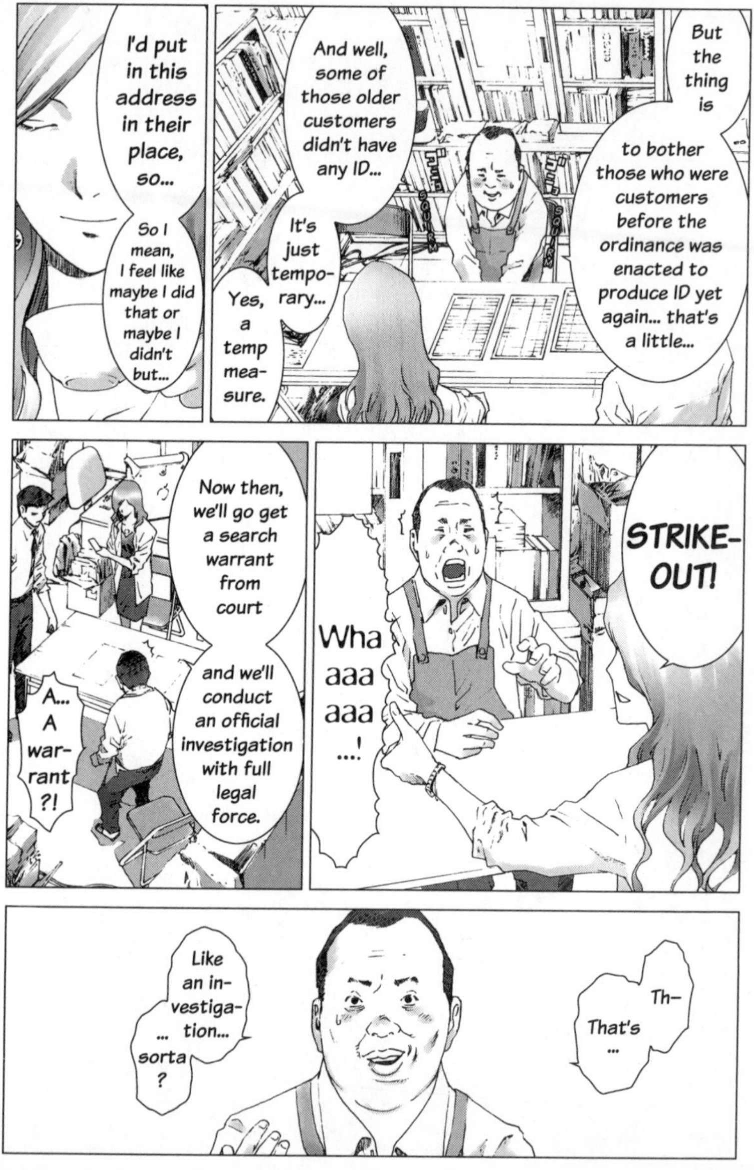
But the thing is
to bother those who were customers before the ordinance was enacted to produce ID yet again... that's a little...
And well, some of those older customers didn't have any ID...
It's just temporary...
Yes, a temp measure.
I'd put in this address in their place, so...
So I mean, I feel like maybe I did that or maybe I didn't but...
STRIKE-OUT!
Whaaaaaaa...!
Now then, we'll go get a search warrant from court
and we'll conduct an official investigation with full legal force.
A... A warrant?!
Th- That's ...
Like an investigation... ...sorta?

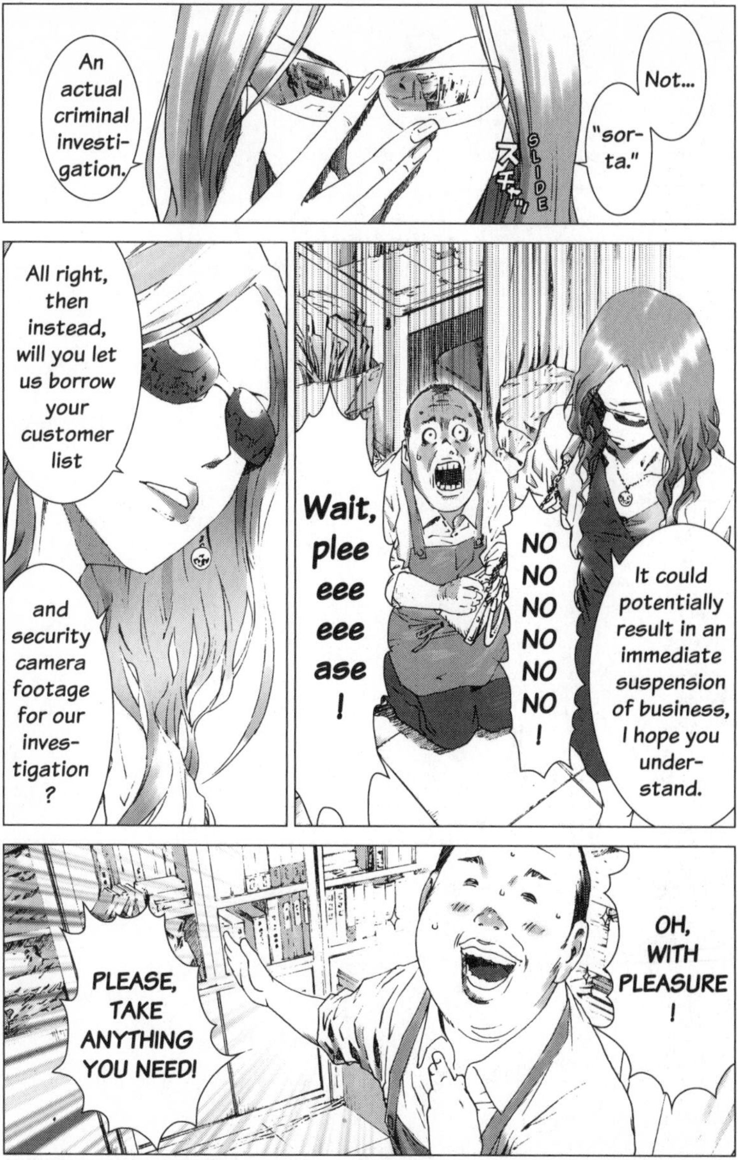
Not... "sorta."
SLIDE
An actual criminal investigation.
It could potentially result in an immediate suspension of business, I hope you understand.
NO NO NO NO NO NO!
Wait, pleeeeeeeease!
All right, then instead, will you let us borrow your customer list
and security camera footage for our investigation?
OH, WITH PLEASURE!
PLEASE, TAKE ANYTHING YOU NEED!

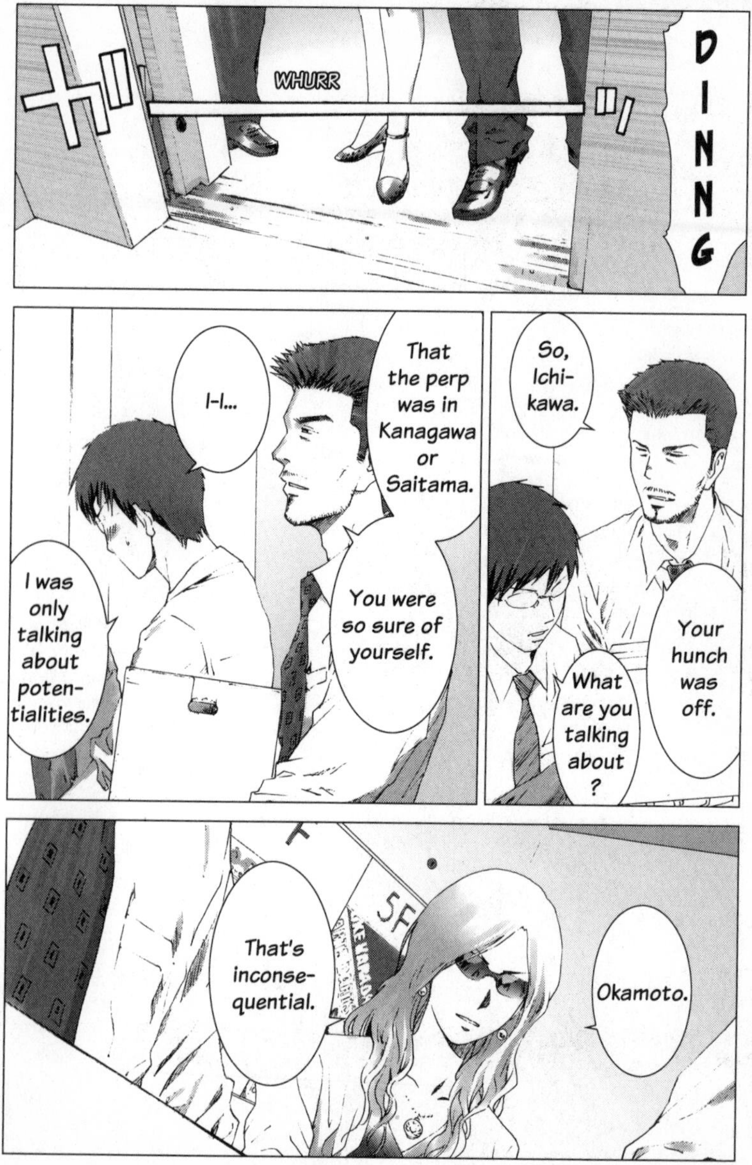
DINNG
WHURR
So, Ichi-kawa.
Your hunch was off.
What are you talking about?
That the perp was in Kanagawa or Saitama.
I-I...
You were so sure of yourself.
I was only talking about poten-tialities.
Okamoto.
5F
That's inconse-quential.

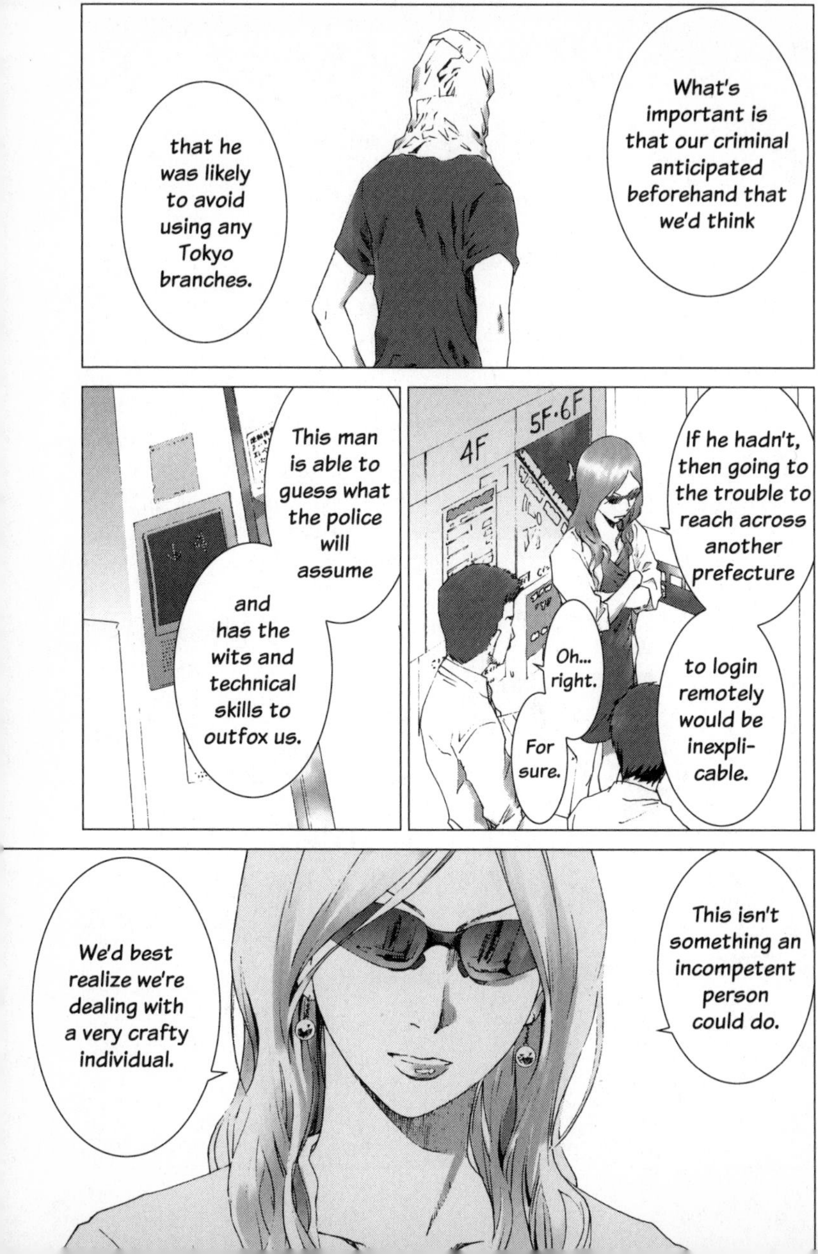
What's important is that our criminal anticipated beforehand that we'd think
that he was likely to avoid using any Tokyo branches.
If he hadn't, then going to the trouble to reach across another prefecture
to login remotely would be inexplicable.
Oh... right.
For sure.
This man is able to guess what the police will assume
and has the wits and technical skills to outfox us.
This isn't something an incompetent person could do.
We'd best realize we're dealing with a very crafty individual.

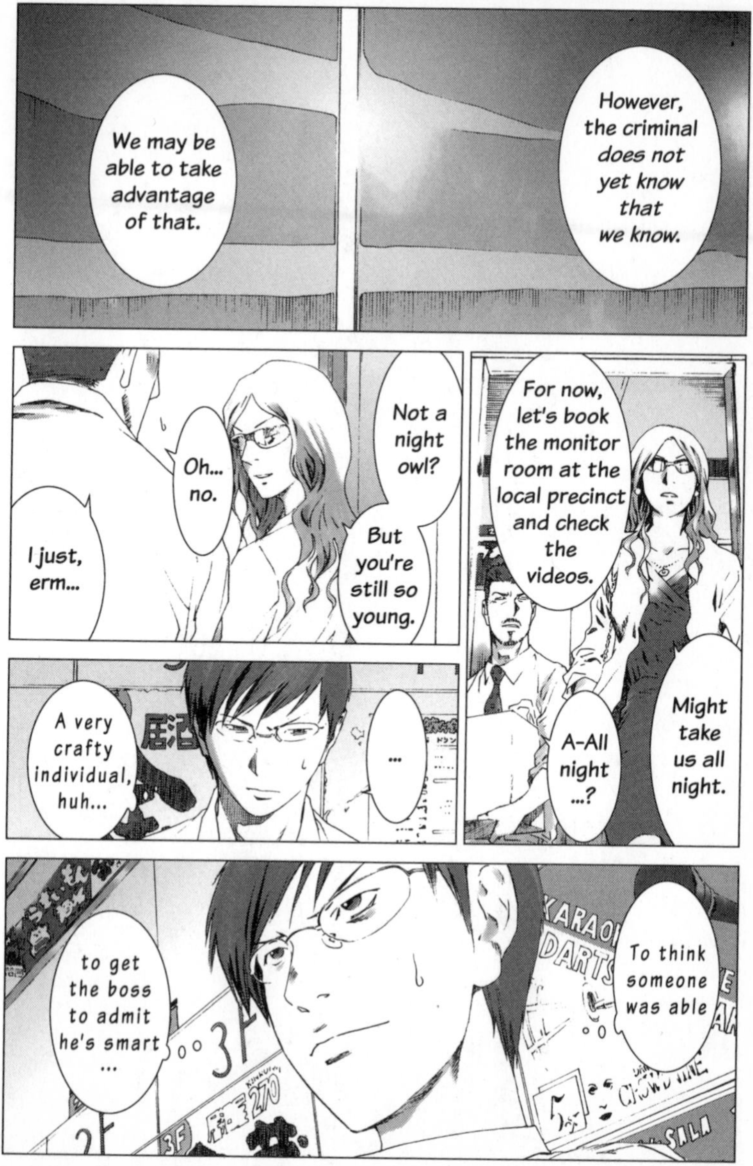
However, the criminal does not yet know that we know.
We may be able to take advantage of that.
For now, let's book the monitor room at the local precinct and check the videos.
Might take us all night.
A-All night ...?
Not a night owl?
But you're still so young.
Oh... no.
I just, erm...
...
A very crafty individual, huh...
To think someone was able
to get the boss to admit he's smart ...

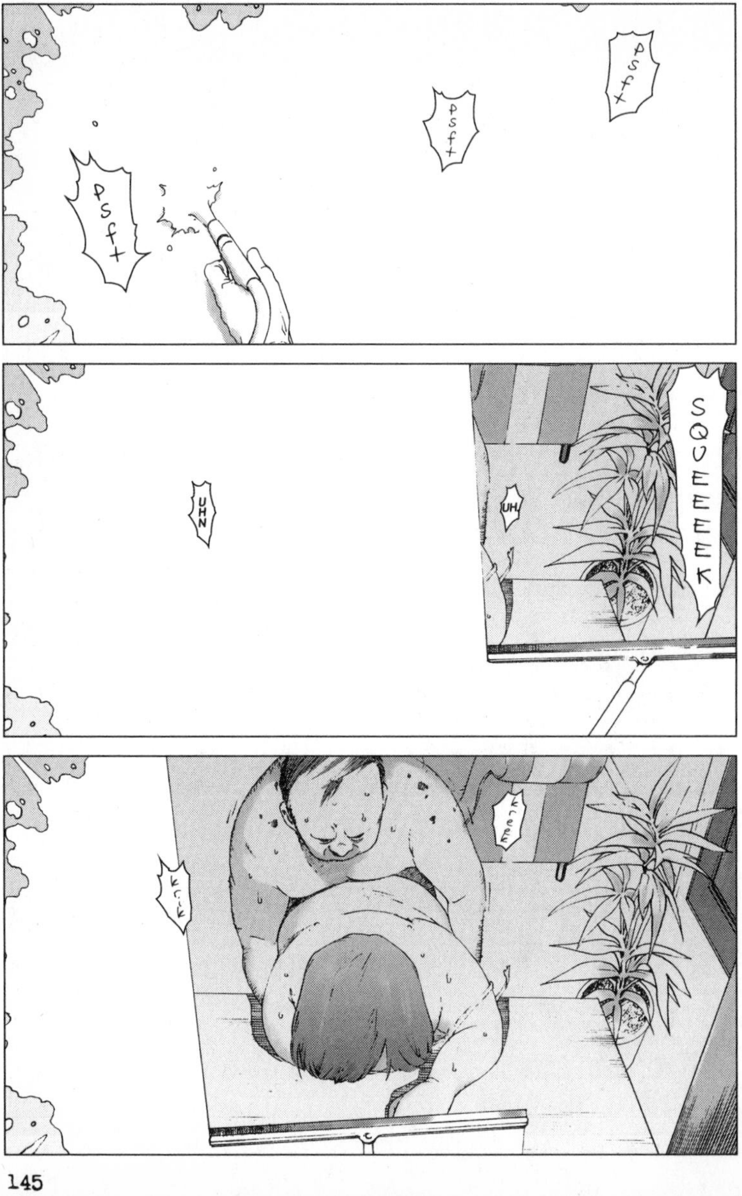
psfft
psfft
psfft
SQUEEEEK
UH,
UHN
kreek
krik

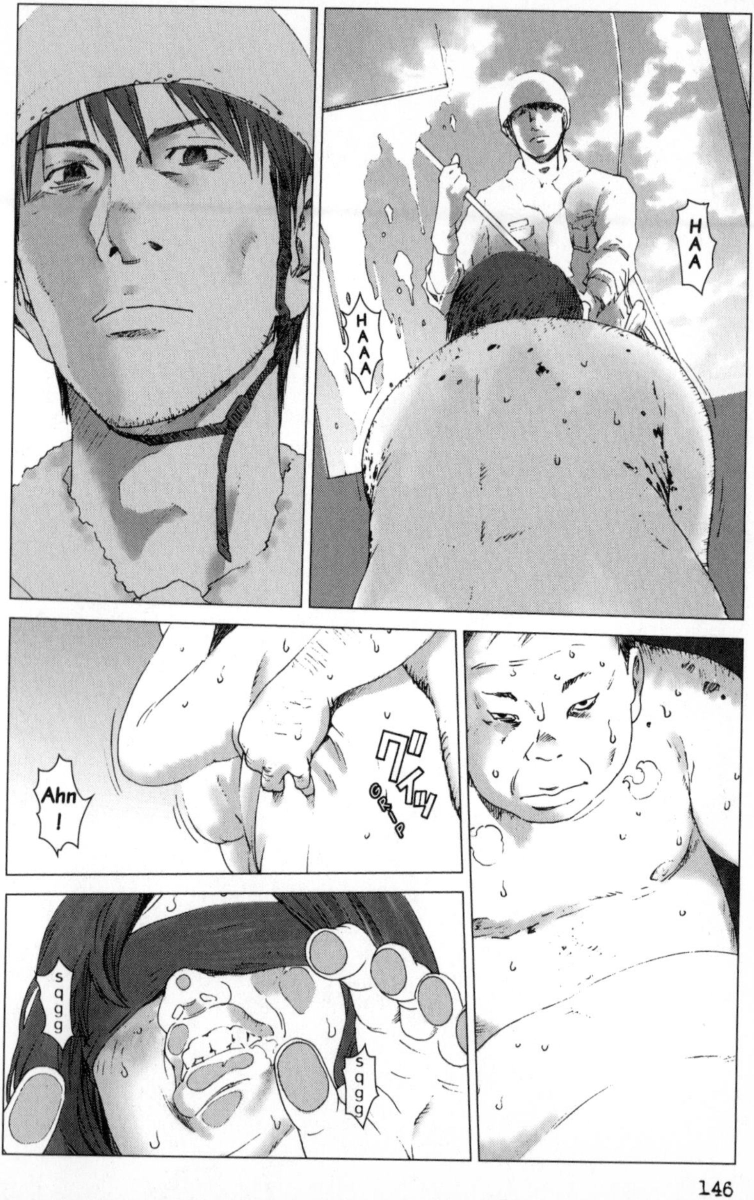
HAAA
HAAA
グイッ
GR-P
Ahn!
sqgg
sqgg

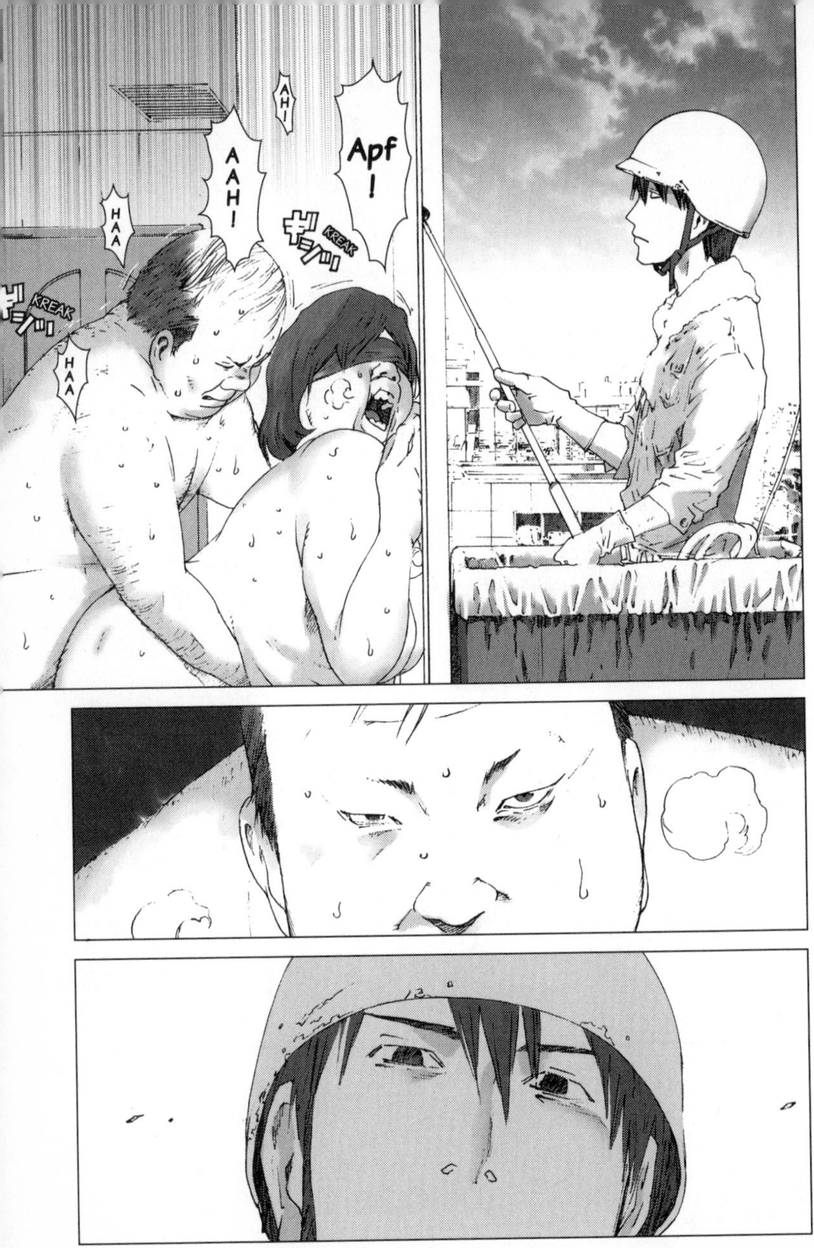

Apf !
AH!
ギシッ
KREAK
AAH!
HAA
ギシッ
KREAK
HAA

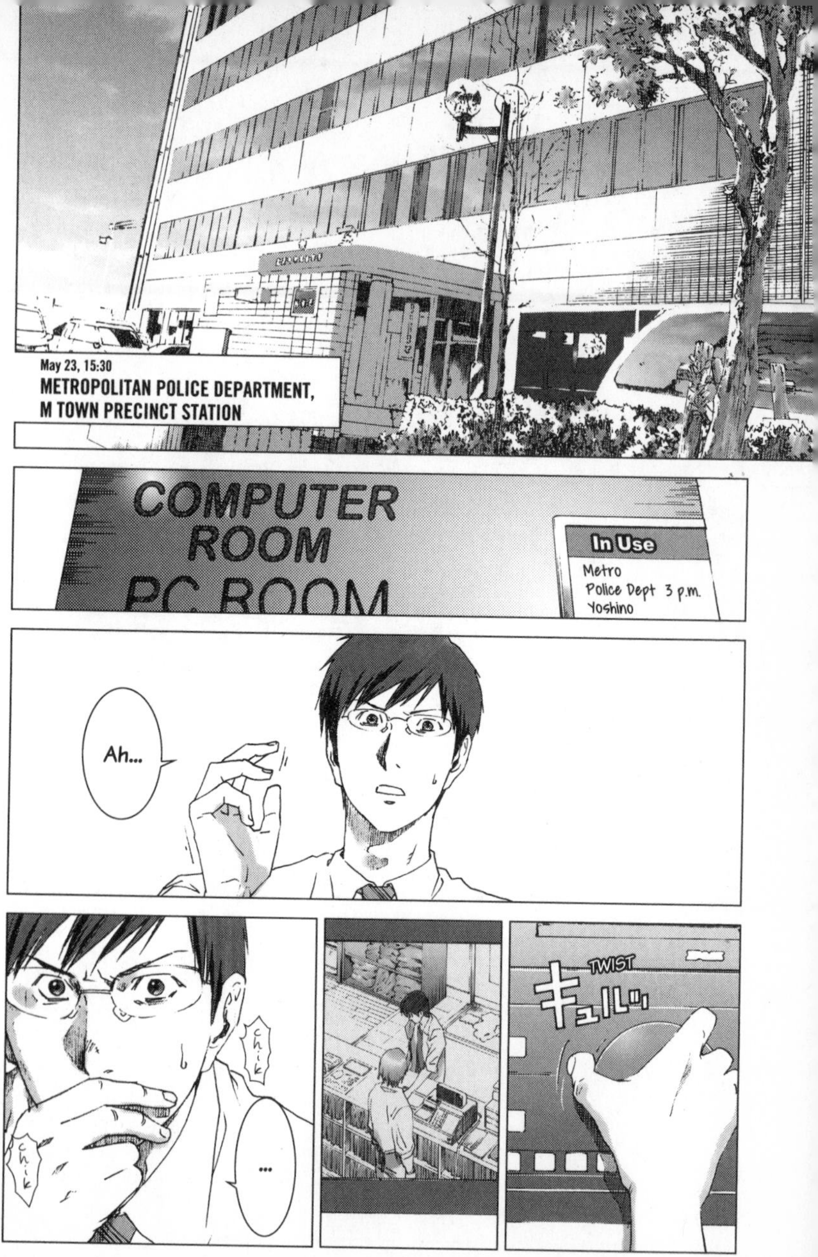
May 23, 15:30
METROPOLITAN POLICE DEPARTMENT, M TOWN PRECINCT STATION
COMPUTER ROOM
PC ROOM
In Use
Metro Police Dept 3 p.m. Yoshino
Ah...
TWIST
chik
...
chik

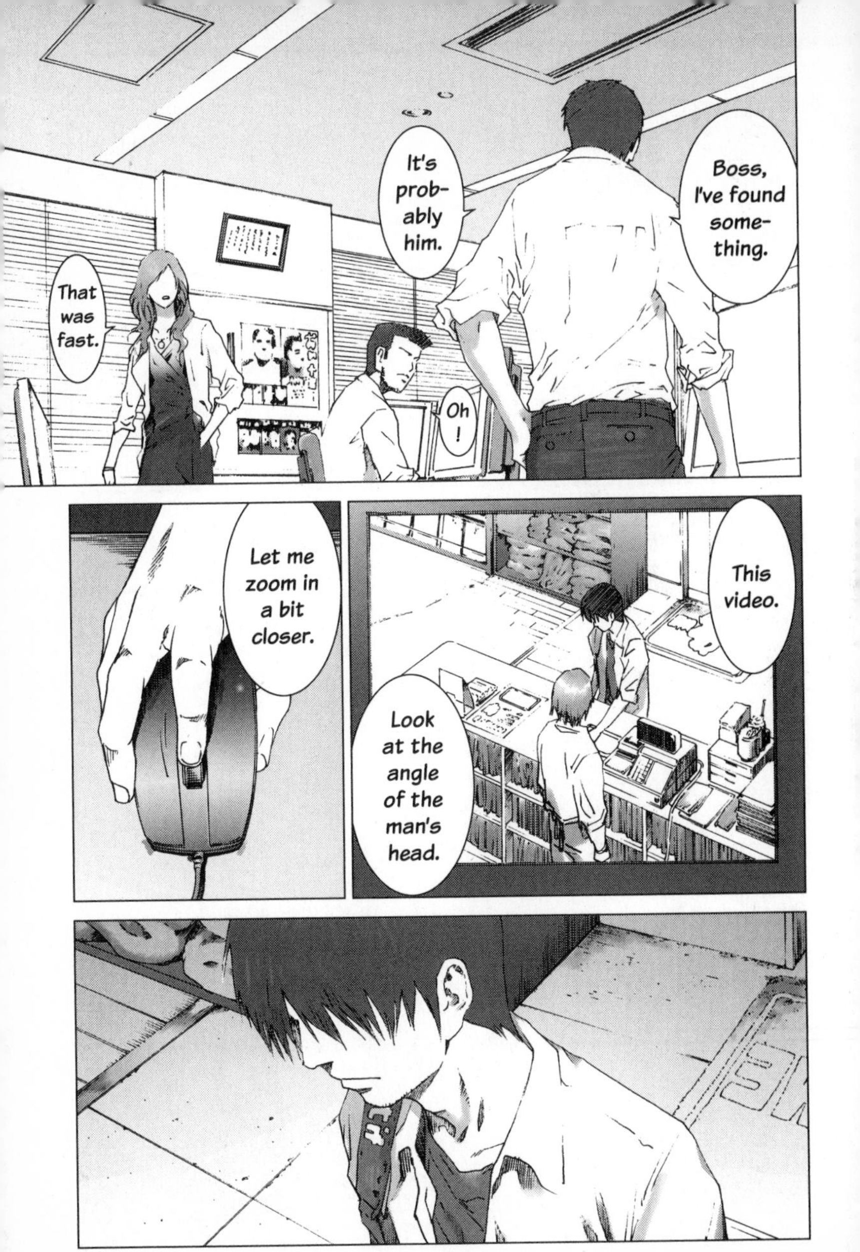
Boss, I've found some-thing.
It's prob-ably him.
Oh!
That was fast.
This video.
Look at the angle of the man's head.
Let me zoom in a bit closer.

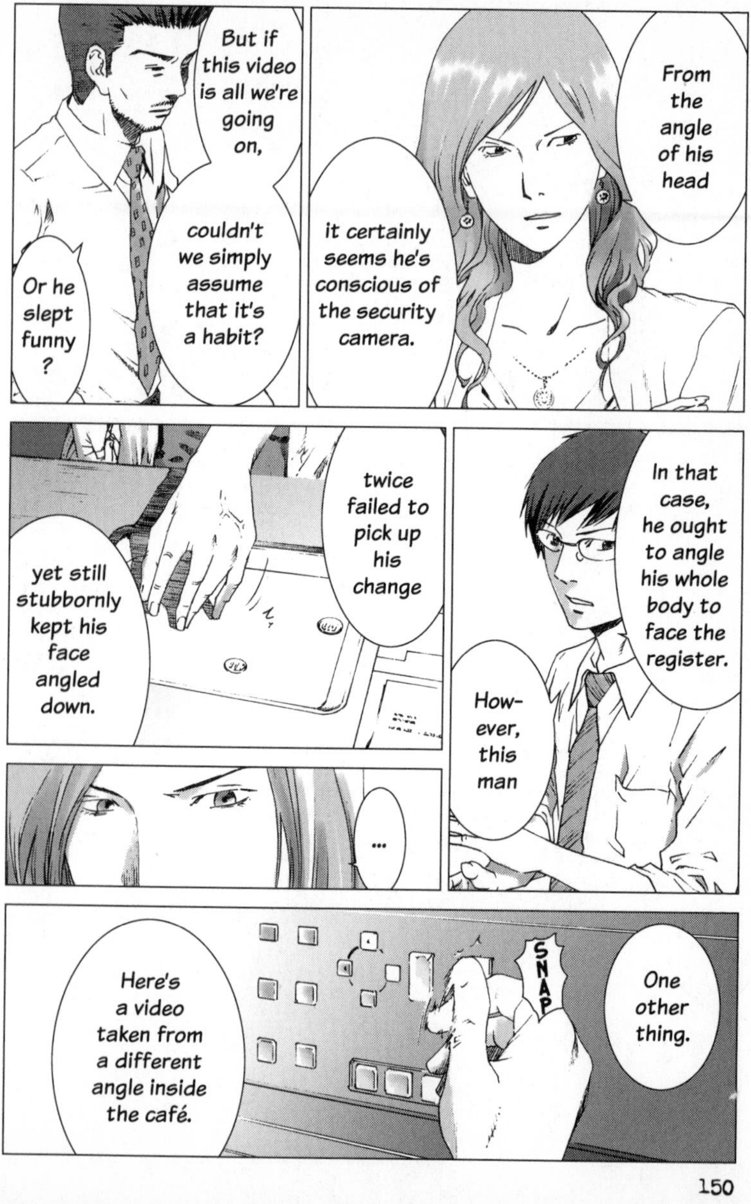
From the angle of his head
it certainly seems he's conscious of the security camera.
But if this video is all we're going on,
couldn't we simply assume that it's a habit?
Or he slept funny?
In that case, he ought to angle his whole body to face the register.
However, this man
twice failed to pick up his change
yet still stubbornly kept his face angled down.
...
One other thing.
SNAP
Here's a video taken from a different angle inside the café.

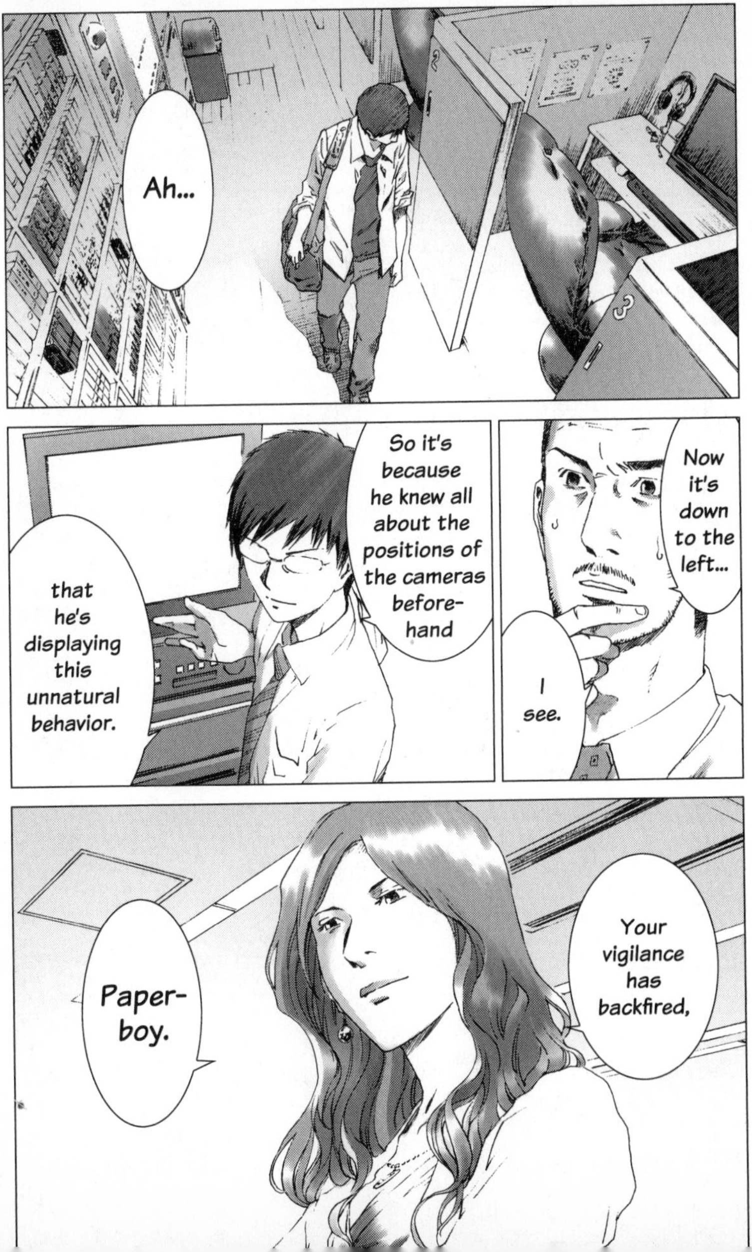
Ah...
Now it's down to the left...
I see.
So it's because he knew all about the positions of the cameras beforehand
that he's displaying this unnatural behavior.
Your vigilance has backfired,
Paper-boy.

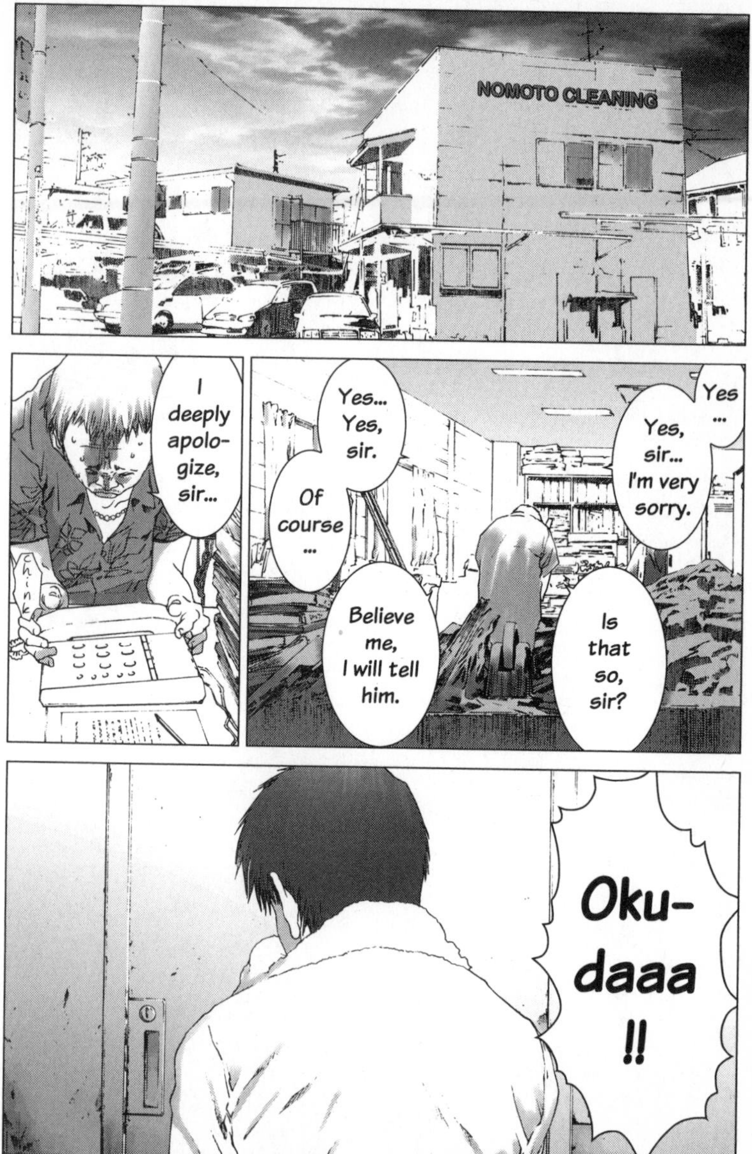
NOMOTO CLEANING
Yes ...
Yes, sir... I'm very sorry.
Yes... Yes, sir.
Of course ...
Is that so, sir?
Believe me, I will tell him.
I deeply apologize, sir...
chink
Oku-daaaa!!

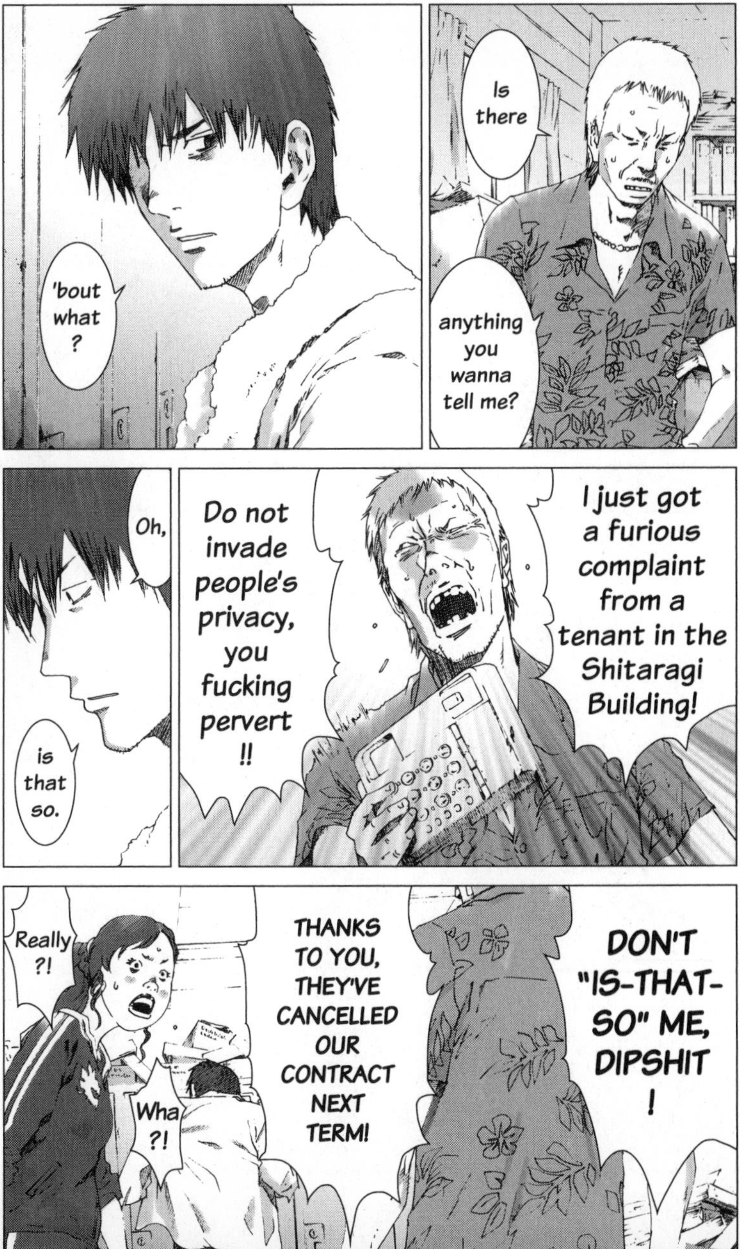
Is there
anything you wanna tell me?
'bout what?
I just got a furious complaint from a tenant in the Shitaragi Building!
Do not invade people's privacy, you fucking pervert!!
Oh,
is that so.
DON'T "IS-THAT-SO" ME, DIPSHIT!
THANKS TO YOU, THEY'VE CANCELLED OUR CONTRACT NEXT TERM!
Really?!
Wha?!

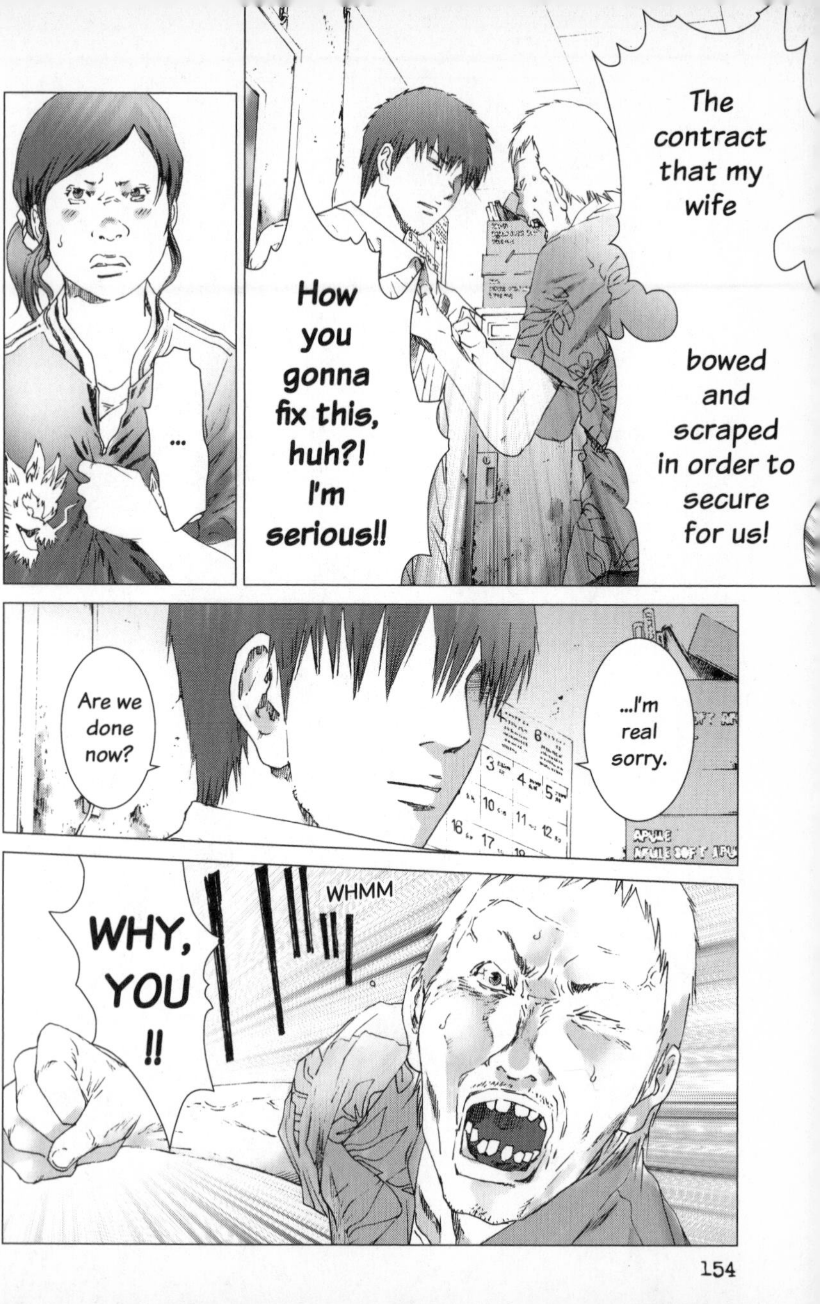
The contract that my wife
bowed and scraped in order to secure for us!
How you gonna fix this, huh?! I'm serious!!
...
...I'm real sorry.
Are we done now?
WHMM
WHY, YOU !!

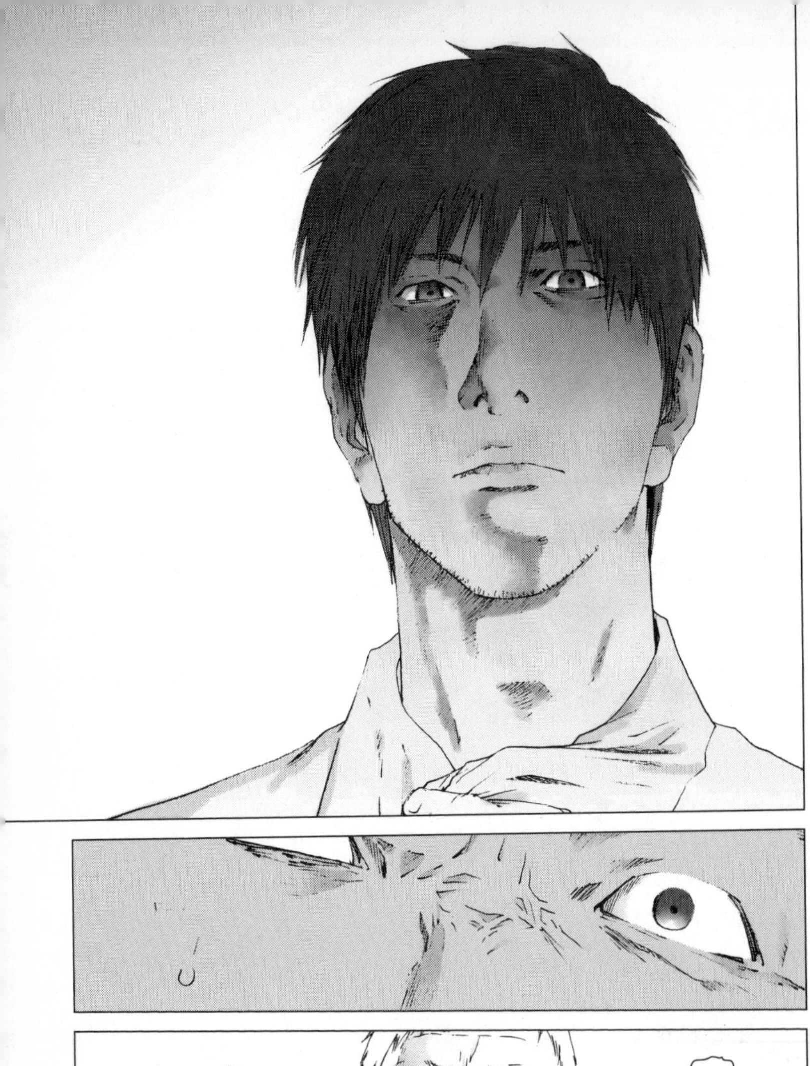
...You.
No, it can't be...

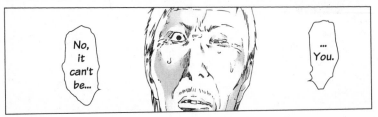

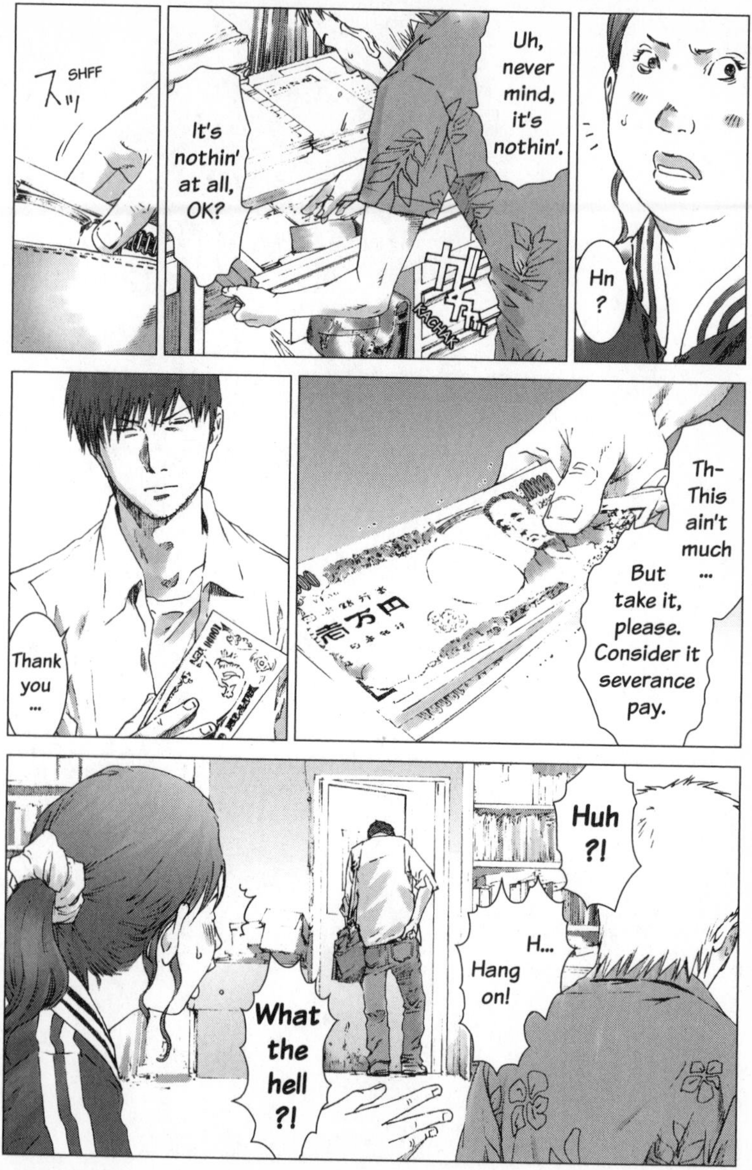
Hn ?
Uh, never mind, it's nothin'.
It's nothin' at all, OK?
KACHAK
スッ
SHFF
Th- This ain't much ...
But take it, please. Consider it severance pay.
Thank you ...
Huh ?!
H... Hang on!
What the hell ?!

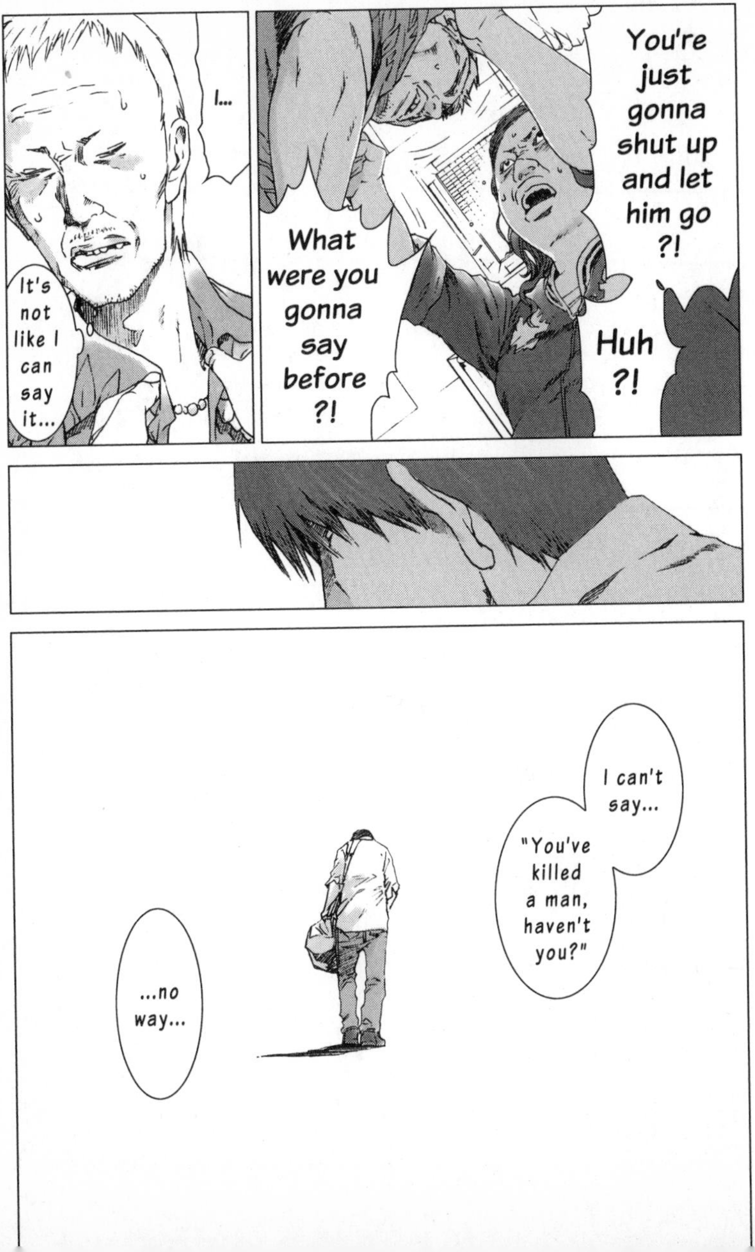
You're just gonna shut up and let him go?!
Huh?!
What were you gonna say before?!
I...
It's not like I can say it...
I can't say...
"You've killed a man, haven't you?"
...no way...

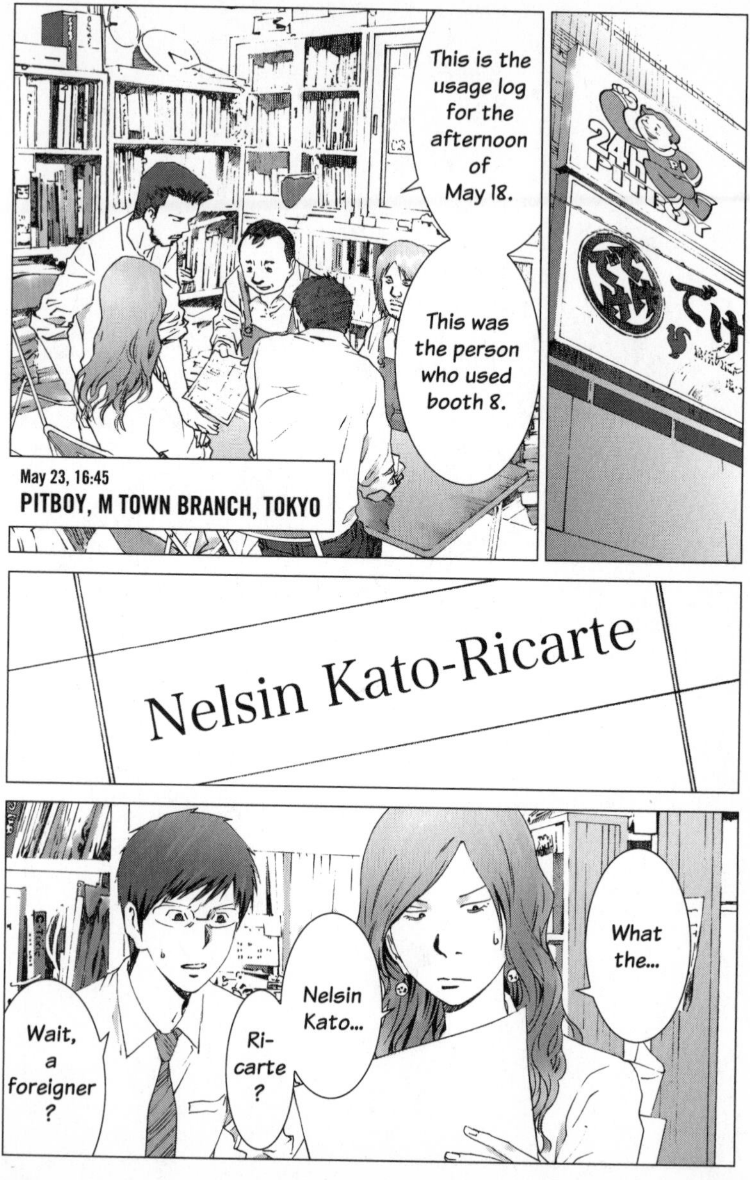
24h
PITBOY
This is the usage log for the afternoon of May 18.
This was the person who used booth 8.
May 23, 16:45
PITBOY, M TOWN BRANCH, TOKYO
Nelsin Kato-Ricarte
What the...
Nelsin Kato...
Ri-carte?
Wait, a foreigner?

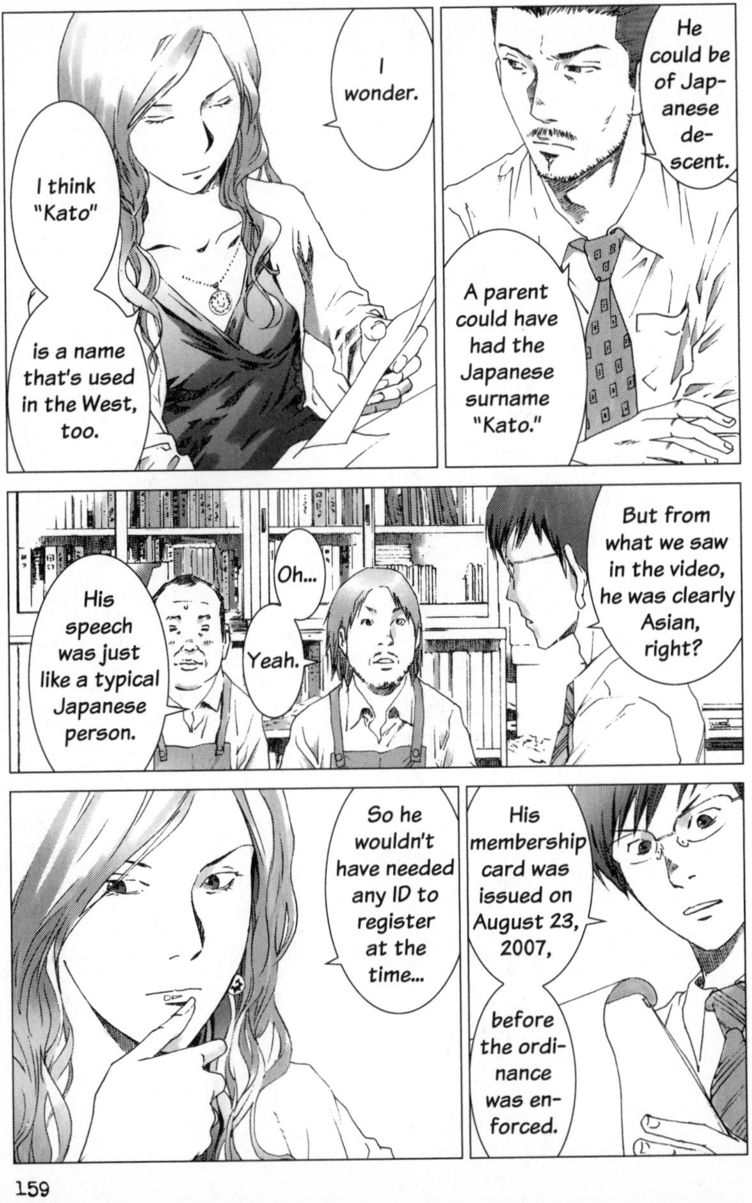
He could be of Japanese descent.
A parent could have had the Japanese surname "Kato."
I wonder.
I think "Kato"
is a name that's used in the West, too.
But from what we saw in the video, he was clearly Asian, right?
Oh...
Yeah.
His speech was just like a typical Japanese person.
His membership card was issued on August 23, 2007,
before the ordinance was enforced.
So he wouldn't have needed any ID to register at the time...

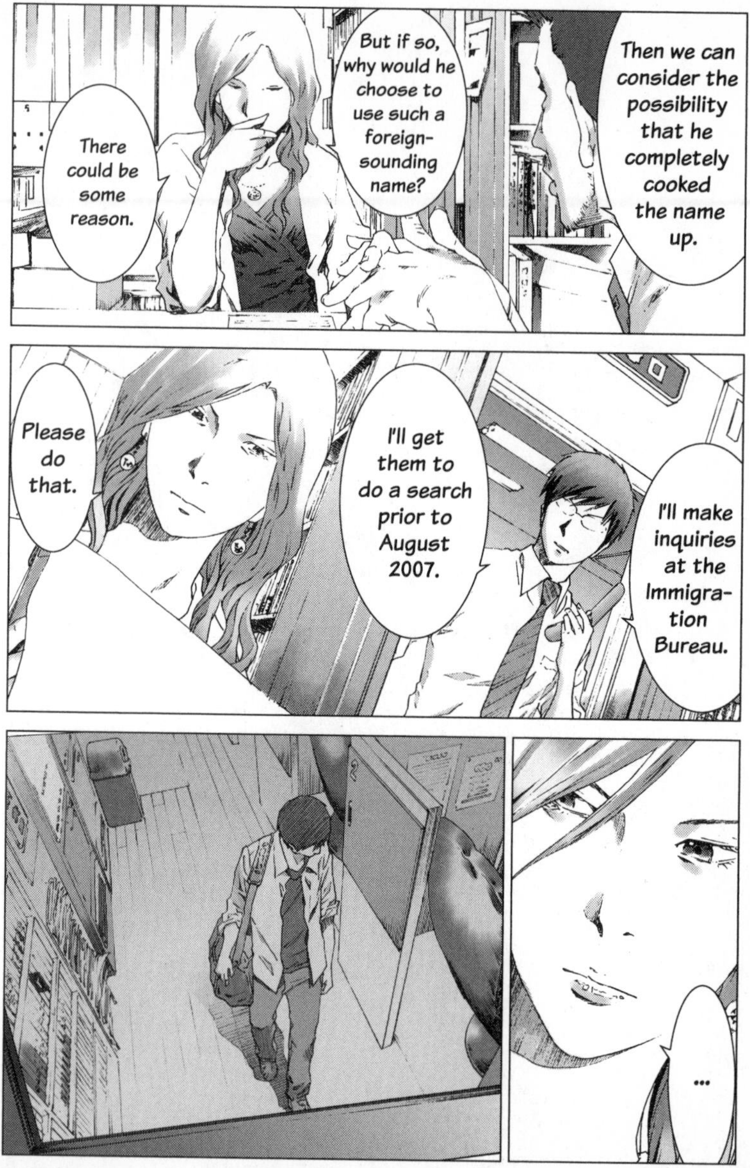
Then we can consider the possibility that he completely cooked the name up.
But if so, why would he choose to use such a foreign-sounding name?
There could be some reason.
I'll make inquiries at the Immigra-tion Bureau.
I'll get them to do a search prior to August 2007.
Please do that.
...

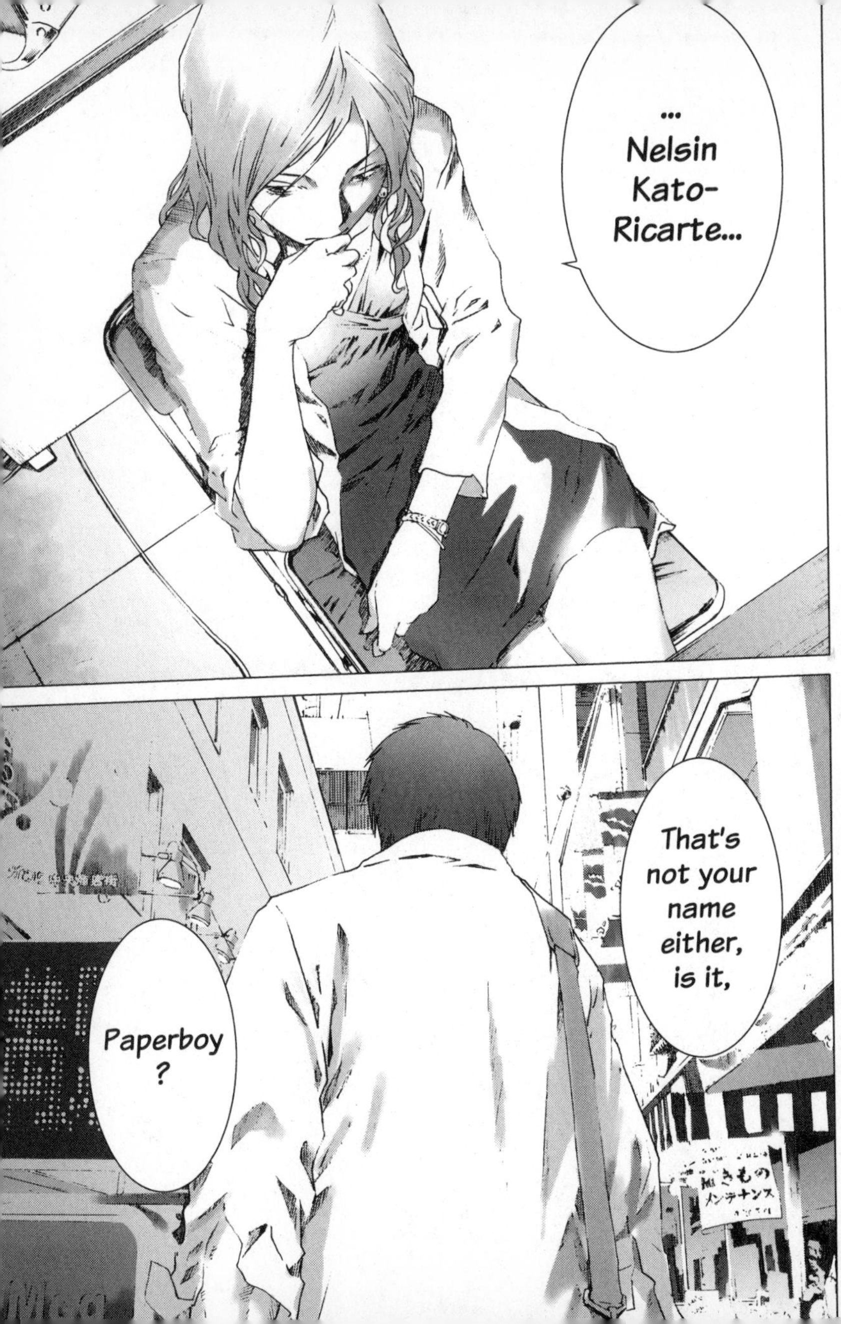
... Nelsin Kato-Ricarte...
That's not your name either, is it,
Paperboy ?

PROPHECY

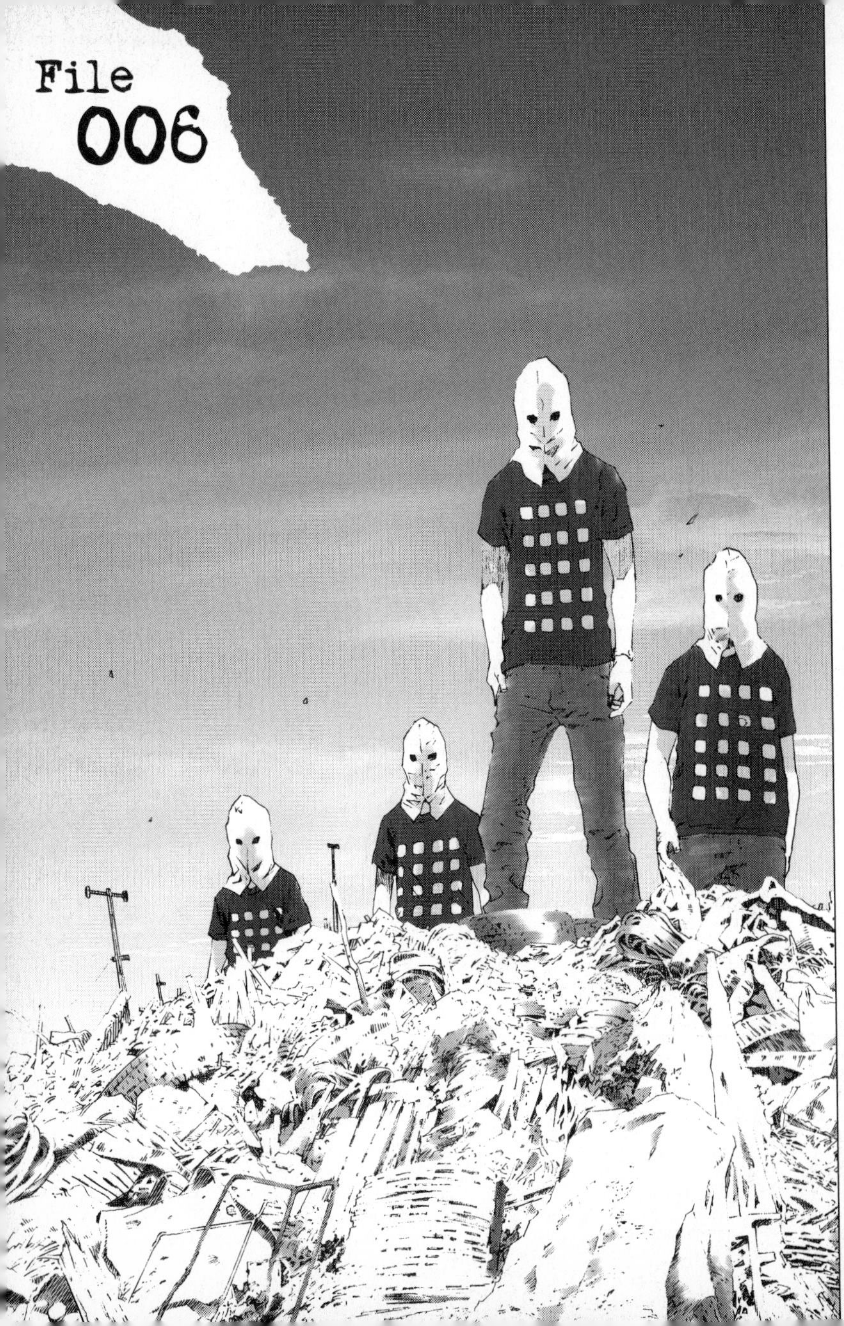
File
006

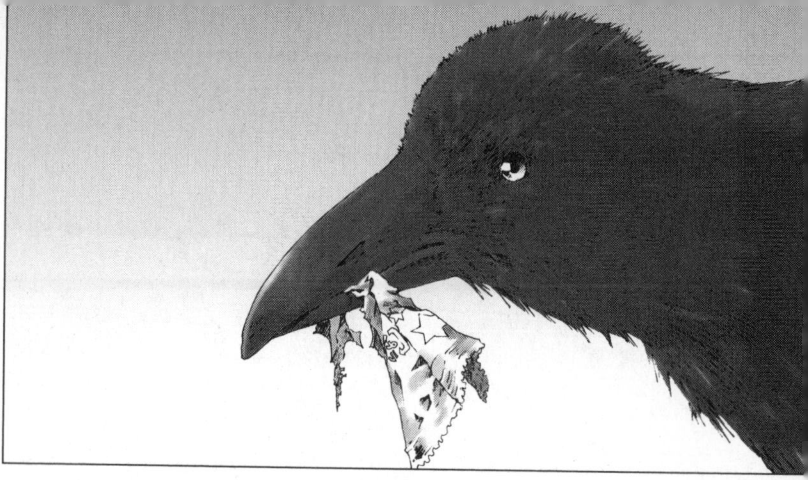

September 20, 2008
4:30 AM

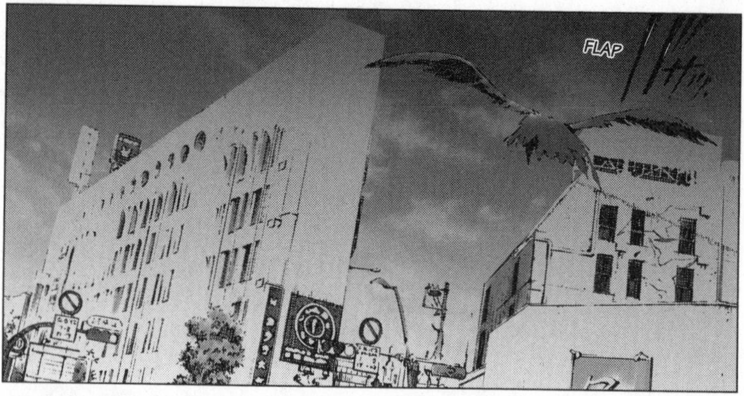
FLAP

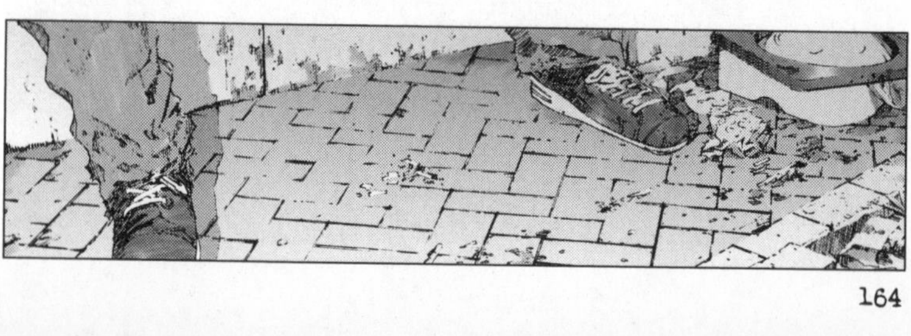

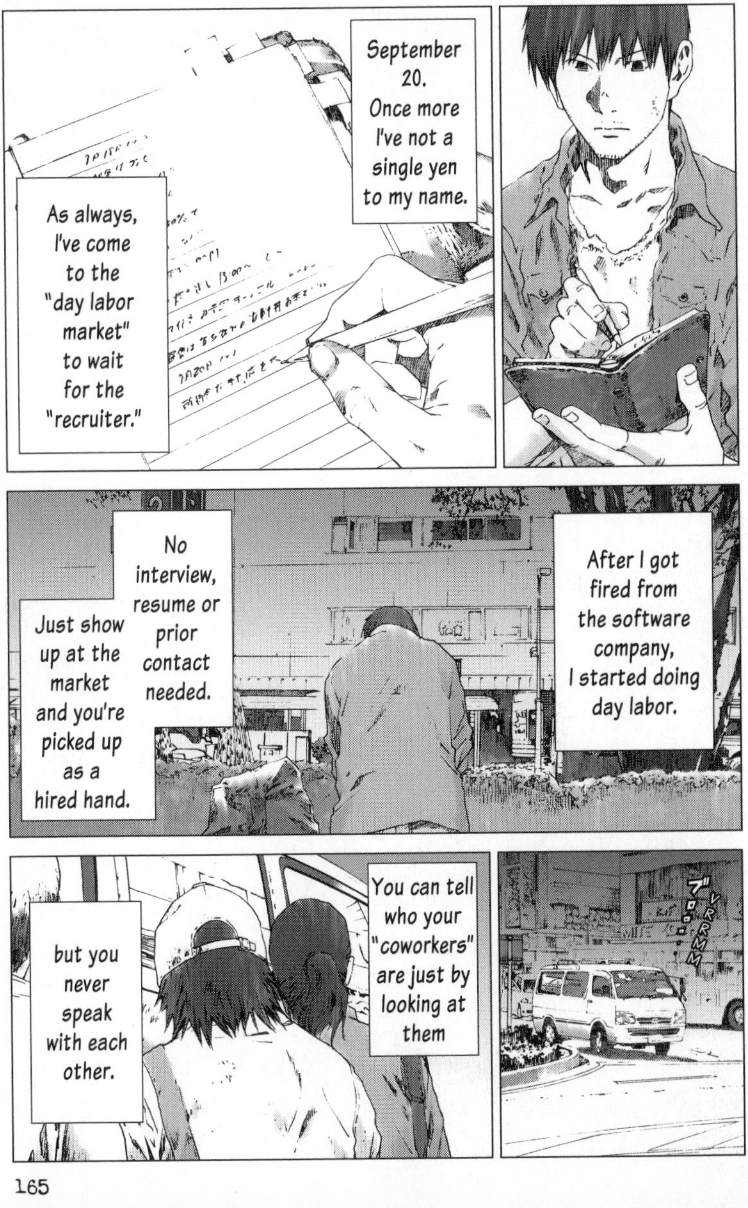
September 20. Once more I've not a single yen to my name.
As always, I've come to the "day labor market" to wait for the "recruiter."
After I got fired from the software company, I started doing day labor.
No interview, resume or prior contact needed.
Just show up at the market and you're picked up as a hired hand.
VRRRMM
You can tell who your "coworkers" are just by looking at them
but you never speak with each other.

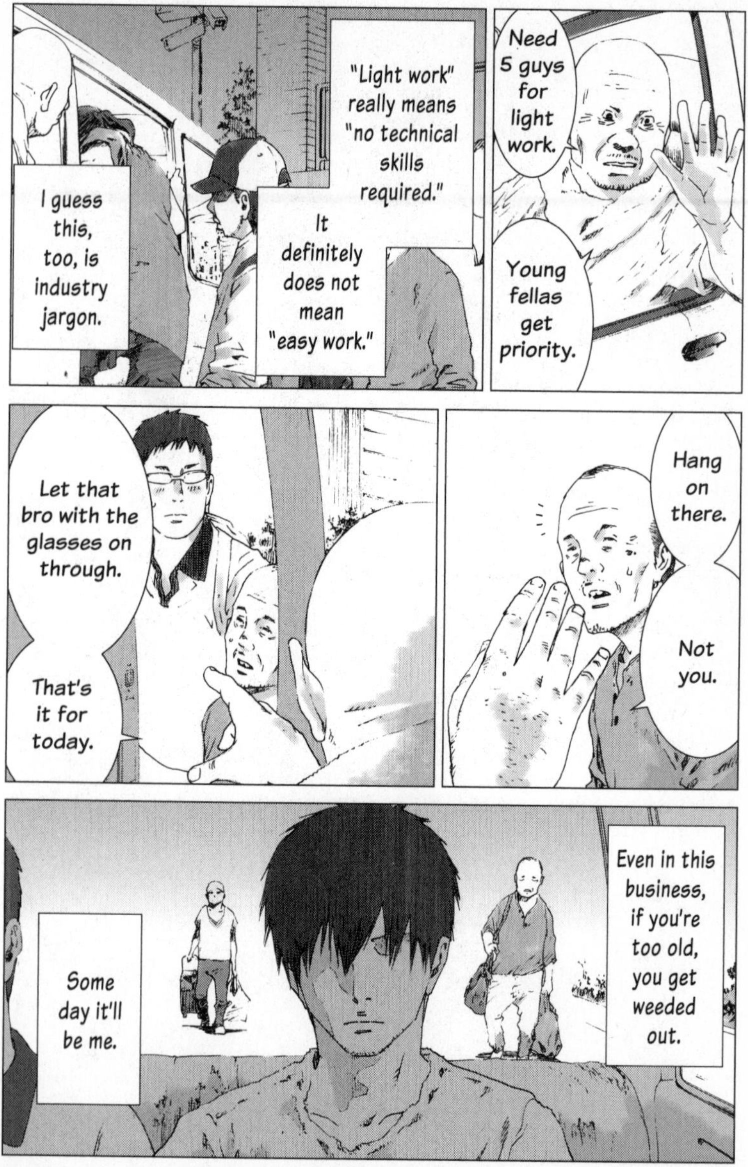
Need 5 guys for light work.
Young fellas get priority.
"Light work" really means "no technical skills required."
It definitely does not mean "easy work."
I guess this, too, is industry jargon.
Hang on there.
Not you.
Let that bro with the glasses on through.
That's it for today.
Even in this business, if you're too old, you get weeded out.
Some day it'll be me.

However, we later learned that on this occasion

those who had been weeded out were the lucky ones.

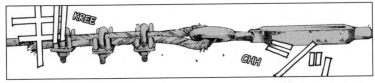

KREE

CHH

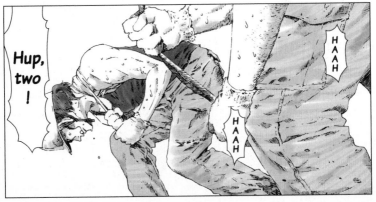

Hup, two!

HAAH

HAAH

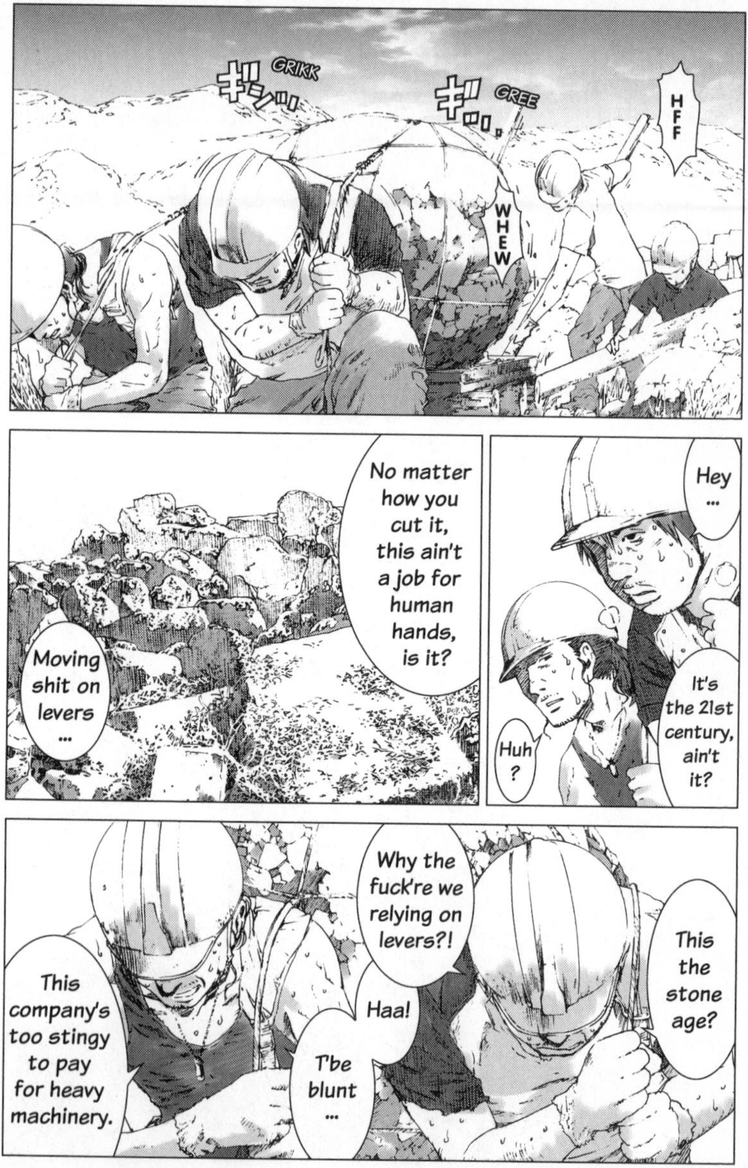
HFF
WHEW
GREE
GRIKK
Hey ...
It's the 21st century, ain't it?
Huh?
No matter how you cut it, this ain't a job for human hands, is it?
Moving shit on levers ...
This the stone age?
Why the fuck're we relying on levers?!
Haa!
T'be blunt ...
This company's too stingy to pay for heavy machinery.

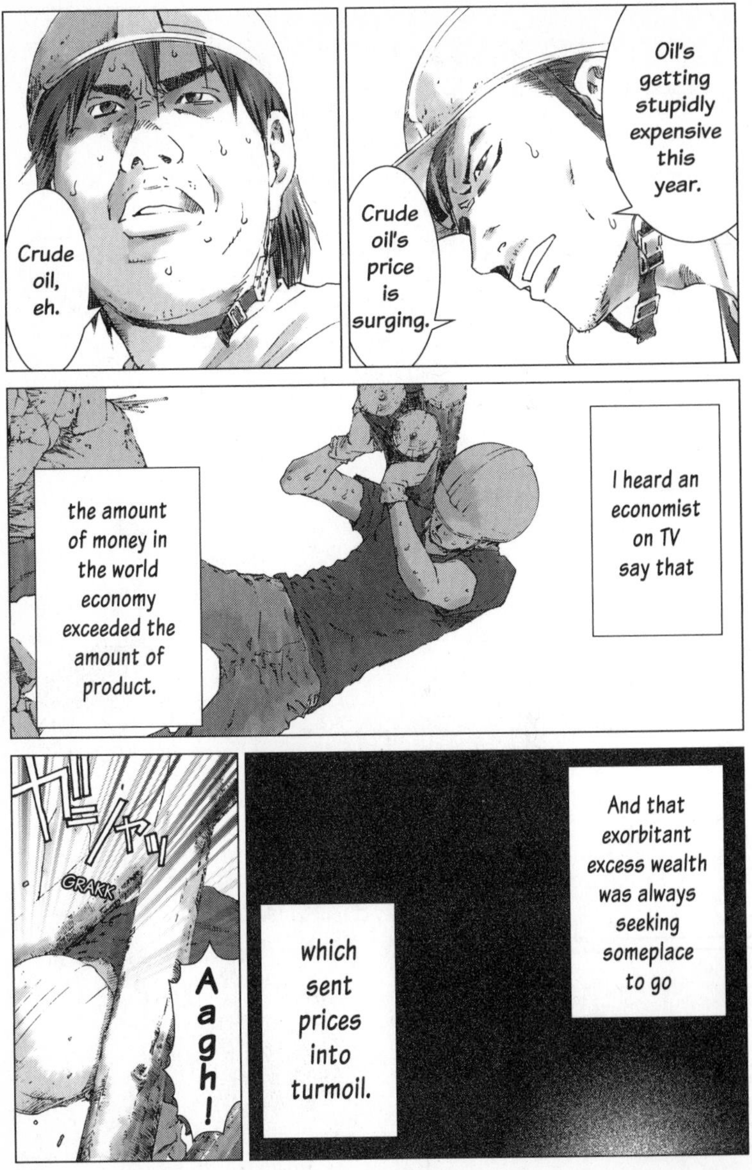
Oil's getting stupidly expensive this year.
Crude oil's price is surging.
Crude oil, eh.
I heard an economist on TV say that
the amount of money in the world economy exceeded the amount of product.
And that exorbitant excess wealth was always seeking someplace to go
which sent prices into turmoil.
GRAKK
Aagh!

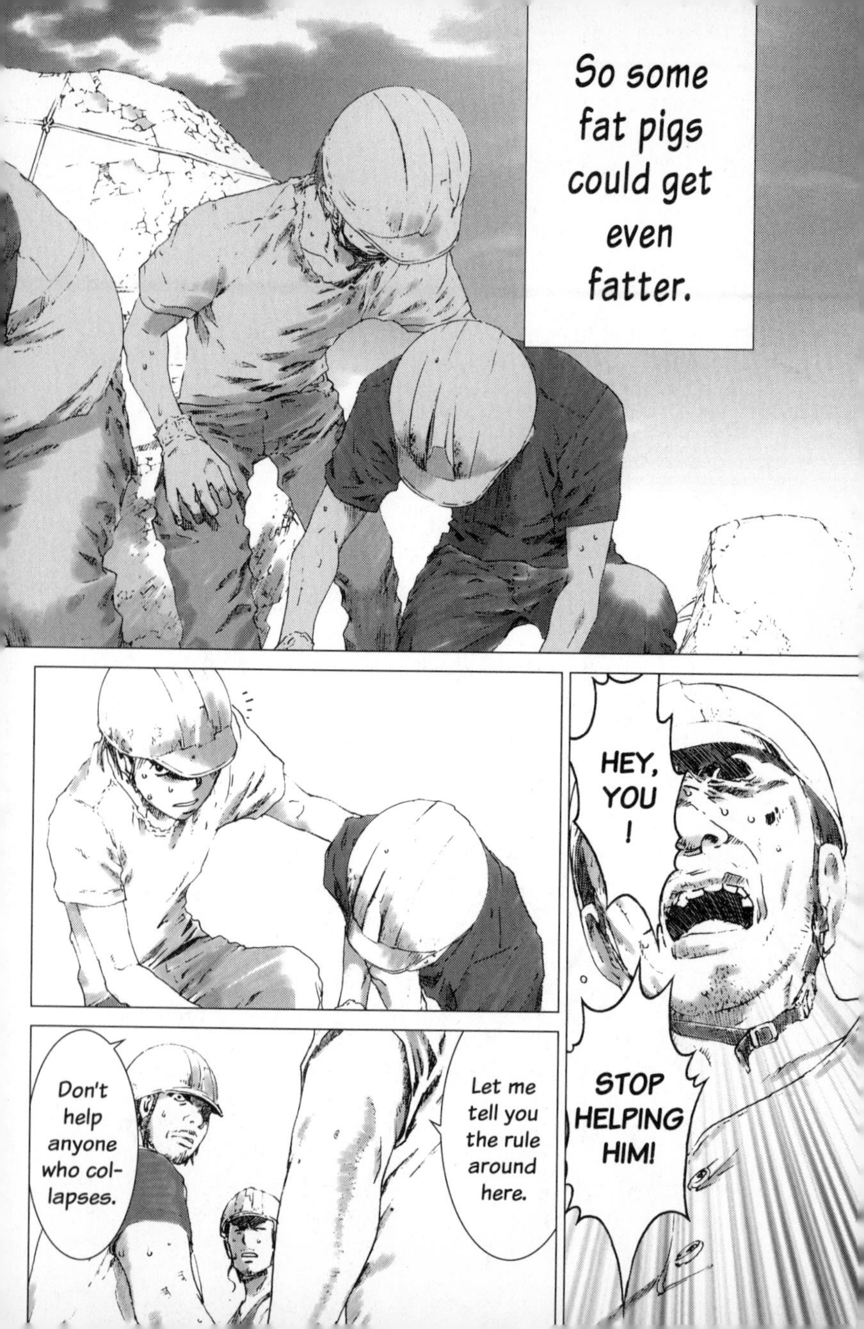
So some fat pigs could get even fatter.
HEY, YOU!
STOP HELPING HIM!
Let me tell you the rule around here.
Don't help anyone who collapses.

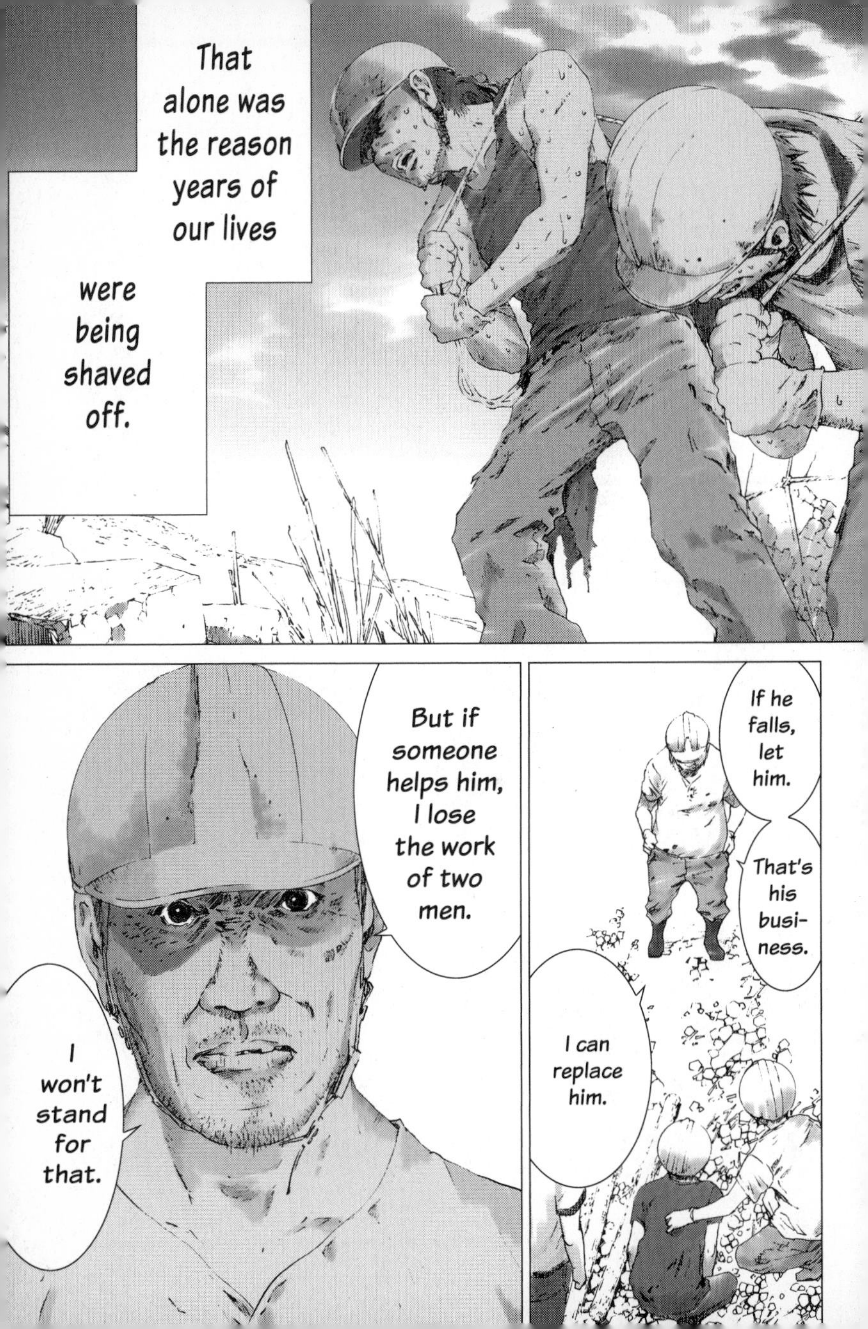
That alone was the reason years of our lives
were being shaved off.
If he falls, let him.
That's his business.
I can replace him.
But if someone helps him, I lose the work of two men.
I won't stand for that.

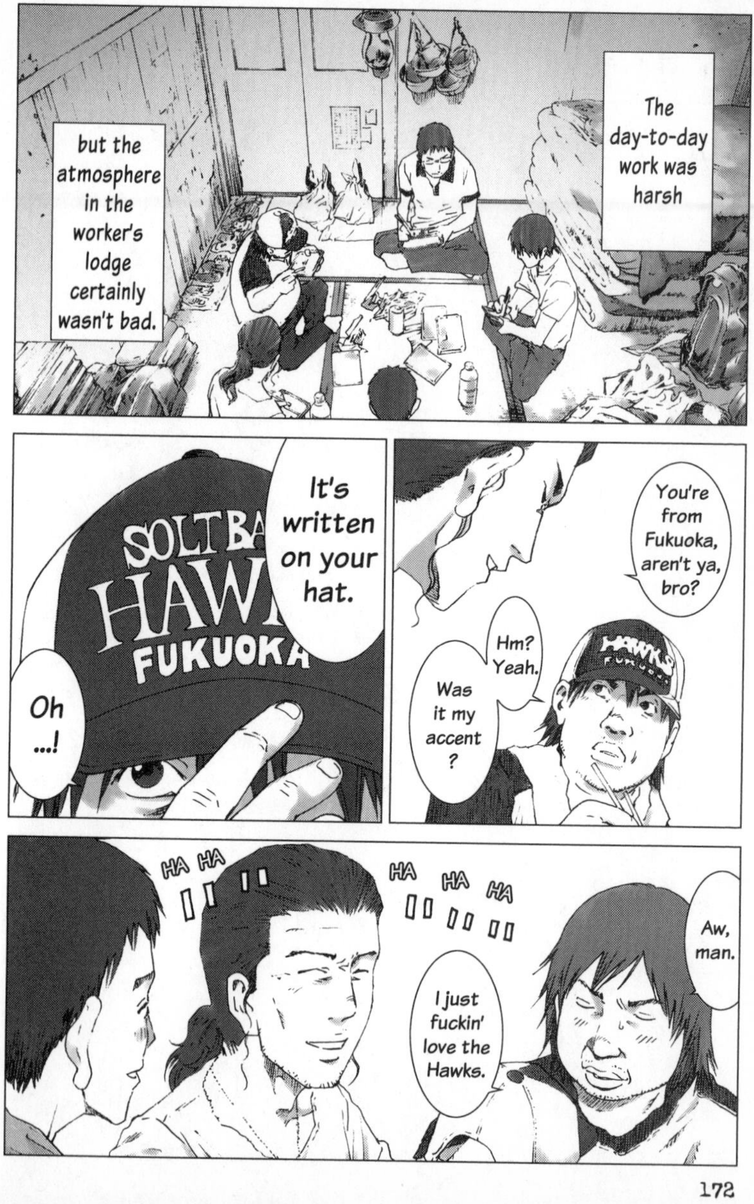
The day-to-day work was harsh
but the atmosphere in the worker's lodge certainly wasn't bad.
You're from Fukuoka, aren't ya, bro?
Hm? Yeah.
Was it my accent?
HAWKS
It's written on your hat.
SOLT BA
HAWK
FUKUOKA
Oh ...!
Aw, man.
HA HA HA
I just fuckin' love the Hawks.
HA HA

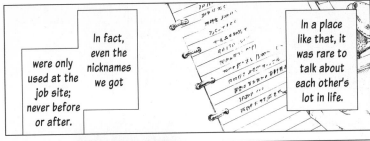

In a place like that, it was rare to talk about each other's lot in life.

In fact, even the nicknames we got

were only used at the job site; never before or after.

Word got out that I had worked in IT

so they just started calling me "Gates."

...Well, nicknames are never all that serious.

This guy was born in Osaka, so we called him "Kansai."

He'd come to Tokyo to try to make it as a musician, but apparently failed.

If you got him started on the corrupt nature of the Japanese music industry, he'd rant for hours.

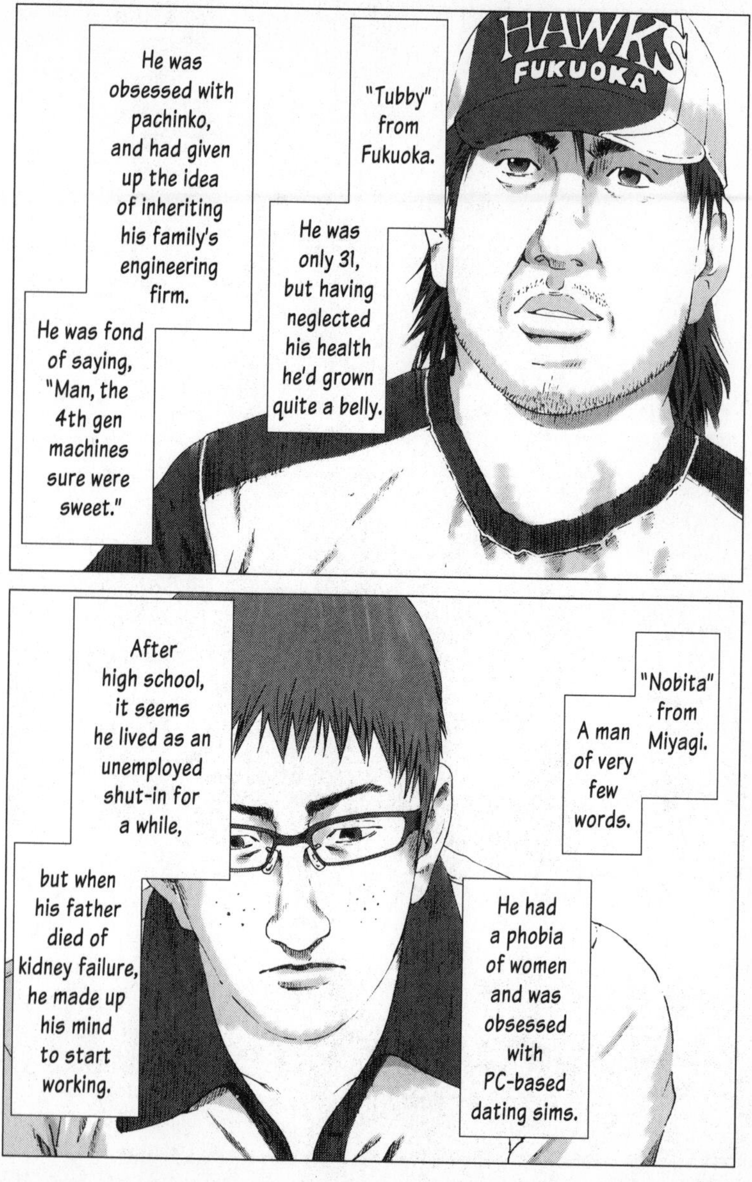
HAWKS
FUKUOKA
"Tubby" from Fukuoka.
He was only 31, but having neglected his health he'd grown quite a belly.
He was obsessed with pachinko, and had given up the idea of inheriting his family's engineering firm.
He was fond of saying, "Man, the 4th gen machines sure were sweet."
"Nobita" from Miyagi.
A man of very few words.
He had a phobia of women and was obsessed with PC-based dating sims.
After high school, it seems he lived as an unemployed shut-in for a while,
but when his father died of kidney failure, he made up his mind to start working.

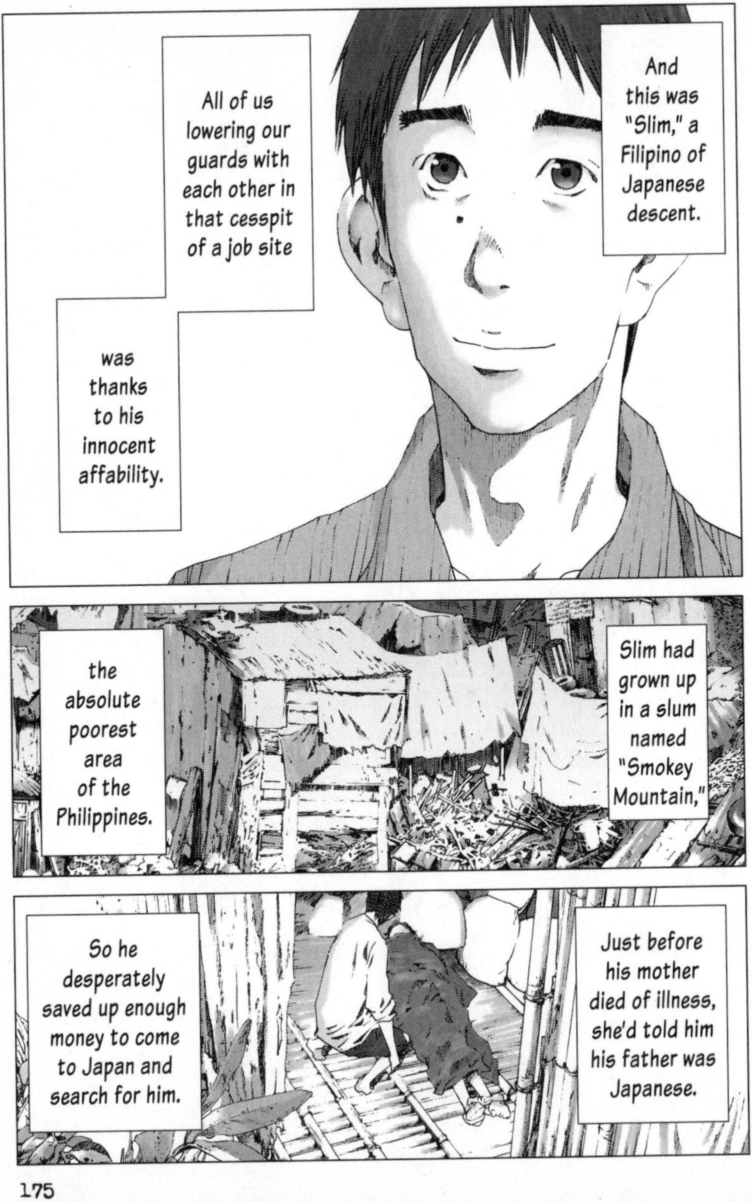
And this was "Slim," a Filipino of Japanese descent.
All of us lowering our guards with each other in that cesspit of a job site
was thanks to his innocent affability.
Slim had grown up in a slum named "Smokey Mountain,"
the absolute poorest area of the Philippines.
Just before his mother died of illness, she'd told him his father was Japanese.
So he desperately saved up enough money to come to Japan and search for him.

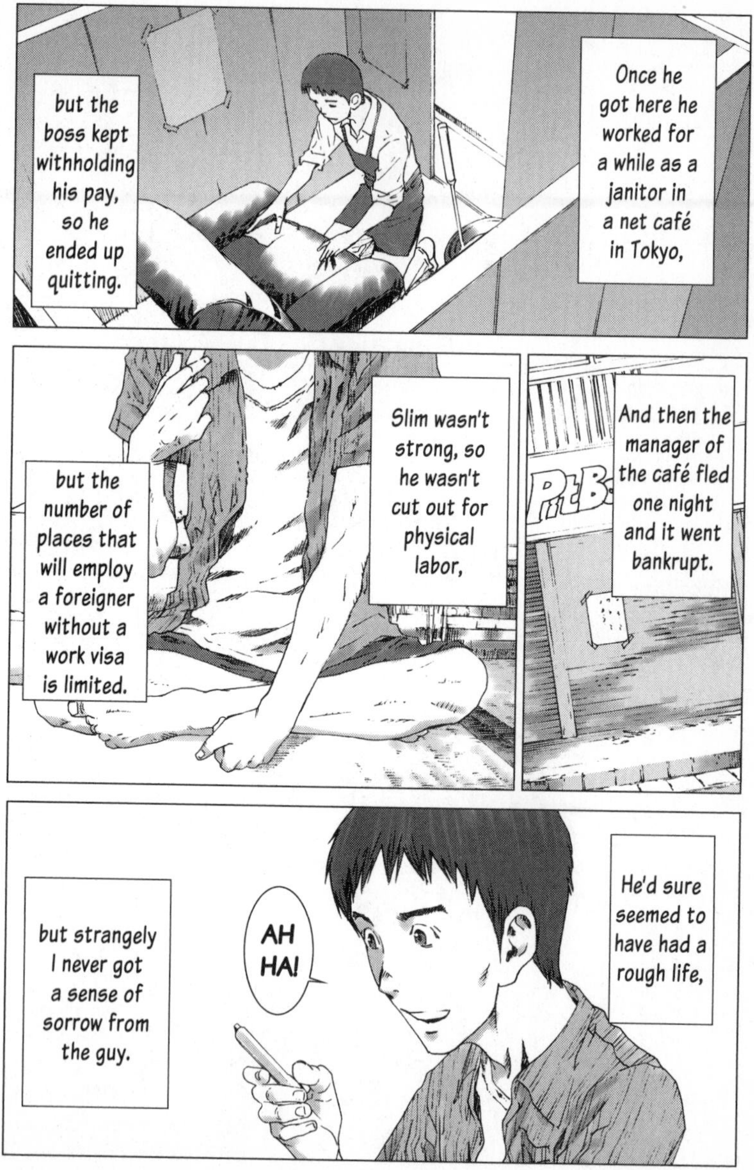
Once he got here he worked for a while as a janitor in a net café in Tokyo,
but the boss kept withholding his pay, so he ended up quitting.
And then the manager of the café fled one night and it went bankrupt.
Slim wasn't strong, so he wasn't cut out for physical labor,
but the number of places that will employ a foreigner without a work visa is limited.
He'd sure seemed to have had a rough life,
AH HA!
but strangely I never got a sense of sorrow from the guy.

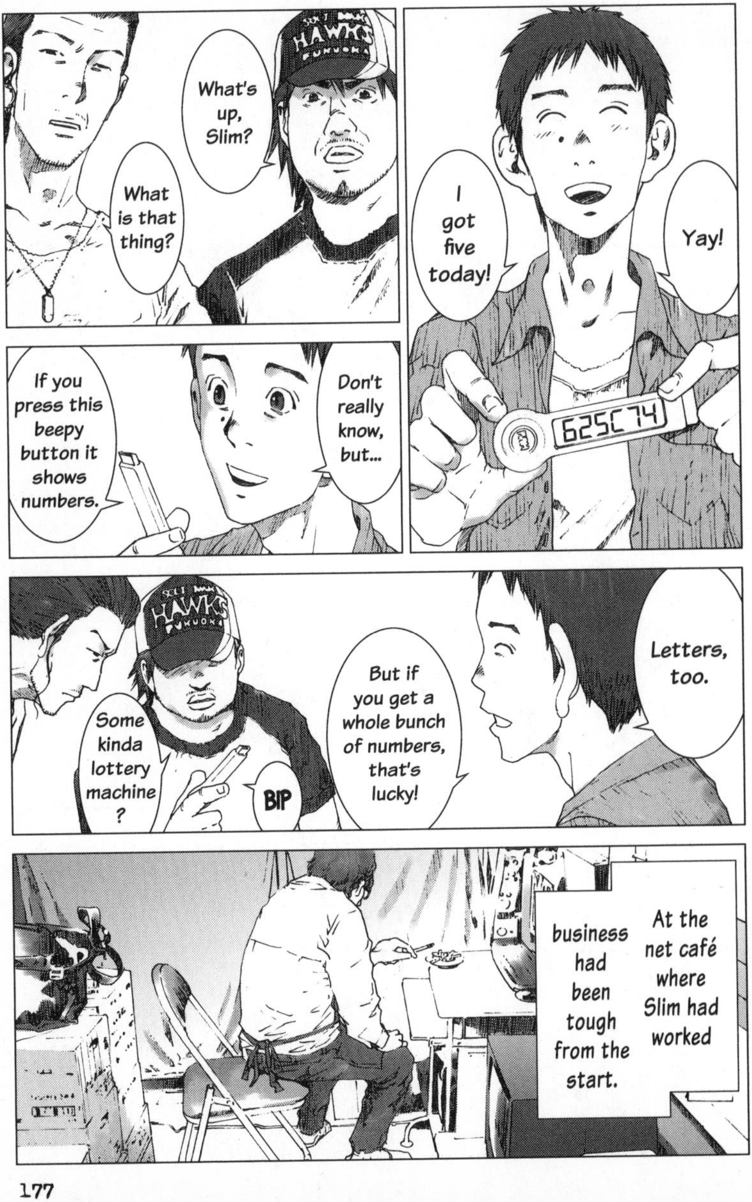

Yay!
I got five today!
625C74
What's up, Slim?
What is that thing?
Don't really know, but...
If you press this beepy button it shows numbers.
Letters, too.
But if you get a whole bunch of numbers, that's lucky!
BIP
Some kinda lottery machine?
At the net café where Slim had worked business had been tough from the start.

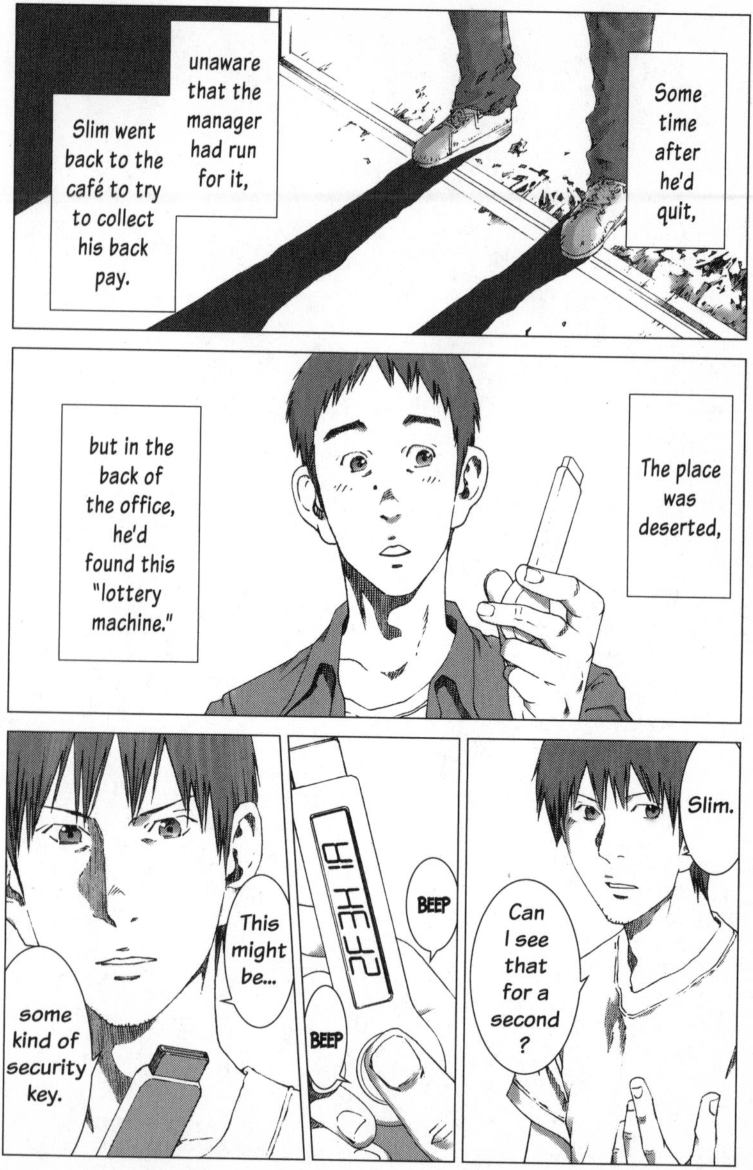

Some time after he'd quit,
unaware that the manager had run for it,
Slim went back to the café to try to collect his back pay.
The place was deserted,
but in the back of the office, he'd found this "lottery machine."
Slim.
Can I see that for a second?
BEEP
BEEP
This might be...
some kind of security key.

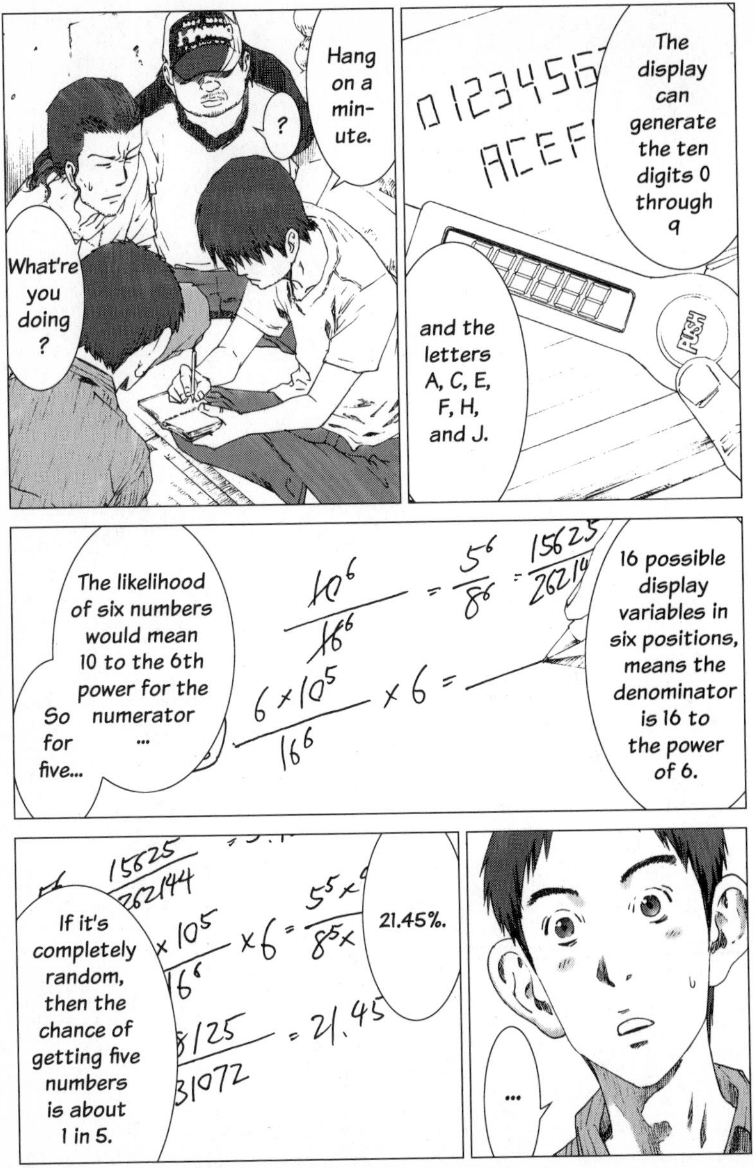

The display can generate the ten digits 0 through 9
and the letters A, C, E, F, H, and J.
Hang on a minute.
?
What're you doing?
16 possible display variables in six positions, means the denominator is 16 to the power of 6.
The likelihood of six numbers would mean 10 to the 6th power for the numerator...
So for five...
...
21.45%.
If it's completely random, then the chance of getting five numbers is about 1 in 5.

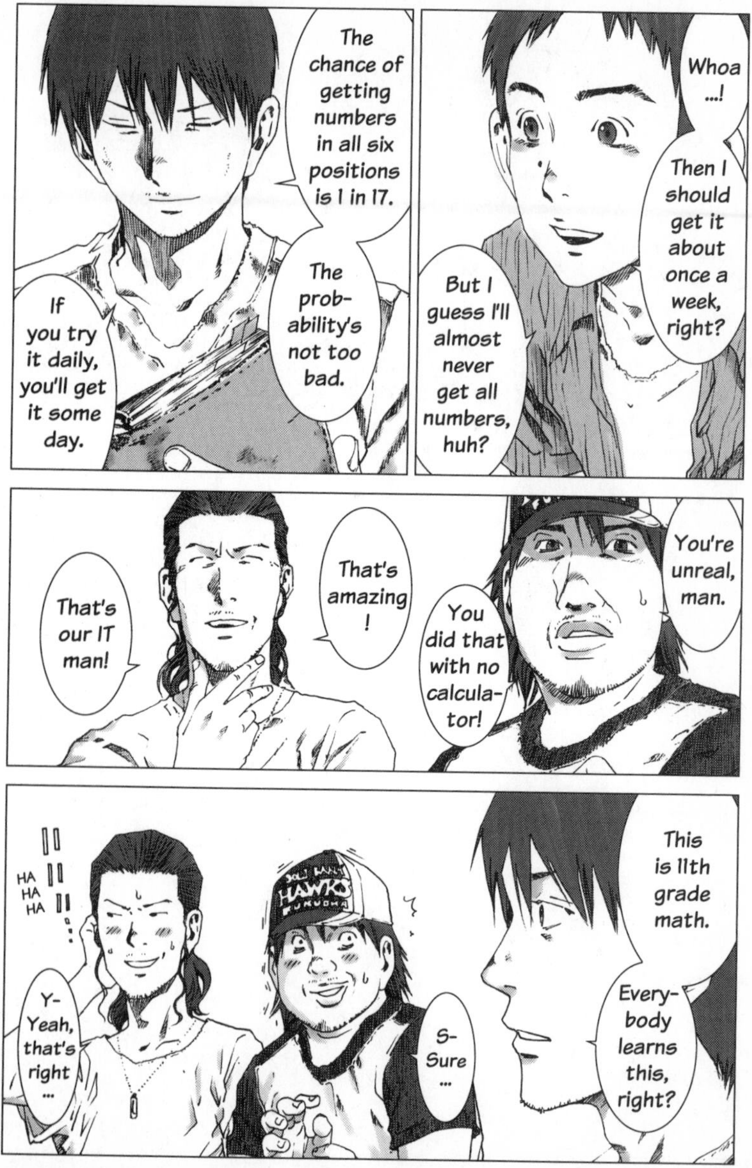
The chance of getting numbers in all six positions is 1 in 17.
The probability's not too bad.
If you try it daily, you'll get it some day.
Whoa ...!
Then I should get it about once a week, right?
But I guess I'll almost never get all numbers, huh?
That's amazing!
That's our IT man!
You're unreal, man.
You did that with no calculator!
This is 11th grade math.
Everybody learns this, right?
S-Sure ...
Y-Yeah, that's right ...
HA HA HA

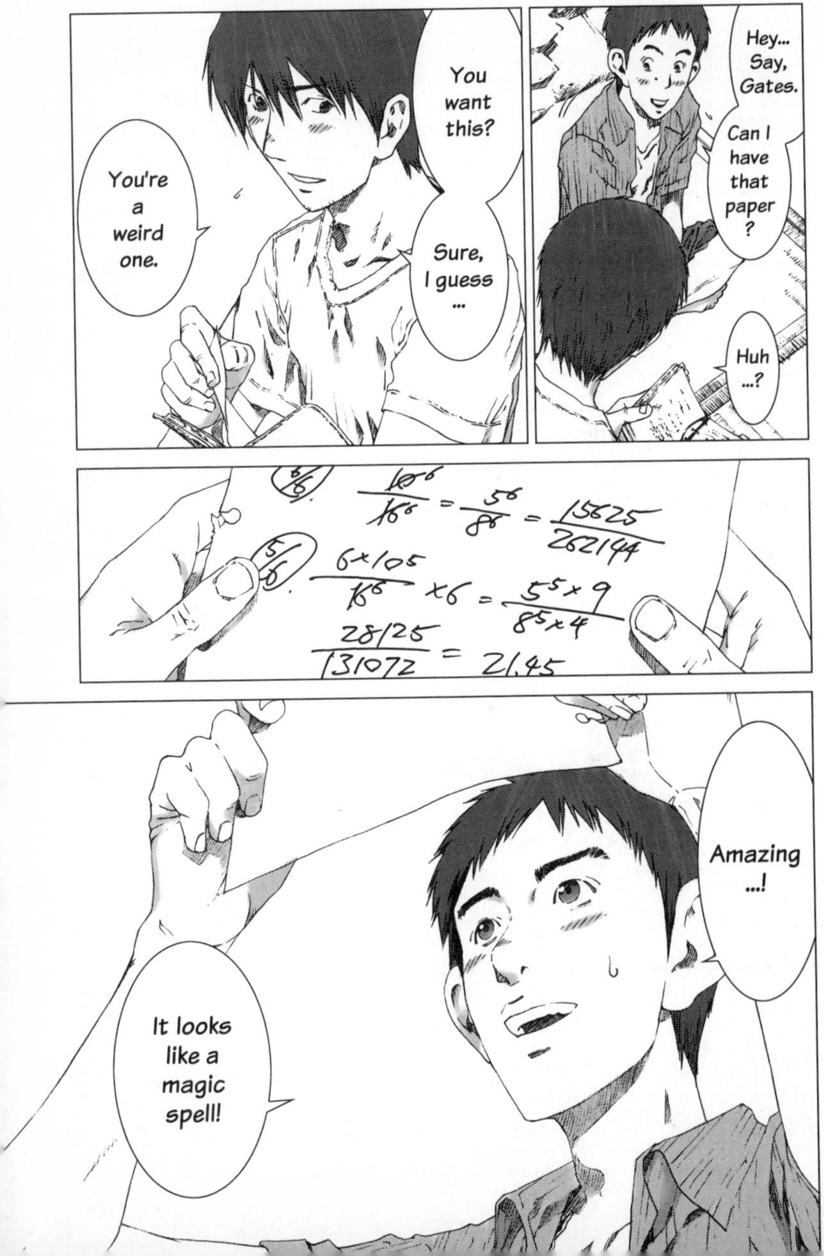
Hey... Say, Gates.
Can I have that paper?
Huh ...?
You want this?
Sure, I guess ...
You're a weird one.
Amazing ...!
It looks like a magic spell!

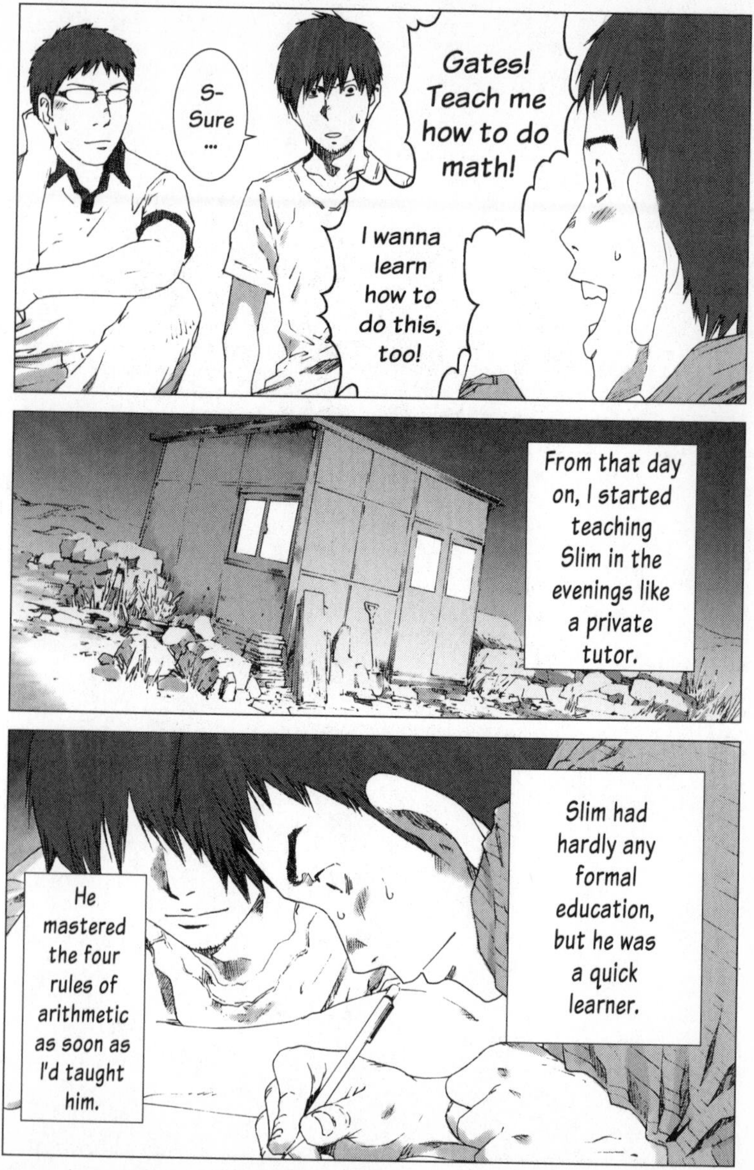
Gates! Teach me how to do math!
I wanna learn how to do this, too!
S- Sure ...
From that day on, I started teaching Slim in the evenings like a private tutor.
Slim had hardly any formal education, but he was a quick learner.
He mastered the four rules of arithmetic as soon as I'd taught him.

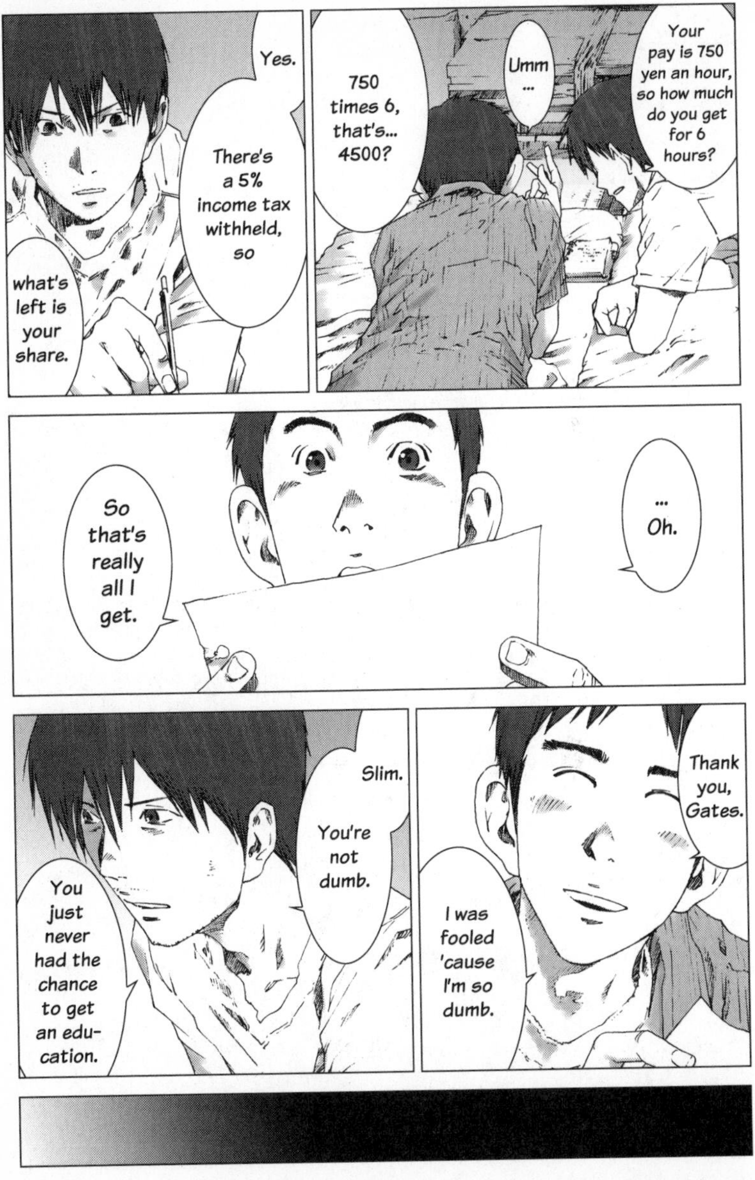
Your pay is 750 yen an hour, so how much do you get for 6 hours?
Umm ...
750 times 6, that's... 4500?
Yes.
There's a 5% income tax withheld, so
what's left is your share.
... Oh.
So that's really all I get.
Thank you, Gates.
I was fooled 'cause I'm so dumb.
Slim.
You're not dumb.
You just never had the chance to get an education.

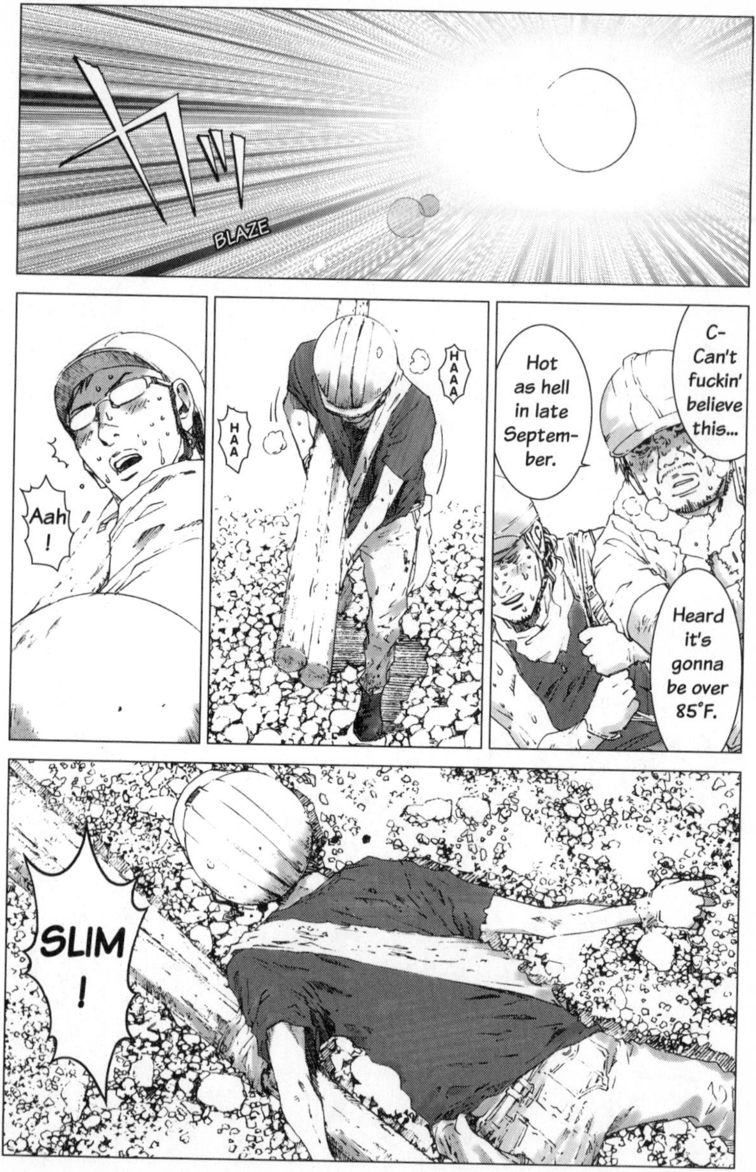

カッ
BLAZE
C- Can't fuckin' believe this...
Hot as hell in late September.
Heard it's gonna be over 85°F.
HAAA
HAA
Aah!
SLIM!

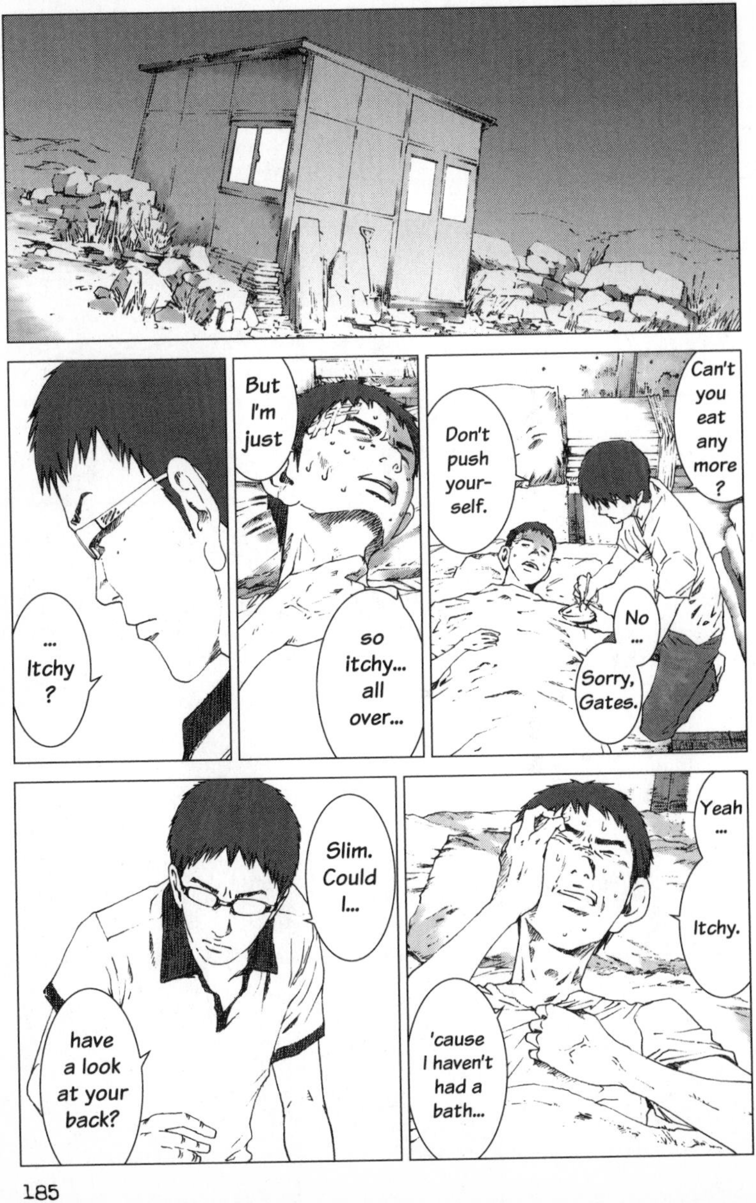
Can't you eat any more?
Don't push yourself.
No...
Sorry, Gates.
But I'm just
so itchy... all over...
...Itchy?
Yeah...
Itchy.
'cause I haven't had a bath...
Slim. Could I...
have a look at your back?

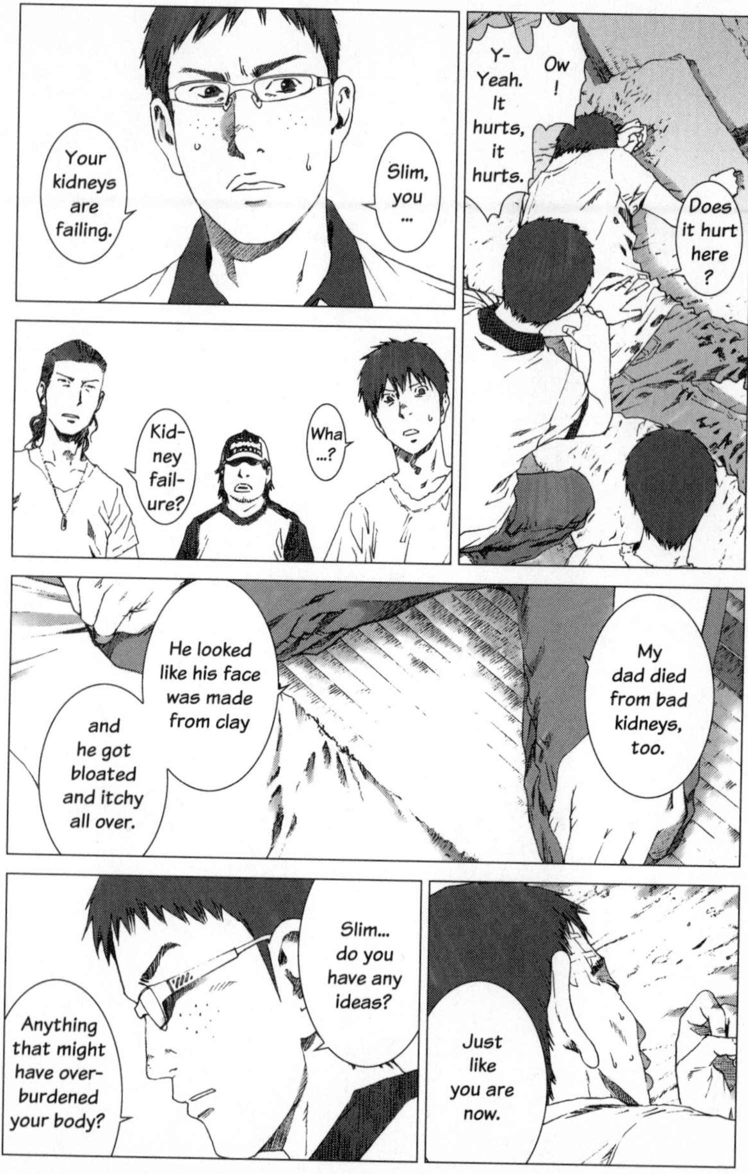
Does it hurt here?
Ow!
Y-Yeah. It hurts, it hurts.
Slim, you ...
Your kidneys are failing.
Wha ...?
Kid-ney fail-ure?
My dad died from bad kidneys, too.
He looked like his face was made from clay
and he got bloated and itchy all over.
Just like you are now.
Slim... do you have any ideas?
Anything that might have over-burdened your body?

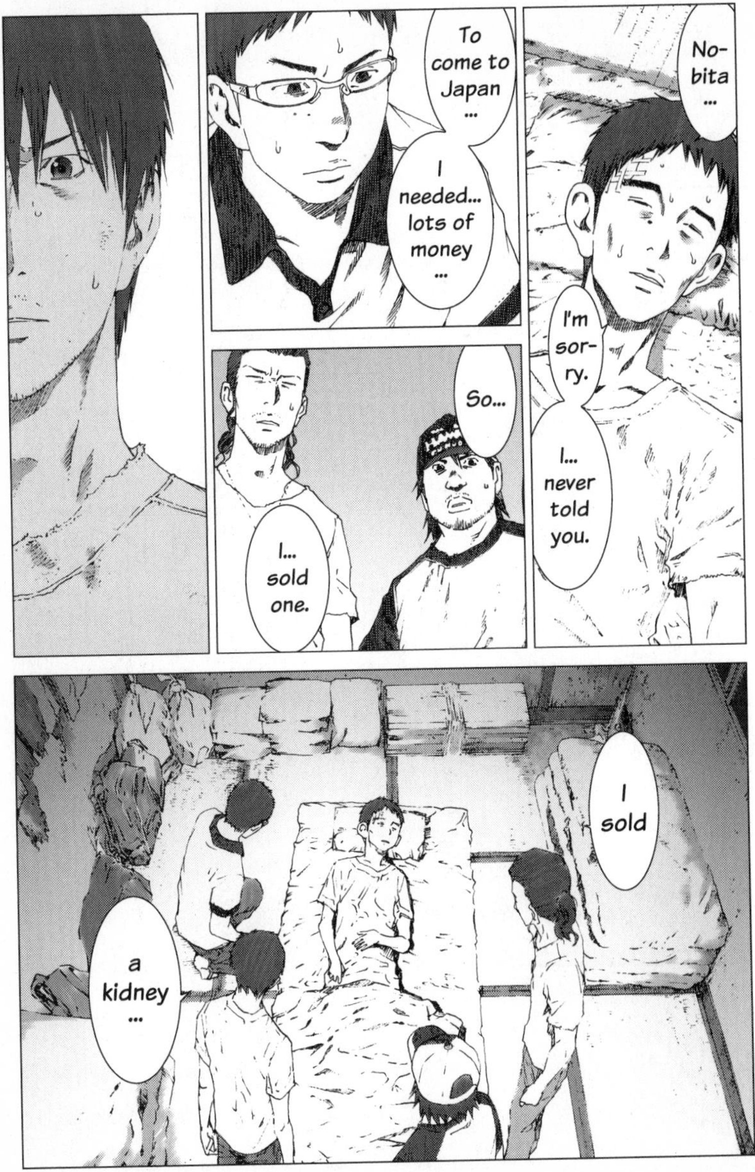
Nobita...
I'm sorry.
I... never told you.
To come to Japan...
I needed... lots of money...
So...
I... sold one.
I sold
a kidney...

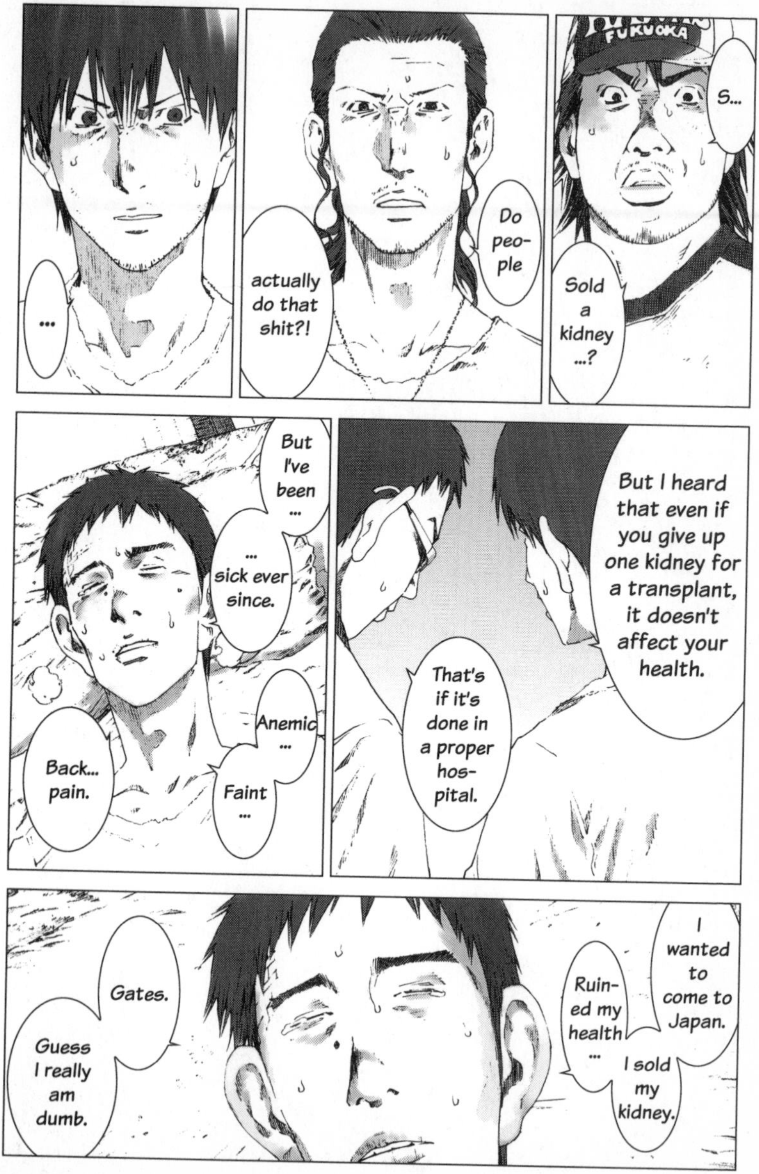
S...
Sold a kidney ...?
Do peo-ple
actually do that shit?!
...
But I heard that even if you give up one kidney for a transplant, it doesn't affect your health.
That's if it's done in a proper hos-pital.
But I've been ...
... sick ever since.
Anemic ...
Faint ...
Back... pain.
I wanted to come to Japan.
Ruin-ed my health ...
I sold my kidney.
Gates.
Guess I really am dumb.

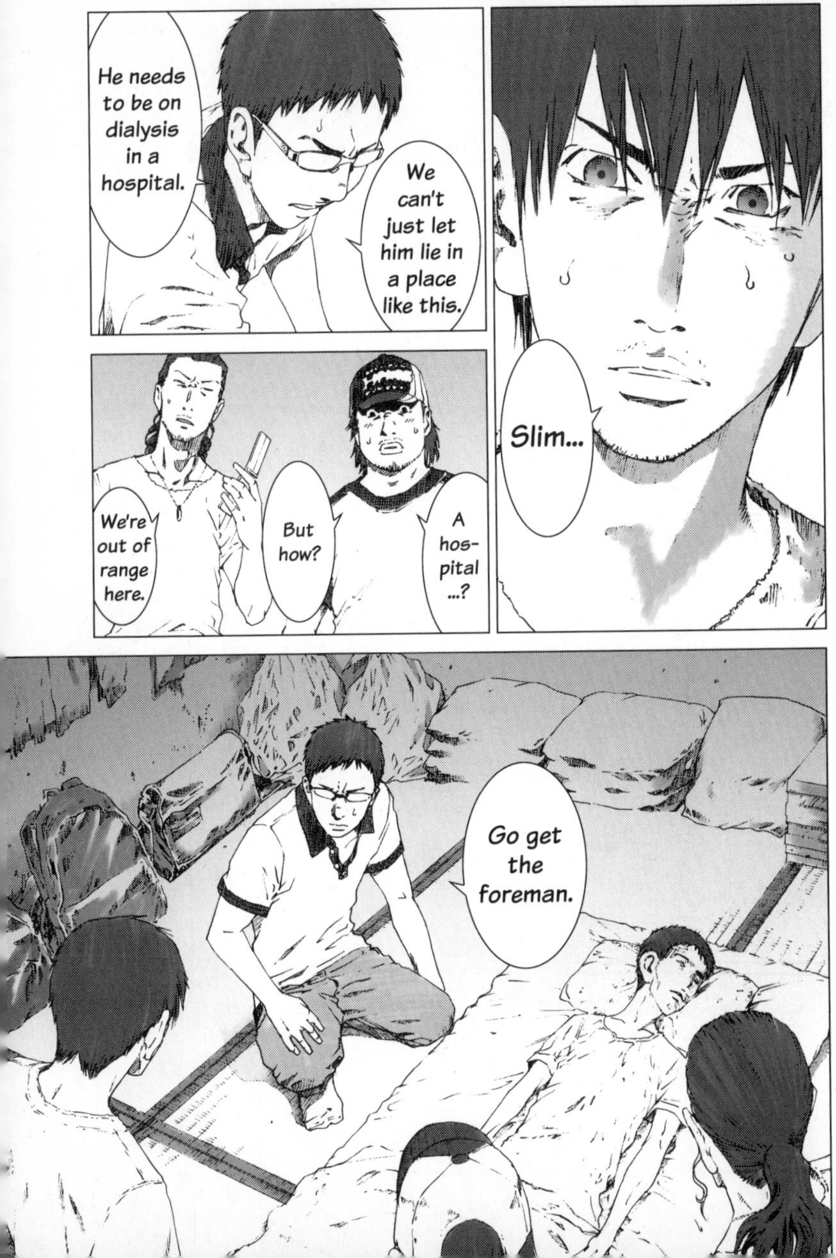
Slim...
He needs to be on dialysis in a hospital.
We can't just let him lie in a place like this.
A hos-pital ...?
But how?
We're out of range here.
Go get the foreman.

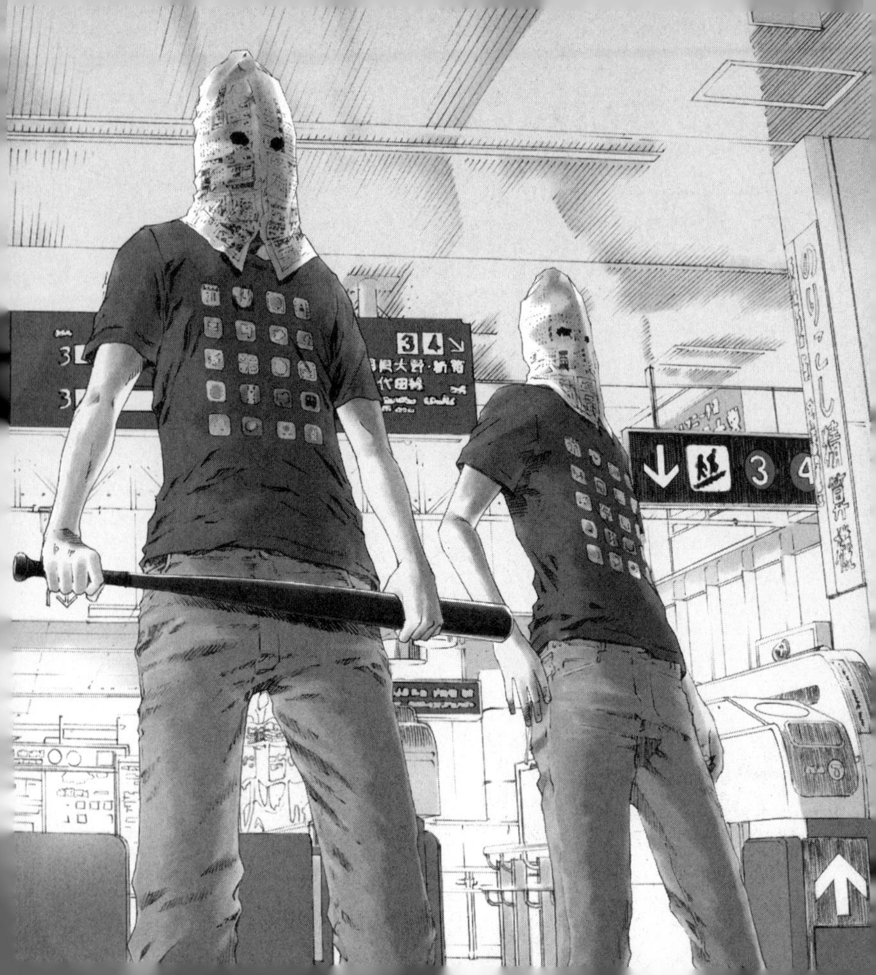

File 007

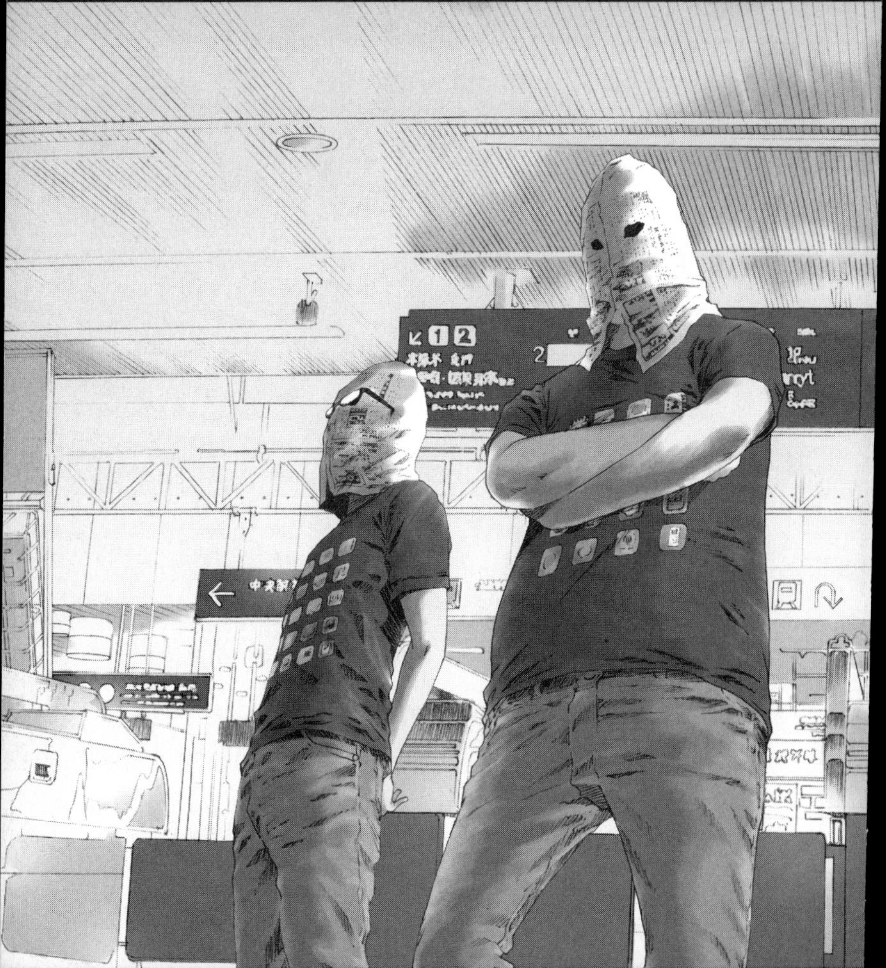

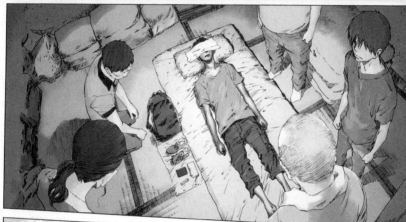

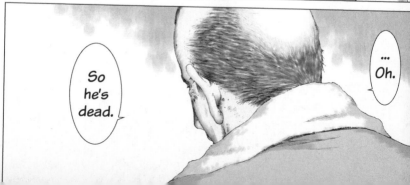

So he's dead.

...Oh.

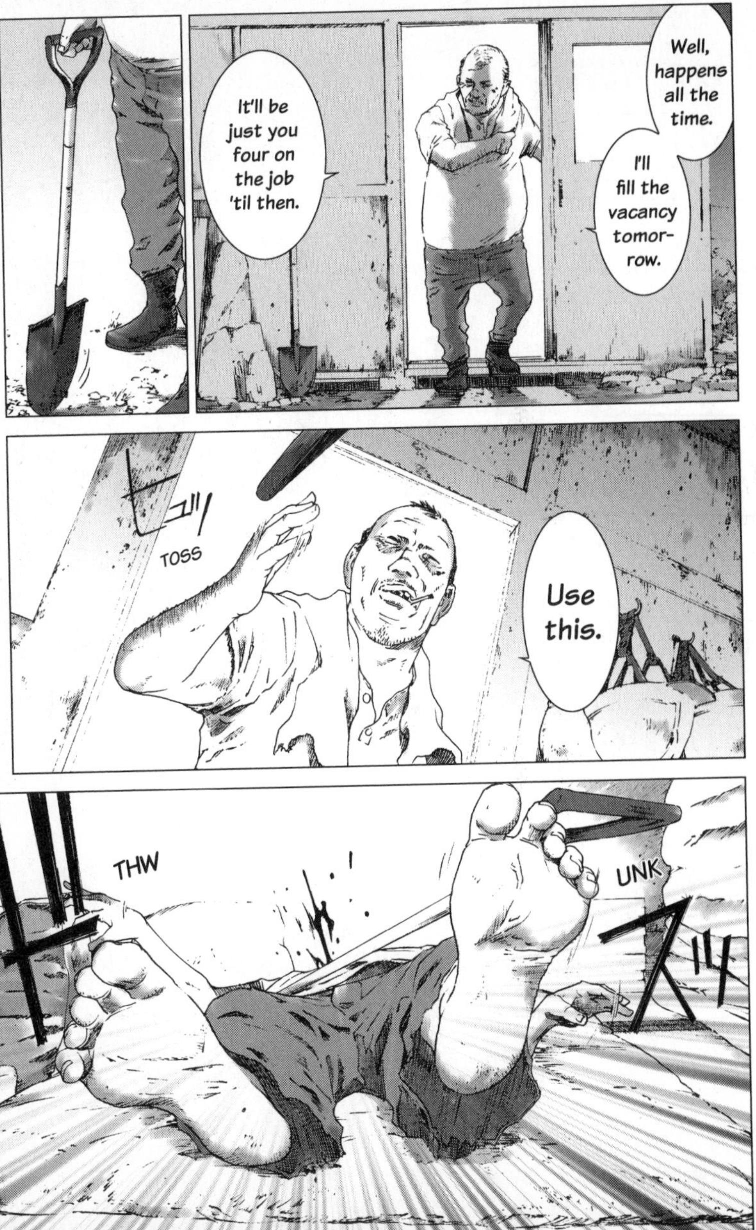
Well, happens all the time.
I'll fill the vacancy tomorrow.
It'll be just you four on the job 'til then.
TOSS
Use this.
UNK
THW

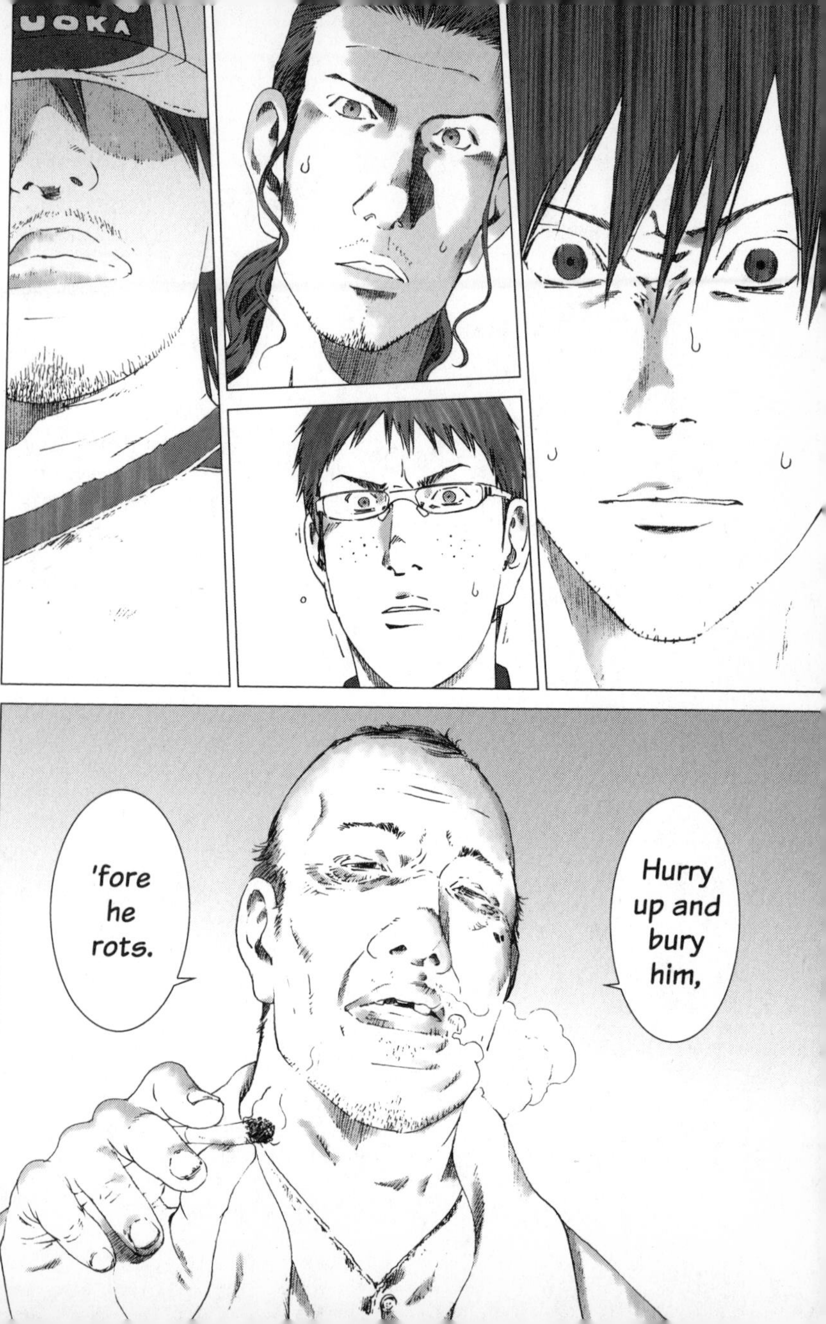
Hurry up and bury him,
'fore he rots.

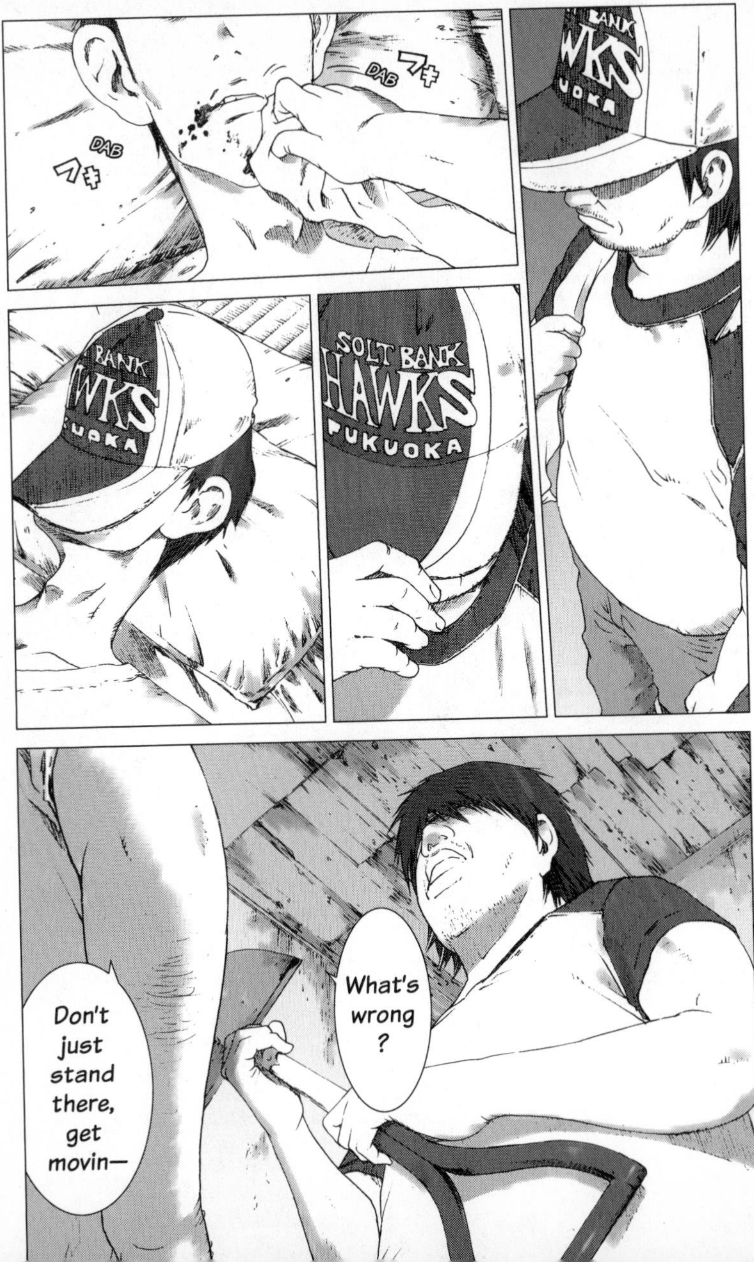
DAB フキ
DAB フキ
SOLT BANK
HAWKS
FUKUOKA
What's wrong?
Don't just stand there, get movin—

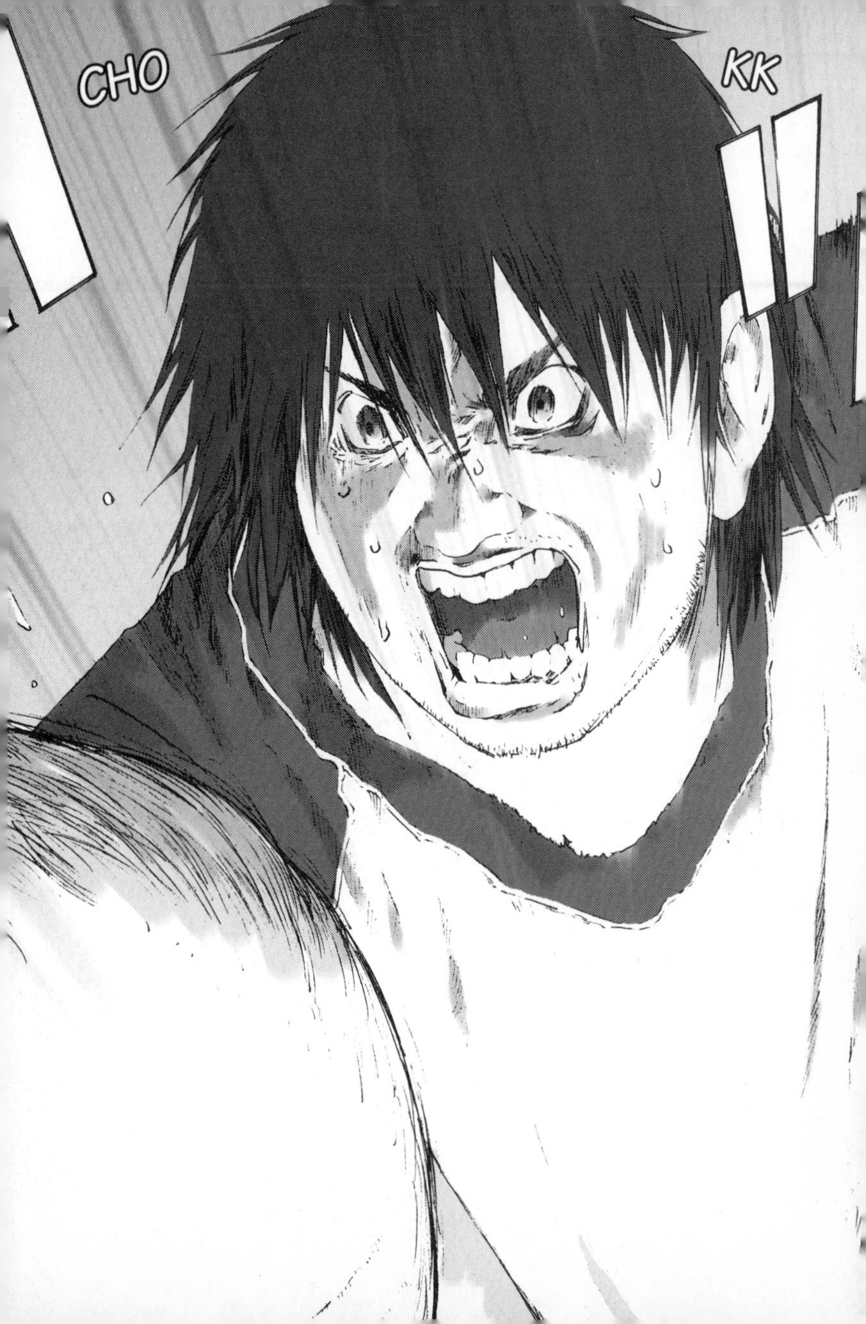
CHO
KK

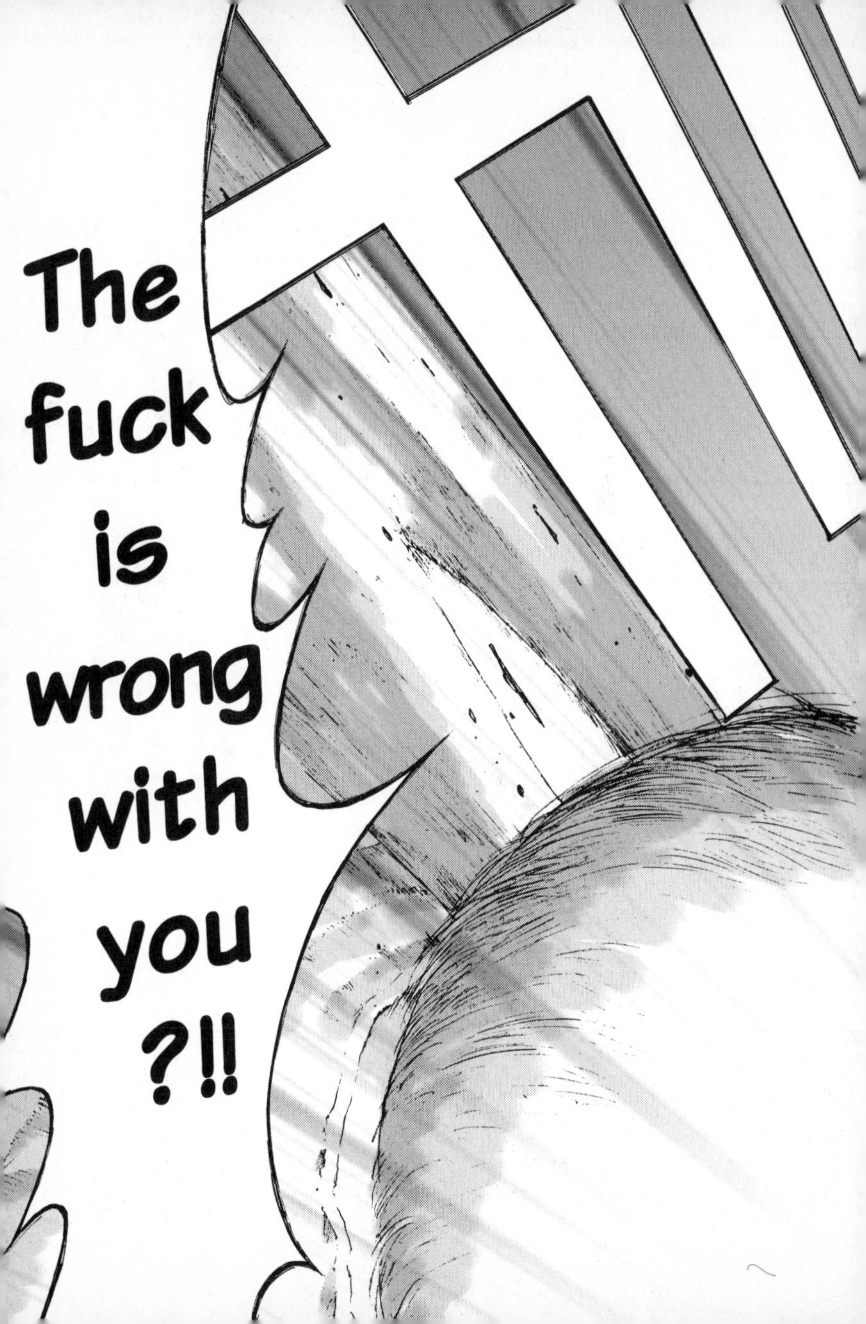
The fuck is wrong with you ?!!

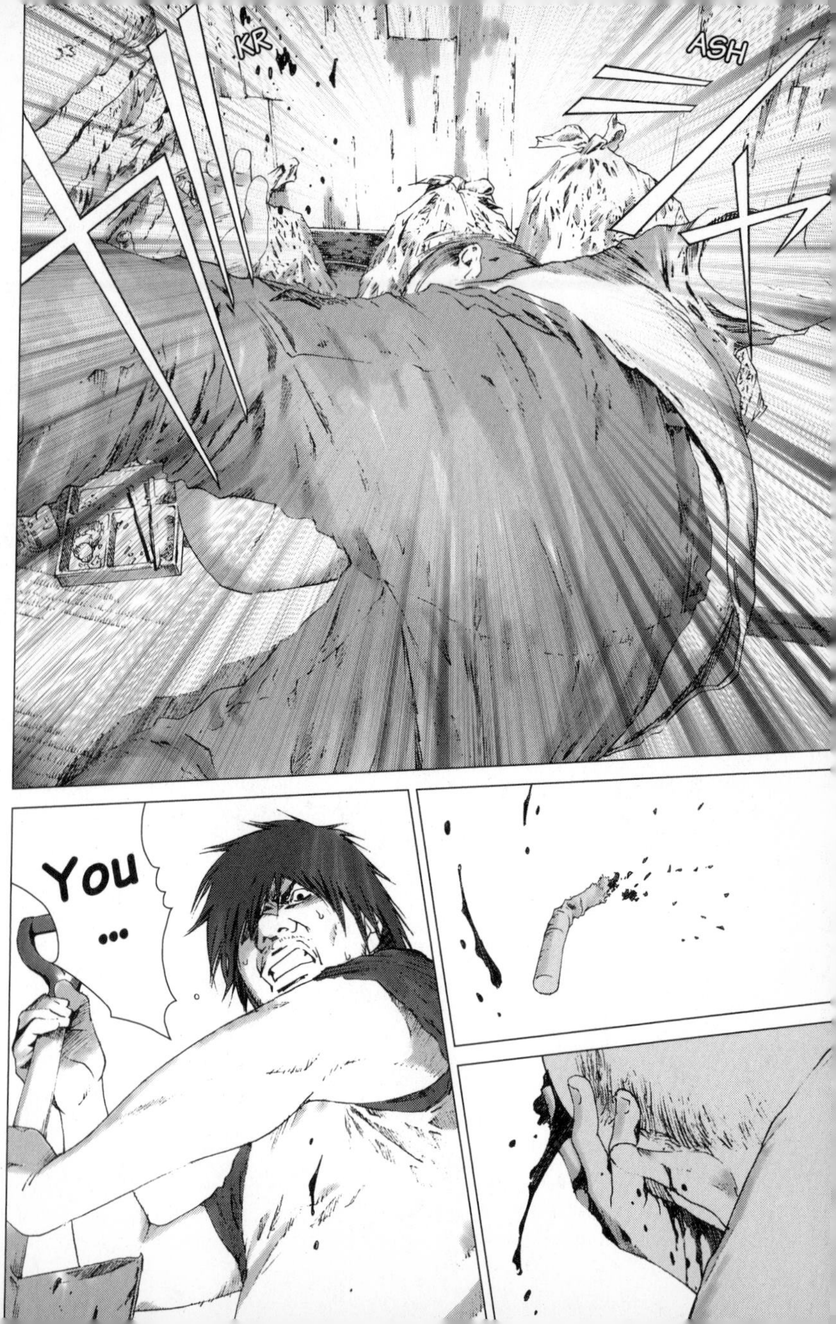
KR
ASH
You ...

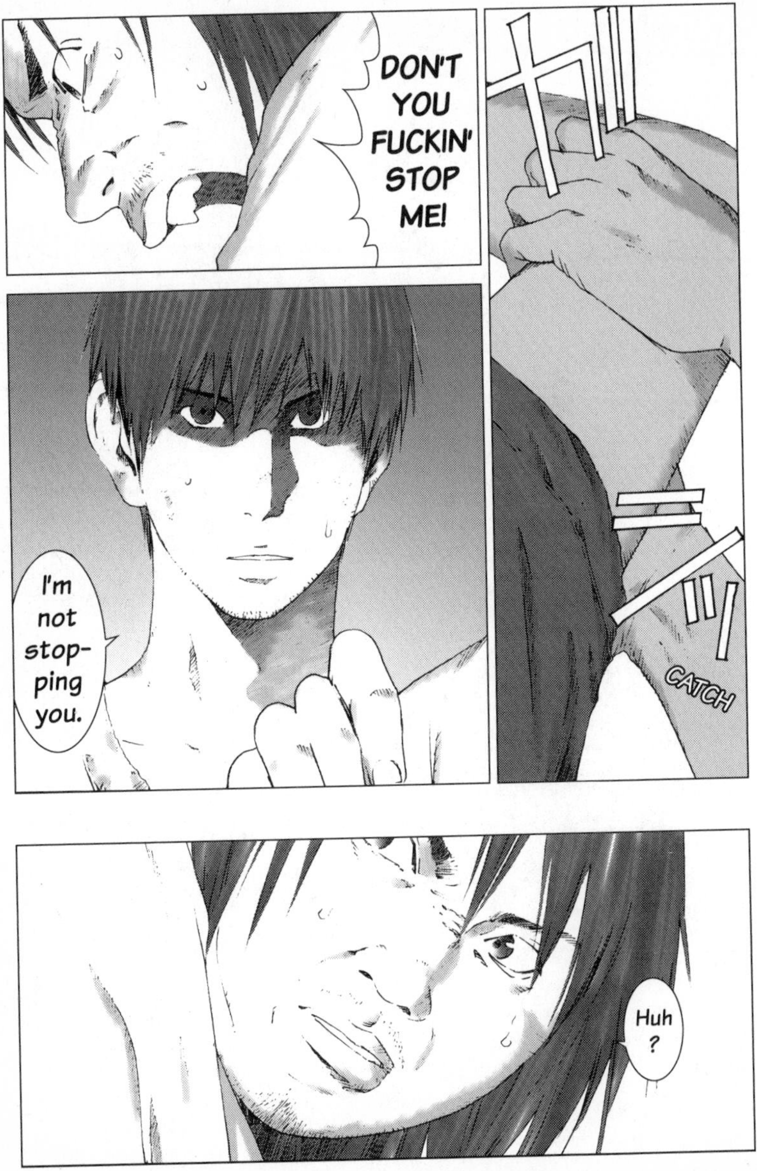
CATCH
DON'T YOU FUCKIN' STOP ME!
I'm not stopping you.
Huh?

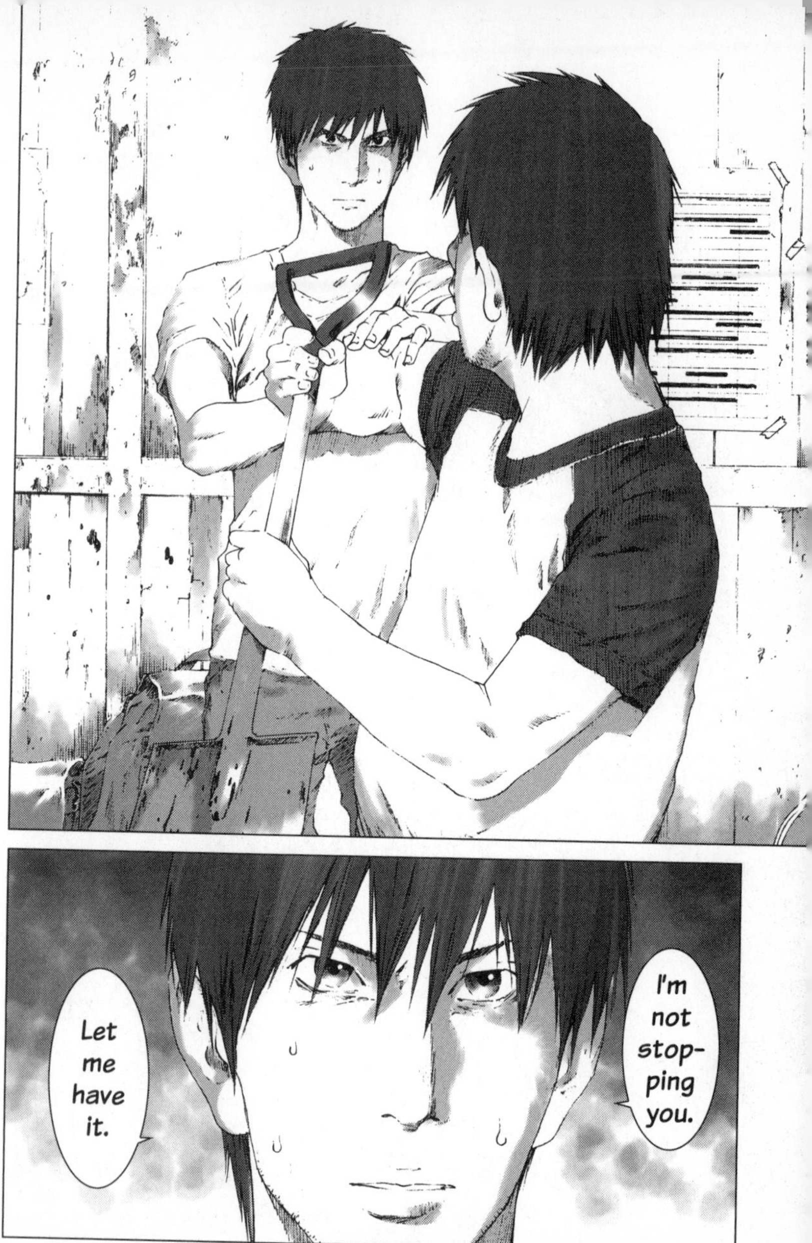
I'm not stopping you.
Let me have it.

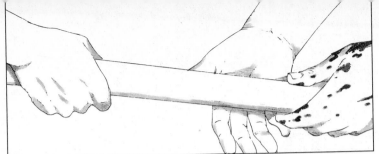

*
koff
*

R
r
g
h

*
hack
*

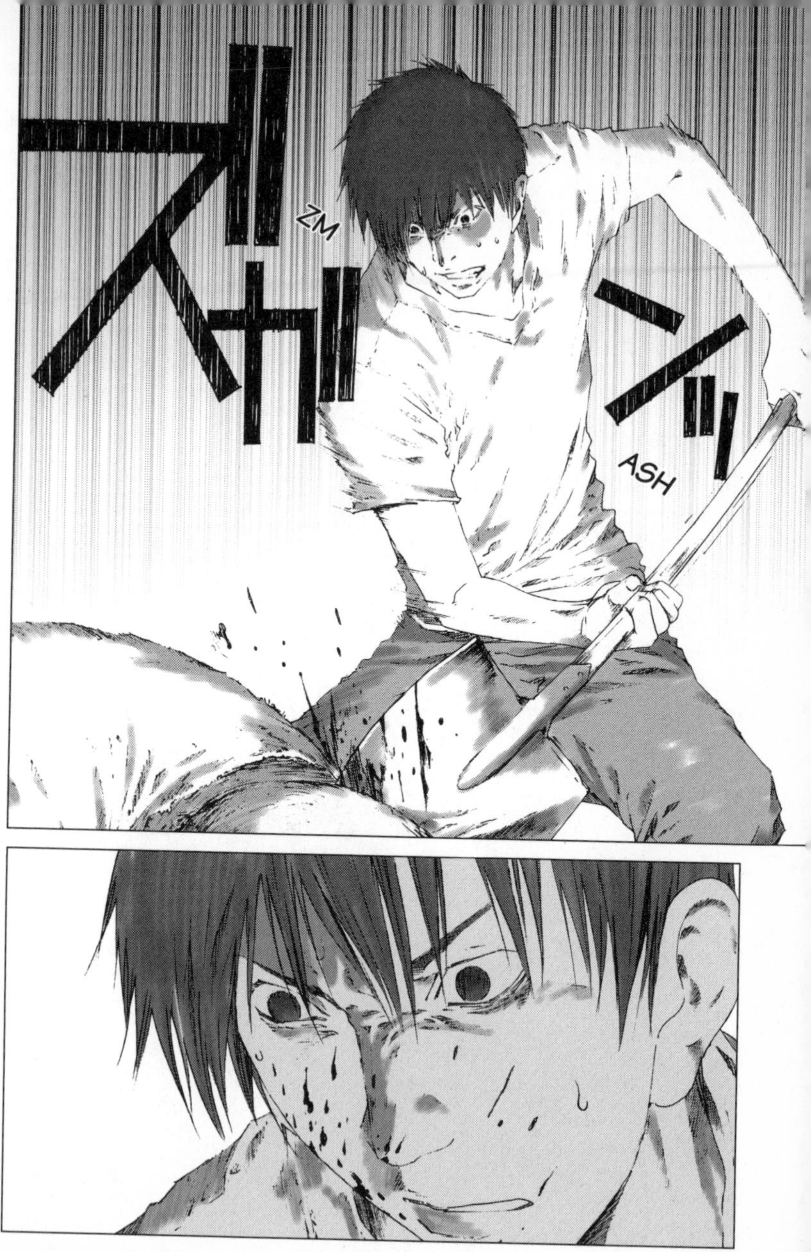
ASH
ZM

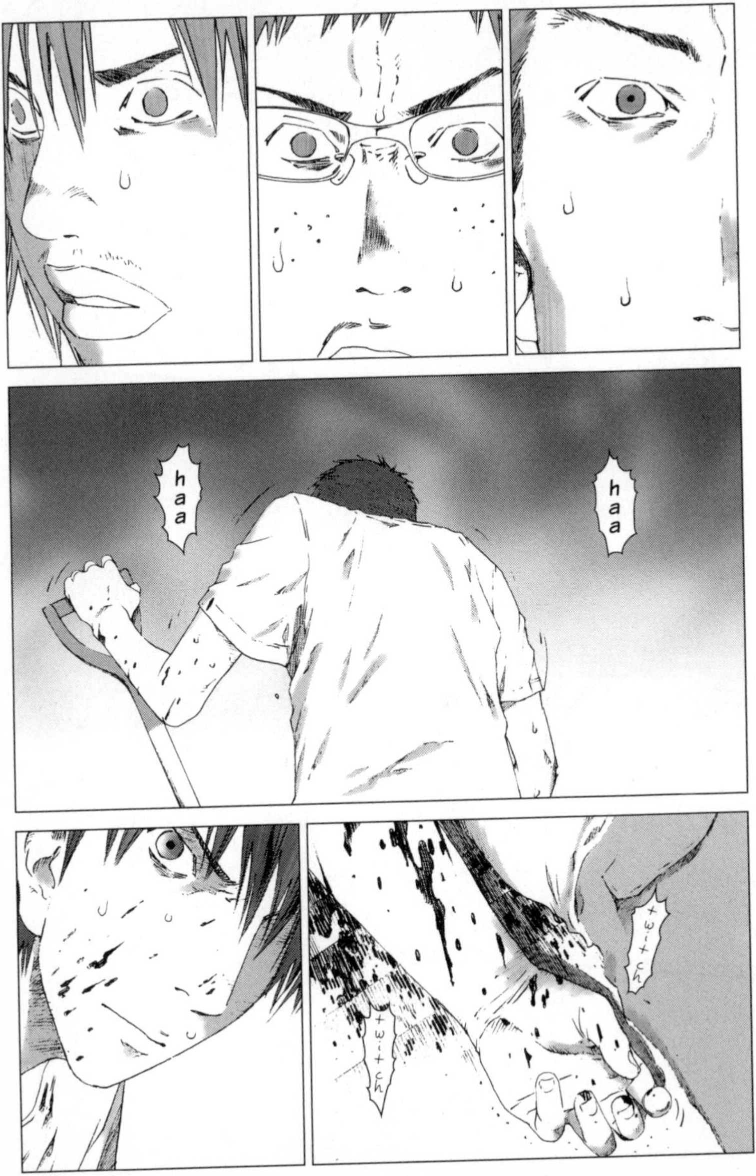
haa
haa
twitch
twitch

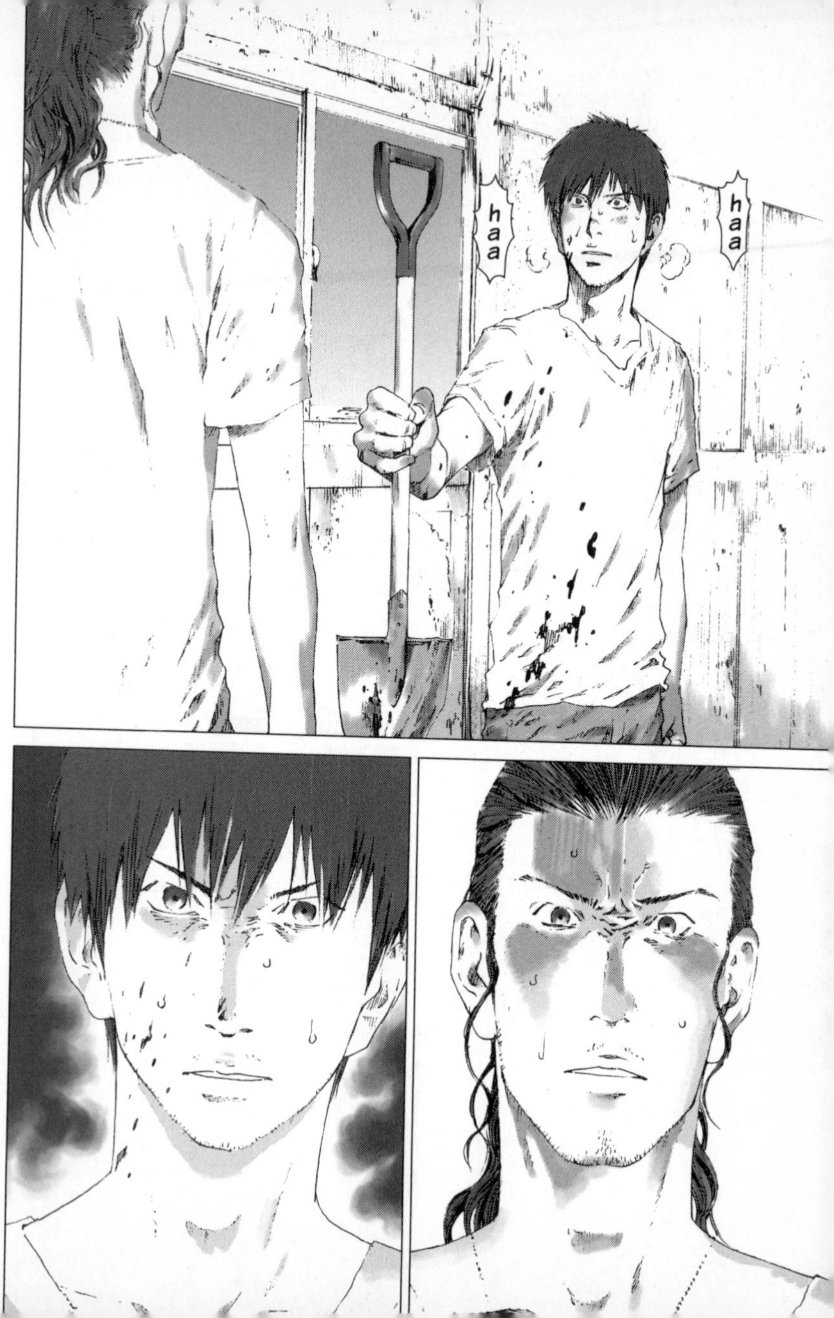
haa
haa

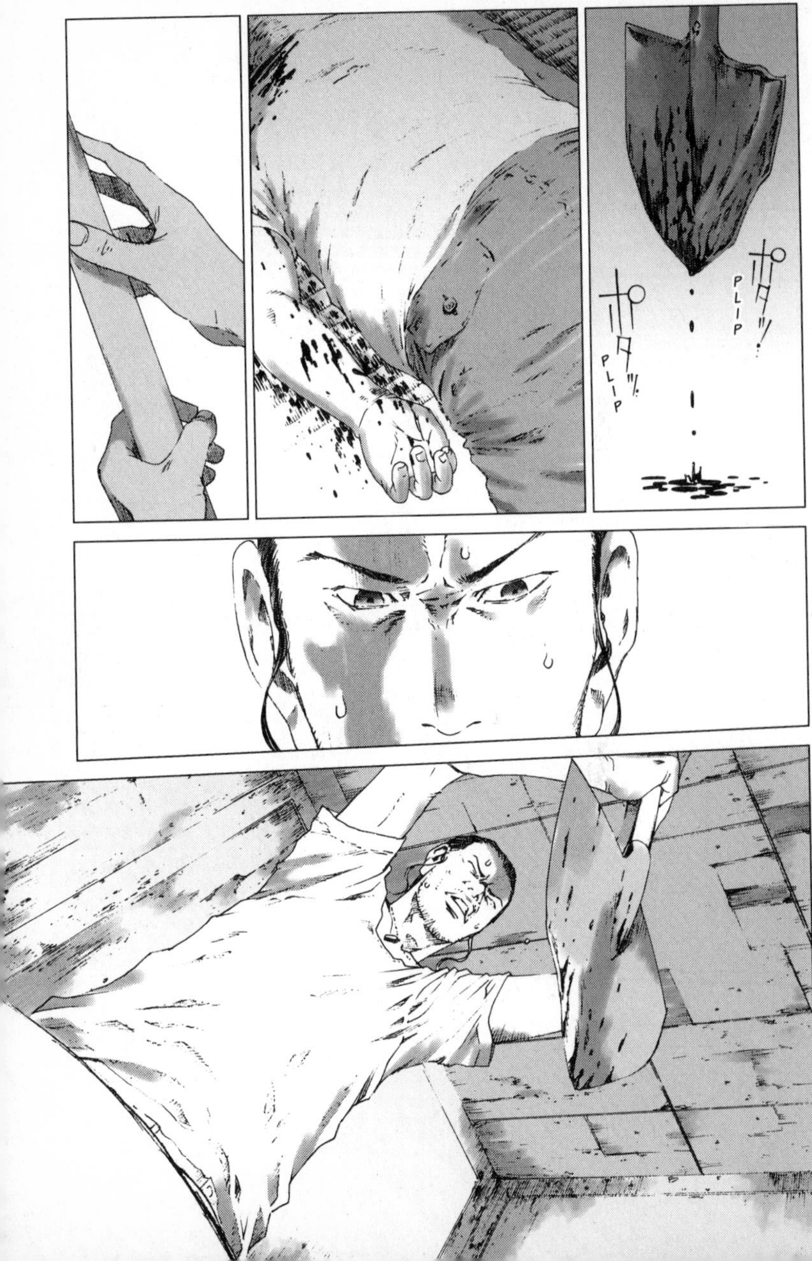
ポタッ!
PLIP
ポタッ!
PLIP

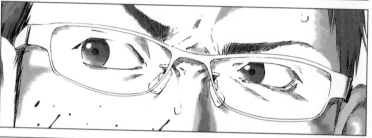

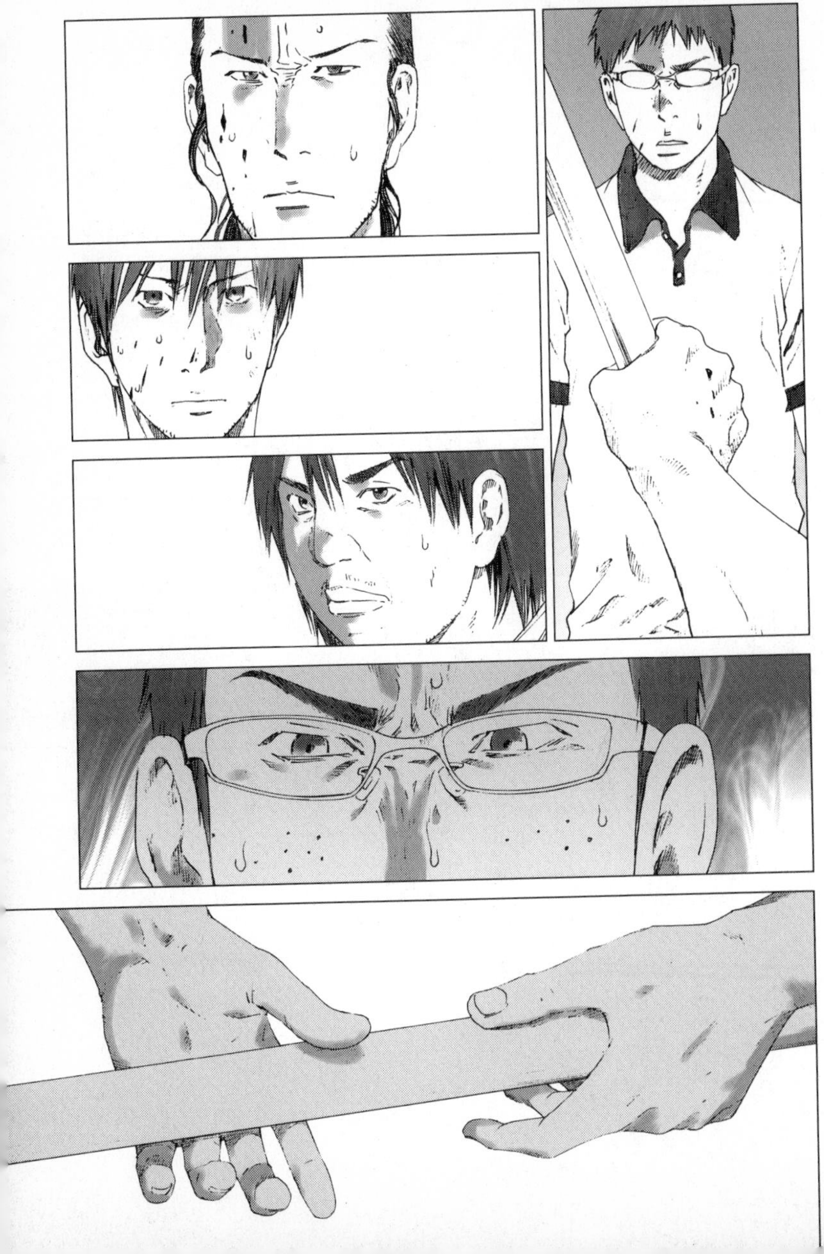

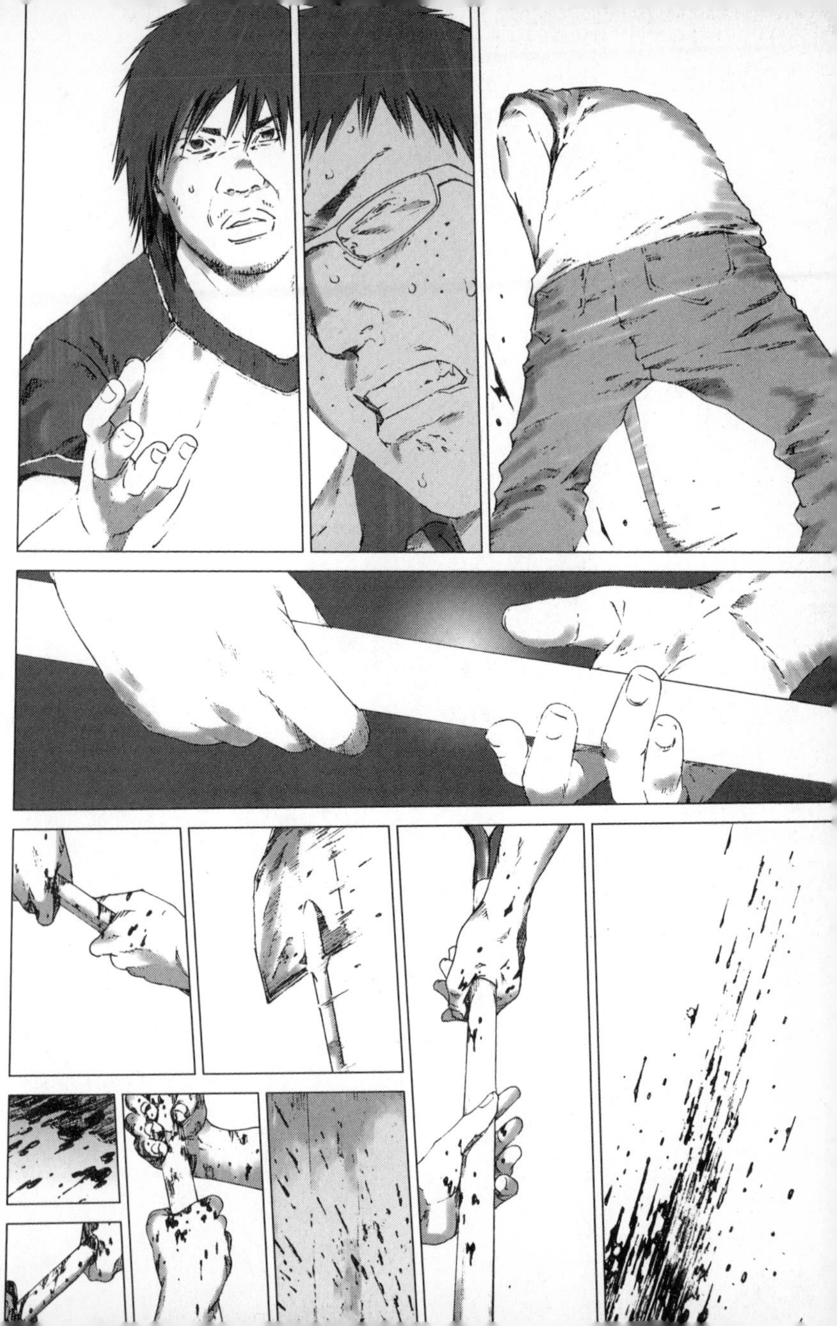

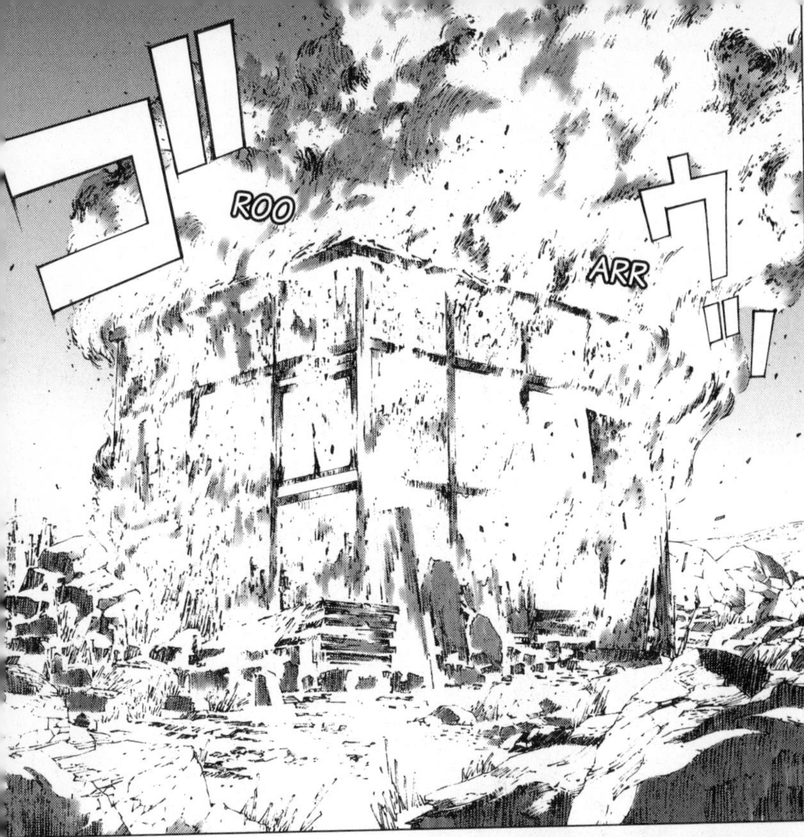
ROO
ARR
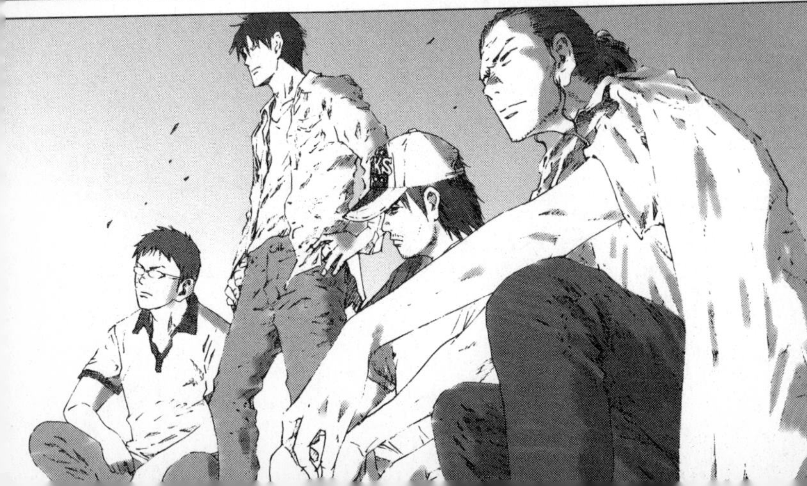

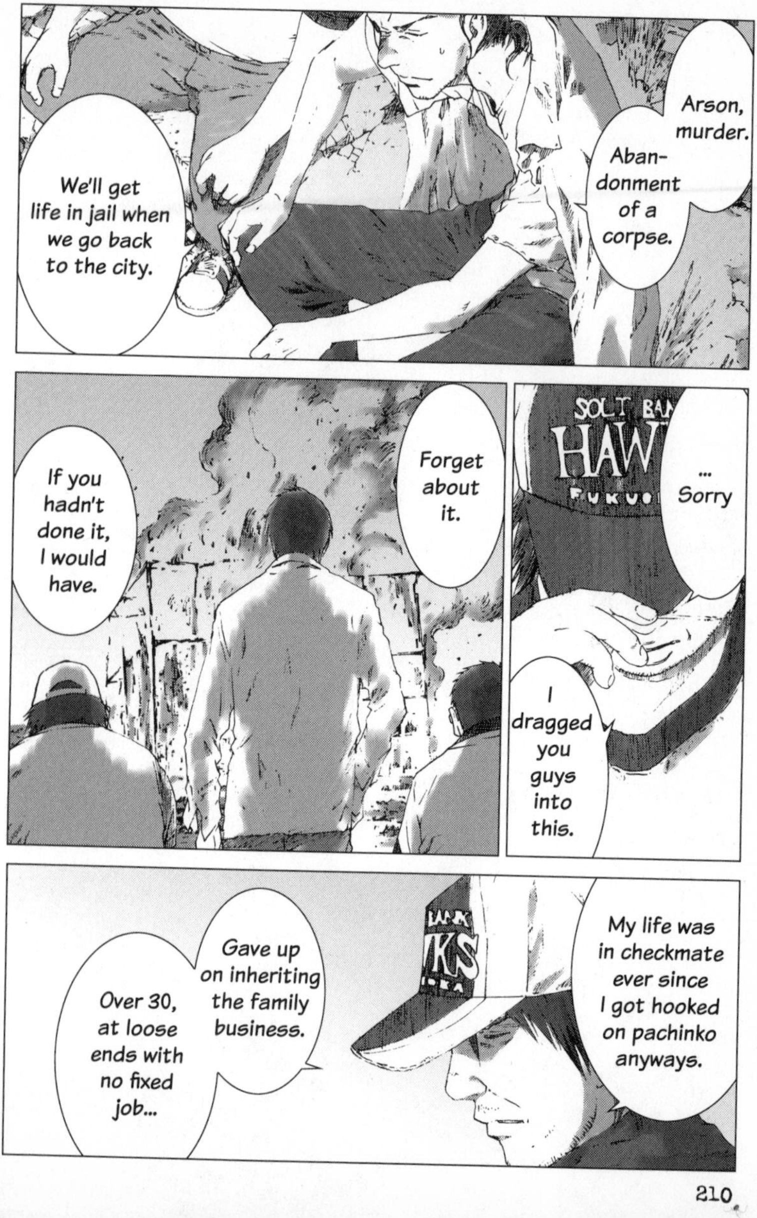
Arson, murder.
Aban-donment of a corpse.
We'll get life in jail when we go back to the city.
... Sorry
I dragged you guys into this.
Forget about it.
If you hadn't done it, I would have.
My life was in checkmate ever since I got hooked on pachinko anyways.
Gave up on inheriting the family business.
Over 30, at loose ends with no fixed job...

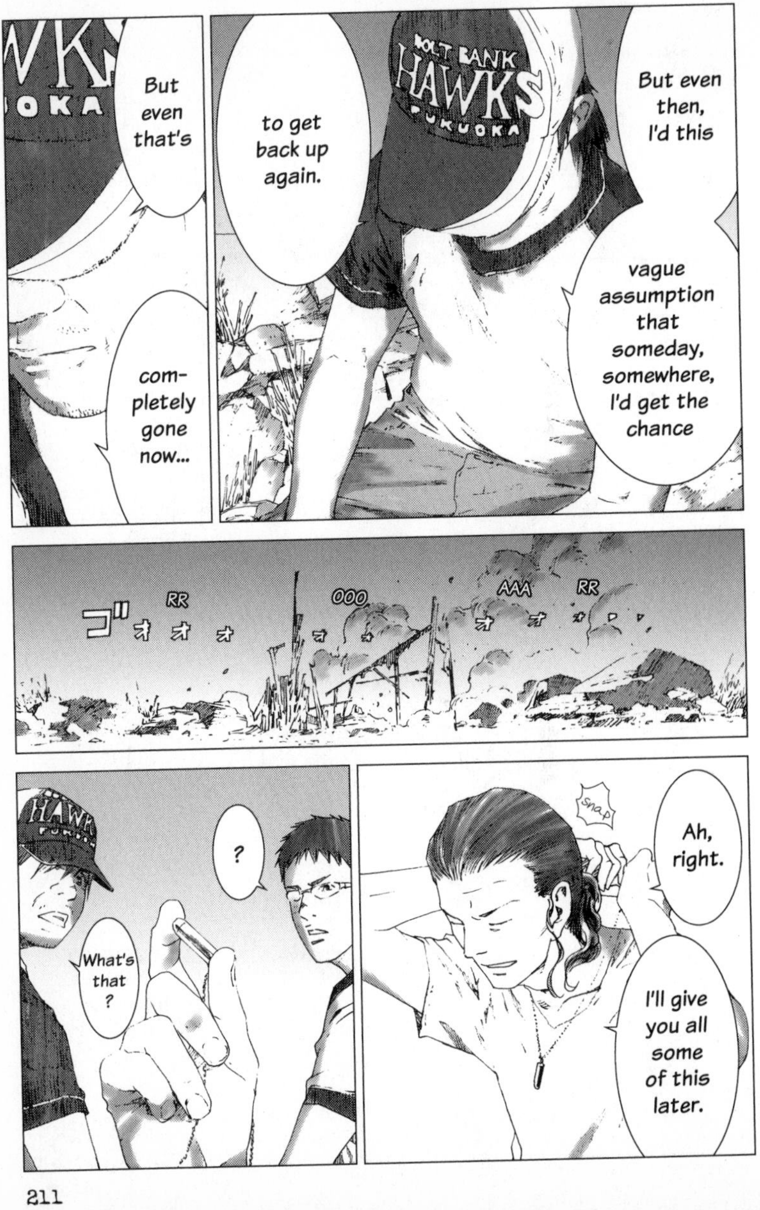
But even then, I'd this
vague assumption that someday, somewhere, I'd get the chance
to get back up again.
But even that's
com-pletely gone now...
RR
OOO
AAA
RR
Snap
Ah, right.
I'll give you all some of this later.
?
What's that?

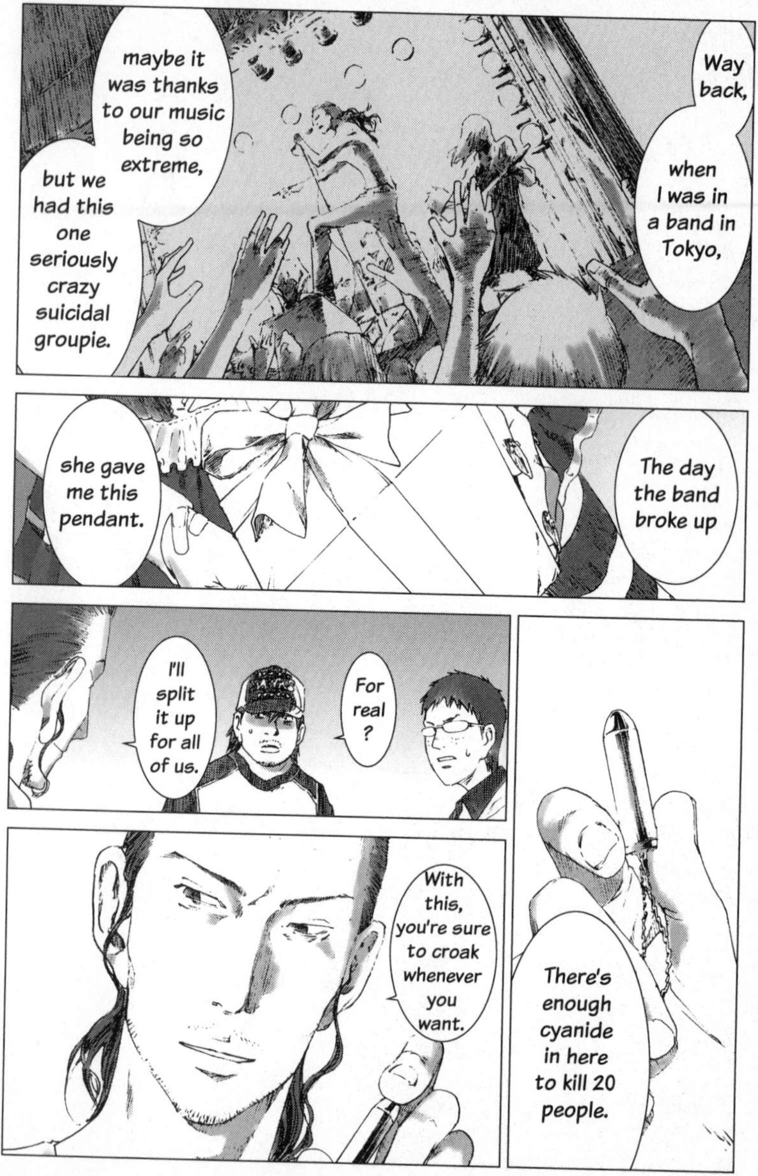

Way back,
when I was in a band in Tokyo,
maybe it was thanks to our music being so extreme,
but we had this one seriously crazy suicidal groupie.
The day the band broke up
she gave me this pendant.
There's enough cyanide in here to kill 20 people.
For real?
I'll split it up for all of us.
With this, you're sure to croak whenever you want.

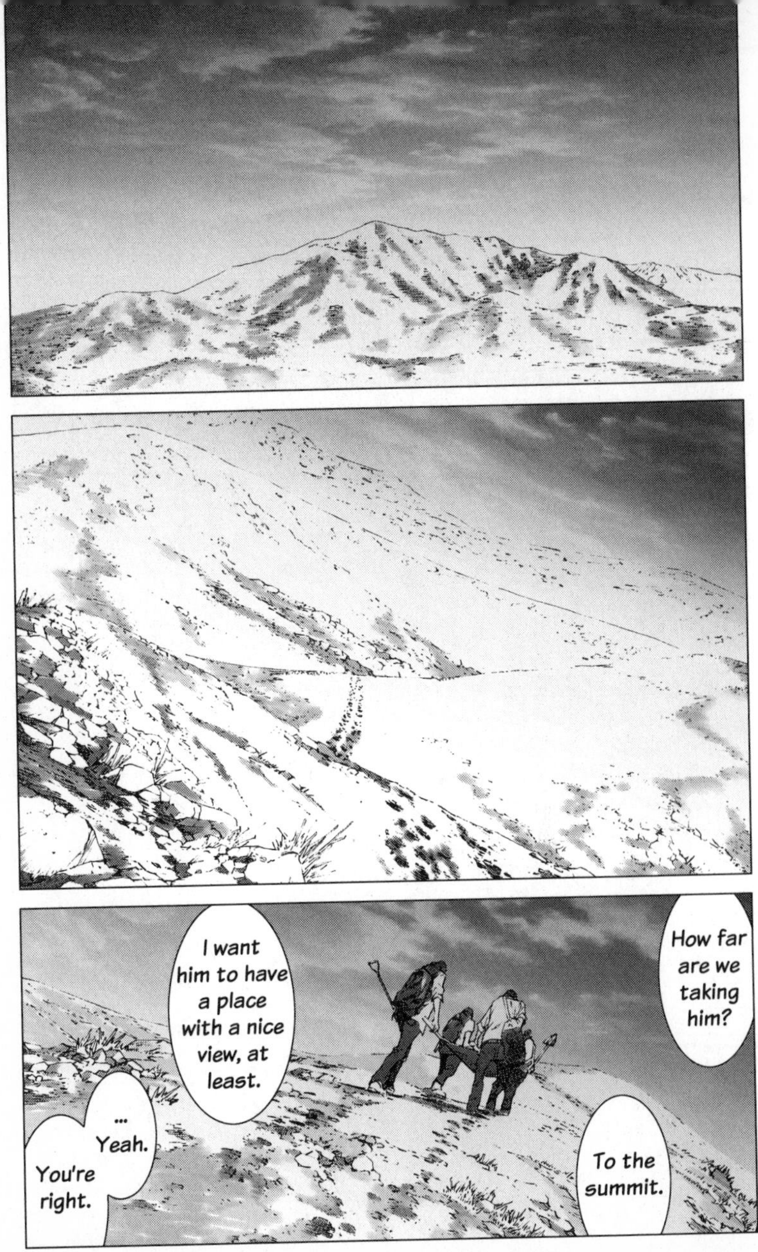
How far are we taking him?
To the summit.
I want him to have a place with a nice view, at least.
... Yeah.
You're right.

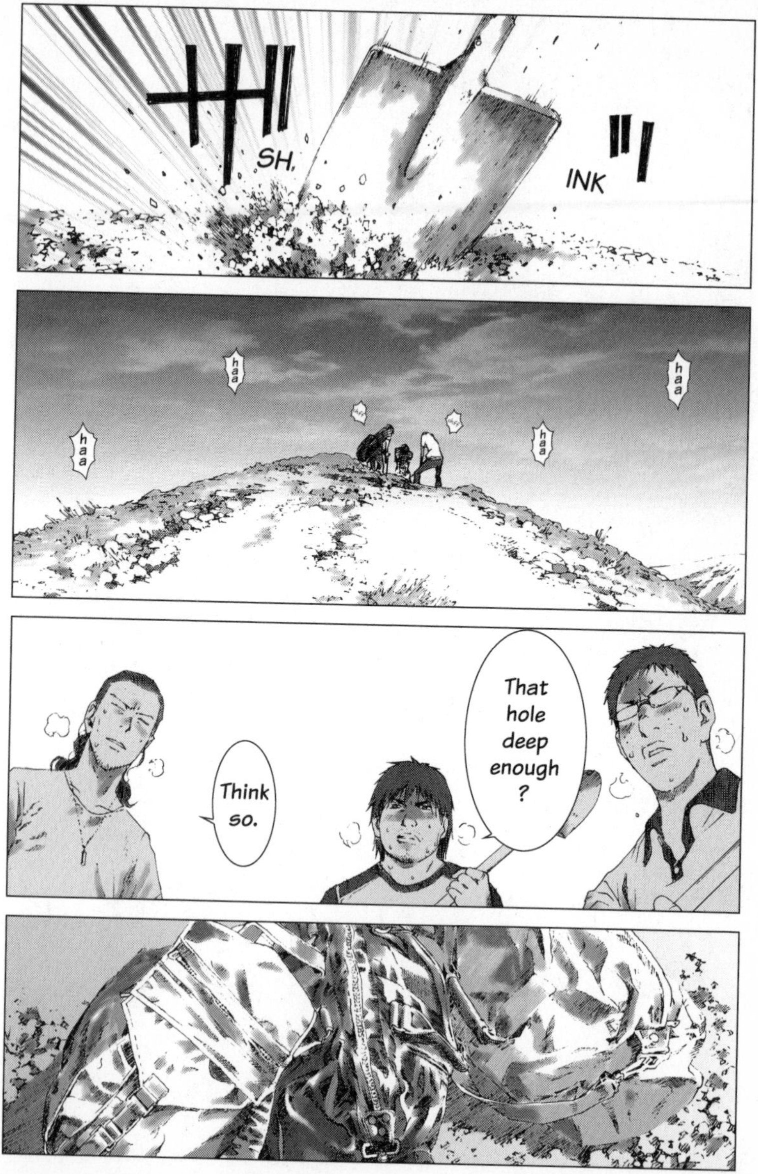
SH.
INK
haa
haa
haa
haa
That hole deep enough?
Think so.

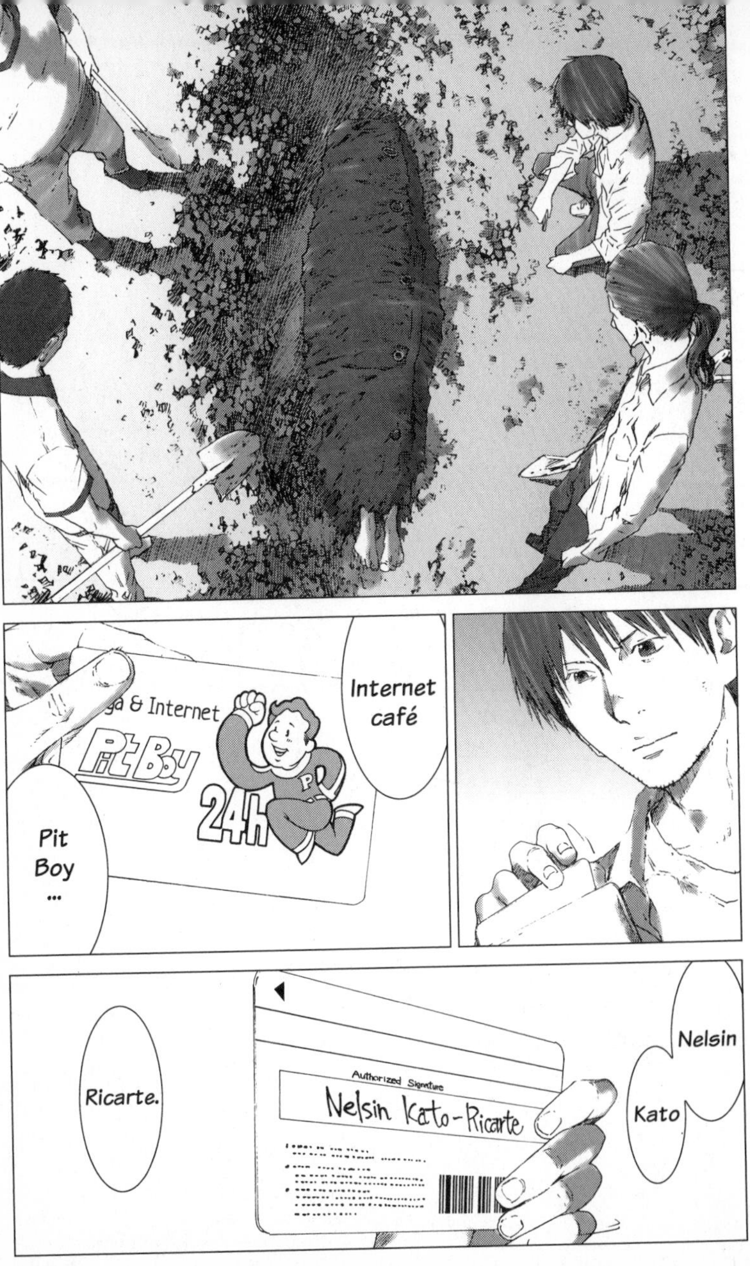
Internet café
ga & Internet
Pit Boy
24h
Pit Boy ...
Nelsin Kato
Authorized Signature
Nelsin Kato-Ricarte
Ricarte.

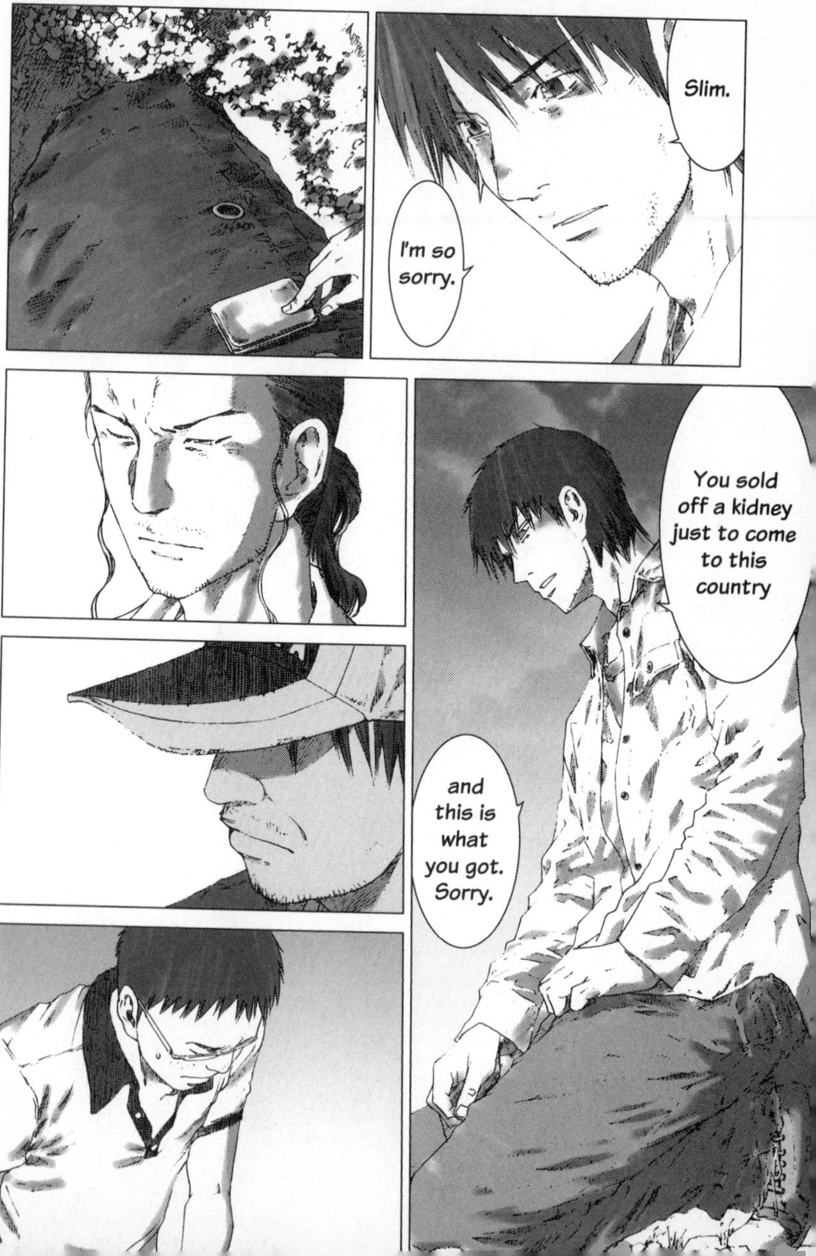
Slim.
I'm so sorry.
You sold off a kidney just to come to this country
and this is what you got. Sorry.

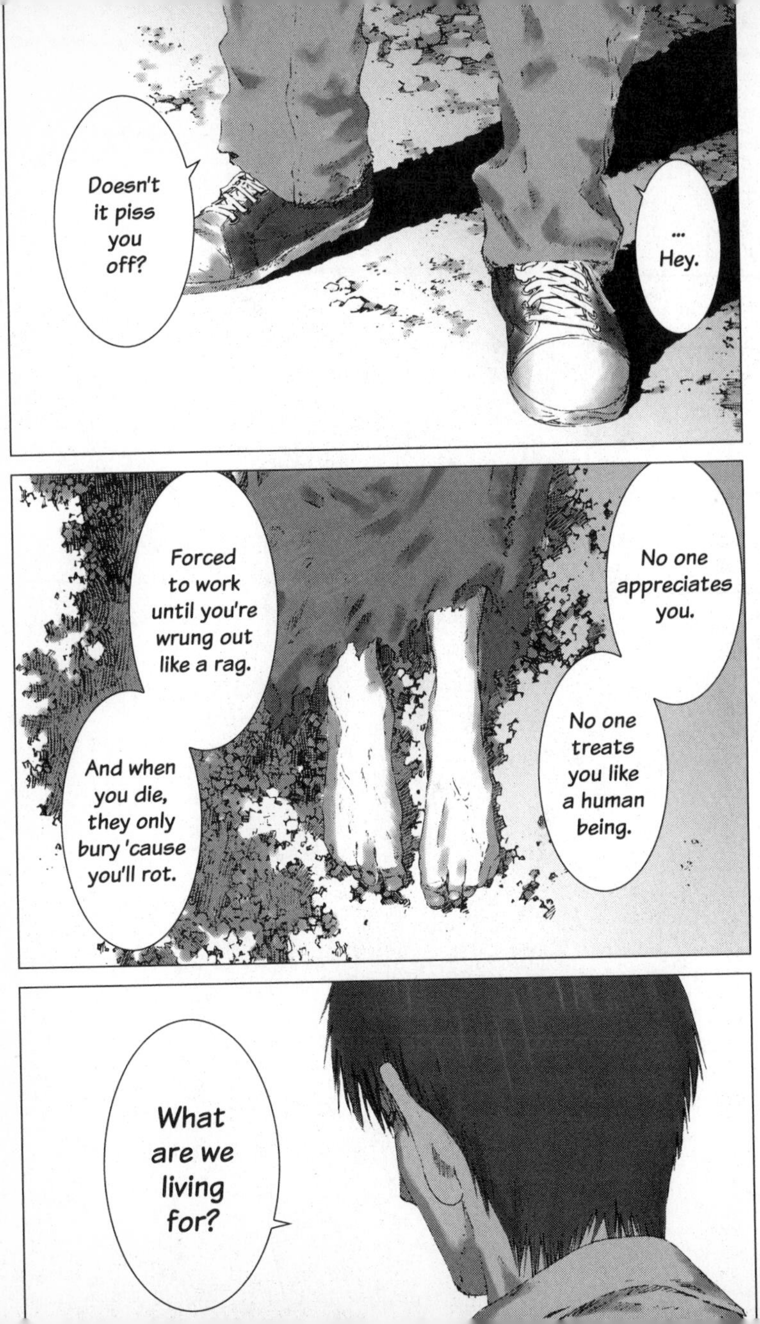
... Hey.
Doesn't it piss you off?
No one appreciates you.
No one treats you like a human being.
Forced to work until you're wrung out like a rag.
And when you die, they only bury 'cause you'll rot.
What are we living for?

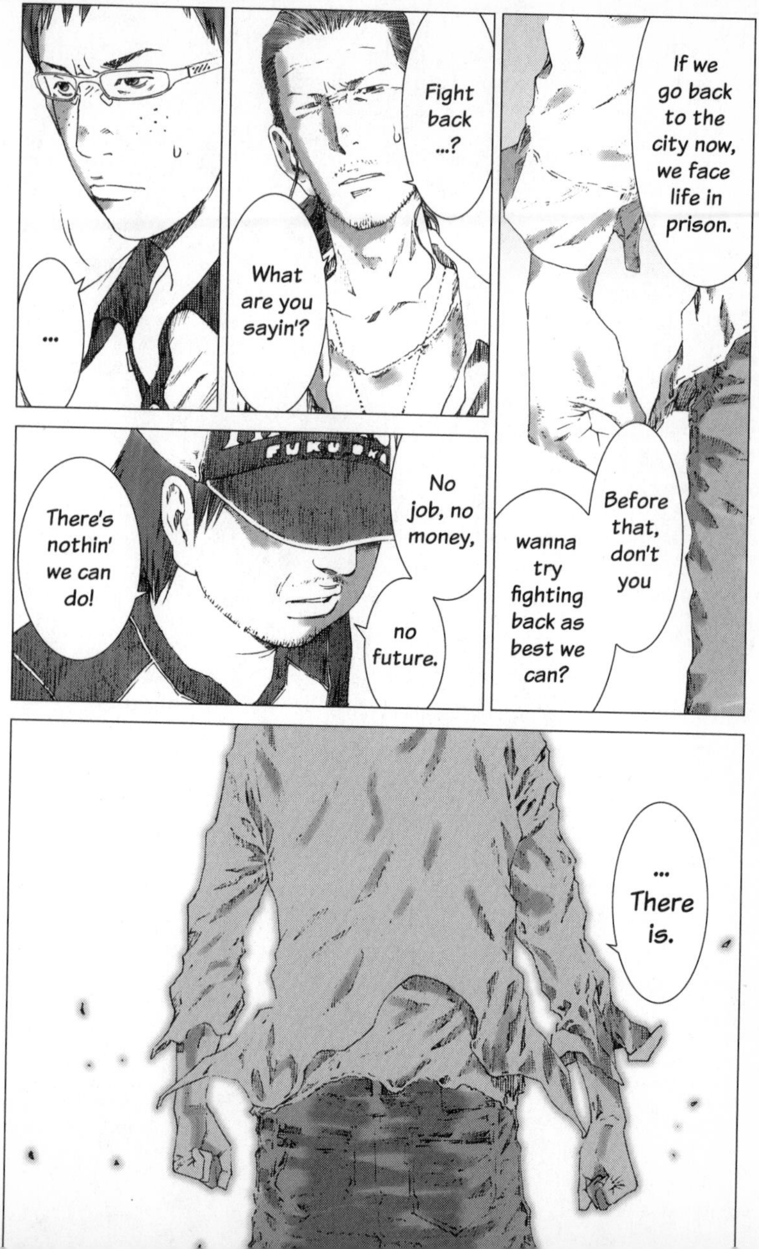
If we go back to the city now, we face life in prison.
Before that, don't you
wanna try fighting back as best we can?
Fight back ...?
What are you sayin'?
...
No job, no money,
no future.
There's nothin' we can do!
... There is.

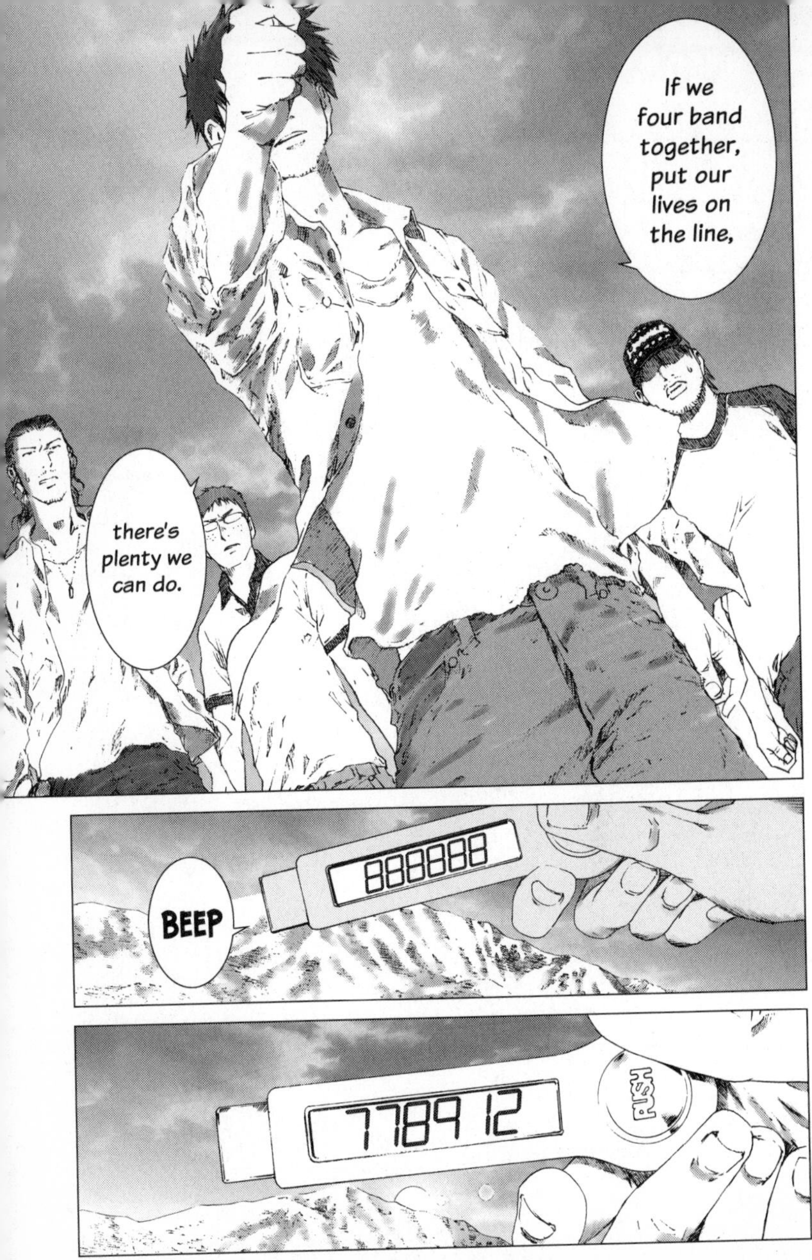
If we four band together, put our lives on the line,
there's plenty we can do.
888888
BEEP
778912

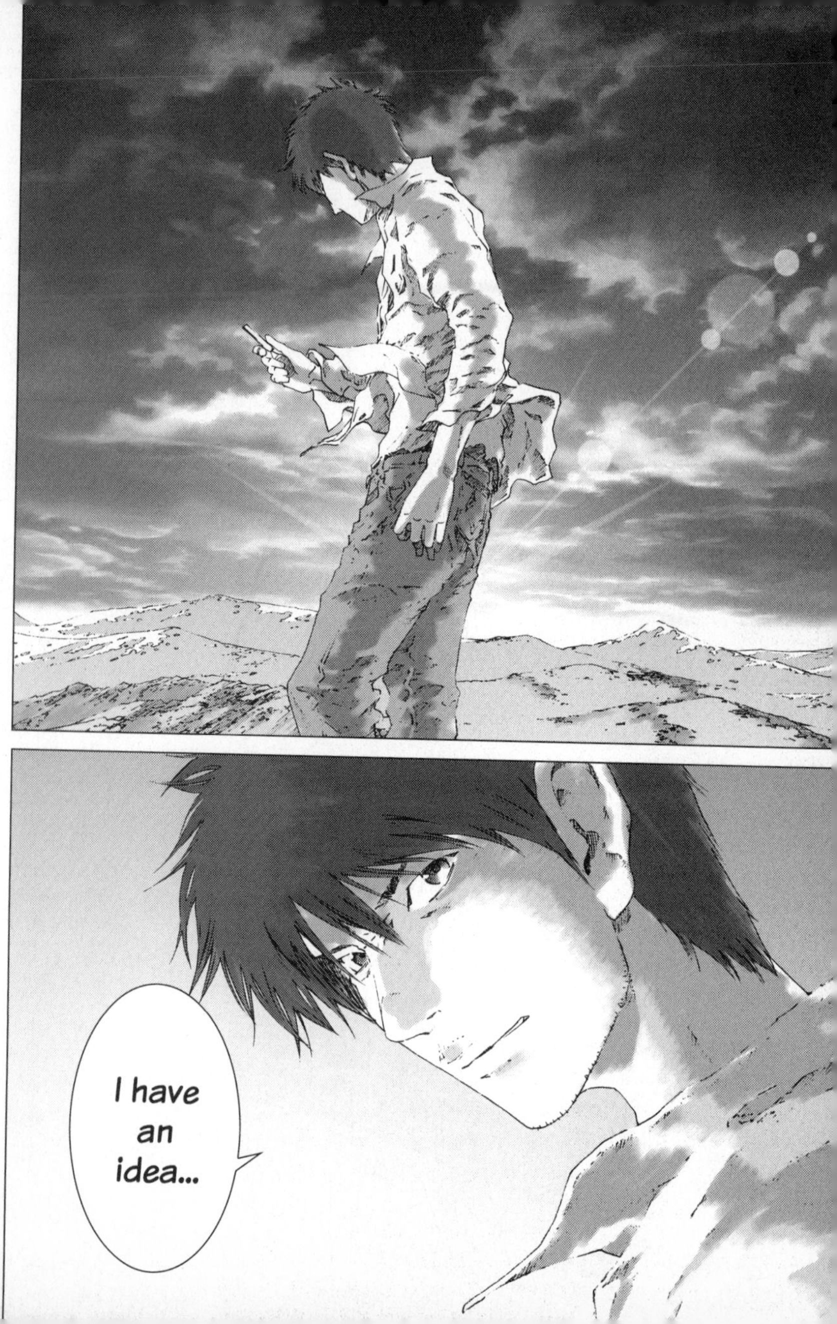
I have an idea...

PROPHECY
01 END

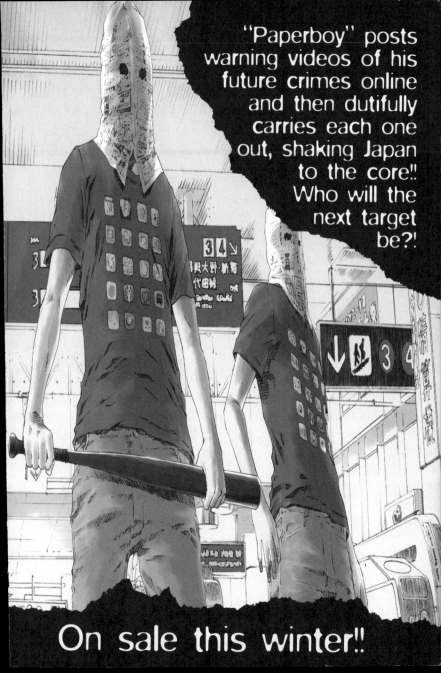

"Paperboy" posts warning videos of his future crimes online and then dutifully carries each one out, shaking Japan to the core!! Who will the next target be?!

On sale this winter!!

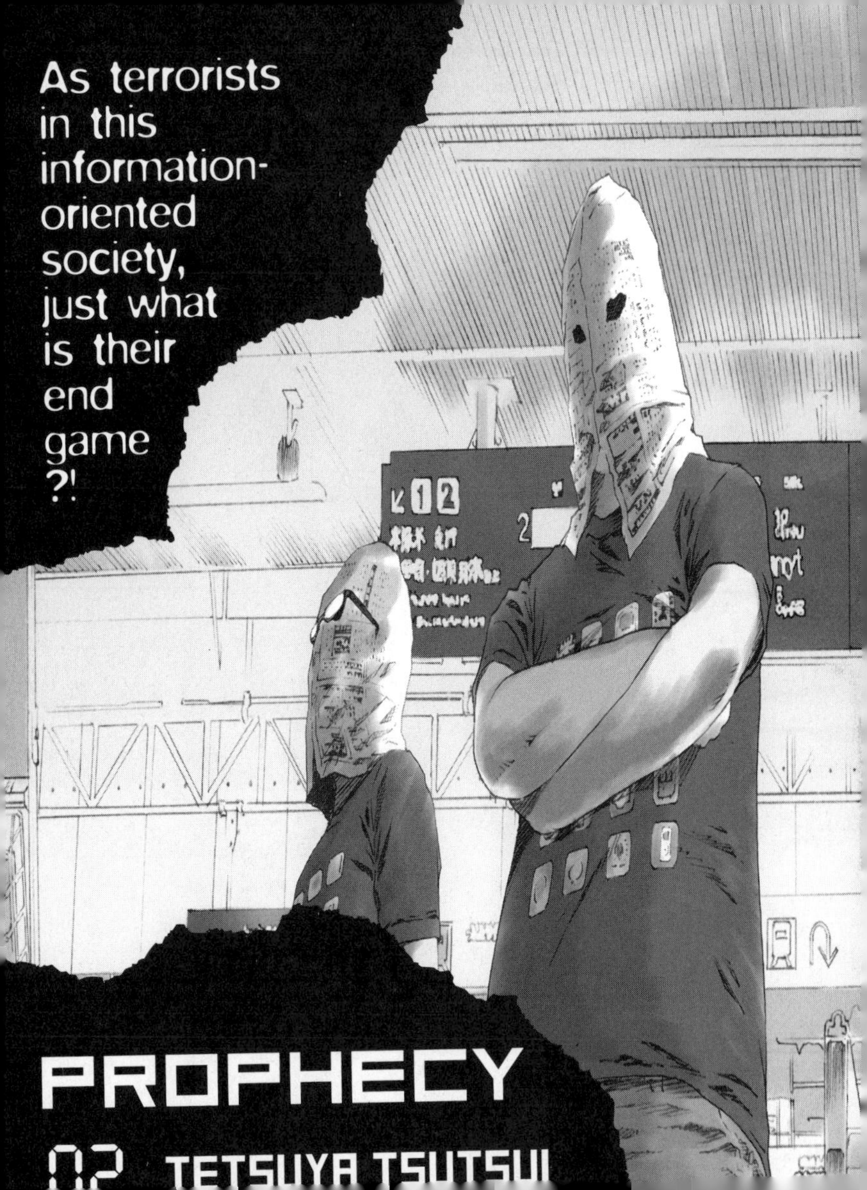
As terrorists in this information-oriented society, just what is their end game?!
PROPHECY
02 TETSUYA TSUTSUI

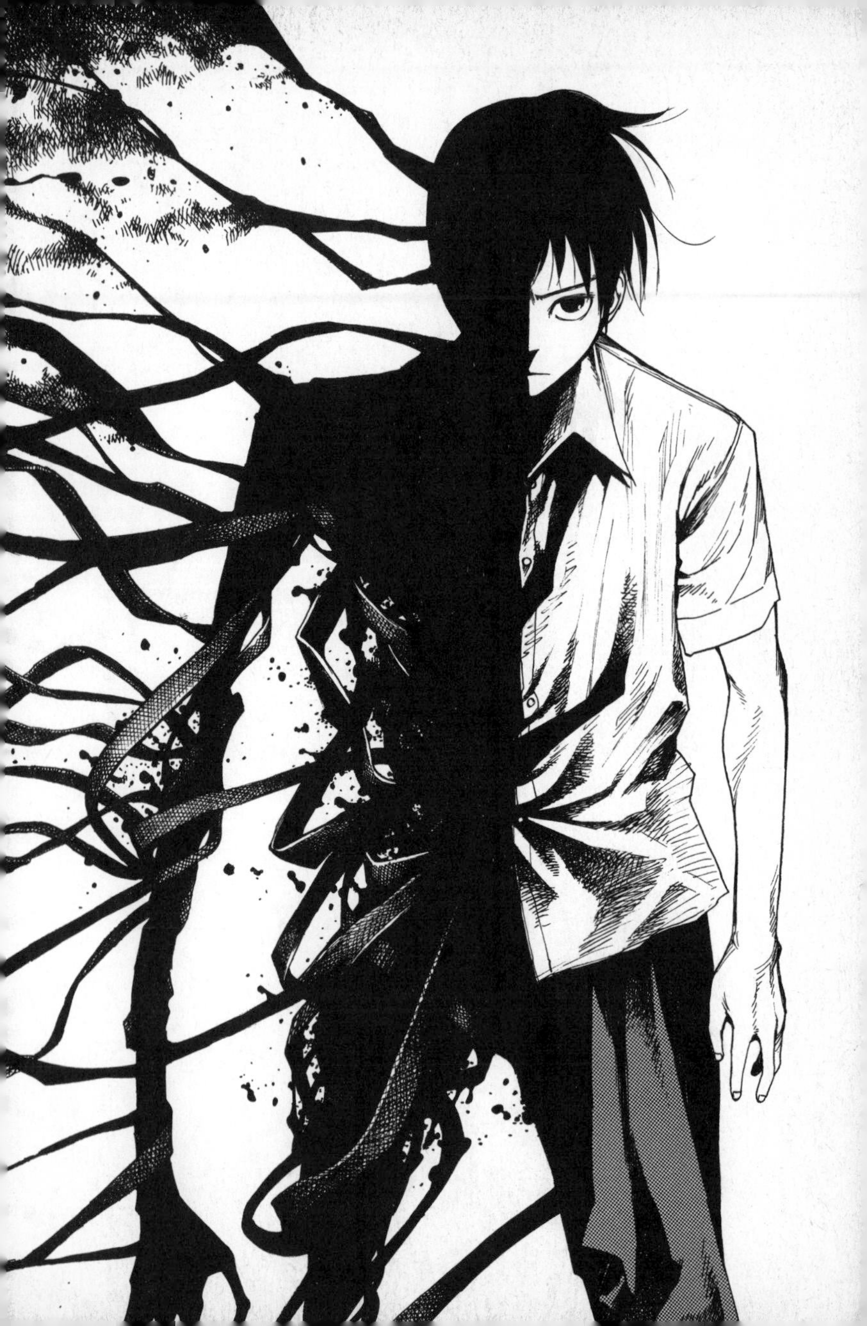

AJIN
DEMI-HUMAN

STORY: TSUINA MIURA
ART: GAMON SAKURAI

SAY YOU GET HIT BY A TRUCK AND DIE. YOU COME BACK TO LIFE. GOOD OR BAD?

FOR HIGH SCHOOLER KEI—AND FOR AT LEAST FORTY-SIX OTHERS—IMMORTALITY COMES AS THE NASTIEST SURPRISE EVER.

SADLY FOR KEI, BUT REFRESHINGLY FOR THE READER, SUCH A FEAT DOESN'T MAKE HIM A SUPERHERO. IN THE EYES OF BOTH THE GENERAL PUBLIC AND GOVERNMENTS, HE'S A RARE SPECIMEN WHO NEEDS TO BE HUNTED DOWN AND HANDED OVER TO SCIENTISTS TO BE EXPERIMENTED ON FOR LIFE—A DEMI-HUMAN WHO MUST DIE A THOUSAND DEATHS FOR THE BENEFIT OF HUMANITY.

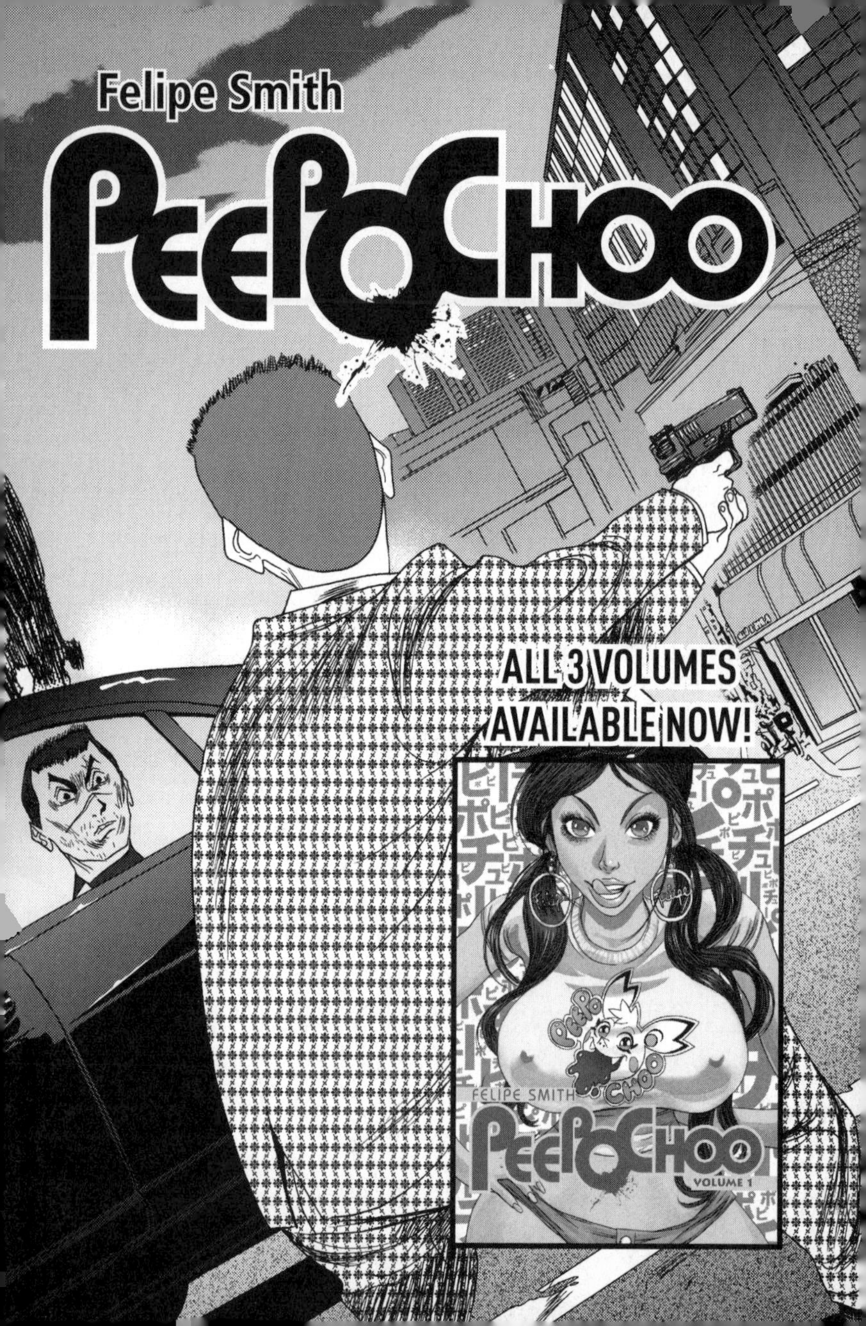
Felipe Smith
PEEPO CHOO
ALL 3 VOLUMES AVAILABLE NOW!
FELIPE SMITH
PEEPO CHOO
VOLUME 1

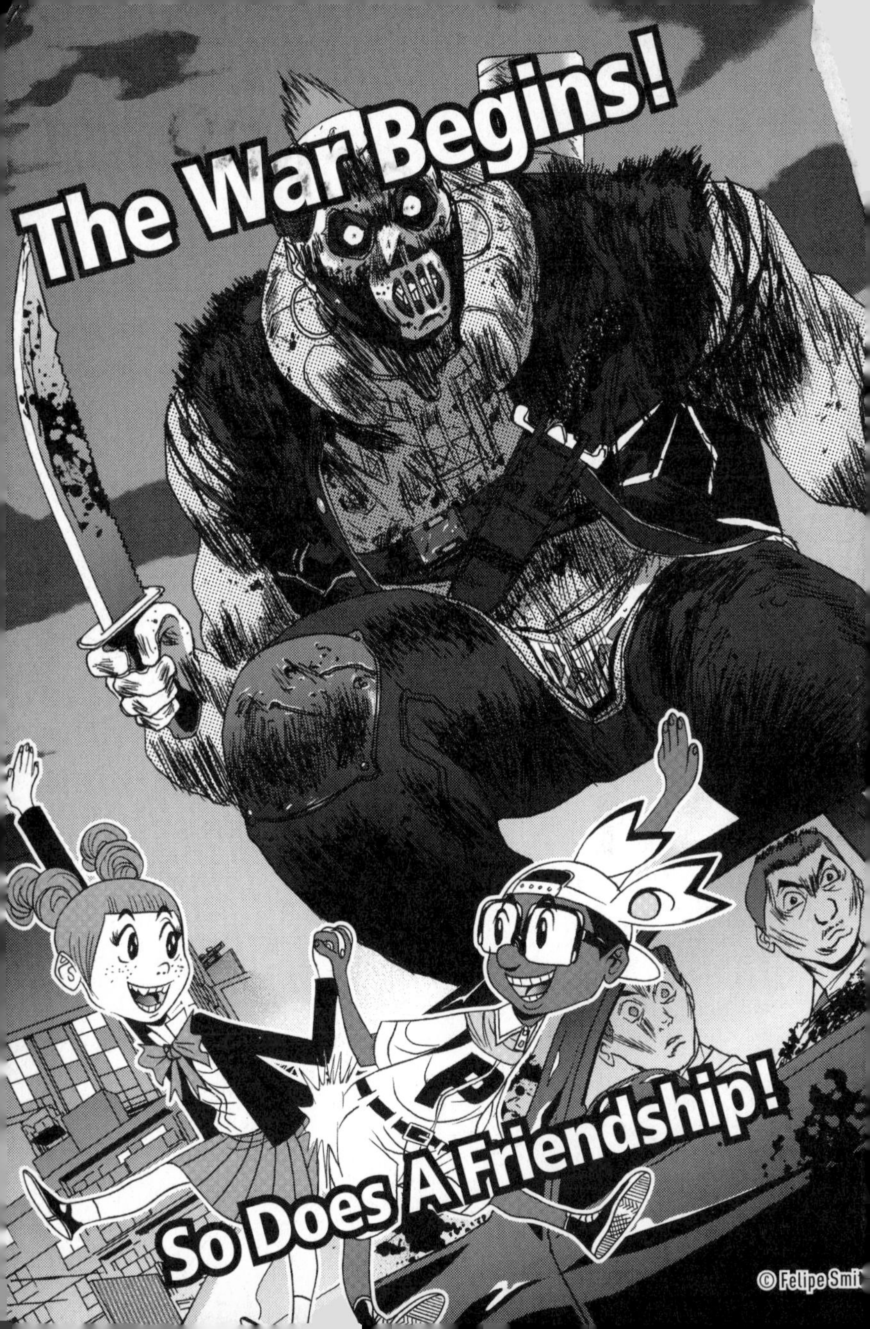
The War Begins!
So Does A Friendship!
© Felipe Smit

Prophecy, part 1

Translation: Kumar Sivasubramanian
Production: Grace Lu
Nicole Dochych
Anthony Quintessenza

Copyright © 2012 Tetsuya Tsutsui / Ki-oon
All rights reserved.
First published in France in 2012 by Ki-oon,
an imprint of AC Media Ltd.
English translation rights arranged through
Tuttle-Mori Agency, Inc.
English language version produced by Vertical, Inc.

Translation provided by Vertical, Inc., 2014
Published by Vertical Comics, an imprint of
Vertical, Inc., New York

This is a work of fiction.

ISBN: 978-1-939130-59-4

Manufactured in the United States of America

First Edition

Vertical, Inc.
451 Park Avenue South
7th Floor
New York, NY 10016
www.vertical-inc.com